Sumner Welles

# THE TIME

# FOR

# DECISION

Harper & Brothers Publishers

NEW YORK and LONDON

*For*
M. T. W.

# Foreword

This book is divided into three parts.

In the chapters comprising Part I, I attempt to survey the course of events in Europe between the two great wars and the gradually changing policy of the United States as the world approached catastrophe. I then go on to describe my mission to Europe in the spring of 1940, when the President sent me to ascertain, by interviews with the heads of states, whether there still remained any possibility of establishing just and permanent peace. The last chapter of this part deals with the momentous decisions taken by this government prior to and during our participation in the war.

Part II is concerned with the problems—past, present, and future—in various areas and countries of the world. In each case I have tried to give the necessary historical background. I have expressed my own opinions about the policies that have been pursued and have attempted to outline a just and realistic solution to the problems presented.

Part III has to do mainly with the future. In the first chapter I present a plan for what seems to me an effective world organization. In the second chapter I indicate the part that I feel this country must take in world affairs if we are to have any reasonable hope of enduring peace and security.

S. W.

# CONTENTS

Foreword    vii

PART I

Chapter 1 — It Might Have Been    3

Chapter 2 — The Tragic Years    41

Chapter 3 — My Mission to Europe: 1940    73

Chapter 4 — From Defensive to Offensive    148

PART II

Chapter 5 — The Good Neighbor Policy    185

Chapter 6 — The Area of Discord: Eastern Europe and
the Near East    242

Chapter 7 — The Japanese Threat and the Problem of
Peace in Asia    272

Chapter 8 — The Constructive Power of the U.S.S.R.    306

Chapter 9 — The German Menace Can Be Ended    336

PART III

Chapter 10 — World Organization    365

Chapter 11 — The Part We Must Play    388

Appendix    415

Index    419

# THE TIME FOR DECISION

## PART ONE

CHAPTER I

# It Might Have Been

AS MY generation looks back to the years between the wars I think our one outstanding thought must always be "it might have been."

Most of us who came of age shortly before the outbreak of the first World War passionately believed when the last shot was fired on November 11, 1918, that we were headed toward a new and better world. We were confident that the errors of the past were to be valiantly corrected; that human wrongs would all be righted; that the self-determination of peoples would end oppression; that human freedom and individual security would become realities; that war, in this new dawn breaking over the earth, was now a nightmare of the past.

We had been thrilled to the depths of our emotional and intellectual being by the vision that Woodrow Wilson had held out to us of a world order founded on justice and on democracy. Our imaginations had responded to his ideal of an association of free peoples. Not least was our pride that our United States had asserted leadership in this great crusade, and that it was capable of assuming the vast responsibilities which this implied.

It is because of my abiding confidence that the realization of most of those ideals was well within human capacity—that our hopes need never have become "might have beens"—that I have dared to write this book.

The exuberant hope and confident optimism that was so general in the United States prevailed throughout the Allied countries. Harold Nicolson, in unforgettable pages, has described the scene in the British House of Lords when the leader for the government, Lord Curzon, intoned the words: "The world's great age begins anew; the golden years return." Those words contained the very essence of what tens of millions of men and women hoped and prayed.

3

It was not only among the Allied peoples that these hopes prevailed. Even in the streets of Berlin crowds were marching and shouting, "Nie wieder Krieg"—never again war. And all the separate nationalities that had for so long been dominated from Vienna joyfully acclaimed the dawn of a better day—a day of liberation and of unlimited horizon.

Peoples were not then inured to the tragedies, the privations, the fear and the hopelessness which have afflicted so great a majority of the human race during these past twenty-five years. They remembered so vividly the good years of their youth. It was not astonishing that many of us may have suffered from that illusion of which Alfred Capus once so cynically wrote, when he said that Woodrow Wilson appeared to believe that the war which had destroyed ten million men had at the same time made the human race perfect, whereas, in fact, it had only diminished its numbers.

Armistice Day of 1918 found me in Argentina—a country as remote from the scene of the first World War as any country of the earth; a country which had fanatically maintained its neutrality. Yet I shall never forget the fervor with which the crowds on the Avenida de Mayo greeted the siren signal from the great newspaper *La Prensa* which announced the end of the war. Nor can I fail to remember the almost mystical faith of all elements and of all classes among the Argentine people that the regeneration of mankind was an accomplished fact.

So it was in every part of the globe—for a few brief months. For the wave of idealism which had swept the world between the day when President Wilson proclaimed his Fourteen Points and the conclusion of the Armistice lasted a short time indeed. And the rapidity with which the dreams and hopes of humanity vanished can be readily explained.

The Fourteen Points had a far-reaching effect upon the peoples of the Central powers as well as in the Allied countries. The solutions for a just and practical peace settlement contained in the Fourteen Points were valid. Popular opinion responded to that validity. The promise of a League of Nations, supported as it was by an overwhelming majority of the people of the New World and by a very considerable majority of the peoples of the Old World, gave men and women hope of the only kind of security which could offer any recompense for the sufferings and the sacrifices they had undergone. It was because Woodrow Wilson was regarded as the prophet of a new era that when he reached Europe he was welcomed with almost idolatrous jubilation by the masses of the people everywhere.

As the months passed it gradually became apparent that those gathered at Paris who had the power to shape the future world were departing more and more from the clear-cut principles of the Fourteen Points, partly because of the greed of some of their governments, partly on account of political expediency, and, finally, because of clamor at home for immediate demobilization and a speedy windup of the job of peacemaking. The arbiters of human destiny seemed less and less like prophets and more and more like harassed, tired, and irritable old men. The flood of emotional optimism quickly vanished in a wave of cold and cynical pessimism.

One of the chief reasons for the compromises which President Wilson felt himself obliged to accept at Paris was the fact that the United States had made no effort to reach any prior understanding with its allies concerning political and territorial problems. Nor, until the final months before the Armistice, had this government tried to come to an agreement with the Allies regarding the Covenant of the League of Nations. Wilson claimed that he was uninformed of the nature of the secret treaties, distributing vast territories and their inhabitants in a manner wholly inconsistent with the Fourteen Points; treaties which had been concluded by the Allies prior to the entrance of the United States into the war. On that point there was a difference of opinion between himself and Lord Balfour. In any event, the delegates assembled at Paris with no agreement covering any of these basic problems. While it was undoubtedly true that so long as the war continued the United States was all-powerful in view of the realization that the victories of 1918 could not have been achieved without American help; nevertheless, with the conclusion of the Armistice, the force of American leverage steadily decreased. What the United States could have obtained in the matter of political agreements in the spring or summer of 1918, to ensure that the final peace treaty would embody in letter and in spirit the principles of the Fourteen Points, would have been far nearer to Wilson's desires and to the hopes of the American people than what he was able to obtain when the Paris Conference was under way.

Moreover, an ungovernable popular demand in all the Allied countries for immediate demobilization impeded the framers of the treaty in their efforts to maintain a semblance of order in the countries where radical territorial or political adjustments had to be made.

The difficulties were immeasurably increased by the fact that the representatives of the victorious powers proceeded upon the assumption that the Central powers, as vanquished enemies, would necessarily be obligated to accept the terms imposed upon them. The treaty of peace was actually a series of conditions imposed upon a conquered foe; in form, however, it constituted a treaty negotiated between the representatives of the Allied nations and the representatives of the new German Republic. It is, of course, well-known that up to the last moment the Allied leaders assembled at Paris were not sure whether the German representatives would actually sign the Treaty of Versailles or not. Lloyd George, in the final stages of the conference, was even convinced that many of the terms already agreed upon would have to be modified to obtain the German signature.

In practice, the treaty proved to be neither a negotiated peace nor peace by imposition. At the time of the Armistice Germany was not invaded by Allied forces. So far as the masses of the German people could see, the collapse of Germany and her decision to sue for an armistice had been due to the breakdown of organized resistance within Germany rather than to military defeat. The Allies failed to impose terms of unconditional surrender upon Germany. The prior collapse of Austria-Hungary and of Bulgaria had undoubtedly hastened the end in so far as Germany was concerned. In the case of Turkey, her surrender, brought about by the defeat of these powers before she had been decisively beaten, created a determination to seek—like Germany—every means of evading the logical results of the victory of the Allies.

When the final treaty was signed, people were disheartened because it failed to measure up to the high ideal on which their hearts had been set. They had also persuaded themselves that their victory implied an end to all their burdens. They did not wish to comprehend that, to carry out the terms of the treaty, force would be required for a period of years—and the utilization of force meant additional burdens—both in the shape of taxation and through a continuation of at least partial mobilization. People everywhere, having undergone the sacrifices, the sufferings, the privations, and the nervous strain of four years of war, sought to relapse into what President Harding termed "normalcy." It was not only in the United States that people wanted to forget the war and everything about the war. This tendency was just as apparent in the countries of Europe. The high strain of emotional idealism of the autumn of 1918 was soon lost in the purely material and exaggeratedly nationalistic reactions of every country of the world.

The errors of omission and of commission contained in the Treaty of Versailles are manifold and have often been set forth. The agencies of the Allied governments set up, toward the very close of the war, to undertake preparatory peace planning, such as the United States "inquiry" and the technical staffs of the British and French Foreign Offices, contained many admirably qualified and intelligent technical experts. These experts, however, were called upon to find solutions for such staggering problems as the creation of new states whose precise populations and frontiers had to be reconciled with the heterogeneous peoples involved and with the requirements of those populations for economic and communications facilities. All too frequently they were compelled to decide in a harassed two weeks questions which it might well have taken two years to determine wisely. And even if by some miracle their judgment had been infallible, the experts had to face the dense ignorance of their own chiefs of government concerning the technical problems involved in these decisions.

Such territorial decisions as those which had to do with the frontiers of the new states carved out of the old Austro-Hungarian Empire, the eastern boundaries of Italy, the western frontier of the Soviet Union, and above all the eastern and western boundaries of the reconstituted Poland were cardinal errors calamitous in their effects upon the future peace and stability of Europe. Many other decisions, such as the arrangements for the treatment of minorities and the disposition of dependent peoples under the mandate system proved only too soon their hopeless inadequacy.

But the three major issues raised by the Treaty of Versailles which deserve particular consideration at this time are the Covenant of the League of Nations, the treatment accorded Germany, and the failure of the Allies even to attempt to follow any constructive policy in dealing with the situation created by the Russian Revolution.

In the winter of 1919 the Covenant of the League had the overwhelming support of the people of the United States; and the support of all the peoples of the other Americas, partly due to the thought of the latter that such a world organization would prevent the United States from continuing to assert a right to regional hegemony. It was supported also by a very large mass of public opinion in Great Britain and by a great majority of the peoples in the smaller countries of Europe. The Covenant met with but little response in France. The highly logical French were already beginning to think that a League of Nations such as that devised by its Anglo-Saxon drafters, rather than the type of League demanded by Léon Bourgeois (which was based upon the utilization of an international police force), was not likely to offer the French nation the concrete form of armed security which they regarded as essential. If the Covenant of the League met with but scant enthusiasm in France, it met with none whatever in either Japan or Italy. The League of Nations was bound to run squarely counter to the policy of aggrandizement which Japan has pursued secretly, and at times openly, since 1895. A League of Nations based upon the principles of self-determination, particularly as interpreted by President Wilson with regard to the control of the Adriatic, was bound to run counter to the Italian demand that Great Britain and France comply with the secret treaties of London.

By the time the Peace Conference met, most of the governments were already seeking what their domestic opinion demanded in the way of individual spoils. The spirit of nationalism rose as the weeks passed. The real cause for amazement, as one considers today the scene of 1919, is not that the Covenant of the League was not better and more effective, but rather that Wilson was able to get it adopted by the Paris Conference at all. Had the Covenant of the League been forged during the war years, had it already been agreed upon by the Allied nations—at least in its main principles—by the time of the Armistice of 1918, the concept of the League would have become so much a part of the very habit of thought of the Allied peoples, and in particular of the men who were doing the fighting, that it would actually have become the heart of the peace treaty. As it was, it was grafted upon the peace treaty, and accepted with reluctance and with but little belief in its efficacy by many of the governments represented.

As I have indicated, the determination of the treatment to be accorded Germany was complicated by the fact that throughout the Peace Conference there was no clear-cut decision as to whether the peace was to be a negotiated instrument or whether it was to consist of terms imposed upon Germany. Part of this difficulty dated back to the Armistice terms themselves. Poincaré had insisted that an armistice should not be granted the Germans until the German armies had been defeated upon German soil. Marshal Foch, however, had expressed the view that if the Germans signed the Armistice terms fixed by the inter-Allied High Command, everything which the Allied nations required would have been achieved and there was therefore no justification for further bloodshed. Clemenceau supported the views of Foch, which were wholly in accord with those of the United States and British governments. Consequently, when the fighting stopped, Germany had not been invaded and the psychological effect of a final and decisive military victory over the German armies within German territory was lost.

The final decision reached was due at least in part to the fact that the chief negotiators had overlooked some salient features of German history during the preceding half century.

There had been no real deviation for nearly fifty years in German policy, which had been consistently directed toward world hegemony. Pan-Germanism was too frequently regarded by public opinion in the Western democracies as a cult preached by a few German extremists. It had been all too often deprecated as merely an unfortunate manifestation of German militarism. As a matter of fact, Pan-Germanism as a national expression of the German people had permeated almost every branch of the German body politic. By 1914, there remained but a bare vestige of the old German liberalism of 1848. Even leaders of the German Socialist parties, in whose steadying effect liberal groups in France, Great Britain, and the United States placed so much faith, proved to be as Pan-German as the German General Staff itself, so long as it appeared probable that Germany would win a speedy and total victory.

In the Conference of Paris, only the French negotiators gave much consideration to these facts. The rest were inclined to believe that once the Prussian Imperial House had been removed from the scene, once the German General Staff had been abolished by fiat, and once the German people had been afforded the opportunity of creating a German Republic, such misguided conceptions as Pan-Germanism would go by the board. Nothing, of course, could have been more lamentably untrue. The German people were sure that they had not been defeated by Allied military might. They were certain that they had failed to conquer their enemies solely because of the breakdown of morale within their own borders. Nothing could have convinced them to the contrary except a smashing Allied victory within Germany, and an immediate military occupation of their chief cities by Allied forces.

The peace treaty contained no terms providing for effective military control of Germany, no stipulations which ensured a continuing imposition of Allied control over German armaments. The Allies took no steps to give any real encouragement to such democratic elements in Germany as might still at that time have proved of some political value; there were no provisions which would enable the German people in the immediate postwar period to voice legitimate grievances and expect thereafter to secure impartial justice from some international tribunal. The treaty did, however, impose reparations requirements which resulted in economic insecurity for every individual German. They paved the way for the later coalescence of all classes behind a movement for national revenge. They increased the already latent popular will to circumvent every form of Allied control.

It is difficult to be dogmatic as to which of two alternative courses it would have been safer for the Allies to have taken in 1919 in deciding upon the kind of treatment to be accorded the German people.

It may be that there were still forces within Germany strong enough to eradicate the Pan-German poison of the preceding fifty years. Had these forces been encouraged, had the Allies made it easier for a real German Republic to succeed, and had such a democratic Government been bolstered in the popular mind by prompt participation in the League of Nations, it is at least conceivable that the temper of the mentality of a majority of the German people might have changed. It is also possible that the views of Poincaré and of the French Right—that the salvation of Europe and world peace depended upon the armed occupation of Germany for an indefinite period; upon the creation of an independent or autonomous buffer state between the Rhine and the Western countries of Europe; and upon an indefinite and rigid supervision by the Allied powers over all forms of German industry capable of producing arms—constituted the only policy which would have prevented a renewal of the German menace. What is, however, unquestionably true is that a combination of the two alternatives was neither workable nor realistic. Unfortunately, it was precisely such a combination of two irreconcilable policies that was determined upon at Paris.

We in the United States must not forget that when Clemenceau, in the name of France, receded from the demands which he had made for French control of the left bank of the Rhine, he did so only because of the treaties guaranteeing French frontiers offered him by President Wilson and by Lloyd George. When these treaties failed to come into force, because the American Treaty of Guaranty was not ratified, British policy, which tended to favor the more lenient of the two courses above outlined, began to separate itself more and more sharply from French policy. The Germans were not slow to derive every possible advantage from this divergence in basic policy. What little control the British and French might still have exercised over Germany went up in smoke as a result of their lack of unity.

The remaining major issue raised by the Versailles Treaty was the attitude adopted by the Allies toward Russia. The collapse of Russian resistance in the spring of 1917 had necessarily prolonged the war by allowing Germany to concentrate all her military strength on the Western Front. The Treaty of Brest-Litovsk had filled Allied public opinion with consternation and indignation. The revolutionary character of the doctrines emanating from Communist Russia had aroused a panic of hysteria throughout Western Europe and the New World. The panic was equaled only by the horror created by the Bolshevik assaults upon religion and by the mass executions which stigmatized the earlier years of the Soviet regime. Russia was treated as a leper and as an outcast among nations. And German propagandists missed no opportunity of turning to their own advantage the excommunication which had been pronounced upon the new Russia by the Allied nations.

The Allied governments grossly underestimated the tremendous hold which the new Russian government had on the loyalties of the masses of the Russian people. Indeed, it is easy to see today the ineptness of Allied policy in its attempt to combat the Soviet government by giving armed assistance to its opponents within Russia. Nothing could have been better calculated to arouse a general nationalistic reaction in support of the Soviet authorities.

What is most difficult to comprehend is the decision of the Allied leaders to deal with European and Asiatic readjustments, both political and territorial, as if Russia were just not there. In all the plans framed for the reconstitution of Poland and for the creation of the new states of Eastern and of Northeastern Europe, no truly wise provision was made for the time when the power most directly concerned, which happened also to be potentially the greatest and the most powerful nation in Europe, would emerge from its international eclipse and demand that its rights must be respected. The ludicrous Prinkipo meeting between Allied and Soviet spokesmen, halfheartedly sponsored by Wilson and Lloyd George, represented the only effort to provide for this contingency. Territories which had been for centuries under Russian sovereignty and which were considered by all nations as integral parts of Greater Russia were disposed of without regard for Russian rights, and without thought of what Russia might eventually do in order to secure their return.

From this condition of amnesia, Great Britain rallied far more rapidly than its allies. Only a year after Versailles, to the vast indignation of the French government, the British government entered into direct commercial relations with the Soviet government. But it was many years before the major Allied powers—the United States last of all—awoke to the fact that whether or not they liked Russian internal or external policy, Russia could not be and would not be ignored.

These three basic errors in Allied policy—the mistakes in planning for and in content of the League of Nations, the inconsistencies and weaknesses in the treatment of Germany, and the failure to take account of Russia—played their full part in making possible the breakdown in later years of the bright plans of 1919 for the creation of an increasingly stable and peaceful world.

Certain purely human equations must not be overlooked in seeking to draw from 1919 a lesson that will be of service when the next peace is made. For instance, there was never any real meeting of minds between the members of the Big Four of 1919. Clemenceau delighted to refer to Lloyd George as the most ignorant man he had ever met. It cannot be denied that Lloyd George's ignorance of European geography and of the racial and economic problems of Central and Eastern Europe was notorious. He was little affected by the thought of how present decisions would affect future generations. He was actuated throughout the peace negotiations by his very British determination to get all he could to the immediate advantage of the British Empire, and by his unwillingness to agree to any policy or any settlement which would in any way jeopardize his popularity at home.

President Wilson has been vituperated by European writers and statesmen because of his unswerving determination that there would be no peace treaty signed by the United States unless that treaty contained the Covenant of the League of Nations. It is undoubtedly true that the Peace Conference was prolonged probably for two or three months because of this determination. Yet had he not insisted on this (granted his initial and fatal error in not obtaining inter-Allied agreement upon the Covenant prior to the Armistice), no League of Nations would have come into being. Given the attitude adopted by the United States Senate, there would have been only an uneasy military alliance between Great Britain, France, and Italy, in which the smaller nations of Europe and the other nations of the world would have had no voice and no share.

Of the Big Four, Clemenceau was undoubtedly the most realistic,

and the most consistent. He never wavered in his determination to
obtain security and reparations for France. Although the security he
did obtain through the British and American Treaties of Guaranty
soon proved to be illusory and the reparations fixed vanished into thin
air, as Foch predicted on the day the Treaty of Versailles was
signed, the French people and the rest of the world were convinced
in the summer of 1919 that French objectives had been attained.
The Italian representative, Signor Orlando, seems today to be merely
a pale shade on the pages of history. But at the time, the fury which
Woodrow Wilson provoked in Italy because of his consistent refusal
to agree to the maximum of the Italian demands for loot did little to
provide for harmonious relationships between the Italian representative and the other members of the Big Four. Furthermore—and
this is a point which can never be sufficiently hammered home—confidence in the delegates to the Peace Conference was shaken because
the assurance of "open covenants openly arrived at," formally proclaimed by President Wilson in the Fourteen Points, was denied
throughout the entire course of the Peace Conference by the most
dense and studied secrecy covering every aspect of the negotiations.
This secrecy imposed by President Wilson and by Lloyd George,
partly because of their fear that any information regarding the
conference would be used to their political detriment at home, reached
so extreme a form that even the other members of the United States
delegation, with the exception of Colonel House, were in total
ignorance of the course of the discussions. What was far more disastrous and even more intolerable, the delegates of the smaller Allied
nations were wholly unable to find out even what the terms of the
peace treaty were until they were confronted with the final document
for signature. In so far as the representatives of the Allied American
republics were concerned, their sole activity, as one or two of them
have so graphically described it to me, was standing around in hotel
corridors, or occasionally, as a great privilege, in the outer waiting
rooms of the Quai d'Orsay, in order to learn by rumor what the
decisions of the Big Four might be.

    With the exception of a few men like M. Venizelos of Greece and
General Smuts, who through their own intrinsic force of character
and intellectual capacity earned the respect and consideration of the

four leaders, none of the delegates of the smaller nations were given any opportunity to discuss questions of major policy other than those directly affecting their national interests. And in such cases their opportunity to "discuss" proved to be their opportunity to "hear" what the Big Four had already decided.

The impenetrable fog of secrecy surrounding the work of the conference had this inevitable result. It poisoned the public mind about the results of the conference before these results had even been determined. For naturally enough, under such conditions, rumor and myth were substituted for the truth. The press published every kind of fantastic report of the commitments which President Wilson was making in the name of this government, of the waiving of United States sovereignty, and of the alleged manner in which Wilson was prostituting the principles established in the Fourteen Points. Some of the newspapers in the European countries, which were desirous of weakening Wilson's influence in the belief that their governments could then more readily obtain the selfish advantages they sought, went to even greater extremes.

Only knowledge of the truth could have operated as an antidote upon public opinion, but every week that passed brought with it more severe measures to prevent the truth from being known. As a consequence, many millions of citizens of this country, who at the outset of the negotiations had earnestly supported the ideals which Wilson preached, found themselves, before the conference was half over, not only uncertain and confused but also prone to a cynical disbelief in the possibility of any fruitful collaboration between nations. There was never a moment when full publicity—within the reasonable limits which any negotiation requires—was more necessary to ensure success for the objectives sought. There was never an international meeting where the public and the press had less guidance and less opportunity to know the truth.

Finally, it cannot be forgotten that the prime negotiators of the Treaty of Versailles were a worn-out and worried group of men. The strain under which they were working, the constant press attacks to which they were subjected both at home and in Paris, the domestic political maneuvers directed against them during their absence, and above all the ever-increasing popular demand for immediate demobilization and for the immediate signature of some treaty—any treaty—harassed them night and day.

The installation of the German Republic—the Weimar Republic, as it has come to be known—was expected by many liberal forces within the Allied countries to bring with it the millennium in which the German lion of the past was automatically to become the German lamb of the future. Had there been enough Karl Liebknechts, the future of Germany and of the world might have been different. What actually happened was that behind the façade of the Weimar Republic the forces responsible for the catastrophe of 1914 remained active and powerful. Where before they had operated openly, they now found it expedient to remain temporarily concealed. They pursued the strategy followed by Prussia when she succeeded in evading the exactions imposed upon her by the first Napoleon.

The terms imposed by Napoleon provided—as did the terms imposed by the Treaty of Versailles—that the Prussian military establishment should be limited to a minimum figure. The Prussians accepted this figure. At the same time they adopted the military system, invented by Scharnhorst, whereby all enlisted men conscripted for the army were replaced at brief intervals with new recruits. Consequently, after a short time, all Germans of military age had received intensive military training. The intent of the Napoleonic edict was thus circumvented.

Precisely the same determination inspired the men operating behind the screen of the Weimar government. The evasion was well thought out, well planned, and carried through with that efficiency in organization which is one of the outstanding characteristics of the German mentality. Within a short time, the forces which these men represented—the General Staff, the big industrialists, the majority of the old political leaders—had reason to believe that the obligations imposed by the Treaty of Versailles could be safely ignored. New German policy reasoned that by paying no attention to German obligations, Germany could nine times out of ten obtain something of advantage, and that even on the tenth occasion she would lose nothing of any material consequence.

Under the terms of the treaty, Germany was required to deliver to the Allied military authorities by March 10, 1920, all war materials over and above a fixed minimum. This obligation was ignored. In July, 1920, the Allied governments ascertained that thousands of airplanes and a very large quantity of additional war matériel was still in German hands. Instead of taking positive action, these governments, as a result of British insistence, granted Germany a further delay of six months to comply with her obligations.

The terms of the treaty likewise obligated Germany to reduce the number of men in the Reichswehr to a maximum of one hundred thousand. Not only were these stipulations not complied with, but through the creation of what were ostensibly police organizations, the armed forces in existence in Germany eighteen months after the Treaty of Versailles amounted to eight times the maximum permitted. For example, in Bavaria alone there existed in the summer of 1921 an armed force of at least three hundred thousand men comprising the Einwohnerwehr. Lloyd George confessed to the House of Commons at that time that these were the facts, and that not only were these so-called irregular forces armed with rifles and machine guns, but that it was believed they had available a number of cannon.

It rapidly became apparent to the Allied governments that this situation was the product of a carefully devised and systematic plan of the German General Staff; that these military forces were being given arms by the very German organization—the Reichstreuhandgesellschaft—that had been established with Allied consent to turn over German war matériel to the Allied military commanders; that these troops were intended to become the nucleus of a future German army; and that the provisions of the Treaty of Versailles which were calculated to render impotent the military power of Germany were being flagrantly evaded.

The disarmament of Germany had been unanimously agreed upon by the Allied governments. As has been seen, Foch had consented to forgo a military occupation of Germany only because of the disarmament provisions in the armistice terms. And yet, except by France, no effort was made to see that German disarmament was actually carried out.

Germany's evasion of the reparations requirements was equally flagrant. Time and time again, German obligations to deliver to the Allies raw materials such as coal were not complied with. And the repeated Allied concessions, made always upon British insistence, invariably were at the expense of France. It was not long before the impression was created that Great Britain was operating as an arbiter, or at least as a mediator, between France and Germany, rather than as the military ally of France in carrying out the clear-cut provisions of the Versailles Treaty.

Whatever may be said about the German's lack of understanding of the psychology of other nations, it must be admitted that the propaganda put out by Germany after her defeat in 1918 was singularly effective. The sympathy of the Anglo-Saxon peoples—which is an honorable one—for the "underdog" was aroused by the constant plaint of German spokesmen that the terms of the treaty were being scrupulously observed but that their observance meant the starvation of innocent millions, and particularly of innocent women and children. Public opinion not only in Great Britain but also in the United States responded rapidly to these German pleas. French demands for British support in procuring Germany's strict compliance with the treaty provisions were often met by the reply that France was motivated by territorial ambitions at the expense of Germany, or else that action could be obtained only through the agency of the League of Nations.

Upon one of the rare occasions when Germany's disregard for the obligations imposed upon her by the Treaty of Versailles was followed by action rather than by concession—when France, upon her own initiative, occupied Frankfurt and Darmstadt in the spring of 1920—not only was American public opinion violently incensed, but the British Prime Minister issued an official statement that the action met with the disapproval of the other Allied governments. (It is interesting to remember in this case that four days later the Polish and Belgian governments publicly announced that they approved the French move, and the Italian government refused to make any statement.)

The future safety of France depended upon the co-operation of the former Allies in forcing Germany to comply rigorously with the conditions of the Versailles Treaty, and upon the ability of the League of Nations to afford her such further security as she might require.

The willingness of the other Allied governments to permit Germany to disregard her obligations—both military and material—with impunity, rapidly dissipated the first of these guarantees. In so far as the League of Nations was concerned, its power to provide security rested upon its ability to utilize the force of public opinion. Actually, the possibility of applying sanctions, either military or economic, became more and more remote as the years passed and the divergence between British and French policy became wider. Moreover, during the first three or four years after the inauguration of the League, Europe, owing to the passion which Mr. Lloyd George developed for the stage which international conferences afforded him, became the scene of an endless number of such meetings. Few of them were held with sufficient preparation. Few of them resulted in any concrete accomplishments. The problems they dealt with should all have been automatically resolved by the League of Nations. This failure of the League to take action in the very matters that it was created to handle impaired its prestige at a time when it should have been afforded every encouragement to assert its authority.

Gradually, the smaller European states lost faith in the League. This was especially noticeable in the case of the new European states which had been created by the Treaty of Versailles. Under such circumstances, nothing was more natural than that Poland should have looked to France for assistance when threatened with defeat by Russia in 1920, rather than to the League of Nations; nothing more natural than that the Little Entente composed of Czechoslovakia, Yugoslavia, and Rumania, should have looked to the same quarter for assistance against a rising Germany. In fact, it was altogether logical that these small countries, which in the concept of the League's founders should have been enabled to devote all their energies to national stabilization, confident in the League's ability to provide them with physical security, should have sought military and economic alliances with the major powers when it became clear that the League of Nations had no physical security to offer.

The creation by the Versailles Treaty of the new European states resulted in a ferment of nationalism. It was only to be expected that such diverse races as the Czechs, the Slovaks, the Ruthenians, the Croats, and the Slovenes, for centuries under the domination of

Austria, should have rejoiced in the liberty accorded them by the Allied powers. Some of them had been given freedom of which they had been deprived for a thousand years. Poland had been for a hundred years partitioned between Russia, Germany and Austria, and Polish patriots rejoiced in the reconstitution of their country as an independent state. They failed to attribute sufficient importance to the fact that the various elements within Poland, stamped with the impress of the cultural and governmental systems of the three empires by which they had been respectively dominated, would need at best a long period for amalgamation. Nor did they realize that each element would have to exercise a large measure of abnegation before the rebirth of Poland could imply an equal measure of security and happiness for all Poles.

Many of the new Succession States, as in the case of Czechoslovakia, were composed of peoples who had for centuries been compelled to eke out the ungrateful existence of racial minorities. But an equal number of new minority problems were created. Rumanian minorities, formerly included within Hungary, were now, it is true, transferred to the new greater Rumania. However, in the distribution of regions and populations, Hungarian minorities were brought under Rumanian rule. The minority problem could have been corrected only by courageous and radical steps providing for the orderly transfer of populations. Only in one instance, however, where Greek and Turkish minorities were involved, was such a transfer undertaken.

The rapid growth of an unhealthy nationalism throughout Central and Eastern Europe persuaded the great powers dominating the Council of the League not only to postpone indefinitely any general transfer of populations, but also to abandon any attempt to further the creation of a Danubian federation of an economic and financial character. And that alone could have resolved the economic chaos resulting from the splitting up of the Austrian Empire.

Most of the Succession States violently opposed any form of Danubian federation. They opposed it because they feared a return to Austrian or Hungarian overlordship and to that financial dependence upon Vienna which had obtained throughout the life of the Hapsburg Empire.

man Austria" was a constituent part of the German Republic. The incorporation of Austria in the German Reich was immediately agreed to by the new German government. The highly intelligent and wholly democratic leaders of the Austrian government saw plainly that the new Austria, as such, could not survive if it was to be economically divorced from all the other constituent parts of the old Austrian Empire. They believed that their sole hope for existence was economic federation with the new Germany. This, however, was expressly prohibited by the Treaty of Versailles. The only sop to Austrian aspirations had been a provision that this prohibition could be set aside by the Council of the League of Nations. However, since the decision of the Council had to be unanimous, and since it was obvious that France would always oppose the so-called "Anschluss" between Austria and Germany, and that French opposition would always be backed by the countries of the Little Entente, there was little hope held out to the Austrian people. As the years passed, although the first political leaders of the Austrian Republic demonstrated both devotion and ability in the manner in which they strove to improve political conditions within the country, economic and financial distress rapidly increased. Upon occasion, both the great powers and the League of Nations rendered a somewhat grudging financial assistance to the Austrian government. For a while complete collapse was postponed. But under such conditions the demand for economic federation with Germany could not fail to continue. It reached its culmination in 1931 when the customs union with Germany, at length officially proposed by Austria, was formally vetoed by France and Great Britain.

In this situation there was only one practical and possible solution, granted France's objection on the ground of her security to any incorporation of Austria in the German Reich. That solution lay in the creation of an economic federation in Eastern Europe, similar to the Danubian federation proposed in 1919. When the French government finally was led to support the proposal for such a federation, because of the constructive economic policy for Europe envisaged by Briand, it was already too late. By that time both Germany and Italy felt themselves powerful enough to block the proposal.

In retrospect, it is obvious that the stability, the prosperity, and the very existence of the Succession States depended upon the ability of the League of Nations to find a way by which their economic security could be assured. The League had also to guarantee them physical security if they were to concentrate their national energies upon finding a solution for their internal problems. The realization of the first of these objectives was defeated when the League failed to create any economic federation of Eastern or of Southeastern Europe. The second of these necessary assurances was never forthcoming, since the League never developed the power to ensure them of physical security.

In 1924 Edouard Herriot became French Prime Minister as leader of a combination of the parties of the Left. In the field of foreign policy, his chief purpose was to bring about a more harmonious relationship between the British and French governments. He believed that France could pursue no effective policy toward Germany until Germany was convinced that the British and French governments could no longer be played off one against the other.

In carrying out this policy Herriot sought at a conference held in London in 1924, at which Germany was represented for the first time since the war, to adjust the differences which had developed between France and Great Britain with regard to the reparations questions.

In pursuit of the same objective, he had at once ordered the French evacuation of the Ruhr. Herriot had been assured by Marshal Foch that from the standpoint of French military security, the occupation of the Ruhr was a source of weakness rather than of strength; that while the French occupation of the left bank of the Rhine was from every military standpoint most necessary, French occupation of the Ruhr was precisely the reverse.

As a result of Herriot's policy, the German government believed the time was ripe for the kind of move by which Gustav Stresemann, head of the German Popular party and at that time Minister for Foreign Affairs, was so often to delude the Anglo-Saxon public as to the real nature of German intentions and ultimate objectives. On February 9, 1925, Stresemann sent a memorandum to Herriot through the German Embassy at Paris. It read in part as follows:

In considering the different possibilities which today exist for the favorable settlement of the question of security, there might be followed a course similar to that contained in the proposal formulated in December 1922 by Herr Cuno, Chancellor of the Reich at that time. Germany could, for example, adhere to a pact by which the Powers directly interested in the Rhine, namely: England, France, Italy, and Germany, would undertake a solemn engagement before the Government of the United States not to make war one against another for a long period, the extension of which might later be determined.

.    .    .    .    .    .    .

Moreover, Germany would deem acceptable a pact which would formally guarantee the actual territorial status quo along the Rhine. Such a pact might be conceived in these terms: That the states interested in the Rhine would obligate themselves reciprocally, rigorously to observe the territorial status quo along the Rhine, and that they would guarantee not only jointly but separately compliance with this engagement, and that they would consider any act infringing upon this engagement as a cause for common action and as a cause for individual action.

.    .    .    .    .    .    .

There should furthermore be examined the possibility of recommending the formulation of the security pact in such a manner as to pave the way for a world-wide convention comprising all states, along the lines of the "Protocol for the Pacific Solution of International Differences" established by the League of Nations, so that the security pact would be backed by such a world-wide convention, or incorporated in it in the event that this convention were to be consummated.

Herriot had been violently attacked in his own country for his decision to evacuate the Ruhr. He was confident that France should take no step such as that proposed by Germany until after relations between the British and French governments had been placed upon a firmer basis. He was consequently predisposed to the counsel offered by his advisers that the Stresemann proposal constituted a German trap. Accordingly, his reply to the German government was limited to a bare acknowledgment of receipt, and a statement that before taking any of the steps proposed France would necessarily have to consult her allies. He was also personally convinced that any such plan as that outlined must be contingent upon the prior entrance of Germany into the League of Nations.

When Briand succeeded Herriot as Prime Minister at the end of 1925, a more comprehensive reply was made to the German démarche. This reply stated specifically that no agreement along the lines proposed was possible unless Germany were a member of the League. Briand also demanded the inclusion of Belgium in any agreement of that character. These negotiations were the first steps along the road which led to the Treaty of Locarno.

In October, 1925, at Locarno in Switzerland, the German, Belgian, British, French, and Italian governments, together with the governments of Poland and Czechoslovakia, signed a series of protocols reiterating their joint intention to seek a pacific solution for all their disputes and providing, on the part of France, Germany, Great Britain, and Italy, for a joint guarantee of French, German, and Belgian frontiers. The credit for this accomplishment was accorded with much popular effusion to Stresemann, Briand, and Austen Chamberlain.

The agreements signed at Locarno were acclaimed throughout the world as a great achievement. Peoples everywhere, as at the time of the Kellogg-Briand Pact, were convinced that peace would now be eternal. Yet in retrospect, one is again bound to ask why, if the provisions of the Covenant of the League, signed only six brief years before, were worth the paper they were written on, the same assurances couched in practically the same terms, save only for the fact that Germany participated in them, were of greater value merely because they were rewritten at Locarno. If, as had already been agreed, Germany was to become a member of the League, and to be bound by the terms of the Covenant, what greater measure of security could then be desired?

In reality the only practical results of the Locarno treaties were to weaken gravely the authority of an already sadly undermined League, and to encourage the belief in the Western democracies that the German leopard had forever changed his spots.

More and more the idea gained headway, particularly among the smaller European states, that while the League Assembly might be a useful place to blow off steam, when it came to the need for finding real solutions for real problems, bilateral or multilateral agreements involving the great powers were the only answer. It is a strange anomaly that during the ten years subsequent to the Treaty of Versailles, the only nations of Europe which acted as if they really had faith in the League as an organization capable of bringing about world stability were the nations which had not participated in the war. In practical forms of League activity it was generally the Scandinavian countries, or Holland, or Finland, that provided leadership and practical co-operation.

Conditions in Eastern and Central Europe, and later in the entire world, were gravely complicated by what at first seemed a transitory phenomenon—the emergence in Italy of the Fascist regime, after Benito Mussolini's so-called march on Rome in 1922. From 1919 until the autumn of 1922, the internal situation in Italy had been utterly chaotic. Economic distress was widespread. The political party system had disintegrated. Italian constitutional government had to all intents and purposes broken down. Neither the influence of the monarchy nor that of the Vatican was any longer heeded. General strikes of revolutionary character succeeded one another. Governmental as well as industrial inefficiency reached a new low. Public opinion, which, outside of the large cities, was still inherently conservative, sought some new panacea for the ills from which Italy was suffering. Opposed to Communism, it was inclined to welcome any form of authority, no matter what its name might be, provided it at least promised some semblance of discipline and some measure of efficiency. And so most of the Italian people, especially the reactionary elements and the larger banking and industrial interests, welcomed the dictatorship of Mussolini, from which they were to suffer for twenty-two years and through which the Italian people were finally forced to their ruin.

In the first years of the Fascist dictatorship, discipline and efficiency were certainly more apparent than they had been. Enjoying some material improvements, a majority of the Italians temporarily condoned such fatal signs as the gradual muzzling of all public opinion, the steady annihilation of representative government, the upsurge of the political murders and exiles decreed by the Fascists, the swelling grasp for personal power of the Fascist leader, and the ever-increasing corruption of his cohorts.

The classic phenomenon which is almost always found in the history of any dictatorship in the Old World was again apparent in the history of Fascism. At first the dictatorship limits itself to domestic affairs. Then internal opposition arises. To quiet public opposition within the country the dictator must then seek to stimulate an artificial patriotism by achieving glory abroad. It was not long before Mussolini was dominating Austria and attempting to dominate Yugoslavia. And the greater the reasons for his unpopularity at home the louder became his bluster abroad.

But the worst phase of Fascism was its effect upon the muddled thinking of the muddled peoples of Europe. In Spain the Primo de Rivera dictatorship had its real origin in Fascism. Later on, the Franco dictatorship gloried in its slavish adoption of Fascist methods. Likewise, many of the smaller countries of Eastern Europe imitated the Fascist experiment. Finally, there can be no doubt that Hitlerism found much of its own inspiration in Fascism.

At first, however, the major powers, and in particular Great Britain, breathed a sigh of relief. From their standpoint Italy had become quiet and orderly. It was in hands that would ruthlessly root out all signs of Communism. Even trains were now running on time. It was only later, when the second phase—the external phase—of Fascist policy became apparent, that doubts of the ultimate outcome of the Fascist experiment became widespread. Only a handful of leaders in Italy, such as Carlo Sforza, Benedetto Croce, Matteotti, and an equally small number of statesmen in the rest of Europe were sufficiently perspicacious to see the inherent danger of Fascism when it first was born.

The entrance of Germany into the League of Nations was obviously a prerequisite to any pacification of Europe. While the step, when it was finally taken, appeared superficially promising, it was in reality already too late. If Germany had entered the League of Nations in 1921 or 1922, it is conceivable that this might have strengthened the few weak elements in Germany which were working for a peaceful co-operation in an organized world. But by 1926, the forces set upon revenge and Pan-Germanism had already regained far too much of a hold on the body politic. From 1925 to 1929, Germany's economic prosperity, largely the result of the millions loaned by American and British bankers, prevented much popular agitation for military revenge. But all hope of popular support for a policy of co-operation rather than aggression vanished with the end of the German boom in 1929.

It was at this time that National Socialism emerged as a dominant factor. The years of world depression and the distress which once more afflicted all classes of German society gave the Nazi party its first great opportunity. In the first national elections in which they took part the total vote which the Nazis had been able to poll amounted to some eight hundred thousand. In 1930, National Socialism obtained six and one-half millions. Docilely led to believe that their misery was largely the result of the Versailles Treaty and that Hitler, the Nazi prophet, would wipe out this evil, the German people three years later not only swept Hitler and the Nazi regime into complete control, but likewise obliterated every vestige of the German Republic and every vestige of their own right to self-government.

It is strange now to recollect how lightly the rest of the world accepted this portentous development. It was only very rarely—and, surprisingly enough, least of all in the Foreign Offices of the Western democracies—that Hitler was seen to be the spearhead of the most evil force which had come out of Europe since the conclusion of the first World War and one which—granted the virility, discipline, and military capacity of the German people—would devastate civilization unless it were checked at the outset. In many quarters, notably in the United States, popular attention was largely focused on Hitler's personal idiosyncrasies and on the similarity between his mustache and that of Charlie Chaplin. Business interests in every one of the democracies of Western Europe and of the New World welcomed Hitlerism as a barrier to the expansion of Communism. They saw in it an assurance that order and authority in Germany would safeguard big business interests there. Among the more reactionary elements of the Church, there was a paean of praise. Strangely enough, even German labor believed that a friendly arrangement between German labor unions and the Nazi regime could be devised, although in their case it was not many weeks before they learned their grievous error.

In the case of Hitler, as in the case of Mussolini, the greedy, the Tories and the shortsighted heralded his rise to power with enthusiasm. I can remember one American Ambassador who publicly applauded Mussolini as the harbinger of a new era of glory, not only for the Italian people but for the rest of the civilized world as well.

The first six months of Hitler's rule should have made the truth plain even to the purblind. Within a few weeks organized labor was abolished and the persecution of the Jewish people began. Every class of German society was regimented; all individual rights obliterated; all individual freedoms destroyed, including the freedom of religious worship, to which many of the German people had been truly devoted. And with each new step toward the final stages of their abject slavery, the German masses became more and more fervid in their adoration of the tyrant.

The announcement of Germany's withdrawal from the League of Nations, made only a few months after Hitler had proclaimed himself chief of the German state, should have been regarded by every government as an unmistakable danger signal. It was tantamount to notice that German rearmament was not only already under way, but would be pursued to the limit. The slogan of "Guns rather than butter" had already captured the imagination of the German people. But to all of this the rest of the world paid but scant heed.

During the years preceding the culmination of Hitlerism, the Soviet Union had gradually emerged upon the European scene. A very considerable portion of Germany's foreign policy in the immediate postwar years had been devoted to finding some ground for an understanding with the Soviet Union as a counterpoise to Germany's weakness in the West. The treaty negotiated in 1922 by the German Foreign Minister, Walter Rathenau, and the Soviet Commissar, Chicherin had spelled Germany's first diplomatic success after the war. The Western powers had also noted that when Germany had entered the League of Nations in 1926, her entry was made contingent upon the agreement of the Soviet Union to the same military obligations as those which might be imposed upon Germany by the League of Nations.

But when the Soviet Union entered the League, even the most obstinate were soon forced to admit that it was the only major power which seemed to take the League seriously. The Soviet government seemed to believe that the Covenant of the League meant what it said. It seemed to feel that the Covenant was not to be regarded merely as a screen for the achievement of each country's individual and selfish purposes. The Foreign Commissar, Maxim Litvinov, the Soviet representative at the sessions of the League, had been kept out of England as a "dangerous alien" by order of the British government when Krassin had been sent to London in 1920 to negotiate the first commercial agreement between England and the Soviet Union. But as one today looks back, that same Maxim Litvinov must be recognized as the only outstanding European statesman who was consistently right during the years between the wars. It was Litvinov's constant appeal that "peace is indivisible"; that the purposes of the Covenant of the League of Nations could be achieved if the European powers complied with its provisions; and that in the increasing welter and turmoil, disaster was inevitable unless the powers of Europe were willing to see that the sanctions set forth in the Covenant were enforced.

Litvinov is a blunt man. He is often brutal. He has never seemed to me to be devious. So long as he represented his government in the League, he strove with all his great ability to make the League work. It should never be forgotten that the Soviet Union did not desert the League. It was the great powers which dominated the League in its later years that deserted the Soviet Union.

In 1931, the international horizon was still further darkened by Japan's decision that the moment had arrived when her ambition to extend her hegemony over the Asiatic continent could safely be carried out. Her rape of the three Manchurian provinces, and her subsequent decision to abandon the League because of the mild reproof administered, brought the League face to face with its greatest issue. The Baldwin government in England refused to countenance any forceful action. Notice was thereby given to the rising forces within Germany and Italy that the League of Nations was impotent in the face of the most flagrant and brutal aggression.

The failure of the League to take action in this case was the chief cause for Mussolini's aggression against Ethiopia; for the triumph of Fascism in Spain; and for Hitler's decision to proceed with the creation by force of his "greater Germany." Never was any decision more fatal in its consequences than that reached in 1932 by the governments of Great Britain and France when they permitted the League to be emasculated.

Within a few years peoples and governments were caught in an ever-surging torrent of events, and swept on to the final tragedy. And still many of the leaders of the Western democracies did not realize the force of the current, nor where it was taking mankind.

In 1934, with every purpose of voiding it as soon as it might prove expedient, Hitler entered into a ten-year pact with the Polish government of Marshal Pilsudski, providing for nonaggression on the part of the two signatories. Temporarily this afforded Hitler some measure of security against the Soviet Union and strengthened Germany's position along her eastern frontier.

In 1935, the plebiscite in the Saar, stipulated by the Treaty of Versailles, had restored the Saar region to Germany by an overwhelming majority of votes.

In 1936, Hitler made his first move toward the creation of the Greater Germany. By now he and the German General Staff saw eye to eye. In order to accomplish the ultimate objective, Germany had to regain full sovereignty over her western marches still subject to the restrictions of the Versailles Treaty, annex Danzig and Memel, recover the provinces which previously had been under German rule and were now comprised within the Polish Corridor, and join to Germany the German populations of Czechoslovakia and the regions of the former Austro-Hungarian Empire now composing the Austrian Republic. The first move in this direction was the reoccupation of the Rhineland. It is recorded that in taking this step Hitler was more hesitant than at any subsequent moment of his career. His officers were likewise divided. But the decision was at last taken. The Rhineland was reoccupied and immediately remilitarized.

Neither France nor Great Britain moved.

The French government, although prodded by French public opinion to take action, was weak and vacillating. It consulted London. The British government was confronted by its own public opinion, which felt quite differently from that of France. To the British people in general, all that was involved was the occupation by the German government of territory that was formerly German. Like the American people, they did not see that if the Western powers failed to prevent Hitler from carrying out his plans, the Treaty of Versailles would be destroyed and the League of Nations would be tacitly admitting that Germany could defy the whole of Europe at any time in the future, whenever she felt powerful enough. Such a failure constituted a welcome notice to Hitler that he might continue with impunity upon his forward march.

Hitler now threw all caution to one side. Military rearmament was no longer surreptitious. The representatives of foreign powers in Berlin were even shown with proud ostentation, in parade after parade, such of the new military equipment as it was not considered necessary to keep secret. The German four-year plan immediately carried into effect a consolidated civil and military organization. It prepared Germany for the outbreak of war by stimulating the development of substitutes for essential materials and through the hurried but most efficient accumulation of stocks of strategic imports from overseas.

The halfhearted and wholly nominal sanctions imposed upon Mussolini after the invasion of Ethiopia had by now persuaded Mussolini to seek support from the country which Italy had traditionally regarded as the chief potential danger to her national interests. In 1937 the Berlin-Rome Axis was proclaimed. It followed by one year the conclusion between Germany and Japan of the Anti-Comintern Pact. By this, the most fatal error of his career, Mussolini abandoned his prior claim to maintain Austria as a buffer state between Germany and Italy. He now gave Hitler preponderance in Austria in return for the promise of support for Italian territorial expansion, not only in East Africa but in North Africa and in the Mediterranean basin as well.

As an integral part of its policy of world domination, the German government, through the devious but incredibly effective systems invented by such of its economic experts as Dr. Hjalmar Schacht, embarked upon a plan of economic penetration and control which literally forced the smaller European powers, the Balkan nations, and many of the South and Central American republics, which were in great part dependent upon the German market for their export trade, to take German goods in preference to goods from other countries. In essence, the arrangements constituted an enforced barter system, since those who sold and exported products to Germany were able to obtain in return therefor only a special form of German exchange, which in turn could be utilized only for the purchase within Germany of special categories of German manufactures. They wiped out all the benefits resulting from triangular or multilateral trade. They brought about a financial and commercial dependence upon Germany which not only greatly increased German influence in many smaller countries but also at once enhanced her political power in those countries. The system also was highly useful in preparing the ground for sub- versive activities and military espionage.

As the months passed, Hitler resorted more and more to the scheme which he had so blatantly proclaimed in *Mein Kampf*—and which the world so blandly ignored. Under this system Germany entered into treaty commitments with other nations for the sole purpose of deceiv- ing them. One of the strangest features of the immediate prewar period was the continued success with which Hitler pursued these tactics. Time and again he violated his solemn official engagements, yet time and again some new victim would willingly enter into a treaty with him, identical to one that he had just violated.

An example of this character was the Naval Agreement concluded by Hitler with England in 1935. This Convention provided that Ger- many's surface armed vessels would in their total tonnage not exceed thirty-five per cent of the total tonnage of the British fleet. Great Britain made this agreement without prior notification to France, and in contravention of the existing understanding between the British and French governments. But a certain section of British public opinion applauded it enthusiastically. Like all Hitler's other treaties, it was thrown into the discard as soon as it had served his purpose.

Simultaneously during these years the German propaganda machine was demanding the return of the colonies seized from Germany in the first World War. Goebbels and Hitler insisted repeatedly that "lebensraum" in Europe, the abandonment by France and Great Britain of their alleged policy of encirclement, and the return of the former German colonies were all that was required to make Germany a peaceful and co-operative member of the family of nations. Yet each time that the British and French governments expressed willingness to discuss colonial adjustment in principle, Hitler and his agents replied that this was not a pressing matter, but one that could be taken up five or ten years later. One of the most amazing features of this particular phase of German propaganda—and one which seemed to make little impression upon the peoples of the Western democracies—was the fact that at the very moment when the Hitler regime was demanding the return of colonies and emphasizing the need for "lebensraum," on the ground of expanding population, it was utilizing every method within its power to increase the German birth rate. In precisely the same manner the Fascist regime in Italy now attempted to justify the invasion of Ethiopia and Italian demands for Tunisia: only in this way, it was claimed, could Italy's excess population find a "little place in the sun." Yet here too the utter hypocrisy of this propaganda was shown by the official encouragement of larger families.

Up until the moment of the final crisis, British, as well as French and American, public opinion was still greatly influenced by many figures in positions of authority who could not understand that Hitler did not care about pacific solutions. They could not see that agreement to any of Hitler's demands would immediately be followed by new and more far-reaching exactions. This habit of thought was never better exemplified than in the very year of the outbreak of war when Lord Halifax, that eminently sincere Secretary of State for Foreign Affairs, officially announced that Great Britain was certain that a reasonable solution could be found for all the outstanding difficulties of Europe if the other European countries "really wanted pacific solutions." Unfortunately, Hitler was willing to resort to pacific solutions only when he could obtain through them every least thing he wanted. The more often he obtained what he wanted by so-called "pacific solutions" the more firmly he became convinced that no power or powers would lift a finger to prevent him from achieving every one of his objectives.

By the spring of 1938, German military and economic preparations had reached the point where Hitler was prepared to make his first move toward world conquest, which was the reconstitution of the greater German Reich. The first step was taken on March 12, 1938, when German troops invaded Austria, and the republic became a German province.

Immediately thereafter, on March 18, in an address to the puppet Reichstag, Hitler gave warning to Czechoslovakia. The moment was well-chosen. The German seizure of Austria had ended Czechoslovakia's ability to defend herself. German accomplices in France were already loudly proclaiming that France's treaty obligation to defend the allied republic should be disregarded, since the defense of Czechoslovakia was not worth a war with Germany. Great Britain, influenced in part by the feeling expressed by Neville Chamberlain that Czechoslovakia was a remote geographical spot, and in part by a latent doubt whether the Sudeten Germans of Czechoslovakia were not entitled to become a part of Germany should they so desire, made it clear that no forceful action could be expected from her.

At the end of May disorders instigated by the Sudeten Germans broke out in Czechoslovakia. Rumors became current that Germany was mobilizing. It seems to be true that Hitler at first was inclined to force the issue with Czechoslovakia without further delay. Simultaneously, however, both the British and French governments intervened in Prague, urging the Czechoslovak government to make ample concessions to satisfy Hitler's demands. These activities resulted in the absurd mission of Lord Runciman. He was supposed to settle the whole problem immediately, but at the same time it was publicly made known that he went to Czechoslovakia in his "personal capacity" and only as an "independent" mediator. The mission disclosed an incomprehensible lack of realism in the British government. Even the man in the street saw more clearly. I happened at the time to visit Holland and Switzerland, and I recall the opinions I heard from all quarters in those two eminently realistic countries concerning the apparent inability of either the British or the French governments to understand that the only policy which could avert the despoiling of Czechoslovakia was the immediate threat to use force against force.

Early in September, at the yearly exercises of the Nazi party in Nuremberg, Hitler openly dared the Western powers to prevent the realization of his ambitions in Eastern Europe. On September 15, Mr. Chamberlain flew to interview Hitler at Berchtesgaden. On September 18, the British and French governments jointly brought pressure upon the Czechoslovak government to agree to cede all that portion of Czechoslovakia in which the German-speaking population was in excess of fifty per cent. The Czechoslovak government was assured that this would satisfy Hitler's maximum demands, and that Czechoslovak security would thereby be assured. Both the British and the French ignored the conversations between the Czechoslovak government and the Soviet government, in which the latter expressed its willingness to give military support to Czechoslovakia in the event of German aggression, provided the two Western powers would do likewise. Representatives of the Polish and Hungarian governments now also rushed to Berchtesgaden to seek German assurance that they would get their share of the spoils.

On September 22, at Godesberg, Mr. Chamberlain learned that Hitler had determined to ask for more as soon as he found out that the Czechoslovak government had been obliged to yield. Thus he flouted completely the positive assurances which he had originally given Chamberlain at Berchtesgaden. The British government then conveyed Hitler's new demands to the Czechoslovak government. When the latter refused to agree to them, the French government finally decreed a partial mobilization. Mobilization of the British Navy was likewise ordered.

On September 26, when Hitler publicly announced that German armies would occupy all of the Sudetenland by October 1 if Czechoslovakia had not previously ceded the territory in question, President Roosevelt addressed a direct appeal to all the governments involved. He urged a conference to bring about a pacific settlement. Immediately thereafter, the British government, finally shocked out of its complacency by Hitler's blatant disregard of promises he had solemnly made, announced that if France should decide to honor its treaty obligation to support Czechoslovakia against German aggression, Great Britain would join France. Mussolini then personally urged Hitler to take no precipitate action, since he was convinced Hitler could obtain the satisfaction of his immediate demands through a conference of the four powers.

The doom of Czechoslovakia was pronounced at the meeting of Munich on September 28. Hitler obtained, as Mussolini had assured him he would, everything he then demanded. He had counted upon the unwillingness of France to go to the assistance of Czechoslovakia and on the unwillingness of both France and Great Britain to align themselves with the Soviet Union in a war in Central Europe. Nor did he underestimate the influence of those in the two Western countries who still believed that German domination of Europe was preferable to the growth of Russian power.

The Sudeten territories were immediately taken over. Not the least contemptible feature of those tragic weeks was the action of the Polish government—at the instigation of Colonel Beck—when it occupied the Czech area of Teschen at the very moment of Czechoslovakia's martyrdom.

For an instant public opinion in the democracies concentrated solely upon the fact that a general war had been averted. Few were witless enough to believe with Mr. Chamberlain that "peace in our time" had been secured, but many did believe that Great Britain and France would now have time to rearm, and thus present to Hitler the one argument that he understood. The British government undertook at long last the rearmament program which had been so fatally delayed.

But the breathing space proved very brief indeed. Hitler moved rapidly, realizing that delay would be to his disadvantage and that public opinion in the democracies would no longer stomach any further concessions without a showdown. For the time being he allayed the fears of some of the members of the Polish government by continuing negotiations with the Polish Foreign Minister, Colonel Beck, for a solution of the problems of Danzig and of the Polish Corridor.

With the resignation and flight of President Beneš from Czechoslovakia, there had come into power in Prague the weak government of Dr. Hacha, pledged to a policy of co-operation with Germany. Grasping the opportunity which the incapacity of the new government afforded, and utilizing the pretext offered by the open dissension between the government at Prague and the Slovak Prime Minister, Father Tiso—who with rare perfidy had appealed to Hitler for assistance—Hitler summoned Dr. Hacha to Berlin, and simultaneously sent German troops to occupy what remained of the Czechoslovak Republic. The following day, March 16, the German Reich announced that it had assumed a "protectorate" over the provinces of Bohemia and Moravia, and that henceforth those Czechoslovak provinces would be governed by a German Protector stationed at Prague.

It is almost incredible now to realize that some people in the Western nations still had a lingering doubt as to Hitler's ultimate aims. No longer could it be claimed that all he sought was the incorporation into the German Reich of German people. By open conquest he had now asserted the right to rule over peoples who were not only non-German but who had for centuries struggled to free themselves from any form of Teutonic domination and to achieve their independence.

The next months were kaleidoscopic. Lithuania was forced by Hitler to surrender Memel. Within two weeks after the occupation of Czechoslovakia, Great Britain announced to the German government that in the event of any act of German aggression against Poland the British government would give all possible aid to Poland. The practical difficulty of getting assistance to Poland at this late date, now that both Czechoslovakia and Austria were in German hands was, of course, obvious. The only solution lay in an immediate, open, and complete understanding with the Soviet Union. This attempt was only now made, and failed for reasons which will be later considered in some detail.

On April 28, 1939, Hitler denounced his ten-year pact of 1934 with Poland, and threatened to solve the question of Germany's eastern frontier by force, if necessary. He ridiculed publicly the urgent representations of President Roosevelt, who had pressed him to agree to a ten-year truce for the gradual and equitable solution of all European problems.

Poland refused to yield to German threats. The Polish government apparently believed that it could hold out, if attacked by the overwhelmingly superior forces of Germany, long enough for the French Army and British air or naval forces to come to her support. A high Polish official at that time informed me with the utmost conviction that the Polish cavalry would be extraordinarily effective in throwing back invading German columns. This attitude was taken in the face of Poland's awareness of Germany's mechanized equipment and the knowledge of most of the world of the crushing might of Germany's air strength.

The German press and radio gave out precisely the same kind of propaganda as at the time of the Czechoslovak crisis the preceding year. Every official propagandist howled that German nationals were being tortured, outraged, and murdered in Poland. The German public again proved that, in its case at least, the greater the lie the more readily it is digested.

While Hitler by this time had reached the conclusion that war with France and Great Britain was almost inevitable, he still made a final effort to postpone it. By a last-minute offer of a German-British alliance, he hoped to persuade the British not to come to the support of Poland. By a similar maneuver he believed he could hoodwink the government of France. But the time for self-deception on the part of the democracies had at last passed. The die was now cast. On September 1, the German armies invaded Poland, and the second World War had begun.

# CHAPTER II

# The Tragic Years

THE detailed account of the events which caused the United States Senate to reject the Treaty of Versailles and the League of Nations has been frequently written, and innumerable explanations of the reasons for that momentous decision have been published.

There is no greater fallacy in American history than the assertion, so often advanced in these accounts, that the refusal of the United States to assume its share of responsibility for maintaining world peace was the result of a solemn referendum held in the Presidential elections of 1920. It is true that the Democratic candidate for the Presidency, Governor Cox, made the League of Nations issue a chief feature in his campaign. It is equally true, however, that, while the Republican candidate declared that the Republican party opposed participation in the kind of League conceived at Paris, he repeatedly asserted that he favored full co-operation by the United States in some other form of international organization. The very platform on which he stood, adopted by the Republican party in its convention in June of that year, contained this plank:

The Republican Party stands for agreement among the nations to preserve the peace of the world. We believe that such an international association must be based upon international justice, and must provide methods which shall maintain the rule of public right by the development of law and the decision of impartial courts, and which shall secure instant and general international conference whenever peace shall be threatened by political action, so that the nations pledged to do and insist upon what is just and fair may exercise their influence and power for the prevention of war.

Nebulous, it is true, but if words mean anything, the words employed could only be interpreted by the average voter as implying that the Republican candidate, if elected, would further the entrance of the United States into "an international association" and that the "influence and *power*" of this nation would be exercised in such an association "for the prevention of war."

The decision of the American electorate at the polls in 1920 was based largely on purely domestic considerations. It was far from being a general vote in favor of "isolationism." It was a vote cast in accordance with the traditional custom of the American people when conditions are not to their liking of holding responsible the party in office; it was due to popular resentment against wartime restrictions and wartime discipline; it was due to the fact that the enthusiasm and cohesion of the Democratic party had broken down. Moreover, the average citizen had had his surfeit of liberalism in the domestic field; and some of the most powerful financial and commercial influences in the nation were determined to stamp out the progressive policies for which Woodrow Wilson stood.

The wave of idealism which had swept the nation in the war years had ended. The lure of "normalcy" held out by Warren Harding was great. The very possibility that the tragedy of war might again shadow the United States seemed fantastically remote.

In 1920 it was not that the majority of the American people disapproved of participation in an international organization to keep the world at peace. That issue just did not seem to be of any importance at the time. But whatever foreign policy the voters thought the Republican party was pledged to carry out, the country as a whole soon discovered what it really was.

With the inauguration of the Harding Administration, every thought of active participation by the United States in world affairs, in so far as any "international association" was concerned, went immediately by the board. It was not long before President Harding's Ambassador to London, George Harvey, was instructed to announce to an astounded Europe that the United States government "could not, without the betrayal of its creators and masters, and will not, I assure you, have anything whatsoever to do with the League, or with any commission or committee appointed by it or responsible to it, directly or indirectly, openly or furtively." This was a flat-footed official declaration of an utterly sterile American foreign policy. It was made less than three months after the new Administration had come to power. It represented the decision of the small but all-powerful group of United States Senators which then dominated the councils of the Republican party and dictated the policy of the government itself. It was far from representing the point of view of the constructive-minded, farsighted leaders of the Republican party for which the new Secretary of State, Charles Evans Hughes, and the former Secretary of State, Elihu Root, were spokesmen. Confronted with the dictatorship of Boies Penrose, Frank Brandegee, and Philander Knox, and the interests which they represented, Secretary Hughes had a grueling task in shaping anything other than a policy of static isolation.

The only constructive note struck by the new Administration lay in its expressed willingness to participate in plans for the reduction of armaments. We can now appraise accurately Mr. Hughes's stupendous accomplishment in this direction in the conference held at Washington at the end of 1921. Both the objectives which he sought and the technique which he employed were bold and imaginative.

I well remember that electrifying inaugural session of the conference when Secretary Hughes announced the willingness of the United States not only to cease building but actually to scrap vessels of the United States Navy, if similar steps were taken by Great Britain, Japan, France, and Italy. I can hear the response of Lord Balfour, made in his halting but extraordinarily graceful delivery; the uniquely beautiful voice of Monsieur Briand, who was of course interested solely in military security for France—an issue which had unfortunately long ceased to concern American public opinion. Most clearly of all do I remember the spontaneous and unruly shouts of applause that came from the seats where members of the American Congress were sitting, and the tears that were streaming down the face of William Jennings Bryan, who was attending as a correspondent of the American press. The agreements met the same spontaneous acclaim throughout the United States.

The criticism made by a few then, and many now, of American policy at this conference seems to me wholly unwarranted. If the vicious circle of armament was ever to be broken, that was the time to make the effort. If any major power should take the initiative it was the United States, for the great powers, members of the League, could naturally take no step toward a reduction of world armaments through the League when the United States not only was not a member but, as George Harvey had said, would have nothing to do with any "committee appointed by it." If disarmament were ever to take place, nations would have actually to disarm, and that was precisely what Mr. Hughes proposed to do.

Mr. Hughes sought a gradual but steady reduction in the back-breaking burden of armaments by firm agreements between the great powers which had major naval forces. This was to be the first step toward the negotiation of similar agreements covering other categories of armaments. He was the last man to fail to see clearly that measures for universal disarmament, to be successful, must be predicated upon two co-ordinate assurances: first, that all the military and naval powers of the world reduced their armaments in the same proportion; and second, that there was some continued and effective international supervision to assure each one of the powers participating in the agreements that the commitments made by the rest were actually carried out. Unfortunately, neither the succeeding Administrations in Washington nor the League of Nations obtained these assurances from the great powers. That fact, not the objectives sought nor the methods employed by Mr. Hughes, is the legitimate ground for criticism. Without these guarantees, the agreements reached at the Washington Conference were not only vain but actually dangerous to our security. For no concrete means was secured of making sure that Japan was carrying out the promises that it had made at Washington. And yet it was well-known that the Japanese delegates who had signed the Treaties of Washington had been excoriated by the controlling elements in their Army and Navy, and were in constant danger of assassination. The exclusion of the Soviet Union weakened gravely the possibility that the conference would create a successful precedent for further steps toward disarmament. And the ever-weakening Allied control over Germany's armament in the years which followed presaged the ultimate failure of the plan so nobly conceived by Mr. Hughes.

An achievement of the Washington Conference, regarded by public opinion at the time as wholly subsidiary, was the treaty concluded between the nine powers having direct interests in the Pacific for the stabilization of that region. This great accomplishment ended the alliance between Great Britain and Japan, which had for many years worried the United States and done much to keep alive anti-British feeling in this country. It brought about the withdrawal of Japan from the Shantung Peninsula; maintained the integrity of China; and gradually eliminated innumerable forms of encroachment upon Chinese sovereignty, of which all the great powers had in varying degree been guilty.

Farsighted and far-reaching as the Nine-Power Treaty and its attendant agreements were, they also had a defective foundation. The treaty abrogation of the right of the United States and British governments to fortify strategic points in the Far East, then under their flags, was undertaken upon the treaty agreement of Japan to take corresponding action. This agreement not to construct military fortifications which could be used by any one of the three powers for offensive military or naval operations was the only basis for a peaceful system in the Pacific. Under the Treaty of Versailles, Japan had obtained the mandate over former German islands in the Southwestern Pacific. Certain of these mandated islands possessed great strategic value. Under the regulations laid down by the League of Nations, League inspection of the mandated territories in all parts of the world was required, and consent thereto by the mandatory was obligatory. Within only a short time, however, the Japanese government sought every available pretext for postponing or limiting such inspections. In later years Japan not only obdurately refused to have such inspections undertaken, but even declined to give any reasons for her refusal. Here again it soon became evident that constructive and desirable as the Pacific agreements might intrinsically be, they constituted a source of weakness to those of the treaty powers that carried out their obligations in good faith. For it did not take long to see that Japan was not carrying out her obligations at all.

Both at the Geneva Conferences and at the London Naval Conferences of 1930 and 1936, the fundamental defects which had vitiated the bright hopes raised by the Washington Conference were again apparent. Without the necessary confidence which a real international supervision of disarmament alone could create, and without an effective agreement on the part of all of the major powers, including Germany and the Soviet Union, no military power could or would agree to undertake any further limitation or reduction of its own armaments.

With the advent of the Coolidge Administration the United States as a world power shrank even farther into its shell. Mr. Coolidge was the most provincial-minded of any of our Presidents since the period immediately subsequent to the Civil War. His aversion to any positive foreign policy was dictated by the habitual caution of the professional politician. It also stemmed from a strong prejudice against any foreign nation.

The debt settlements obtained by this country from the Allied nations had irritated many American citizens. They were unwilling to comprehend why the war debts were not being repaid one hundred cents on the dollar, together with one hundred per cent of accumulated interest. The impoverishment of the European peoples, already staggering under the burdens imposed by their individual economic difficulties and by the costs of reconstruction, made it obviously out of the question for them to meet their obligations to us through the transfer of gold balances. Even if they had been highly prosperous their payments must have represented goods or services. With the increasingly high tariff rates imposed by the Congress, any such form of payment as this was out of the question. Thus the high tariff policies pursued by the Harding, Coolidge, and Hoover administrations killed any chance of debt payments. They also rolled up unemployment in Great Britain and in Western Europe. They encouraged the German government to adopt its autarchic economic policy, which in turn was a contributing factor in bringing about the second World War.

No effort was made by the government to explain these simple economic truths to the American public. But this was hardly surprising when one remembers the statement of President Coolidge when he insisted that the European governments must meet their obligations: "They hired the money, didn't they?"

The only instance of American co-operation in dealing with the problem of world peace, so far as the foreign policy of the Coolidge Administration is concerned, is the negotiation of the Kellogg-Briand Pact. The Pact was the brain child of Senator Borah of Idaho and

Mr. Salmon P. Levinson, a wholly sincere but somewhat ingenuous Chicago attorney. Mr. Levinson earnestly believed that the one great requirement to secure permanent peace was for the nations of the world simultaneously to append their signatures to a document outlawing war as an instrument of national policy. Whether the commitments would be respected by militaristic regimes lusting for power or loot; whether a German General Staff still burning to avenge its defeat in 1918 would permit any German government to respect such pledges; whether such a renunciation would carry any weight at some future time when peoples under the pressure of economic prostration were unemployed and starving; or whether the world had as yet reached the point where it could enforce the sanctity of such engagements by the mere impact of public opinion appeared to be altogether minor problems in the minds of the sponsors of the pact.

Senator Borah, however, persuaded Secretary Kellogg to assume the paternity for the suggested convention. The latter proved a ready and willing convert. As a result of a singular chain of circumstances Monsieur Briand, already engaged upon his infinitely more worthwhile and more practical plan for the creation of a European union, when approached by the American Secretary of State, was led to believe that through this project the people of the United States could be brought into at least some kind of co-operation with other countries in measures affecting the basic interests of them all. He consequently offered the support of the French government.

Eventually, in a gaudy ceremony, most of the sovereign governments of the earth affixed their signatures to the pact. The signing of the Kellogg-Briand Pact was regarded by almost all elements in this country and by many in Europe as a portent of a new epoch. There was going to be no more war because a number of governments had by fiat decreed that war was abolished.

I doubt whether, during the years which have elapsed since the Senate rejected the covenant of the League, any aspect of American foreign policy has proved to be more truly harmful in its effect upon the vital interests of the United States. The Kellogg-Briand Pact stimulated the delusion of a great body of the American people that the mere formulation of a wish is equivalent to positive action. It was regarded by many millions of American citizens as a complete

justification for the refusal of their government to take part in the
League of Nations or to participate actively in any other practical
form of international co-operation which would have required action
and sacrifice. To them it represented a happy and decorous means of
evading rather than accepting responsibility. It lulled to sleep any still
lurking feeling of national obligation. It blinded the American people
to the danger to their own security inherent in an increasingly unstable world. It greatly accentuated the demands of ultrapacifist organizations for total disarmament by this country, whatever else
other nations might be doing. For a time at least, a majority of the
American people were convinced that with such an ironclad guarantee
of safety, they need no longer concern themselves about the kind of
world they lived in. They could be confident that war was a thing of
the past.

The Kellogg-Briand Pact marked a high point in isolationist thinking in this country. It was a fitting climax to a foreign policy which
even in its least harmful aspects was totally negative. During Coolidge's elected term as President from 1925 to 1929, American policy
invariably concentrated upon American rights. It never envisaged any
obligations on the part of this country as a member of a family of
nations.

The inauguration of Herbert Hoover presaged to many a more
realistic and constructive foreign policy. His magnificent record in
relief work in Belgium, as well as his relief measures in other parts
of Europe, and his personal knowledge of world affairs seemed to
indicate a reversal of the Coolidge policies. Still greater hope lay in
the fact that in his Secretary of State, Henry L. Stimson, he possessed an adviser with much practical experience both in the field of
government and in the realm of foreign affairs. Colonel Stimson
was a liberal-minded follower of Elihu Root. He was imbued with
the latter's abiding conviction that our government in its own interest
should take an active part in all forms of international co-operation
which were likely to promote world stability.

However, Herbert Hoover as President proved to be quite distinct
from the Herbert Hoover of the earlier years. It is true that in the
first year of his administration he was confronted with the economic
depression which was spreading over the entire world. But instead

of recognizing that the one remaining hope of lessening its impact lay in speedy and practical measures of international co-operation, he adopted enactments which could only intensify economic distress, promote autarchic policies abroad, and encourage the growth of conditions which led inevitably to world-wide chaos. The Smoot-Hawley Tariff Act of 1930 immediately accentuated the depression throughout the world. It killed any chances still existing of an intergovernmental program for the promotion of world trade. The intergovernmental moratorium, which Mr. Hoover at last somewhat hesitantly initiated, came far too late to have any of the beneficent results that might earlier have been secured.

The Hoover Administration, as did the two before it, stressed the disarmament issue. But, like them, it appeared to ignore what were the basic requirements for disarmament, especially when peoples throughout the world were suffering from the greatest economic depression in history, and when certain governments were already manufacturing munitions rather than butter as a means of offering employment.

In one major issue, however, the policy of the Hoover Administration was directed squarely toward assumption by the United States of full responsibility as a great power for checking international anarchy. An account of American policy with regard to the Manchurian incident of 1931 will be undertaken in a later chapter. But it is important to remember that the effort made by Secretary Stimson to reach an agreement with the British government, which might have averted the later invasion of China by Japan and the subsequent breakdown of the League of Nations, was the first step taken by any American administration since the days of Woodrow Wilson that recognized our obligation to take part in the maintenance of world order. Even though this effort was to fail, there at least emerged from it the American policy of nonrecognition of territory seized by aggression. Had this policy been adopted earlier as a result of an agreement between the United States and the other world powers, the history of the decade which lay ahead might well have been far different.

On a bleak and gray March 4 Franklin Roosevelt assumed the Presidency and gave courage and fortitude to millions of his fellow countrymen who were confronting life with fear and despair. The thoughts of the American people were never farther removed from problems of foreign relations nor from the dangers to them already arising with dizzying rapidity in the rest of the world. The President's classic inaugural address devoted only one brief paragraph to the subject of foreign relations:

> In the field of world policy I would dedicate this Nation to the policy of the good neighbor—the neighbor who resolutely respects himself and, because he does so, respects the rights of others—the neighbor who respects his obligations and respects the sanctity of his agreements in and with a world of neighbors.

During the years preceding his inauguration President Roosevelt had, however, studied every aspect of American foreign relations. The general lines of policy upon which he had determined included an attempt to create a system within the Western Hemisphere through strictly co-operative methods; an increasingly close relationship with the Dominion of Canada; the establishment of firm political and commercial relations with the Soviet Union; a vigorous effort to obtain through a peaceful and equitable approach a settlement of problems in the Pacific; and an eventual understanding between this country and the leading powers of Europe to achieve economic co-operation. Like his predecessors in the Presidency, he also hoped, through the actual reduction of armaments, not only to ease political tensions but also to lessen a budgetary burden that was fast reducing living standards throughout the civilized world. In the realm of world problems, nothing occupied a more prominent place in the President's mind than the fact that almost universally budgetary deficits were precisely equivalent to armaments expenditures.

By education and training, by long experience in government, through personal knowledge of Europe and of the lands of the Western Hemisphere, and above all else by an almost intuitive understanding of the great forces which control human relations, Franklin Roosevelt brought to the conduct of American foreign relations more specialized qualifications than those possessed by any President since the days of John Quincy Adams.

In the initial months of his first administration the clouds upon the international horizon were lowering. While lightning flickered through them from time to time both in Europe and in the Far East, the lightning seemed very far away. A few weeks before the President's inauguration the Nazi Fuehrer had at length grasped the authority he had so long coveted. There were few of us who appraised accurately what Hitler's rise to power was to mean to the rest of the world. Even fewer of us perhaps foresaw clearly the ultimate possibilities in Japan's pretensions. Everyone's mind was concentrated upon relieving the human suffering and economic chaos within our own borders. It was not only logical but clearly desirable that the first move of the new administration in the field of foreign relations should be concerned with international economics.

The President himself was forced to devote almost every one of his interminable working hours to domestic problems. In fact, throughout his first administration the grave social and economic maladies from which the American body politic was suffering were so acute that almost all his time had to be given to the task of internal recovery and reform. The government, however, was immediately confronted with the need to take part in the International Economic Conference of London. Our participation in the conference, convoked by Geneva, had already been pledged by the Hoover Administration.

The program of the conference was grandiose. The nations of the world were to assemble and without further delay find some practical solution for their economic and financial ills. In sober fact, the world would have been far better off if such a conference had been temporarily postponed. The new administration in Washington, plunged into the turmoil of its gigantic domestic problems, had not finally determined the part it could play in such a vast world program. It had not decided the course that in its own interest it must follow with regard to trade policies, monetary policies, or the problem of intergovernmental indebtedness.

The course that the new administration would pursue was the great enigma to all the European powers. The attitude of the United States would decide whether, even at that late hour, international co-operation was practicable as a means of averting a world calamity. If we advanced a constructive and positive policy, there would be hope. If our policy was negative, there would be none.

During the spring months of 1933 delegations from the major European powers, as well as from many other nations, streamed into Washington. The capital became the meeting place of all those who possessed the authority to decide the future of the world. It is tragic when we speculate today as to what the outcome might have been could this government have asserted the same kind of bold, vigorous, and progressive leadership in planning for world economic recovery that the President was asserting in the domestic field. There might have been mistakes but the ultimate calamity might have been lessened.

Order there was none. Of organization there was even less. Conference after conference took place. The foreign emissaries were hopelessly confused. They were either unable to obtain any satisfactory response whatever to questions which to them seemed vital or else they obtained five or six contradictory replies from members of this government, all of whom, ostensibly at least, possessed equal authority. In those weeks in Washington confusion degenerated into chaos. Neither in the Treasury Department nor in the Department of Commerce did there appear to be the slightest comprehension of the crying need for rapid decision on a consistent and constructive American economic policy, as a means of helping to bring about world recovery. In the Department of State the situation was even worse. Individuals who had minor or no official status assumed a greater measure of responsibility than those who filled the highest official positions. Officials in the highest category who were primarily responsible for determining and clarifying policy were either incapable of assuming that responsibility or else unwilling to do so. Consequently, the other powers were unable to discover what attitude the United States would adopt on the major issues of the conference.

The President, in view of the overwhelming burdens which he was already carrying, had a right to look to members of his Cabinet for their concerted advice and to expect of them the capacity and willingness to initiate policy. Such help was never forthcoming. Not only was it not forthcoming, but violent feuds sprang up between his chief advisers.

When the conference in London finally took place, its achievements totaled exactly zero. What was worse, the sessions of the conference aroused a widespread hostility to the United States government which should at all costs, in those crucial days, have been avoided.

The story has been sedulously spread that the failure of the London Economic Conference was due to the fact that the powers given by the President to the American delegation were modified while it was still at sea on the way to London. It is further claimed that the message in which the President refused to agree during the conference to the proposals for currency stabilization which were then advanced was a death blow to the hopes held by the gold-bloc nations. The President has been consequently charged by his critics with "torpedoing" the conference and "sabotaging" his own delegation. Those charges are far from being fair.

The President's own explanation of his much-debated decision to reject the stabilization proposals of the British and French governments may be found in these words:

For two good reasons, the United States could not yield to this demand: first, it would have terminated our national price-level increase which at that moment was restoring our own economic activity more nearly to the pre-depression level; and second, action on reducing trade barriers and on other important matters on the agenda had to be taken up simultaneously with the question of exchange arrangements if the Conference expected to accomplish permanent results.

It is true that my radio message to the London Conference fell upon it like a bombshell. This was because the message was realistic at a time when the gold-bloc nations were seeking a purely limited objective and were unwilling to go to the root of national and international problems.

There is also another highly important consideration to be borne in mind.

The President appointed a delegation headed by the Secretary of State, composed in its majority of competent and influential members of Congress, and containing as well so distinguished a public servant as former Governor Cox, Presidential candidate of the Democratic party in 1920. As responsible officials, including members of both the executive and legislative branches, and fully aware of the significance of the duties they were called upon to carry out, it was surely the obligation of the delegates before leaving Washington to assure themselves that the policy of their government was not only positively established in their instructions, but also that these instructions represented the final considered decisions of the President himself. They knew that the President, under the stress of the burden he was then carrying, had not had a chance to determine finally to his own satisfaction the domestic financial policies of the new administration. Therefore, they should have insisted upon having the time necessary to canvass with him fully every aspect of the all-important stabilization issue, as well as of other major problems likely to arise in London, particularly as it was obvious that the President was not wholly aware of the controversies that had arisen between his own advisers. This was not done and the failure of the conference is in great part due to that fact.

The inability of the London Economic Conference to achieve practical results, save perhaps upon the secondary issue of silver, greatly reduced the chances of any further attempt to check what was fast becoming a stampede toward autarchy. Moreover, foreign attacks upon the United States, because of the breakdown of the conference, increased American distaste for any form of international co-operation.

This distaste was later accentuated by the inability of the United States to make any headway in the field of disarmament. One of the most constructive suggestions for disarmament offered by President Roosevelt in his first years of office was that which he made in 1933 to the armaments conference in Geneva. He proposed that any state that sent its armed forces across the frontiers of any other sovereign state be automatically regarded by the other nations of the world as an aggressor. Upon this proposal, had it been accepted, there at least could have been erected a program for the gradual abolition under international control of offensive armaments. But the proposal was shelved. It was already too late to expect either

Hitler's Germany or Mussolini's Italy, let alone the Japan which had invaded China, to heed any argument save force.

The greatest positive achievement of the first Roosevelt Administration in the realm of international co-operation lay in the trade agreements policy for which Secretary of State Hull is wholly responsible, and which he has furthered with a single-minded and indefatigable devotion. It has been the one program of an economic character which, during the last years before the second World War, struck a note of constructive sanity in international trade relations. It lowered commercial barriers at the very moment when all nations seemed most bent upon increasing them. It greatly assisted in establishing the good neighbor policy in the Western Hemisphere. It helped materially to lessen the stranglehold which Hitler was endeavoring to exercise over the smaller countries of Europe. It arrested a runaway trend on the part of many peoples toward the belief that autarchic trade systems were inevitable. The Trade Agreements Act in which the policy has been incorporated has been repeatedly extended by the Congress. The continuance of the Act will operate as a wholesome and constructive factor in molding international commercial policy in the postwar years.

Outside of the sphere of inter-American policy, the years of the first Roosevelt Administration saw no change in this government's policy of refraining from any form of organized international co-operation. In his well-remembered speech at Chautauqua in 1934, which dealt more than any of his other first-term addresses with issues of foreign policy, the President delivered an eloquent denunciation of war and of all that war implies. He indicated, however, no specific policy by which this country could best be safeguarded against involvement in war. Had he done so, it is wholly improbable that it would have met with popular understanding and, even less, with popular approval.

Those were years which today seem incredibly remote. Congress was devoting a large part of its time to the enactment of so-called "neutrality" legislation, which its sponsors assured the American people would keep the United States out of war. Senate committees were indulging in long-drawn-out sessions to prove that the country had been plunged into the first World War solely because of the Machiavellian machinations of the arms manufacturers and of the international bankers. The cash-and-carry provision inserted in the first "neutrality" act, providing that no belligerent could procure arms or ammunition within the United States unless cash were paid for each shipment, and unless such shipments were carried in vessels other than those of United States registry, was the panacea which the authors of these measures proclaimed would end all danger of war for this country. This legislation was a humiliating admission of the extent of America's delusion. It also reversed our traditional policy which admitted the right of any sovereign government to obtain war matériel within the United States on such terms and in such manner as that government and the American manufacturers concerned might deem advisable.

This legislation, and the amended acts succeeding it, were adopted by overwhelming majorities in both Houses of Congress. They were acclaimed by a substantial majority of the American people and by all but a small section of the press. As one looks back at the record of those years, what is especially surprising is how little attention was paid to the obvious fact that such a policy encouraged rapid rearmament in Germany, in Italy, and in Japan. For it gave warning that such powers as China, France, Great Britain, and the smaller countries of Europe, in the event of aggression, would be unable to secure more than a minimum of airplanes or arms in the United States. By constructing aviation and munitions factories and naval bases within their own boundaries as rapidly as possible, the Axis countries would be soon assured of a volume of military and naval production far superior to that of the peaceful powers which still looked to the League of Nations for security, and which had for so long obtained political support from their taxpayers by repeated reductions in their military and naval estimates.

In view of the popular feeling in the United States, it is all the more remarkable that the President, upon the failure of the London Naval Conference of 1936, was able to secure the appropriations necessary for the construction of additional battleships and airplane carriers. Those additions to our Navy, laid down as a result of the continued insistence of the President and the Navy Department, played a vital role in our defense in the months after Pearl Harbor.

The Presidential campaign of 1936 revolved around wholly domestic issues. And yet that year marked the last stage of the world race toward the precipice of 1939.

The American public strongly condemned the Italian invasion of Ethiopia. But their sympathy, although aroused by the plight of the Ethiopian people and by the shocking cynicism of the Italian attack, was purely platonic. Great Britain and France have never played a more pusillanimous part in world affairs than they did in the face of Mussolini's aggression. The Hoare-Laval deal for the appeasement of Mussolini by carving up the independent state of Ethiopia, although defeated by an outraged moral opinion in England, nevertheless was indicative of the deterioration of international standards. And, unfortunately, the role of the United States in 1935 was nothing to be proud of. The best that the Department of State could devise to uphold the rule of decency in international affairs was the policy of the "moral embargo." It further recommended that American exports to the two belligerents of oil or of other raw materials which could be utilized in military operations should be limited to the average shipped to them in the years immediately preceding hostilities. Since Italy normally imported large quantities of oil and other raw materials needed for her war purposes, and since Ethiopia had never imported any, the result was obvious. Italy continued to obtain at least a substantial quantity of imports which greatly helped to keep her military machine functioning. Ethiopia obtained nothing. But even these steps, hypocritical as they were, were vehemently denounced by many sturdy isolationists as measures likely to incur Mussolini's wrath and thereby endanger the future peace of this country.

Of all our blind isolationist policies, the most disastrous was our attitude on the Spanish civil war.

The constitutional Republican government of Spain had been officially recognized by this government. While it was guilty of various excesses, it was undoubtedly a popular government. Franco's revolt against this legitimate government gained headway. His rebellion, connived at by agents of Mussolini, obtained financial support from the Italian government. Military support was made available both by Mussolini and by Hitler. A state of civil war broke out. Within a short time Italian and German munitions poured into the ports which Franco's forces had succeeded in occupying. Italian and German aviators and troops, at first under the guise of "technicians," later with no effort at concealment, increased tremendously the striking power of Franco's forces. The Republican armies had neither airplanes nor modern equipment except for the very small quantities in their hands at the outbreak of the revolt. The Soviet government, much more farsighted than the Western democracies as to the ultimate consequences should Fascism succeed in dominating Spain, made available to the Loyalist forces some quantities of munitions and war matériel. However, because of the far greater distances involved in the shipment of such supplies from the Soviet Union than from Germany and Italy, the assistance obtained by the Loyalist forces was only a token compared to that obtained by Franco.

Shortly after the outbreak of the civil war, the British and French governments invited the other powers of Europe to adopt a common policy of "nonintervention." The Nonintervention Committee, which sat in London, composed of delegates from all the major European powers, was supposed to prevent both the legitimate government as well as Franco's forces from obtaining military supplies abroad. From the outset Italy and Germany brazenly disregarded their pledge of so-called nonintervention and whenever remonstrances at this flagrant breach of their commitments were politely conveyed by the British or French governments to the delinquent powers, the explanations given were such glaring prevarications as to insult even the most moderate intelligence. Under the circumstances, the Soviet government increased its help to the Loyalists.

Fearing some open clash between the Soviet Union and the Central European powers as a result of the continued sinking in the Mediterranean of merchant vessels, believed to be carrying supplies for the Loyalist forces, by "mysterious" submarines, the British government proposed a conference. The meeting took place at the Swiss village of Nyons. With the loud applause of the British and

French press, Mr. Eden succeeded in obtaining once more high-sounding assurances. Actually the situation continued unchanged.

Faced with these conditions, as a result of which armaments and troops from Germany and Italy were pouring into the regions of Spain held by Franco, and unable to obtain more than a handful of military supplies for its own defense, the legitimate Republican government placed orders for airplanes and munitions in the United States.

It has been our traditional policy to permit the legitimate and recognized government of a foreign country, confronted by a revolt within its own borders, to obtain from this country such military supplies as it may require. It has also been our traditional policy, reinforced by our own experience in the American Civil War, not to grant belligerent rights to the rebel forces in such cases unless the rebellion has gained control of the greater part of the national territory and has acquired such proportions as to warrant regarding those who are participating in it as actual belligerents.

By the autumn of 1936 the civil war in Spain had aroused deep popular feeling in the United States. It could not be denied that horrifying atrocities had been committed upon priests and nuns by groups who alleged that they were operating under the orders of republican officials. Churches and monasteries had been despoiled. It appeared that the position of the Catholic Church in Spain was being deliberately destroyed. These actions had aroused a strong antagonism in many quarters against the constitutional government. Furthermore, the fact that some of the political groups supporting the Republican government were avowed Communists or anarchists, and that the Soviet government was openly supporting the legitimate authorities created suspicion and hostility here.

On the other hand, many Americans were beginning to realize more accurately what the ultimate aims of Fascist and Nazi policy actually were. They saw with increasing clarity that, if Spain were dominated by the Fascist and Nazi governments, the Mediterranean would be closed from the Atlantic; it would become the Italian lake of Mussolini's ambition; and the vital lines of communication between Great Britain and the Suez Canal would be severed. Any such shift in strategic positions in Europe would necessarily endanger

American political and commercial interests. Finally, they began to
see that the real issue was not one that arose as a result of a bona
fide revolution in Spain, similar to so many other bloody revolts
which had marred the pages of Spanish history. They now saw
that the real question was whether a popular government elected by
the people, representing in many of its elements democratic ideals and
aspirations, should be overthrown with impunity, not by a rebellion
of the Spanish people but by the armed forces of Hitler and Mussolini, intent upon dominating Spain for their own ends. The crucial
point was whether in a crisis such as this, where our own interests were involved, the traditional policy of the United States should
be reversed—to the great benefit of the Nazi and Fascist governments.

With the reopening of Congress immediately after the Presidential elections of 1936, there was a stampede to Washington of
the peace-at-any-price organizations; of all the groups which had
been outraged by the treatment of the Catholic Church in Spain; and
of countless individuals who were clamoring that unless the existing
"neutrality" legislation were amended to prevent the Republican
government of Spain from purchasing munitions here, the United
States would be drawn into a European war.

When the Senate Committee on Foreign Relations requested
advice from the Department of State as to the desirability of amend-
ing the "neutrality" legislation as demanded by the pacifist organizations, the following reply was made by the official spokesman for
the Department:

> You are trying to protect the neutrality of this country, to prevent
> this country from being involved in war, and at the same time not
> sacrificing unduly the interest of our own people by the enactment of
> this domestic legislation. It is a tremendous step forward, and it is a
> tremendous task to enact the wisest legislation that you can devise.

With this stamp of approval, the revised "neutrality" legislation
was enacted on January 8, 1937, with the almost unanimous approval of the two Houses of Congress.

It is to the credit of the President that, when the measure came
to him for approval, he expressed in writing the deep disquiet it
caused him and the regret with which he signed it. He recognized

that in the face of the popular agitation which had arisen a veto would not only have been overridden by Congress, but would have been misunderstood by the people. The public had not been really enlightened about the actual issues involved.

During the time that the legislation was receiving final consideration in Congress, and at the moment when the official spokesman for the Department of State was making the statement above quoted, the President and the Secretary of State were absent from the country, attending the opening session of the Inter-American Conference for the Maintenance of Peace at Buenos Aires. I have always believed that if the President had been in Washington during those weeks he would at least have explained to the American people why the measure was unwise and why it was so extremely prejudicial to the national interests of this country. In the long history of the foreign policy of the Roosevelt Administration, there has been, I think, no more cardinal error than the policy adopted during the civil war in Spain.

Partly because of the issues involved in the Spanish civil war, and partly because the real nature of Hitlerism was becoming increasingly apparent, the President determined to make a vigorous effort to persuade public opinion that in its own interest the United States should propose some constructive plan for international action to check the forces of aggression before they succeeded in engulfing the world. For this effort he selected the very heart of isolationism —the city of Chicago. In an address delivered there in October of 1937, which aroused great opposition, he said:

The political situation in the world, which of late has been growing progressively worse, is such as to cause grave concern and anxiety to all the peoples and nations who wish to live in peace and amity with their neighbors.

Some fifteen years ago the hopes of mankind for a continuing era of international peace were raised to great heights when more than sixty nations solemnly pledged themselves not to resort to arms in furtherance of their national aims and policies. The high aspirations expressed in the Briand-Kellogg Peace Pact and the hopes for peace thus raised have of late given way to a haunting fear of calamity. The present reign of terror and international lawlessness began a few years ago.

It began through unjustified interference in the internal affairs of other nations or the invasion of alien territory in violation of treaties, and has now reached a stage where the very foundations of civilization are seriously threatened. The landmarks and traditions which have marked the progress of civilization towards a condition of law, order and justice are being wiped away.

Without a declaration of war and without warning or justification of any kind civilians, including women and children, are being ruthlessly murdered with bombs from the air. In times of so-called peace ships are being attacked and sunk by submarines without cause or notice. Nations are fomenting and taking sides in civil warfare in nations that have never done them any harm. Nations claiming freedom for themselves deny it to others.

Innocent peoples and nations are being cruelly sacrificed to a greed for power and supremacy which is devoid of all sense of justice and humane consideration.

.     .     .     .     .     .     .

If those things come to pass in other parts of the world, let no one imagine that America will escape, that it may expect mercy, that this Western Hemisphere will not be attacked and that it will continue tranquilly and peacefully to carry on the ethics and the arts of civilization.

.     .     .     .     .     .     .

If those days are not to come to pass—if we are to have a world in which we can breathe freely and live in amity without fear—the peace-loving nations must make a concerted effort to uphold laws and principles on which alone peace can rest secure.

.     .     .     .     .     .     .

Those who cherish their freedom and recognize and respect the equal right of their neighbors to be free and live in peace, must work together for the triumph of law and moral principles in order that peace, justice and confidence may prevail in the world. There must be a return to a belief in the pledged word, in the value of a signed treaty. There must be recognition of the fact that national morality is as vital as private morality.

.     .     .     .     .     .     .

I am compelled and you are compelled, nevertheless, to look ahead. The peace, the freedom and the security of ninety per cent of the population of the world is being jeopardized by the remaining ten per cent who are threatening a breakdown of all international order and law. Surely the ninety per cent who want to live in peace under law and in accordance with moral standards that have received almost universal acceptance through the centuries, can and must find some way to make their will prevail.

· · · · · · ·

It seems to be unfortunately true that the epidemic of world lawlessness is spreading.

When an epidemic of physical disease starts to spread, the community approves and joins in a quarantine of the patients in order to protect the health of the community against the spread of the disease.

· · · · · ·

Most important of all, the will for peace on the part of peace-loving nations must express itself to the end that nations that may be tempted to violate their agreements and the rights of others will desist from such a cause. There must be positive endeavors to preserve peace.

The statements were made solely upon the President's own initiative. Among certain members of his own administration—those who should have been most ready to support his position—they were met not only with deep-rooted antagonism, but with a deprecation that was by no means hidden. The result was that throughout the very large Democratic majority in both Houses of Congress there was current an uneasy spirit of uncertainty as to the need for any forthright foreign policy such as the President proposed. The public, stimulated by isolationist leaders and the pacifist organizations, clamored against his proposals. Throughout the entire country, save for a small section of the press which had consistently supported international co-operation for the maintenance of peace, there was hardly a voice raised to express agreement with the President's views. The leader was still far ahead of popular sentiment. Bitter experience and popular education would be required before any basic change in foreign policy could be successfully undertaken.

The President was only too fully aware that the peace was daily being more gravely imperiled by the German and Italian governments. Their course had its Japanese parallel in the Far East, and as the bandit nations drew together, their respective policies became more and more clearly synchronized. Even though public opinion here was not yet alive to the danger, and even though the American people were not yet willing to support any forthright and preventive policy on the part of their government, the President was convinced that, because of his responsibility to defend the national interests, he should nevertheless try by every possible constitutional method to check the progress of the totalitarian powers in their aim of world domination.

In October, 1937, he considered one step of this kind which he could take at once. On the coming Armistice Day at a White House meeting of all the Diplomatic Corps, he would deliver a message to the other governments of the world. He would state that he had reached the final conclusion that, unless the nations of the earth speedily resumed their observance of those fundamental rules of conduct which the judgment of nineteen centuries and the experience of recent years had demonstrated as being necessary in relations between states, world peace could not much longer be maintained. He would continue by saying that doubtless some would predict that, because many efforts to better the chances of preserving world peace had failed, this new effort would also fail. He was unwilling to accept any such prediction as an excuse for a failure on his part to make one more fervent appeal. He would state that he was making this appeal in the knowledge held by every man and woman in every nation that if new wars broke out, and no binding accord existed covering rules and measures to mitigate their horrors, especially the horrors involving civilian populations, no man could say that such a war would not destroy all that which was salvaged from the first World War.

He intended to state specifically that every citizen in the civilized world was suffering from the increasing armament burdens. The cost of these armaments was consuming an ever-greater share of productive income, and destroying the higher standards of living which might otherwise be attained. He would express his understanding of the fact that, since many nations of the world could obviously not undertake overnight a complete reversal of their present policy of military production without simultaneously dislocating their economic structure, it seemed clear that ways and means should be discussed looking to an agreement upon a gradual transition period toward an ultimate international economy based upon reduced armaments, a greater common use of world resources, and the improvement and simplification of economic relationships between all peoples.

The President planned to conclude this message by urging that all the governments strive to reach at the earliest date unanimous agreement upon the following matters: first, the essential principles of international conduct; second, the most effective methods for achieving a general limitation and reduction of armaments; third, effective ways of promoting the economic security, stability, and welfare of all nations through equality of treatment and opportunity; and, finally, effective measures for ensuring that in the event of war maximum respect would be given to humanitarian considerations.

The President intended to end his appeal with the assurance that, should the governments of the world be favorably disposed to his major proposals, the government of the United States would, if they wished, request a number of other governments to join it in drawing up tentative proposals which would be submitted to all nations as a basis for universal agreement. He would make it clear that he was not proposing any general international conference.

At the time that the President was considering this plan, the Nine-Power Conference was about to inaugurate its sessions in Brussels in order to make a final attempt to prevent Japan from continuing her policy of armed expansion in Eastern Asia. If the President's world-wide appeal had been made, its impact upon Japan would have strengthened the hands of the powers at Brussels.

Were his proposals to be accepted, the President was considering the creation of a working committee of ten nations, representative of all regions of the world, to elaborate a clear-cut agenda on the basis of which a world agreement might later be obtained. To this executive committee the President would have invited representatives of the European powers not already directly involved in acute major controversies, together with representatives of the American republics and of nations of the Near East. Simultaneously he would have advised the governments of the other powers that they would be kept completely informed of all developments taking place in the executive committee in order that their suggestions and views might be given full consideration. It was hoped that the proposal in itself would lend impetus to the efforts of Great Britain and France to prevent any further deterioration in European affairs.

The President believed that, even if the major powers of Europe, including the Soviet Union, did not succeed in making any progress toward understanding, the United States would at least have obtained the support of all governments, except the Berlin-Rome Axis, for her efforts to maintain world peace. He felt that the rousing of public opinion on a world scale would in itself be productive of practical good and would have instant repercussions on the German and Italian peoples. It would have a tonic effect upon the smaller countries of Europe which had felt increasingly during the preceding three years that the great democracies had surrendered all initiative and all semblance of leadership.

Finally, if the policies of Germany and Italy were halted through an understanding with Great Britain and France, the support which the former two powers were giving Japan would be weakened at least sufficiently to oblige Japan to make peace with China upon terms consistent with the Nine-Power Treaty.

The project which the President had under consideration was almost hysterically opposed by certain of his closest advisers. They insisted that it involved great dangers to the prestige of the United States. They argued that any such dramatic appeal to the nations of the world on Armistice Day would be highly unwise unless the President had earlier received, at least confidentially, the assurance that the British or the French government would not regard it as running counter to negotiations which they already had in hand or to policies upon which they had previously determined.

Consequently, the President for a short while reluctantly postponed action. On January 12, 1938, he secretly sounded out the views of the British Prime Minister as a preliminary step. Unfortunately, the Chamberlain Cabinet was not the Churchill Cabinet. The reply made by Neville Chamberlain was in the nature of a douche of cold water. While courteously expressing appreciation of the President's purposes, he voiced the fear that were the President to put forward his proposals at that time, Germany as well as Italy would take advantage of them to delay consideration of specific points which must be settled between Great Britain, France, Germany, and Italy "if appeasement were to be achieved," and to make demands over and above those which they would make if no other negotiations existed. The Prime Minister further said that he would keep the President informed of the steps already taken and under contemplation by the British government. In the same message, he gave the President the startling information that under certain circumstances the British government was prepared, if possible with the authority of the League of Nations, to recognize the Italian conquest of Ethiopia as "de jure."

By sounding the British government in this manner the President was now confronted with a positive warning that British support for his proposals would not be forthcoming. It has always been my conviction that had the President not been advised to make these preliminary confidential soundings, and had he carried out his original idea of a world-wide appeal on Armistice Day of 1937, neither the British government nor the Axis powers could then have refused, under the pressure of circumstances and public opinion, to lend at least apparent co-operation.

However, in view of the situation created by Mr. Chamberlain's reply, the President felt he had no alternative but to defer "for a short while" the proposal he had hoped to make. But in his reply to Mr. Chamberlain he took occasion to state clearly that he was deeply concerned by the indication that the British government might give official recognition to the Italian conquest of Ethiopia. He warned Mr. Chamberlain that a surrender by the British government of the principle of nonrecognition of territories seized by aggression would at that time inevitably have a serious effect upon public opinion in the United States. The American people, he said emphatically, would not support their government in measures of specific co-operation with other nations unless those measures were destined to re-establish and maintain principles of international law and morality.

It happened that at the time the President's confidential enquiry was received in London, Mr. Eden, then Secretary of State for Foreign Affairs, was absent in the south of Europe. As soon as he was advised of the proposal and of Mr. Chamberlain's reply, he at once returned to London. It is generally understood that it was due to his direct intervention that, at the end of the same month of January, Mr. Chamberlain sent a new and different message to the President. In this message the Prime Minister stated that, as a result of a few days' reconsideration, he had reached the conclusion that he should welcome the President's initiative and that the British government would do its utmost to contribute to the success of the scheme whenever the President decided to launch it. He insisted, however, that since de jure recognition had already been given by a great many other governments to the conquest of Ethiopia, the Italian government would regard the continued failure of Great Britain to recognize the conquest as positive proof that she desired no general understanding with Italy governing the Mediterranean and the Red Sea. The present tension would thereby not only be continued but aggravated to an extreme degree. Mr. Chamberlain expressed the opinion that no economic concessions would be sufficient in themselves to satisfy the Axis powers. He felt certain, nevertheless, that if they could be brought to a co-operative frame of mind in the settlement of political problems they would also desire co-operative assistance on the economic side. He said he believed that there was a chance to bring them to that point of view.

By this time, of course, many invaluable weeks had passed. The situation within Germany was reaching a boiling point. In an interview which the British Ambassador in Berlin had with Hitler on March 3, Hitler dismissed as unimportant the question of colonial adjustments and insisted upon the need for an immediate solution, in a manner satisfactory to him, of the problems of Austria and Czecho-slovakia. Hitler stated that, in so far as the limitation of armaments was concerned, Germany would refuse to deal with Great Britain (against whom, he alleged, Germany was not arming) unless Great Britain had previously begun satisfactory discussions with the Soviet Union. It was already apparent, therefore, that the German government was about to seize Austria and the Sudetenland as its first step toward the creation of a greater Germany. The time for such constructive and preventive remedies as those embodied in the President's proposals had passed.

This chapter in the President's efforts to avert the impending world crisis must always remain a subject for speculation. In November, 1937, the European situation was still fluid. While Hitler had undoubtedly already fully formulated his plans in co-operation with the German General Staff, the policies of Italy were far from crystallized. The full participation by the United States in such a world-wide effort to keep the peace as that envisaged by the President might have given Italy pause. It might have resulted in a radical modification of Japanese policy. Under those conditions Hitler would have been forced to think far more carefully before embarking on his last moves toward world war. In November, 1937, an appeal by the President, and the constructive program he had in mind, might well have rallied a still vocal public opinion in Europe sufficiently to have changed the course of the events of the next two years.

With the annexation of Austria and with the threatened attack upon Czechoslovakia in the spring of 1938, the President had no longer any real opportunity to arrest impending calamity. At the beginning of the crisis which culminated at Munich, the President at one o'clock in the morning of Monday, September 26, sent similar messages to the Prime Ministers of Great Britain and France, to President Beneš, and to Hitler. In this message he urged that negotiations for a peaceful solution of the controversy should not be broken off and that there be no resort to force. The President said:

> The fabric of peace on the continent of Europe, if not throughout the rest of the world, is in immediate danger. The consequences of its rupture are incalculable. Should hostilities break out the lives of millions of men, women and children in every country involved will most certainly be lost under circumstances of unspeakable horror.
>
> The economic system of every country involved is certain to be shattered. The social structure of every country involved may well be completely wrecked.
>
> The supreme desire of the American people is to live in peace. But in the event of a general war they face the fact that no nation can escape some measure of the consequences of such a world catastrophe.

It is my conviction that all people under the threat of war today pray that peace may be made before, rather than after, war.

On behalf of the one hundred thirty millions of people of the United States of America and for the sake of humanity everywhere I most earnestly appeal to you not to break off negotiations looking to a peaceful, fair and constructive settlement of the questions at issue.

I earnestly repeat that so long as negotiations continue differences may be reconciled. Once they are broken off reason is banished and force asserts itself.

And force produces no solution for the future good of humanity.

The British and French Prime Ministers at once assured the President of their desire to find a peaceful solution. A profoundly touching message in the same sense was received a few hours later from President Beneš. Later the President received a reply from Hitler admitting that the consequences of a European war were unforeseeable, but advancing the argument that the present situation was a result of the injustices of the Versailles Treaty and of the failure of the League of Nations to carry out its obligations. (At this time, of course, Germany had already left the League of Nations.) He concluded by asserting that it did not rest with the German government, but with the Czechoslovak government alone, to decide whether there was to be peace or war.

Early in the afternoon of September 27 the President sent urgent instructions to American diplomatic representatives throughout the world to express the belief of the government of the United States that the consequences of war would be so disastrous that no steps should be overlooked which could possibly contribute to the maintenance of peace. He expressed the hope that all governments would send similar messages since even at that late date a united world public opinion might conceivably influence the course of events.

The President also sent a personal appeal to Mussolini urging that Mussolini help in seeing that negotiations were continued. Mussolini had received this appeal from the President when he repeatedly urged Hitler by telephone, on the morning of September 28, to avoid an outbreak of war and to continue negotiations with the British and French governments.

On the afternoon of September 27, the President received direct word that Hitler had fixed the hour of two o'clock in the afternoon of September 28 for the entrance of the German armies into Czechoslovakia. (It is now believed that the date actually fixed by Hitler for the invasion was October 1.) The President consequently sent a further appeal to Hitler on the night of September 27. He urged that should the need for supplementing the negotiations already under way become evident, their scope might well be widened into a conference of all of the nations directly interested. If such a meeting could be held immediately in some neutral spot in Europe, the present problems might be solved in a spirit of justice and with a promise of permanence.

In a moving paragraph he expressed his conviction that the soul of every man, woman, and child whose life might be lost in the threatened war would hold him and all other chiefs of government accountable should they omit any appeal for its prevention. To this final appeal from the President, Hitler made no reply.

The hideous series of atrocities committed by the German government upon the Jews later in the autumn of 1938 raised public indignation in the United States to fever pitch. The decision of the American government to withdraw its Ambassador from Berlin, as an official indication of the general horror of the American people, was supported throughout the United States, save by the isolationists and blindly pacifist elements.

Hitler's occupation of Czechoslovakia on March 15, 1939—an almost immediate violation of the engagements entered into at Munich—at length proved to that portion of the American public which still hoped to combat Hitlerism with reason that only force could convince the Nazis. The feeling became general that war in Europe was inevitable, and that nothing could be done to prevent it.

That considerable segment of the American public sympathetic to the Soviet Union was profoundly disheartened, although still confident that, notwithstanding the errors of policy which the British and French governments had committed during the preceding eighteen months, it would ultimately, in the final crisis, align itself with the Western democracies. Accordingly, the conclusion in the latter days of August of the agreement between the Soviet Union and Germany caused great shock and increased the feeling of fatal-ism. The Soviet-German Agreement confused and discouraged the liberal groups in the United States. When the invasion of Poland became imminent, the President felt it useless for him to do more than again appeal to the heads of the governments for a breathing space that would provide opportunity for further negotiation. Should war break out, he urged at least an agreement to respect the lives of civilian populations by the elimination of bombing from the air.

As we look back over the years between 1933 and 1939 I believe many of us have gained the conviction that the United States might even then have changed the trend of events had public opinion in this country grasped more clearly how desperately serious the world situation had become, and that in its own interest alone this country should share actively and effectively in international affairs.

That of course is a large "if." During those years among the highest officials of this Government only the President himself clearly and emphatically sounded the note of danger—and he was at once accused of "warmongering." For in a democracy such as ours the people must be kept fully and continuously informed. Except by the President they were not so informed. Even after the President's "quarantine" speech they could not fully comprehend the great issues which this country faced, and the magnitude of the dangers which threatened them unless the United States took a hand in remedying the conditions which had brought these dangers into being.

There could never be clearer proof of the crying need for both Houses of the Congress, as representatives of the people, to be kept frequently and fully informed by the Department of State of every aspect of our foreign relations, and of every menace, however remote, that may threaten the well-being of our country.

Only an enlightened public opinion can be held responsible for its mistakes.

# CHAPTER III

# My Mission to Europe: 1940

IN THE first days of January, 1940, the President sent for me to talk with him in his office at the White House. He told me that for some time past—in fact, since soon after the outbreak of the European war—he had been asking himself whether there still remained any step which he, as President of the United States, could take to avert the dangers that would so clearly confront the people of this country, as well as of the civilized world, if the European war continued. It seemed to him that, if the long-expected all-out offensive by Germany upon the Western powers should take place, the results of the war would be unpredictable. With its continuation there would be ever greater danger that the United States would be involved.

Even though by some miracle that might be avoided, one of two major dangers would be inevitable. The first: a victory by Hitler would immediately imperil the vital interests of the United States. The other: an eventual victory of the Western powers could probably be won only after a long and desperately fought contest which would bring Europe to total economic and social collapse, with disastrous effects upon the American people.

The President told me that he had been canvassing the possibilities still open to him. He admitted frankly that the chances seemed to him about one in a thousand that anything at all could be done to change the course of events. On the other hand, he felt that no possibility, however remote and however improbable, should be overlooked. He believed that his obligations to the American people made it imperative for him to leave no stone unturned. He said that, consequently, he had decided to send a personal representative to Germany, England, and France, as well as to Italy, since Italy, although not a belligerent, was an Axis partner. Under the conditions which had existed since the agreement of the previous August between Germany and the Soviet Union, he did not feel that a visit to Moscow would serve any useful purpose, at least for the time being. His representative would offer no proposals and no suggestions. He would find out only what the views of the four governments might be as to the present possibilities of concluding any just and permanent peace. He himself had no interest in any temporary or tentative armed truce.

For various reasons the President believed that I was the most available person within the government to undertake this mission for him.

Owing to an attack of illness I was obliged to leave Washington for a brief period. Upon my return the President informed me that, after giving the matter further and very careful thought, he believed that my trip should be undertaken without delay.

First of all, I had to find out whether the governments which the President wanted me to visit would be willing to receive me in the capacity indicated, and would enable me freely to obtain from them the information which the President desired.

While the British, French, and Italian governments immediately gave a most cordial response, it was clear that both in England and in France considerable perplexity and some apprehension were created by the announcement of my visit. Certain quarters in both countries expressed fear that this government might be intending to throw all its influence behind peace at any price, which, under the conditions then obtaining, could result only in strengthening Germany's position. It was also feared that, if the two Western powers refused for that reason to consider what would be tantamount to submission to Hitler's plans for the domination of Europe, public opinion in the United States would interpret their refusal as an evidence of blind intransigence and modify the openly expressed sympathy for the Western powers which had so far prevailed.

As was to be anticipated, the response received from Berlin was both cold and noncommittal. While the German government agreed to receive me, no indication was given that Hitler himself would see me. Unless I could talk with Hitler, my visit to Germany would scarcely yield an authoritative impression of the views of the German government.

For some reason which still seems inexplicable public imagination in this country had been captured by the phrase employed by Senator Borah when he referred to the European war as a "phony" war. It was true that after the devastation of Poland the Germans had refrained from undertaking any air offensive against the Western powers. Nor had the German armies as yet made any move to invade the Low Countries or to break through the Maginot Line. But even to the most casual observer familiar with the working of Hitler's mind it was obvious that Hitler was waiting for two developments. First, he hoped that Germany's overwhelming superiority in the air and in mechanized equipment, as evidenced in the invasion of Poland, would persuade Great Britain and France that a negotiated peace granting Germany, as a first step, hegemony over Europe would be preferable to the probability of annihilation and occupation. Second, should this hope fail, he knew that the winter months would give his propaganda and subversive agencies much valuable time in which to break down the morale of the French armies. In this manner he would improve his chances for a military pushover as soon as the approach of summer made weather conditions more propitious for an all-out offensive.

Why any considerable segment of public opinion in the United States should have regarded the war as a "phony" war in view of constantly accumulating evidence of Hitler's military strength, and in view of the ruin which Poland had already suffered, must always remain a mystery. Moreover, many people appeared to feel, like Senator Borah, that the failure of Great Britain and France to undertake the offensive was somehow reprehensible. This feeling was almost sadistic. It had in it something of the "boos" howled out by the spectators at a prize ring when the two contestants are not putting on as bloody an exhibition as they have paid to witness.

At the same time, and this was perhaps more understandable, American public opinion had at this moment, except in one or two sections of the country, reached another climax of out-and-out isolationism. Popular feeling demanded that this government refrain from any action, and even from any gesture, which might conceivably involve the United States with the warring powers. A few vigorously asserted that my mission was extremely dangerous in view of the fact that it was an evidence of direct interest on the part of this government in the European tragedy. The charge was made, even in Washington, that such a mission could only result in stirring up antagonism against the United States on both sides, and that it would be far better for the President to let us "mind our own business."

The situation in Europe, as seen from Washington, did not offer much ground for optimism. While Mr. Chamberlain himself had long since decided that there was no hope for British security so long as Hitlerism remained in the saddle, powerful elements in financial and industrial circles still believed that the domination of Europe by Hitler and the survival of a free British Commonwealth of Nations were not necessarily contradictory. In France the political chaos which had existed during the preceding six years, the steady boring from within in every part of the French national structure carried on by Germany's direct and indirect accomplices, and the disastrous corruption of French national sentiment had all contributed to a state of affairs giving little promise of any real resistance to Germany.

Along the Siegfried and Maginot lines the opposing armies lay immobile, with only rare and sporadic exchanges of artillery fire. But, while on the German side the morale of the forces had never been higher, it was already becoming notorious that the discipline of the French troops was giving their officers grave concern, and that the inefficiency and dubious loyalty of some of the French officers were giving equal concern to many of the patriots whom they were commanding.

American relations with Germany had become purely nominal. The glaring evidences of Hitler's ultimate ambitions, the nature of the attack upon Poland, his persecution of the Jewish people, and the knowledge we possessed of the subversive activities conducted by the Nazi regime in many other states of Europe and within the Americas, had removed all reasons for preserving anything more than nominal relations with Berlin.

Only in Italy was it remotely conceivable that the policy of this government might have some concrete effect. If by some means the United States could prevent Italy from actually taking part in the war against France and Great Britain, if Hitler could not obtain the active participation of his southern partner in an attack upon France, the outcome of the war might be less certain than it then seemed. American influence in Italy might have weight. Italian immigrants to the United States had created a very real friendship for this country among the Italian people, which had not been modified by the rise of a strong Anglophobe feeling in Italy after the Ethiopian overture.

The government of the United States at that moment was in no way empowered by public opinion to exercise any real influence in Europe. This country was not bound by any treaty to join in international action against the Nazi aggressor, even though that aggressor had made it plain that he desired to dominate the globe. Congress had gone still further, through the cash-and-carry and other similar provisions of the so-called neutrality legislation, to make it clear that the United States would not even help the nations attacked by Hitler to obtain means of self-defense in this country.

Looking back now, with a fuller knowledge of the overwhelming confidence of the Nazi leaders, it is obvious that no verbal interposition by the United States in the winter of 1940 would have been effective. Only one thing could have deflected Hitler from his purpose: the sure knowledge that the power of the United States would be directed against him if he attempted to carry out his intention of conquering the world by force. And only that same knowledge could have dissuaded Mussolini—as distinguished from the Italian people—from his fatal adventure at the side of Hitler.

At that time no representative of this government could have been authorized to intimate any such thing. Even if he had been, both the Nazi and Fascist regimes would have discounted his assertions because of their knowledge of the state of public and Congressional opinion in this country. Had any representative of the President attempted to give such an impression without authorization, not only would he have been dishonorably derelict in his obligations to his own government, but he would likewise have knowingly disregarded popular sentiment in the United States.

My mission, therefore, was a forlorn hope. However, even at the worst, it could yield information that would be valuable to the President in his conduct of foreign relations during those inestimably difficult days.

I arrived in Rome, the first stage of my journey, on February 25. Our ambassador in Rome at that time, William Phillips, had been my predecessor as undersecretary of state and possessed a longer experience in the Foreign Service of this government than any other of our ambassadors. With an unwavering sympathy for the Italian people, he had been deeply antagonized by all aspects of Fascist policy and by the subservience of the Italian government to Hitler's dictation. For more than a year prior to my arrival in Rome, Mussolini had shown his displeasure with American policy by ignoring the American Ambassador and by evading his frequent requests for interviews. The Ambassador's relations with the Foreign Minister, Count Ciano, however, had remained unbroken.

My first interview, to which the Ambassador accompanied me, was with Count Ciano, on the morning after my arrival. Since the permanent ministry was under construction in what the Italian government hoped would be the 1942 Rome Exposition Grounds, I was received in the temporary Ministry of Foreign Affairs in the Chigi Palace.

The impression Count Ciano made upon me was quite different from what I had anticipated. From the accounts given to me by many who had talked with him, as well as from his photographs, I had pictured him as overbearing and as filled with an egregious sense of his own importance. In my numerous conversations with him I found him quite the reverse. He seemed older than his thirty-six years. His manner was always cordial and entirely unaffected. He could not have been simpler or more outspoken in the expression of his views. He spoke colloquial English.

In accordance with the line which I had decided to follow, I tried to stress in every possible way the advantage to Italy of a policy of real neutrality in the European war. I made it clear that all of us in the United States had the utmost regard for our fellow citizens of Italian origin or birth and that all of us shared their satisfaction in the fact that Italy had not entered the war and had made efforts to avert it. The United States, in complete harmony with all the other American republics, constituted one great neutral influence in the world. Italy so far had constituted another powerful nonbelligerent influence. If an opportunity should arise to establish a permanent and stable world peace, the efforts of those two neutral influences to lay the groundwork could be more effective if they would co-operate than if they took different roads.

At that moment all neutral countries found their normal export trade severely curtailed. It would surely be helpful to Italy as well as to the United States if some satisfactory method of enlarging the volume of trade between them were found. I emphasized that to make such an arrangement possible the two governments must agree on principles and policies, but that I hoped friendly study and consideration of all the factors might bring this about. I, of course, made it clear that such benefits could be obtained only through the continued neutrality of Italy.

I said to the Minister that he was, of course, already fully familiar with the purpose of my mission. I was directed by the President to report to him upon the possibility of establishing lasting peace; the President was not interested in any precarious or temporary peace which would be no more than a patched-up truce. I was not empowered to offer any proposals nor enter into any commitments, but I would value any opinion which he might care to express as to the views of the Italian government with regard to such possibilities.

Count Ciano said plainly that he was glad that I did not intend to offer any proposals or set formula as to a possible peace treaty; that he doubted whether the moment was propitious for any effort of that character.

I observed that from Washington we had followed his own efforts at the end of the previous August to prevent war, and since that date, to limit the spread of war. I was particularly interested in knowing whether the Italian government was still considering the possibility of the kind of meeting between representatives of the belligerent powers which it had suggested on August 31, 1939.

Count Ciano said that that initiative had been his, taken after consultation with Mussolini.

He then got up and took out of a safe his famous red diary in which he recorded in his own handwriting his daily activities. This memorandum book was well-known to many of the American correspondents stationed in Rome, with most of whom Ciano had continued to maintain friendly personal relations. The Minister read excerpts to me from the diary covering the period in question. It appeared that during the three days commencing August 31 he had been constantly on the long-distance telephone speaking personally with the Foreign Ministers of Great Britain and France, Lord Halifax and Georges Bonnet, and with Hitler himself, urging a meeting between them and Mussolini to be held at Stresa on September 1. Count Ciano had recorded that Hitler had agreed to such a meeting on September 1, but that he had not been able to obtain replies from the British and French Ministers until September 2. While the latter had been agreed in principle, Lord Halifax had made the condition that German troops must first be withdrawn beyond the German-Polish frontier. Ciano felt that if the reply from Lord Halifax had come on September 1 Hitler might have agreed, but that by September 2 German troops had advanced so far, and German military enthusiasm had reached such a pitch, that it was physically impossible for him to accept this condition. The Minister doubted whether a similar meeting at the present moment would serve any useful purpose.

Count Ciano then spoke at considerable length of German-Italian relations. He made no effort to conceal his hearty detestation of Ribbentrop. He said: "If Hitler wants anything—and God knows he always wants enough—Ribbentrop always goes him one better." He made it clear that he bitterly resented not only Hitler's lack of proper consideration for his Axis partner in failing to consult the Italian government with regard to German policy, but also what he claimed was Hitler's complete disregard for the specific terms of the treaty between Italy and Germany.

During the preceding summer, when he had twice conferred with Hitler and Ribbentrop, the subject of the negotiations then progressing between the Soviet Union and France and England had, of course, come up for discussion. The Germans had told him that in order to impede these negotiations they were attempting to conclude a commercial agreement with Russia, but that this was merely in the nature of a "petit jeu."

"Do you further realize," he asked, "that Hitler called me on the telephone only on August 21 last to announce the conclusion of this alliance to me, and that before I had even had time to get Mussolini on the telephone to break the news to him this very radio in my own office here was carrying the report broadcast to the whole world?" "That," he said, "was the way in which Italy was advised as to German foreign policy. And with regard to Poland," he continued, "the clear-cut terms of our understanding with Germany provides that, if Germany undertakes any military venture, Italy must be first afforded an opportunity for consultation. We would, if we could, have prevented the invasion of Poland, but we were never given any chance to exert any influence on Hitler to prevent it."

Count Ciano insisted that the Italian government had the deepest sympathy for the "real Poles." He believed that Poland must be reconstituted. And as an indication of its policy, the Italian government continued to recognize a Polish Embassy in Rome and he, Ciano himself, was spending much time in bringing what influence he could to bear on Germany to mitigate the brutality of the treatment of Polish nationals in occupied territory.

"No country," Count Ciano declared, "would want to have Germany as a neighbor. Italy now has her as a neighbor and we must do the best we can to get on with her.

"You will wonder why Italy did nothing at the time of Dollfuss's assassination and nothing later when Hitler occupied Austria. I will tell you, for there is a great deal of misunderstanding on that score. There are many people in Austria today who are unhappy, who are tormented; many who wish that Hitler's kind of Anschluss had not taken place. But, as an Italian, I tell you the great majority of Austrians would even today rather be a part of Germany than have to live the life of starvation and of progressive exhaustion they were forced to lead in independent Austria.

"Before the occupation of Austria, Dr. Schuschnigg came to Rome. He admitted to me frankly that, if Germany occupied Austria, the majority of Austrians would support the occupation and, if Italy sent troops into Austria to prevent the occupation, the Austrians as one man would join with the Germans to fight Italy.

"For that reason, when peace terms are considered, it would be stupid—except on one condition—to support the French thesis that an independent Austria must be reconstituted. An independent Austria can be successful only if the Austrian people are given a real chance to live and a new opportunity to develop a stable and prosperous country.

"If any country could logically desire the reconstitution of an independent Austria, it would be Italy. But Italy knows that the Austrians are primarily German and that the Austrian people will never be content to go back to the state of inanition and of lingering death which they endured for twenty years after 1918."

Count Ciano told me that he had spent two days in Berlin the preceding October conferring with Hitler. At that time he believed that Germany would still have been willing to agree upon a peace based upon the retention of Austria, or a plebiscite in Austria—since he felt that Hitler was convinced that a real plebiscite would result in an overwhelming vote in favor of continued amalgamation with Germany; an independent Slovakia and an independent Bohemia-Moravia, both under the protectorate of Germany; and the reconstitution of a completely independent Poland, Germany retaining Danzig, the Corridor, and the territory in Western Poland occupied by German minorities, and Russia retaining Eastern Poland, removing the inhabitants of Polish nationality to the new Polish state, which would be given access to the sea. The terms would also have included the return of Germany's former colonial possessions, or their equivalent. Count Ciano was by no means sure that Germany would still agree to such terms.

Throughout the conversation Ciano revealed not only his contempt and hatred for Ribbentrop but also an underlying antagonism toward Hitler. He did not hide his anxiety in so far as Italy was concerned, with regard to Germany and his fear of her military power. But neither did he show the slightest predilection toward Great Britain or France.

As soon as the conversation ended, the motion-picture men were sent for, and the Minister posed with me for an unduly protracted period. That was the only time I saw the "chest out, chin up" Ciano of whom I had been told. Until the cameras began clicking he could not have been more human or more simple.

At the outset of our interview Ciano had told me that I was to be received that same afternoon by Mussolini at the Palazzo Venezia. The hours between were crowded. I had the opportunity of talking with several of the American correspondents who were stationed in Rome or who were there temporarily, among them Herbert L. Matthews and Camille Cianfarra of the New York *Times*, John T. Whitaker, William Philip Sims, and the Packards of the United Press. During this first stage of my Roman visit the Embassy offices were picketed by agents of the Fascist government. Few Italians were willing to run the gantlet and I was thus kept away from Italian visitors. It was rather noticeable upon my second visit, three weeks later, that these restrictions had been relaxed. By that time the regime had reached the conclusion that the true purpose of my mission was that stated in my original conversation with Mussolini and that no ulterior purposes were envisaged.

I was enabled, however, to talk with various Italians at the Ambassador's private residence, as well as with the French and British Ambassadors, M. François-Poncet and Sir Percy Lorraine.

From these varied and divergent sources I obtained precisely the same point of view: that not only the vast majority of the Italian people but also the key figures within the Italian government itself —save those notoriously under the Nazi influence and, of course, Mussolini himself—were totally and even violently opposed to the entrance of Italy into the war.

Nor was there any discrepancy in the viewpoint expressed concerning Italy's preparedness for war. The members of our own Embassy staff who, I think, were singularly well-informed, coincided in the opinion that the preparedness, morale, and discipline of the Italian armies were approximately the same as they had been in 1915. I was told, however, that Italian aviators were of superior quality, and that the Italian navy was well-prepared. The modern warships constructed by Mussolini were admirably equipped for operations in the Mediterranean. The one salient weakness of Italian naval preparedness lay in her dependence upon German sources of supply for fuel oil.

At five o'clock in the afternoon, accompanied by Ambassador Phillips, I was received by Mussolini.

I entered the palace by the side entrance used by the Duce and, going up in a small elevator, was escorted through a long corridor hung with paintings and filled with vitrines containing examples of old Italian porcelain to a reception room where Count Ciano was waiting to receive us. From there we passed to the Hall of the Grand Fascist Council which, while on a far smaller scale and hung in blue instead of red, was reminiscent of the Hall of the Doges in the Doges' Palace at Venice. At the end of the Hall was a raised—and a very large—armchair set aside for the use of the Duce. On a lower level around a horseshoe table were other chairs for members of the Grand Council. The walls were covered with superb portraits.

Mussolini received me in his office in the "Sala Mapa Mondo." The Hall, of which so much has been written, was very long, but did not seem of that ominous length so often emphasized by those who in earlier days had been granted interviews by Mussolini. There was no furniture in it except a desk at the extreme end and three chairs placed in front of it for the Ambassador, Count Ciano, and myself. A small reading lamp on the desk was the sole illumination in the whole vast room, already darkening in the winter twilight.

Mussolini met me cordially at the door, saying he was very happy to welcome me, and walked with me the length of the hall to his desk. Although he had not been willing to receive Ambassador Phillips for over a year, he made no reference to that fact.

My first impression was one of profound astonishment at Mussolini's appearance. In the countless times I had seen him in photographs and in motion pictures and in the many descriptions I had read of him I had always gained the impression of an active, quick-moving, exceedingly animated personality. The man I saw before me seemed fifteen years older than his actual age of fifty-six. He was ponderous and static rather than vital. He moved with an elephantine motion; every step appeared an effort. He was heavy for his height, and his face in repose fell in rolls of flesh. His close-cropped hair was snow-white. During our long and rapid interchange of views he kept his eyes shut a considerable part of the time. He opened them with his dynamic and often described wide stare only when he desired particularly to underline some remark. At his side was a large cup of some hot brew which he sipped from time to time.

Mussolini impressed me as a man laboring under a tremendous strain. One could almost sense a leaden oppression.

Ciano commenced the conversation by saying Mussolini desired him to act as interpreter since, in view of the importance of the conversations, he would prefer to speak in his own language rather than in French or in English.

Our conversation dealt almost entirely with the problems of economic policy and the armament question. I reminded Mussolini of the enquiry addressed by the United States to the other neutral powers, suggesting an exchange of views on a sane international economic system and the possibility of postwar reduction and limitation of armaments. He said that Italy's reply would be tantamount to asking what the views of my government might be on these questions. I stated that I had brought with me a brief written statement of the views of the United States on international economic relationships and that, since I was fully familiar with the opinions which Mussolini himself had expressed in his address to the Chamber of Deputies on May 26, 1934, I wondered if the ideas of my government did not very generally coincide with his own.

He at once asked for the paper and read it word for word. As he read, he commented. His comment on the first paragraph was: "Molto bello, I agree with every word. Unfortunately, however, Italy has never been in a position where she could anticipate having access on equal terms to raw materials."

When he came to the portion which related to discrimination, he said: "And could there be greater discriminations than those found in the Ottawa Agreements? Or in the tariff policy pursued by the United States prior to the Roosevelt Administration?"

When he had concluded his reading, he said: "I subscribe to every word in this. It coincides completely with what I said in 1934, and what I believe now. But you must remember that Italy was the last country to embark upon an autarchic system, and that she did so solely as a last resort and in self-defense. A poor country like Italy had no other course after Britain had entered upon the Ottawa policy, and after the other European nations had adopted autarchy, and France had imposed her quota system and other restrictions. The policy outlined in your government's document represents the ideal which nations must come to, but I want to remind you, if and when the time comes that the nations can again trade freely with each other, no such ideal as this can be realized unless the powers agree simultaneously upon a practical and positive disarmament plan. So long as peoples are draining their national economies in the construction of armaments, there can be no hope of a sane international economic relationship."

I said that it was precisely for that reason that the government of the United States had suggested that, if the neutral powers could now agree upon the principles I had just listed, neutral influences might be of great service when peace came in bringing these ideals to practical realization.

To that he replied that, in his opinion, the only neutral powers having any influence were the United States, Japan, and Italy, and that Italy was not technically a neutral because of her relationship to Germany. (It was notable that this was his only reference throughout the conversation to his Axis ties.) He said that when peace came the influence of the United States would be decisive, and that our views on economic relations, which he himself would support, would have to be accepted. He added that this would take place only if the United States insisted.

He then continued by asserting that no moral influence at that time would prove effective. In his judgment the basis for a just political peace would have to be found before any constructive steps could be taken.

I interrupted, saying that, as he already knew, I was charged by the President with the duty of reporting to him on the present possibilities of establishing the basis for peace in Europe. A part of my task necessarily was to learn what Mussolini's own views on the subject might be.

Mussolini then set forth what he believed to be the terms Germany would accept. He repeated the statements regarding Austria,

Slovakia, and Bohemia-Moravia previously made by Ciano. When it came to the question of Poland he drew himself up and with much vigor said: "The Polish people have a right to their untrammeled independence and sovereignty and I will support them in that endeavor. But that does not mean that Poland should again become a crazy quilt of diverse nationalities. The poison of Europe during the past twenty years has been the question of minorities. That cardinal error must not be committed again. The real Germans of Danzig, of the Corridor, and of Posen should remain in the Reich, but the real Poles should have their Free Poland with access to the sea." I asked: "How about the real Poles who are now under Russian domination?" Mussolini answered that they could emigrate from Russian-controlled Poland to the new Polish state in the same manner in which Germans were then emigrating from the Upper Adige back to Germany. "What other solution is there," he said, "unless we are all prepared to fight Russia?"

He then continued by insisting that I should attribute great importance to Hitler's speech of February 23. That speech had been precise. "Vital interests in Central Europe" meant what Mussolini had just indicated. The restoration of German colonies was another indispensable factor. Germany, he believed, had every right to the position which Hitler demanded in Central Europe, and there could be no lasting peace unless such a solution were found. He then quickly said: "And when peace negotiations are undertaken Italy's just claims must be satisfied. I have not raised them now because the madhouse which is Europe will not stand further excitement. But there can be no peace which is real until Italy has free egress from and access to the Mediterranean."

At this stage and throughout the conversation the Duce spoke with the utmost bitterness concerning the British.

He continued by expressing the belief that the Allied nations gravely underestimated the military strength and the efficiency of the German organization.

I then asked him a flat question: "Do you consider it possible at this moment for any successful negotiations to be undertaken between Germany and the Allies for a lasting peace?"

His answer was an emphatic "Yes." He said that of one thing he was profoundly certain: that none of the peoples at war desired to fight. The situation, in his belief, was utterly different from that which existed in 1914. "But," he continued, "I am equally sure that if a 'real' war breaks out, with its attendant slaughter and devastation, there will be no possibility for a long time to come of any peace negotiation."

At the end of our conversation he told me that he would be glad to talk with me again at any time and that he believed he would probably receive reports from Berlin, Paris, and London after my visits to those capitals which would be of value to the President before I returned to Washington. It was agreed that I would see him again upon my return to Rome before my return to the United States.

The Duce got up and joined me on the other side of his desk. For a while he spoke to me in English, then broke into French. I asked him if he still rode every morning and he said he did, but that he had now taken up a new sport, tennis; that he had always thought of tennis as a young lady's game, but he had now discovered it was almost as hard exercise as fencing. He was delighted to say that that very morning he had beaten his professional 6 to 2. He walked with me to the door, gave me a powerful handshake, and said he would look forward to seeing me again.

The Italian censors that evening received an indication from the Palazzo Venezia that they could now refer with moderate cordiality to my visit. Up to that time the press had been silent about me. Evidently Mussolini had decided that nothing should be published until he himself had learned whether there was anything more to my visit than was told in the announcement he had received from Washington.

For obvious reasons it had been decided that, after leaving Rome, I should proceed to Berlin before visiting Paris and London so that no false inferences could be drawn from my itinerary.

The hand of Fascism lay heavy over Italy. Even in passing through the streets one could sense the restiveness of an inherently simple and natural people under an ever-tightening control to which they were neither accustomed nor adapted. The few hours I spent in

Switzerland on the way to Germany were a breath of fresh air, even though my brief stopover in Zurich was made exasperating by the persistent and all too apparent efforts of various categories of German agents to form some contact with myself or with the members of my staff. Two Germans whom I had known slightly many years before sent me letters by messenger alleging that through their intimacy with powerful figures in the Nazi regime they could be of great service in the accomplishment of my mission. Other individuals, with patently concocted stories of distress, attempted to play upon the sympathies of my secretaries. Still others never let me out of their sight during the time of my short stay in Switzerland.

But if Italy had seemed to be weighted down by unaccustomed restrictions, my first step upon German soil made the atmosphere within Italy seem light and carefree in comparison.

Throughout most of the trip from the Swiss frontier to Berlin the blinds of the railway carriage in which I traveled were kept drawn because of wartime restrictions, but upon the few occasions when I was able to set foot on the station platform, my feeling of oppression was almost physical.

This feeling was heightened upon reading the German newspapers brought to me by Herr von Struwe, who had been sent by the German Foreign Office to accompany me from the frontier. In Washington, I had, of course, seen excerpts from the German press, but I had never before realized so vividly what an amazing document a German newspaper under Hitler actually was. I remember that on the first page of the very first paper I picked up there were three items, written with ponderous solemnity, which purported to describe events alleged to have taken place recently in England and in the United States. All of them were not only untrue, but fantastically untrue. I think this detail had as great an impact on my consciousness as any other experience I had while I was in Germany. On occasion, one has to undergo certain experiences personally in order to grasp fully what one may already know and tacitly admit to be the case. Like hundreds of thousands of my fellow citizens, I had known that the press in Germany was entirely controlled by the Nazi regime and that the German people were permitted to read only what the Nazi leaders wanted them to. But until that moment I had not fully realized the tremendous power such authority gives to a government. Under those conditions, and at a time when listening to a foreign radio broadcast was a capital offense, punishments for which were reported in the very newspaper I was then reading, how was it conceivable that the people of Germany could ever move except as their masters instructed them? From that moment I have been convinced that when this war is over the peoples of the earth must never again permit a situation to arise where any people shall be deprived of their inherent right to know the truth.

I arrived in Berlin at the Friedrichstrasse station in the early morning of March 1. Almost the first thing I saw, as I drove down the familiar Unter den Linden to the Hotel Adlon, was a group of Polish prisoners, under armed guards, shoveling snow from the streets.

The German government had permitted no word of my arrival in Berlin to appear in the German press. The public had no knowledge of my mission or its purpose. The Adlon Hotel ostentatiously displayed a flag indicating the presence of some emissaries of the so-called republic of Slovakia, but it was not permitted to put out an American flag.

The time of my reception by Hitler's Minister for Foreign Affairs, Herr von Ribbentrop, had been fixed for noon. I was escorted to the Foreign Office Building by the Chief of Protocol, Herr von Doernberg. Alexander Kirk, the American Charge d'Affaires, who had never previously been received by Ribbentrop, accompanied me to the interview at my request.

Every official of the Foreign Office was dressed in military uniform. After we passed the two sphinxes at the portal dating from Bismarck's time, we came upon storm troopers in stained uniforms, stationed at the top of the stairs. Their faces were subnormal in their startling brutality.

My reception by Ribbentrop was in some ways the most astonishing experience of my entire mission.

Backed by Herr Schmidt, the well-known official interpreter, he received me at the door of his office, without even the semblance of a smile, and without even a word of greeting. After a moment's pause, I spoke a few words in English, since I knew that he spoke English fluently. In addition to his brief service in London as ambassador, he had spent several years in England as a wine salesman and four years in the United States and Canada in the same capacity.

Ribbentrop looked at me icily and barked at Dr. Schmidt the German word "interpret." We then sat down. The Minister turned to me and asked me in German whether I had had a comfortable journey. I turned to Dr. Schmidt and said in English that I had now lost all facility in speaking German and to be good enough to interpret my reply to the Minister.

I set forth the nature of my mission, emphasizing that my government was solely interested in the establishment of permanent peace in Europe and had no interest in any temporary truce. I concluded by making it very clear that I had no proposals to offer and no commitments whatever to put forward on the part of the United States.

Ribbentrop then commenced to speak and never stopped for well over two hours, except to request the interpreter from time to time to translate the preceding portion of his discourse. The Minister sat with his arms extended on the sides of his chair and his eyes continuously closed. The pomposity and absurdity of his manner could not be exaggerated. One could only assume that he envisioned himself as the Delphic oracle. It would be unduly tedious to relate in any detail the harangue which then ensued. The early part of the discourse had to do with German-American relations, and the entire burden for their deterioration was put on the United States. The remainder of Ribbentrop's outpourings was such an amazing conglomeration of misinformation and deliberate lies that I could not possibly have remained silent if I had not been afraid of jeopardizing the arrangements for the interview which I was scheduled to have with Hitler on the following morning. Among other things, Ribbentrop asserted that German foreign policy conflicted in no way with the interests of this country and that the German government never had and never would interfere directly or indirectly in the domestic affairs of the United States, nor in those of any other American republic.

He then began an account of Germany's participation in European history from the day Hitler became chancellor on January 30, 1933. The occupation of the Rhineland and the manner in which it had been carried out was alleged to have been accepted by the entire world as a rightful step. According to him, the consolidation of Austria into the German Reich had marked the union of two severed portions of the old German Empire, and had brought back into one German family German peoples who desired such union. It had been attained without the shedding of blood, and in accordance with the will of the overwhelming majority of the Austrian people. I then was obliged to listen to what was almost a verbatim recital of the pages in the German White Books which had published the German version of the steps leading up to the Munich Agreements. The atrocities which he alleged had been committed by the government of Czechoslovakia upon the Sudeten people were, he maintained, the primary reason for the occupation of Czechoslovakia, and Ribbentrop insisted that Hitler's sole desire had been to achieve a "friendly solution" of this problem.

He brought up the bilateral agreement between Neville Chamberlain and Hitler. What, he asked, had happened only a few weeks later? Chamberlain and the Churchills, Edens, and Duff-Coopers had dared to announce in the British Parliament that Great Britain was embarking on the biggest armament program of its entire history, so that "no agreement like that of Munich would ever again be forced upon the British Government."

From this point on in the Minister's monologue, the word "England, England, England" punctuated every sentence of his speech. He insisted that the keystone of Hitler's foreign policy had been the desire to create close and co-operative relations with England. His overtures had not only been repulsed with scorn—and the German word "hohn" came out like the hiss of a snake—but England had "with craft and with guile" done her utmost to prevent the German people from once more assuming their rightful place in the family of nations.

He asserted that Hitler had no ambitions which threatened the integrity of the British Empire; on the contrary, he believed the integrity of the British Empire was a desirable factor from the standpoint of Germany. For that reason he had entered into the naval agreement of 1935 with Great Britain, voluntarily pledging Germany to keep to a minimum naval ratio, as a pledge to England that Germany had no designs upon the Empire. Until the last moment Hitler had sought peace and understanding with England, always to find hatred, scorn, and trickery as his reward.

It was admitted that Germany had offered to guarantee the frontiers of the new Czechoslovakia agreed on at Munich, but how could this commitment be carried out? The new Czech authorities had proved weak tools of the enemies of Germany. They had been unable or unwilling to prevent foreign agents from stirring up agitation or from concocting plots against Germany. How could Germany guarantee the frontiers of a nation which was being deliberately turned into a menace to the heart of Germany? That was the sole excuse Ribbentrop offered for Hitler's flagrant violation of the obligations he had contracted at Munich.

And then the Minister turned to Poland. Ribbentrop insisted that Hitler had always maintained that the separation of the German city Danzig from the Reich and the complete divorce of East Prussia from Greater Germany were provisions of the Versailles Treaty which could not endure. But at the same time he had been convinced that these questions could be solved satisfactorily by means of a direct understanding between Poland and Germany. In that spirit the nonaggression pact between Germany and Poland had been concluded. As far back as 1938 negotiations had been begun between the German Foreign Office and Colonel Beck, for the purpose of restoring Danzig to the Reich and granting to Germany an extraterritorial motor road and railroad across the Corridor between Greater Germany and East Prussia. These conversations had prospered; they had reached a complete agreement in principle when Colonel Beck had visited Berlin and Berchtesgaden early in 1939. In a few months, Ribbentrop maintained, had it not been for foreign interference, the entire arrangement would have been concluded to the satisfaction of Poland, and Germany would have abided permanently by this settlement. (This flat contradiction of what he had said only a moment before with regard to Hitler's insistence that the Polish Corridor could not endure was only one of an infinity of similar contradictions throughout the interview.)

And what had happened? The German government now had the complete archives of Warsaw. He wished me to know that it possessed incontrovertible proof that England had incited the Polish government to refuse to conclude this agreement; that England had incited the Poles to determine upon war against Germany. Looking pointedly at me, Ribbentrop added that the German government likewise had incontrovertible proof that officials of governments in no way connected with the issues involved had urged the Polish government to make no concession of any nature to Germany. (It will be remembered that shortly after my visit to Berlin the German Foreign Office published records alleged to have been found at Warsaw which purported to show that diplomatic representatives of the United States in Europe had intervened in this manner.)

Finally, the German government, he said, had proof that the British guarantee of military support had been thrust upon Poland against the wishes and advice of Colonel Beck, solely as a means of persuading her to refrain from making any fair settlement with Germany.

When this stage had been reached, the Poles, he asserted, had undertaken every kind of cruel repressive measure against the German minorities in Poland. The German government had attempted time and again to point out to Poland the dangerous results of such a policy. The torture and mutilation of Germans, Ribbentrop declared, was so unbelievable that he would be glad to furnish me with documentary evidence and photographs of these alleged atrocities.

And finally, "solely to protect the Germans in Poland" and as a means of self-defense against Polish mobilization, Germany had been forced to take military action. But even at this last moment Hitler had attempted to keep the peace with England and France. He had made it clear to both the Western powers that Germany wished in no way to endanger British or French security. It had been England and France who had insisted upon declaring war on Germany. Germany under no conditions would have declared war on them.

Ribbentrop then went on to say that Germany wished for nothing more in Europe than the United States had in the Western Hemisphere through the Monroe Doctrine. As a great power she was entitled to safeguard her vital interests. He himself had been in the United States and he knew that every American citizen felt, and he thought quite legitimately, that the preservation of the Monroe Doctrine was fundamental in assuring the safety of the United States' world position. Surely Germany was entitled to the same position in Central Europe. Germany, he proclaimed, desired nothing more than the unity under the German Reich of the German people in Europe; the return of the colonies which had been stolen from her, so that she might obtain from them the raw materials she could not herself produce, and make possible the profitable emigration to them of German nationals; the official recognition by the other great powers of Germany's sphere of influence in Central Europe; the independence and autonomy of the smaller states of Europe which had a clearly established historic right to independence.

With regard to these latter nations, the Minister said (and this was barely two months prior to the German invasion of these smaller powers, for which at that very moment plans were fully prepared), Germany had not the faintest design upon them. She expected, of course, the independent powers "within her sphere of influence" to have close economic ties with the Reich. And I should not forget that one thousand years ago German emperors had been crowned in Prague. Germany, however, had no desire or intention of preventing the Czech people from having their complete autonomy.

Germany must have her Monroe Doctrine in Central Europe. She would never again discuss any question affecting her interests in Eastern Europe except with the Soviet Union; and with Russia, Ribbentrop alleged, Hitler had already reached a complete and permanent delimitation of interests in that area. But the days of encirclement—of British and French political meddling in Central and Eastern Europe—had passed, and forever.

(It was particularly significant that Italy was never once mentioned by Ribbentrop throughout the entire conversation.)

British policy made any such recognition of German rights impossible. Only the night before, Ribbentrop said, Eden had publicly declared that the war aim of England was to destroy Hitlerism. Ribbentrop wished me to know that every German national was a part of Hitler. The destruction of Hitlerism could only mean the destruction of the German people, for Germany would never again be governed by any form of government other than Hitlerism.

Germany was strong and completely confident of ultimate victory. She had immense military superiority, and from her eastern and southern neighbors she could obtain the raw materials she required. She was prepared for a long war. But the Minister was confident it would be a short war. Germany wanted peace, but only on condition, Ribbentrop said, "that the will on the part of England to destroy Germany is obliterated once and for all. I see no way in which that can be accomplished except through complete and total German victory."

By the time this stage had been reached Ribbentrop's voice had become almost exhausted, and he paused.

I said I would not attempt to reply at any length, but that I could not refrain from making certain comments upon what the Minister had said.

First of all, the Minister had referred to American-German relations and had declared that propaganda was responsible for the fact that the United States had permitted their deterioration. I said I had no doubt that propaganda was active in almost every part of the world and I felt very deeply, as President Roosevelt had said, that the more peoples were enabled freely to drink from the well of truth, and had means of access to true information, the more peaceful and happy the world would be. But, if the Minister thought that the unsatisfactory state of American-German relations was due to propaganda, he was sadly deceived. The American people, I said, were idealistic people, profoundly moved by humanitarian considerations. They resented in their inmost soul ill-treatment of human beings in any part of the world. The cruel treatment of the Jewish people, and of other minorities in Germany, was one of the two compelling causes of American feeling toward Germany.

The other was the overwhelming feeling in the United States that international controversies can and must be settled by pacific methods, and that the use of force, such as had been exercised by Germany in recent years, destroyed the very foundations of international relations and those bases of international life which alone could give real security to the United States and to other nations. Those, I said, and not propaganda, were the real reasons for the feeling existing in the United States toward Germany. So far as trade relations were concerned, which the Minister had asserted Germany desired to maintain with the United States, he must know that so long as Germany pursued her present autarchic policy and indulged in every form of discrimination against us there was no opportunity offered the United States for improved trade with Germany.

I said that I further desired to refer to the Minister's statements about the Monroe Doctrine. It seemed to me very clear that he was laboring under a complete misunderstanding of the nature of that policy. Many years ago, I was quite willing to admit, the Monroe Doctrine had been occasionally misinterpreted as entitling the United States to exercise some form of hegemony in the Western Hemisphere. But the doctrine had never in reality been other than a unilateral declaration by the United States that it would not permit any non-American power to exercise any kind of sway, military or political, within the Western Hemisphere. It had never implied the intention of the United States to prevent non-American powers from having the same trade relations with the other American republics as we ourselves possessed, and on equal terms. It had never rightfully implied the assumption of any political control by us over our neighbors.

At this moment, I was glad to say, a new relationship existed in the Western Hemisphere. The Monroe Doctrine was now reinforced by the common agreement of all the American republics that they would regard any extracontinental danger to the peace of any one republic as a menace to the peace of them all. The United States was an equal partner in an association of twenty-one partners. Consequently, if the Minister used the term "Monroe Doctrine" as synonymous with the term "sphere of influence," whether political or economic, he should find some more accurate synonym for what he had in mind.

I went on to say that, if a war of devastation were now to take place, all that civilization held most dear, all the remaining material and social structure of Europe, would in great part be destroyed. The loss of lives would be appalling. No country on earth would remain unaffected, and the United States, as the most powerful neutral, could not possibly avoid suffering every form of repercussion upon its own political, social, and economic structure. It was for that reason my government hoped most earnestly, while there was still time, that some way might be found for the construction of a durable and just peace. The President of the United States had officially stated in the preceding year, as the Minister knew, that if the way to such a peace could be found by the nations directly involved, of which the United States was not one, my government would participate wholeheartedly in a common attempt to bring about a real limitation and reduction of armaments, as well as a return by all nations to a sane economic system of international trade relations. On these two latter points, as the Minister doubtless knew, my government was even now discussing the possibility of reaching some common understanding with the neutral powers. All of these opportunities to return to a world of security, sanity, and prosperity would be grievously, if not fatally, prejudiced if a war of devastation now broke out.

To these brief remarks, the sole rejoinder made by Ribbentrop was the constant repetition of the words: "We have not attacked England. She has attacked us. I see no way by which we can attain the peace we want and which we seek save through German victory."

I then terminated the interview, which had lasted almost three hours.

In the notes which I made immediately afterwards, I used these words: "Ribbentrop has a completely closed mind. It struck me as also a very stupid mind. The man is saturated with hate for England to the exclusion of any other dominating mental influence. He is clearly without background in international affairs, and he was guilty of a hundred lies in his presentation of German policy during recent years."

Late that same afternoon I went to see State Secretary von Weizsaecker in his office at the Foreign Office. In the German official hierarchy the position of state secretary has corresponded since the days of Bismarck to that of undersecretary of state in our own country.

Herr von Weizsaecker was a typical example of a German official of the old school. Although his early service had been in the German Navy, he had been transferred to the diplomatic service at a time when the German government had decided to increase its Foreign Service by using suitable officers of the German Army and Navy. In the intervening years von Weizsaecker had become wholly imbued with the traditions of the Wilhelmstrasse. In his schooling, in his mentality, and in his general approach he was reminiscent of the Bernstorffs and of the Bülows.

He spoke to me of his own home life. His greatest pleasure, he told me, had been when he and his wife and his three boys could have an evening of chamber music together in their house. The family had now been shattered. His youngest son of twenty had been killed in the Polish war, and his other two sons were serving on the Western Front.

I spoke with Herr von Weizsaecker of my earlier conversation with Ribbentrop and, after hesitating a moment, Weizsaecker said: "I am going to be quite frank with you. I have been strictly instructed not to discuss with you in any way any subject which relates directly or indirectly to the possibility of peace."

He then drew his chair toward the center of the room and motioned to me to do likewise. It was evident that the omnipresent German secret police dictaphones were installed in the walls rather than in the central lighting fixtures.

We had for a while a desultory conversation. I then reverted again to my conversation with Ribbentrop. I said that, if the feeling of the German government as a whole was as decisive as that of Herr von Ribbentrop that a war of devastation and of conquest was the only course for Germany to follow, I would be needlessly taking up the time of the German authorities by prolonging my stay.

Herr von Weizsaecker thought a good three minutes before replying. He then leaned toward me and said: "It is of the utmost importance that you say that personally to the Fuehrer when you see him tomorrow."

I waited a moment myself and then asked him:

"Let me have your personal advice, for I am now asking an entirely personal question. Do you believe that any suggestions for peace conversations proffered by Mussolini would have any favorable reception here?"

This time Herr von Weizsaecker again waited before answering. His reply when it came was: "What I have already said about the Fuehrer answers a part of your question. But," and here he motioned to the Foreign Office in which we were, "here the relations between Germany and Italy have *narrowed* greatly."

The only interpretation which could be drawn from his statement was that in Weizsaecker's opinion, if the Duce were to approach Hitler directly and secretly, it might have some effect. If Ribbentrop knew of the approach he would do his utmost to block it.

During the remainder of the day I had the opportunity of seeing and of talking with the members of our own Embassy staff, and with the American press correspondents still stationed in Berlin. I think that any American citizen would have had reason to be proud of the officials of our Foreign Service and of the American correspondents who were trying to keep the American people informed of what was going on inside Germany.

The American Charge d'Affaires, Alexander Kirk, had spent his entire life in the Foreign Service. He had served in every part of the world. Brilliantly intelligent, with a highly accurate and penetrating mind, he was impelled by a consuming hatred for the Nazi regime and all its manifestations, and eagerly anxious that the people of the United States might become aroused to the danger which he so clearly foresaw for the United States in Nazi policy.

With few exceptions, the American press correspondents saw eye to eye with the head of our own Embassy. The services which both groups rendered, under singularly trying conditions, confronted by hostility and suspicion at every turn, doing their utmost both officially and through the press to tell the people of the United States the truth, cannot be overestimated.

At eleven o'clock on the morning of March 2 several Foreign Office officials, dressed in uniform and headed by Herr von Doernberg, came for me at the Adlon Hotel to take me to my interview with Hitler at the new Chancellery. This monstrous edifice had been completed the previous year within a period of eight months. Workmen had toiled night and day in order to have it ready for the Chancellor's New Year's Day reception for the Diplomatic Corps, so that the foreign representatives might obtain an idea of what the new Hitlerized Berlin was to look like. Kirk accompanied me to the interview at my request. He had never previously been permitted to see Hitler except at a distance.

The façade of the new Chancellery on the Wilhelmstrasse could remind one only of a modern factory building. My car drove into a rectangular court with very high blank walls. At one end was a flight of broad steps leading into the Chancellery. Monumental, black, nude statues flanked the portico to which the steps led. The impression the court gave was that of a prison yard. A company of soldiers was drawn up on each side to give me the Nazi salute as I entered. At the head of the steps I was greeted by Reich Minister Meissner, the head of Hitler's Chancellery, who, chameleon-like, had maintained his position under Ebert, under Hindenburg, and now under Hitler. A group of flunkies in the entrance hall were dressed in light-blue satin liveries with powdered hair.

We then formed a procession of some twenty couples, headed by Meissner and myself, and with slow and measured tread first traversed a tremendously long red marble hall, of which walls and floor were both of marble; then up a flight of excessively slippery, red marble steps into a gallery which, also of red marble, had windows at one side and tapestries on the other. The gallery, like the main salons in German ocean liners, was lined with an interminable series of sofas, each with a low table and four chairs in front of it. From the gallery there opened off a series of drawing rooms. Finally the procession deployed into one of these, where I was requested to sit down until Hitler was ready to receive me.

In a very few minutes Meissner came to announce that Hitler was waiting. I was shown into the adjoining room, a rectagonal drawing room furnished with comfortable upholstered sofas and chairs, over-looking the garden of Bismarck's old residence in which Hitler was then living.

Hitler received me near the door. He greeted me pleasantly, but with great formality. Ribbentrop and Schmidt, the interpreter, were the only two German officials present at the interview.

Hitler was taller than I had judged from his photographs. He had in real life none of the ludicrous features so often shown in his photographs. He seemed in excellent physical condition and in good training. His color was good and, while his eyes were tired, they were clear. He was dignified, both in speech and in movement. His voice, in conversation, was low and well-modulated. It had only once during our conversation of an hour and a half the raucous stridency which is always heard in his speeches, and it was only at that moment that his features lost their composure. He spoke with clarity and precision and I was able to follow every word in German, although Dr. Schmidt interpreted—and at times inaccurately.

After we were seated Hitler looked at me to indicate that I was to commence the conversation.

(It must here be emphasized once more that the limitations properly placed upon my mission by the President precluded my making any proposals to Hitler. My sole function was to learn from him what the purpose of the German government actually was, in order that the President might determine whether there existed even a remote chance for the negotiation of any just or durable peace.)

I set forth the detailed purposes of my mission as I had already explained them to Ribbentrop. I made particular reference to the fact that I was authorized to make no proposals. In as eloquent terms as I could command I set forth the President's hope that there might still be a way open for a stable, just, and lasting peace and not a truce or a precarious breathing spell. I pointed out that, if a war of annihilation now broke out, whether it was short or whether it was long, it would definitely preclude for the present the negotiation of such a peace because of the human suffering it would create and because of the human passions it would arouse. Inevitably, I said, it would exhaust the economic and financial resources which still existed in Europe. In such a war as that, I said, who would be the victors? It seemed clear that all would be the losers and in that sense not only would the belligerents be the losers but also the neutrals, of which the United States was the greatest and most powerful. We, as a people, now realized fully that such a war must inevitably have the gravest repercussions upon our vital national interests.

The President of the United States had, in communications addressed to the Chancellor himself, made it clear that if a just political peace could be found—and in the negotiation of such a peace we could not be directly involved—the United States would play its full part in co-operating toward the achievement of two fundamental requirements in the establishment of any sane and ordered world : the limitation and reduction of armaments, and sound international economic relationships. If such bases could still be found, was it not worth every effort to seek the way of peace before the war of devastation commenced and before the doors to peace were closed? I spoke only of a just peace, I said, a peace which promised stability and security for the future. I could conceive of no lasting or real peace until Germany was no longer regarded by her neighbors as a threat to their independence or to their security and, unless Germany made it evident that she was not in fact striving for constantly increased objectives— objectives which necessarily involved aggression and a threat to the rights of free peoples.

Hitler knew that I had been given the opportunity of speaking with Mussolini in Rome. I had gained the impression from my conversation with Mussolini that the latter believed the foundations of a durable peace might still be laid. I said that I would welcome any views which Hitler cared to express to me for the information of the President in that regard.

Hitler then outlined what he claimed had been his foreign policy during the preceding seven years. The outline pursued exactly the lines followed on the previous day by Ribbentrop, and it was note-worthy that every conversation I had with members of the German government was prefaced by exactly the same historical survey. It was obvious that Hitler himself or Ribbentrop had dictated the course which members of the German government were to follow in their conversations with me.

Hitler, however, emphasized even more strongly than Ribbentrop his desire to reach an understanding with England. He claimed par-ticularly that the Naval Agreement of 1935 should be regarded as an indication that Germany had then had no intention of challenging British naval supremacy or impairing the security of the British Empire. When he came to the account of the negotiations with Po-land which had terminated in the German assault upon that country, the preceding September, he turned to me and said: "I have never in my life made a more earnest or more sincere appeal than I did to the British Ambassador when I sent for him just prior to the break with Poland. He was sitting in the same place where you are now sitting, and I besought him to tell his government that Germany had no in-tention of attacking England or of directly or indirectly impairing British interests, but that Germany could not permit continuing domination by Western European powers of the small states of East-ern Europe, nor continuation of the state of affairs which resulted in an ever-increasing threat to German vital interests. That appeal, like every other approach I have made to England in seven years, was rejected with derision."

Hitler then continued by saying that I had referred to the problem of limitation and reduction of armaments. Time and again, he said, he had offered England and the other powers of the world the op-portunity for a real and practicable reduction of armies. He had guar-anteed that Germany would limit her standing army to two hundred thousand men; then to three hundred thousand men; he had expressed German willingness to outlaw certain types of munitions and implements of war. Never once, however, had these offers on his part received the slightest attention or, much less, consideration as a possible basis for agreement. He went on to say: "The present armament burden is crushing the life out of all peoples; it cannot continue much longer. The national economy of every nation will crash before much further time elapses."

He stated that he believed there were two practicable methods of securing real disarmament. The first was for the great powers of Europe to agree upon their minimum ratios of military and naval strength, outlawing all but a minimum of offensive armaments, and upon that basis further to agree that, in the event of any threat to their security or to the peace of Europe, these powers would pool their military and naval resources as a police force. He had formally made this proposal to Great Britain and to France. He had never received the slightest response.

The other alternative was for the powers to agree upon a progressive and gradual reduction in their respective military strength; with the gradual elimination at the same time of certain categories of offensive armament. This, he believed, would take a very long time and was the less satisfactory of the two methods.

I had also mentioned, he continued, the problem of a liberal, unconditional most-favored-nation international trade relationship as an objective toward which the nations of the world should strive. He felt quite in accord with me. He said that that was a desirable goal, and Germany, under more normal conditions, would gladly co-operate toward that end. He did not, however, believe that unrestricted international trade was the cure for all of the world's economic problems. He said that, for example, while Germany would doubtless profit by taking a considerable portion of America's agricultural surpluses, an industrial country like Germany could not take any large part of America's industrial production, nor could the United States import Germany's manufactured products on a big scale. It was, consequently, necessary for Germany to intensify her trade relations with countries in Central and Southeastern Europe which desired Germany's industrial exports, which they themselves did not produce, in return for raw materials needed by Germany.

At this point I interrupted to say that Hitler appeared to overlook the fact that, while the United States, it was true, was a large industrial producer as well as an exporter of agricultural surpluses, nevertheless trade between the United States and Germany over a period of many generations had been highly profitable to both sides. He must not forget that Germany manufactured many commodities either more cheaply or in more efficient form than similar items were manufactured in the United States, and that such exports from Germany had always been profitably sold to my country. The question, moreover, I said, was not one of a purely bilateral nature, but a question which necessarily involved the problem of profitable triangular trade which had always entered into the picture of Germany's trade relations with the United States. Furthermore, for Germany to be able to sell profitably the bulk of her luxury products she had to find countries where the standard of living was relatively high. I believed the standard of living in the countries of Southeastern Europe was not sufficiently high to make it possible for Germany as yet to find there a very profitable market for any large percentage of her industrial products.

Hitler did not seem to comprehend this problem and dropped the subject after remarking that a country with a population of one hundred and forty individuals to the square kilometer must increase its production if those individuals were to find the wherewithal to survive. I replied that it seemed to me there was no country in the world that would profit more immediately and more greatly than Germany from a restoration of liberal international trade relations, as this would enable the one hundred and forty individuals in each square kilometer to increase their standard of living and their purchasing power, particularly if their work was dedicated to constructive production rather than to the sterile manufacture of munitions.

Hitler then said that Germany's objectives were simple and that he would outline them to me. He would classify them as (a) historical; (b) political; and (c) economic.

From the historical aspect, Germany had existed as an empire five hundred years before Columbus discovered the Western World. The German people had every right to demand that their historical position of one thousand years should be restored to them; Germany, he alleged, had no aim and no ambition other than the return of the German people to the territorial position which historically was rightly theirs.

Germany's political aims were co-ordinate. Germany could not tolerate the existence of a state such at Czechoslovakia, which constituted an enclave created at Versailles solely for strategic reasons and which formed an ever-present menace to the security of the German people; nor could Germany tolerate the separation from Greater Germany of German provinces by corridors under alien control and likewise created solely for strategic reasons. No great power could exist under such conditions. Germany, however, did not desire to dominate non-German peoples and, if such peoples adjacent to her boundaries did not constitute a military or political threat to the German people, she had no desire to destroy permanently or to interfere with their independence.

From the economic standpoint Germany must claim the right to profit to the fullest extent through trade with the nations close to her in Central and Southeastern Europe. She would no longer permit the Western powers of Europe to infringe or impair her preferential position in this respect.

In brief, the German people intended to maintain the unity which he had now achieved for them. They intended to prevent any state on Germany's eastern frontier from constituting again a military or strategic threat to German security. Finally, Germany intended to obtain recognition for her economic supremacy in Eastern and Southeastern Europe.

Germany, further, would insist that the colonies stolen from her at Versailles be returned to her. Germany had not obtained these colonies through military conquest. She had obtained them through purchase or pacific negotiation. She had never utilized her colonies for military purposes. She now required them to obtain raw materials which could not be produced in Germany, and as a field for German emigration. Such a demand, he insisted, was not only reasonable but just.

At no time during the course of our conversation did Hitler mention the subject of German-American relations. Nor did he refer in any way to German relations with Soviet Russia or with Italy.

Hitler then passed to the subject of the war aims of the Allies. He asked me if I had heard or read the speech made in England the night before by Sir John Simon. I replied that I had not. He said that when I read the speech I would gain from it the same clear understanding which he had gained, namely, that it constituted a clear-cut definition of British aims and that these aims were the total destruction of Germany.

He said: "I am fully aware that the Allied powers believe a distinction can be made between National Socialism and the German people. There was never a greater mistake. The German people today are united as one man and I have the support of every German. I can see no hope for the establishment of any lasting peace until the will of England and France to destroy Germany is itself destroyed. I feel that there is no way by which the will to destroy Germany can itself be destroyed except through a complete German victory. I believe that German might is such as to make the triumph of Germany inevitable but, if not, we will all go down together." —And here he added the extraordinary phrase: "Whether that be for better or for worse."

He paused a moment and then said textually, rapidly, and in high and raucous pitch: "I did not want this war. It has been forced upon me against my will. It is a waste of my time. My life should have been spent in constructing and not in destroying."

I said that Hitler would, of course, understand it was the belief of my government that, if some way could be found to a peace which promised security to all peoples, no nation would have to "go down," let alone all of them. For that reason I earnestly trusted that such a way and such a peace might still be found. Hitler remained quiet for a moment or two. He then said: "I can assure you that Germany's aim, whether it comes through war or not, is lasting peace."

The interview then ended. Throughout the conversation Ribbentrop had remained silent. Most of the time he had kept his eyes closed, but occasionally he had leaned forward to nod his approval of some point or other made by Hitler in his declarations.

When I left the room where Hitler had received me, the procession re-formed and once more with slow and measured tread we passed through the hall and antechamber.

I remember thinking to myself as I got into the car that it was only too tragically plain that all decisions had already been made. The best that could be hoped for was delay, for what little that might be worth. With regard to Hitler himself, words which General Moreau had once used of Napoleon kept ringing through my mind:

"Il hait la liberté, et tout ce qui en porte l'empreinte lui déplait."

That same afternoon I went to have talks with the Italian and Belgian Ambassadors, the two most experienced members of the Diplomatic Corps then in Berlin. Both of them were confident that, whatever signs of army or other internal opposition there may have been to Hitler upon the conclusion of the Polish campaign, such opposition had died away. They told me that both the German Army and the German people had become thoroughly convinced by Goebbels' highly effective propaganda that the only aim of the Allies was the destruction of Germany and the enslavement of the German people. They both were confident that the Allied governments had grossly underestimated Germany's military strength as well as the ability of the Germans to withstand a protracted war.

The Belgian Ambassador assured me that Germany's stores of oil were far greater than either the British or the French government realized, and that Germany not only could undertake a large-scale offensive but could maintain it for a long period before the German Army would be in the slightest degree hampered in obtaining every one of its requirements.

As I walked back alone that evening to the Adlon Hotel across the snow-covered Pariser Platz, I came across a group of four old German women who had paused to rest for a moment. All were carrying heavy bags and satchels. They were evidently country women, dressed in the tight corsets and long heavy skirts of forty years before. Each one of them was in deep black. I stopped to speak with them and asked them if they were making a long journey. They had the decent, kindly faces I had seen so often in the early years when I had lived in Germany. They were going, they told me, to the railway station to visit members of their families in Southern Germany. Three of them had already lost a son in the Polish war. One of them had lost three.

That night through the completely dark streets, where not another automobile except our own was moving, I went to the Opera House to hear a magnificent performance of Mozart's *Marriage of Figaro*. The house was filled to the last seat. The audience was rapt. It had forgotten for the moment the war and the blackout and its apprehension of the future.

These two incidents stand out in my recollection of those grim hours in Berlin. They seemed to emphasize the strange, incongruous, and paradoxical aspects in the character of the German people—an incongruity so difficult for other races to understand. It is, I suppose, because of these very traits of human kindliness and of devotion to many of the higher cultural forms that the Anglo-Saxon peoples, at least, have for so long underestimated the danger of the German people in the mass as a disintegrating factor in modern civilization.

On the following morning, Sunday, March 3, again accompanied by officials of the German Foreign Office and by the ubiquitous Dr. Schmidt, I called upon Rudolf Hess, then Deputy to Hitler in his capacity as head of the Nazi party.

Hess received me in his offices in the party headquarters. They were built in the modern German style which Hitler was impressing upon the face of Berlin. The walls were completely bare of molding or of decoration. Hess and I, during our conversation, were seated, with Dr. Schmidt at my right. Behind Hess stood a somewhat disorderly and intrusive group of four or five youthful Nazi party leaders who, while not actually joining in the conversation, appeared to have previously rehearsed with Hess every word of what he was to say.

Notwithstanding the impression so often given me previously that Hess possessed a powerful and determining influence in German affairs, the effect he made upon me at the time was that of a man who had only the lowest order of intelligence. His forehead is low and narrow and his deep-set eyes are very close together. There was no sign of the "fatuous smile" of which Nevile Henderson has written.

At the outset of our conversation Hess took out of his pocket a collection of typewritten cards, and during the whole time we were talking he never took his eyes from them. His statements to me followed precisely the lines adopted by Ribbentrop, and there was no deviation from that outline, other than a paragraph or two which related to the Nazi party organization.

According to Hess, the German people were convinced that the Allies had no war aims other than the destruction of Germany and the obliteration of the German people. The German people, he said, stood as one man behind their Fuehrer. Hess impressed upon me that, as active head of the Nazi party, he was in a better position than anyone else to know what the real feeling of the German people was, since every district leader and every local leader under his jurisdiction was in turn in touch with the unit leaders who were in hourly contact with the German masses. He could assure me, he insisted, that never before in the history of the Nazi party had the German people as a whole been so completely identified with their Fuehrer as they were at that moment. As head of the Nazi party, he could state flatly that there was only one possible way through which Germany could achieve a lasting peace, and that was through a total and crushing German military victory. At that every one of the heads behind him nodded emphatic approval and the eyes burned with an almost insane fanaticism.

It was so obvious that Hess was merely repeating what he had been told to say to me and what I had already twice heard, and that he had neither explored the issues at stake nor thought anything out for himself, that I made no attempt to enter into any discussion with him. At the conclusion of the interview I merely stated that I regretted to learn his opinion that there existed no hope of any outcome save military conquest.

Hess was patently of abnormal mentality. His was a personality easily subject to domination by a stronger character. It has always, consequently, been incredible to me that his notorious flight to England could have been undertaken on his own initiative. He went as an emissary.

Immediately after the end of my interview with Hess I was scheduled to leave in the company of Dr. Schmidt for Karinhall, the palace built by Field Marshal Goering at the Schorfheide, which lies at a motoring distance of about an hour and a half to the north of Berlin.

As we came out of the Nazi party headquarters, the snow was commencing to fall in whirling gusts. The car provided for me was an open touring car enclosed with flapping canvas curtains through which the wind and snow persistently drove.

There was no traffic on the road. The flat North German wastes of birch and pine stretched out interminably as we reached the entrance of the National Game Reserve, which Goering had selected as the place for his home.

The entrance drive continued for many miles. It was blocked at intervals by closed gates which opened automatically upon our approach by the electric eye device. The loud clangor of a signal bell rang as soon as the car had passed. As we approached the residence, the road was lined on each side with enclosures surrounded with high wire fences where Goering kept his menagerie, and where he preserved his herd of European aurochs, now nearly extinct.

Karinhall was built by Goering around a log cabin which he had used in earlier years on hunting trips. The stone building which he had constructed was already immense, and at the time of my visit he was adding a new wing which should have made the entire building, when completed, about the size of the National Art Gallery at Washington.

Upon my arrival I was shown into a waiting room by Goering's aide, the brother of a German who had settled in Kentucky and was interned when we entered the war. He showed me with great pride the glass cases surrounding the walls of the room, filled with cups, bowls, beakers, and other objects of solid gold, which, he assured me, had been given to the Marshal by organizations and communities throughout Germany as a "spontaneous" indication of their admiration and affection for him.

Goering received me almost immediately. By his express desire there was no one present at our interview except Dr. Schmidt and Kirk.

Goering looked exactly like his photographs. His thighs and arms were tremendous, and his girth was monstrous. His face gave the impression of having been heavily rouged, but since, at the end of our three-hour conversation, the color had vanished, the effect was probably due to some form of physical maladjustment.

He wore a white tunic on which were plastered various emblems and insignia in brilliants, and over the Iron Cross which hung from his neck dangled a monocle on a black cord. His hands were shaped like the digging paws of a badger. On his right hand he wore an enormous ring set with six huge diamonds. On his left he wore an emerald at least an inch square.

His manner was simple, unaffected, and exceedingly cordial, and he spoke with far greater frankness and clarity than any other German official whom I met. We dispensed with the services of the interpreter except for the translation by Dr. Schmidt into German of what I had to say.

After I had once more set forth the nature and purposes of my mission, the Field Marshal reiterated the history of German foreign policy during the past seven years, following exactly the same lines as Hitler and Ribbentrop.

At one point, however, Goering deviated from the account given by the two others. That was in his discussion of the causes of the war against Poland. Goering stated with the utmost emphasis that at the time Ribbentrop visited Paris on December 6, 1938, to sign the nonaggression pact between France and Germany, Georges Bonnet, then French Foreign Minister, had assured him in the name of the French government that, as the result of the agreements at Munich, France would renounce all further interest in Eastern Europe and had stated specifically that France would refrain from influencing Polish policy in the future. While I had, of course, seen the official publications of the French and German governments on this question, which were diametrically opposed one to the other, I had not previously received from any German source so detailed a statement of the commitments which it was alleged Bonnet had made at that time.

I consequently asked the Marshal to repeat his statement. Goering turned to Dr. Schmidt, who it appeared had been present at Paris at the interview between Bonnet and Ribbentrop when the alleged commitments were made, and Schmidt related what he claimed had been said upon that occasion. According to him, the exact statement that Bonnet had made was that France thereafter renounced all political interests in Eastern Europe and specifically agreed not to influence Poland against the conclusion of an agreement with Germany whereby Danzig would be returned to Germany and whereby Germany would receive an extraterritorial means of access to East Prussia across the Polish Corridor.

In his statement of German objectives the Field Marshal was most explicit. Germany had forever renounced any ambitions with regard to Alsace-Lorraine. Germany had no desire to impair the integrity of the British Empire; she believed that in her own interest the British Empire should be maintained intact; Germany must retain as an integral part of the German Reich, Austria, the Sudetenland, and all those portions of Poland inhabited by German people. During the war Germany would continue her military occupation of Bohemia-Moravia and of Poland. If peace came, Germany would grant independence to the Czechs, but upon the understanding that they would remain demilitarized so that never again could either the Czechs or the Slovaks constitute a threat to Germany's military security in Central Europe. The Polish people who were actually Poles would be installed in a free and independent Poland with access to the sea. Germany must regain her colonies. In addition to this she must obtain a recognized position of economic preference in Eastern Europe.

From this point the Field Marshal went on to discuss British policy. He complained of the inability of Hitler to reach any form of understanding with England. Goering said he knew Hitler so well that he realized that, as a result of many years of failure in this direction, Hitler had now hardened. He doubted whether Hitler could bring himself to believe that there was any way of obliterating the British will to destroy Germany except through a German military victory. He recounted to me his own conversation with Lord Halifax when the latter had visited Germany two years before. He told me he had warned Lord Halifax time and again not to encourage Poland and Czechoslovakia to refuse to reach a reasonable and basic understanding with Germany. He had told him that if England persisted in this course war was inevitable, but that there was no justifiable need of war.

Both the problem of the German minorities in Czechoslovakia and the Czechoslovak military threat to the security of Germany, as well as the problem of Danzig and the Corridor in its relation to Poland, could have been settled readily if England and France had not refused to permit such a settlement.

The Field Marshal himself had never believed there was any possible justification for war, and he had done everything within his power to avert it. But England and France had persisted in bringing it about.

Now the situation from the military standpoint was this: Germany's air force was supreme and would remain supreme. Her military strength was far greater in proportion to the strength of the Allies than it had been in 1914. Today Germany had "all the trumps in her hands." In 1914 Germany had been attacked on all fronts. Today Russia and Italy were friendly, and the Balkans were neutral. The British blockade had already proved ineffective, and every day that passed made it easier for Germany to procure the raw materials which she required from the east and from the south. He could assure me that the stocks and supplies on hand in Germany were more than sufficient to meet every requirement. I might be interested to know that the Germans were now even manufacturing butter and other fats in great quantities from coal. While the Marshal believed the war would be short and a German victory soon attained, nevertheless, if the war were prolonged five or even ten years, Germany would strengthen and consolidate her position with every month that passed.

We were seated in front of an open fireplace in low easy chairs. Outside, through the huge windows, the snow was falling in ever-thickening gusts. As Goering went on speaking, it became more and more clear to me that, while he was quite as ruthless, quite as impervious to sentiment or to any humane influences as his colleagues in the Nazi machine, he at least had some conception of the outside world and of the psychology of other peoples. If anyone of real authority in the German state at that moment could grasp the eventual impact upon the people of the United States of a German war of devastation, Goering would be that individual.

I said to him that it seemed to me that no matter who would win such a war the devastation and loss of life, the human suffering, and the destruction of material resources would inevitably be so vast that much of what modern civilization had slowly and painfully built up during the ages would be obliterated. In that way the American people were directly concerned. I said that we in the United States already realized that the repercussions from such a war would affect us profoundly in many ways, that in a world where war reigned supreme, where the rule of force replaced the rule of reason, security for all peoples, no matter how remote they might at first be from the scene of actual hostilities, was inevitably undermined. If a war of devastation broke out, the vital interests of all neutral peoples, no matter how much they were determined to keep out of war, could not but be jeopardized.

The Field Marshal interrupted to say that he did not see how the American people could feel that their vital interests were affected through a war in Europe. He said: "It is needless for me to say to you that Germany has no ambitions of any kind other than those I have indicated to you, and least of all any ambitions which could affect the Western Hemisphere."

I replied that Goering must remember that, while the American people were overwhelmingly determined at that moment not to be drawn into the war, and while it was the consistent policy of the government to keep the American people from being drawn into war, nevertheless in 1916 President Wilson had been re-elected under circumstances not dissimilar on a platform which amounted to "He has kept us out of war"; and the Republican candidate, Mr. Hughes, had announced in his platform that he, if elected, would keep the American people out of war. Yet six months after the elections of 1916 the American people had overwhelmingly supported the entrance of the United States into the war. I said it must never be forgotten that the American people are quick to act when they believe that their vital interests are at stake.

I went on to say that the Marshal must also remember that the American people, as a whole, are profoundly moved by what they regard as inhumanity or cruelty to human beings. The measures taken by the German government against the Jewish people, and the hideous cruelties perpetrated upon them, had created a revulsion of feeling on the part of all the American people which could be best appreciated by those who could estimate the depth and strength of this feeling at first hand. I said that the Marshal would be wise not to minimize the importance of this issue.

Goering made but a halfhearted attempt to defend the position of his government. He said that I was complaining of an intense racial feeling which existed not only in Germany but in many other parts of the world as well. He wondered if the American people were consistent. He went on to say that not long before he had seen an American motion picture which had to do with discrimination against an individual thought to be white but who was found to have colored blood. He wanted to know whether the same kind of discrimination against which the American people were now protesting was not in fact practiced by themselves.

I replied that, while it was true, unfortunately, that in a few isolated instances people of the colored race had been subjected to cruelties, the tremendous majority of the American people not only deplored them but were doing everything within their power to correct the conditions from which they arose. I said that it was ludicrous to compare such incidents with an official policy initiated and persisted in by a government itself, which was carried on with the utmost barbarity and which was aimed at the actual extirpation of hundreds of thousands of decent law-abiding citizens.

Goering did not pursue the subject any further.

I then discussed with the Field Marshal the conversations which the United States government had recently undertaken with other neutral governments to try to find an agreement in principle upon the problems of the limitation and reduction of armaments and of a sound international trade policy. I had brought with me a brief memorandum setting forth the views of our government on this subject. The memorandum was read to him. Goering quickly said he was entirely in accord with every word, and that the German government at the time of any peace negotiations would wholeheartedly co-operate in establishing that policy. He said there was no country on earth that would stand to gain more from it than Germany. At the first appropriate opportunity he himself in a public speech would indicate Germany's intention to co-operate toward that end.

As for the question of limiting and reducing armaments, Goering made much the same statement as that made to me by Hitler the day before. He said that the armament race was ruining the economy of the entire world, and that no people could stand the strain much longer. He insisted that the German government had time and time again offered to participate in any reasonable plan for disarmament, but that its offers had always been rejected. If peace came, he said, Germany would enter into any practical plan which would make possible a real reduction of armaments.

He then reverted to British war objectives. He said that he was entirely convinced that the British and French governments were determined to destroy National Socialism, to subjugate the German people, and to split Germany into small units under military control. He said: "The English say that that is the way to get a lasting peace, because early in the nineteenth century when Germany was a collection of small independent states with an infinity of customs barriers, the Germans were only a race of musicians and poets. But they have never made a greater mistake. If they succeed in carrying out that plan, they will find not a race of musicians and poets, but a horde of Bolsheviks and Communists."

At the close of our conversation Goering said: "When you visit Paris and London you will realize that there is no hope for peace. You will there learn what I now know, and that is that the British and French governments are determined to destroy Germany, and that no peace, except on that basis, will be acceptable to them. If there is any way by which your government can avert the war, which I myself believe to be inevitable, it will have accomplished the greatest thing which human beings could desire."

When our interview was over Goering insisted upon showing me the vast and innumerable rooms of his palace. It would be difficult

to find an uglier building or one more intrinsically vulgar in its osten-
tatious display. The walls of the reception rooms and of the halls
were hung with hundreds of paintings. Many examples of the best
Italian and old German masters were placed side by side with daubs
by modern German painters. He had made a specialty of collecting
Cranachs. Two of them I recognized as being from the collection in
the Alte Pinakothek in Munich.

In the entrance hall, lined like the first reception room with glass
vitrines, there were displayed gifts presented to the Marshal by foreign governments. In this collection were shown a large number of
objects recently given to him by the government of Japan. Goering
told me that he had personally arranged the placing of every object
in the house.

In March the twilight sets in early in North Germany. It was
already getting dark as we came out through the entrance gate of
Goering's preserve. I had ample time for meditation on the long drive
back to Berlin.

Various things had become fully clear. The key to the question
whether Hitlerism was going to dominate Europe, and possibly succeed in dominating the rest of the world, was to be found in Berlin
and nowhere else. It was far more evident than I had previously
realized that Mussolini's influence, if it had ever possessed even some
slight weight, had vanished. It had all along been more than obvious
that both the British and French governments had kept on appeasing
until, if they were to retain even a semblance of independence, they
could appease no longer. But never before in the history of Europe
had the Western powers fought a more wholly defensive war than
that in which they were now engaged. The allegations of Hitler, Ribbentrop, and Goering that the Western powers wanted the war might
have had some deceptive effect in 1914. They were farcical in 1939.

There was only one power on earth which could give Hitler and
his associates pause. That would be their conviction that, in a war of
devastation forced upon Europe by Germany, the United States, in its
own interest, would come to the support of the Western democracies.
Equally clearly, however, there was at that moment not the remotest
chance that our government could tell the Nazi government that this

would prove to be the case. The great majority of the American people were altogether confident that they could keep out of the war. No executive in Washington with any sense of his responsibility to the American electorate, or with any regard for his constitutional limitations, could assume the authority for bluntly informing the government of the Third Reich that the United States would support Great Britain and France should Germany persist in her policy of world conquest. And yet it was only that threat which would have the remotest chance of averting the greatest calamity that the modern world had known.

As we drove through the dreary Berlin suburbs, night was just settling down. Long queues were patiently standing in the streets, as they had been when I had earlier passed through, waiting to obtain provisions or to enter a motion-picture theater. It struck me that the temper of the Berlin people had radically changed during the years since I had last been there. Even in the inflation days and in the days of desperate poverty of my last visits the crowds in the streets had seemed good-natured. One saw smiling faces. Through the miles of Berlin streets that I traversed on this final visit I never saw one smiling face.

That night I left Berlin.

The following morning when the train reached Freiburg as we neared the Swiss border on our way to Basel, the shades, which until that time had sealed the windows, were raised.

During the last miles of the journey the railroad line followed the Rhine valley. The women, and even small children, were out in the early morning sunlight pruning the vines in the hillside vineyards. The scene seemed very peaceful; peaceful, until one saw that in every vineyard, on every slope throughout the entire countryside there were continuous fortifications. This farmhouse on closer inspection was surrounded by pillboxes. That grove of trees, which in the distance seemed so harmless, half concealed gun emplacements. Only a few hundred yards away on the other side of the river was the camouflaged line of French military defenses. There was not a sound as we passed. Not even an airplane was to be seen in the sky.

It is, of course, impossible for me to recount in any detail the conversations I had in Paris or in London. Many of them dealt with questions which could in no event be made public until after the conclusion of the war. Furthermore, tragically enough, the great majority of the French officials with whom I talked during my two visits to Paris are now imprisoned and in German hands. While the Gestapo presumably has obtained the French records of the conversations I had, at least of those I had with members of the French government, it would be unthinkable for me to write anything here that might even remotely add to the suffering they have already undergone. Every word they uttered when I was with them was wholly legitimate and fully justified, but we have seen enough of German reactions to realize the distortions and perversions of truth of which Germans are capable.

I arrived in Paris in the early morning of March 7. It was a Paris wholly changed. There was no semblance of the fervor and high spirit of the Paris I had known in the early months of the first World War. One could almost sense in the very houses the feeling of sullen apathy which marked most of the faces that one passed in the nearly deserted streets. There was a sensation of a general waiting; of an expectation of some dire calamity. Among the innumerable persons with whom I talked, only in the rarest instances, outside of a few governmental departments, did I obtain the impression of hope or vigor, or even, tragically enough, of the will to courage.

The first visit I made was to the President of the Republic, Albert Lebrun, at the Elysée Palace.

The President spent much of the time that I was with him in telling me of his own life. He spoke of his having been born in the extreme eastern part of France, in a region adjacent to the German border, and of his earliest recollections being overlaid with the memory of the occupation of that region by German troops after the war of 1870. The point he wished to drive home, and with so much reason, was that the oldest generation of living Frenchmen had seen three wars, in each of which France had been attacked by Germany, and that France could not survive unless at least one generation of Frenchmen could live a normal span of life without having seen their country devastated as the result of German aggression.

President Lebrun was the type of high-minded, honorable Frenchman so often seen in the past in French public life. It is, however, an understatement to say that he possessed neither the character, the ability, the hard-driving energy, nor the vision which Poincaré, President of France during the first World War, possessed in so high a degree. President Lebrun's memory was evidently failing rapidly. It was difficult for him to remember with any accuracy names, or dates, or even facts.

In fact, it was highly embarrassing when, at the conclusion of our interview, as he was taking me on a tour of the main rooms of the palace, he attempted with a good deal of insistence to tell me the names of the subjects of the portraits hanging in the various rooms. For he was quite unable to remember the names of any of them, and was forced in each case to have recourse to one of his aides in order that I might be properly informed.

As soon as I left the Elysée Palace I was taken in charge by the French secret service and driven at lightning speed to keep my appointment with Prime Minister Daladier.

We passed down the Avenue Gabriel, deserted and sad in a bleak March light, through an empty Place de la Concorde to the narrow Rue St.-Dominique, where the Prime Minister spent most of his working days in the Ministry of National Defense.

Daladier was somewhat crippled from an accident he had had some little time before and was suffering, he told me, almost continual pain.

He started the conversation by reminding me of the talk I had had with him in Paris in the critical days of September, 1938, and of the tragic events which had taken place since that time. He laid great stress on what he claimed would prove to be the undying gratitude of the French people for the sympathetic and understanding attitude of the President of the United States and of his government, and for the invaluable help which France had been given by the revision of the American neutrality legislation.

The Prime Minister felt that the repeated efforts of the President to prevent the outbreak of war and to bring about a just settlement of

European controversies had been of great value in making men and women throughout Europe aware of the moral issues involved.

During the two hours that I talked with Daladier we covered a very wide range indeed. The Prime Minister was lucid, vigorous, and realistic. He was singularly frank in criticizing French foreign policy in the years that had just elapsed. His analysis of Hitler's policy was, I think, perhaps more precise and more accurate in its appreciation than that presented to me by any other European statesman. He had not believed at the time of Munich, and he did not believe now, that unification of the German people of Central Europe was all that Germany really desired and, much less, all that her present leaders desired. At Munich Hitler had personally said to him that the Czechs were an inferior people and that Germany would never consent to defile the purity of the German race by incorporating Bohemia and Moravia in Greater Germany. Hitler had now, of course, proved that the assurances then given had been lies. The Prime Minister believed that the German government had been very cleverly following a policy which had but one objective, and that was the ultimate domination of the whole of Europe and of the whole of the Near East. He was by no means sure that the ultimate ambitions of the German government did not go still much further. In any event, he said, the point had been reached where France could no longer survive the kind of existence which the Nazi regime was forcing upon Europe. France must fight until she had gained actual security for herself.

Daladier knew well that Hitler's reiterated assurances that he had forever renounced any aspirations covering Alsace and Lorraine were as untruthful as those he had earlier given with regard to Czechoslovakia. He possessed absolute evidence that long before the outbreak of war, German subversive agents had been attempting to create the same kind of emotional ferment among the German-speaking people in Alsace that they had in Czechoslovakia in 1938. He had documents showing that these German agents had been instructed to follow exactly the same lines as those followed by Henlein in the Sudetenland.

When I asked for his views on the kind of international machinery that would afford France the actual physical security she craved, the Prime Minister replied that the real problem was that the military forces of the opposing powers were roughly equivalent. Clearly disarmament was the only solution; and yet how could France and England take any actual step toward disarmament unless they were confident that Germany and Italy were in reality disarming at the same time. How could France have confidence in any disarmament which Germany might claim she was undertaking in view of the experience that France had had during the years following the close of the first World War, and especially during the latter portion of that period? He was referring, of course, to the years prior to the public declaration by Hitler that Germany was rearming. The French military mission sent in 1919 to Germany under General Nollet had been perfectly well aware that every time stocks of German armaments were destroyed, equivalent or greater stocks were being constructed secretly in other parts of Germany. It seemed that the one solution for ensuring actual disarmament lay in an international assumption of responsibility by the most powerful neutrals—those neutrals being prepared to use force if necessary.

To the Prime Minister aviation was the crux of the problem. He said that he thought it was entirely possible, as he himself had indicated in Geneva on earlier occasions, for an aviation force composed of units of various European powers to be set up, under some form of international authority, as a police power in Europe, to maintain peace and to ensure that all the powers complied with the disarmament commitments into which they might enter. He was confident that such a police force, if properly administered, would be sufficient to prevent any nation in Europe from undertaking aggressive action. Modern aviation being what it was, he believed the threat which the use of such a police force involved would have prevented the aggressor European powers in recent years from carrying out their acts of aggression.

He believed, he said, as President Roosevelt had so often insisted, that a clear distinction could be made between offensive and defensive categories in armaments. Security could be obtained by destroying, except for the use of a police force, all offensive types of armaments and retaining only those which were clearly defensive in nature.

Daladier, with much candor, gave me his own account of his experiences at Munich and his estimate of the other statesmen who had taken part in those negotiations.

That evening I had the opportunity of continuing my talk with the Prime Minister, since he had asked me to dine with him at the Quai d'Orsay with Chautemps, the Vice-Prime Minister; Georges Bonnet, former Foreign Minister and Ambassador in Washington and at that time Minister of Justice; Alexis Leger, the Secretary General of the Foreign Office; Champetier de Ribes, the Parliamentary Vice-Minister for Foreign Affairs; and Coulondre, the last French Ambassador to Germany. General Gamelin, the Chief of the General Staff, was expected but had suddenly been called to the northern front.

Conversation during the evening covered much the same ground as the talk I had had alone with the Prime Minister. Leger, as always, displayed magnificent clarity and logic in his thinking, as well as the innately liberal nature of his political philosophy.

There was the same general uncertainty as to the ultimate policy which Mussolini would force Italy to pursue as I later found in London. There was no difference of opinion as to the opposition of the Italian people, except for a thin Fascist veneer, to being drawn into a European war. The uncertainty was whether Mussolini would risk an adventure counter to the underlying sentiment of his own people, until he possessed positive assurance that he would win the gamble.

On the following day I visited the President of the Senate, Senator Jules Jeanneney. The Senator received me in his official residence in the Luxembourg Palace overlooking those familiar gardens of which I had known every corner from my earliest childhood.

Senator Jeanneney prefaced our conversation by calling my attention to the fact that the bust of Clemenceau stood on the chest of drawers which towered over his head. He said that Clemenceau had been the dominating influence in his life, and now that he had reached the ripe age of seventy-seven he appreciated more vividly than ever before how intrinsically right Clemenceau had been, and what a prophetic vision he had possessed in 1919.

The Senator told me that he, like President Lebrun, came from a border province, and that his earliest recollections had to do with the German military occupation of the village where he was born. He reminded me that since that time France had been forced by Germany into two more wars. He assured me that he spoke the sentiment of a unanimous French Senate in favoring the continuation of the present war until Germany had been defeated, and until she had been taught such a lesson as to make it impossible for her ever again to bring about a European conflagration.

As I listened to him it seemed to me that I was again hearing the voice of Clemenceau himself: "There is only one way in which to deal with a mad dog. Either kill him or chain him with steel chains which cannot be broken."

I was equally moved by my next conversation, which was with Edouard Herriot, President of the Chamber of Deputies. M. Herriot spoke with the deepest admiration of the President, of what he had done, and of what he stood for. He kept a very warm recollection of his own visit to Washington in 1933.

During his entire public life, and in particular during the past twenty years, he said, he had devoted himself to the attempt to lay the foundations for a lasting friendship and understanding between the German and the French peoples. His efforts had wholly failed. Time and again German statesmen, like Stresemann and Marx, had lied to him and deceived him. He had reached the positive conviction that the German people were themselves the cause of the present situation, and not their leaders alone.

He wished me to know that in 1924, when he was Prime Minister, at a time when the government of the Weimar Republic was putting its best foot forward and had almost persuaded the Western world that Germany was sincere in desiring the pacific adjustment which Locarno should have brought about, he had agreed to meet the members of the German government who were then visiting London upon the invitation of Ramsay MacDonald. Stresemann, he said, had been the principal figure in the German delegation. Soon after Herriot's arrival in London, Stresemann had invited him to a secret meeting. Reluctantly he had accepted, only to learn when they met that Stresemann wanted Herriot to agree to the conclusion of a secret alliance between Germany and France from which Great Britain would be excluded. How, he wished to know, could any nation have faith in Germany when a German leader, who was above all others identified as the prophet of German regeneration, was willing to stoop to treachery of so low and so grotesque a character?

Herriot saw no present solution other than a military defeat of Germany. As the result of a "real war," devastation would once more sweep over France. The Republic would be in ruins for many decades to come. As a further consequence of the war the social and economic structure of the whole of Europe would be completely changed. He was utterly pessimistic and utterly without hope.

Later in the day I had separate interviews with the Deputy Prime Minister, Camille Chautemps, and with Georges Bonnet.

M. Chautemps reflected much the same views as those expressed to me by Daladier. Bonnet gave me his version in full detail of the history of the negotiations between Germany and France during the months subsequent to the Munich agreements. It is fair to him to state that of his own initiative and, without his possessing, so far as I know, any knowledge of my conversations in Germany, he denied categorically what had been told me in Berlin regarding the pact of non-aggression which he had signed with Ribbentrop in December, 1938. He insisted that when the question of French policy in Eastern Europe had arisen, he had never directly or indirectly given Germany any assurance that France would wash her hands with regard to the fate of Poland. The only statement which he had made to Ribbentrop in that connection, he said, had been that the French government was signing the pact with the sole reservation that it should not be construed as impairing France's obligations under her two treaties of alliance with the Soviet Union and with Poland.

According to Bonnet, Ribbentrop had replied that this declaration on the part of the French government could in no sense be regarded as prejudicial to Germany in so far as Poland was concerned, since Germany also had a pact of non-aggression with Poland and since the

German government believed that relations between Germany and Poland would be increasingly friendly during the next four or five years. Bonnet asserted that Ribbentrop had, of course, lied brazenly and openly, and that in the French Yellow Book, already published, the French government had set forth the facts as they really were.

Of the remaining conversations which I had in Paris during those crowded few days, two stand out particularly in my memory.

I had known Paul Reynaud for many years. I had always had a very real admiration both for the calibre of his mentality and for the position which he had taken with regard to French foreign policy during the preceding ten years.

We had lunch together in the offices of the Louvre which he occupied as Minister of Finance. They were formerly an apartment, used during the time of Napoleon III by the Prince Imperial, and overlook the Louvre Gardens and the Tuileries beyond.

The larger part of our talk was devoted to the economic and financial questions in which he was then primarily concerned. But at the close of the luncheon he turned to me and said, "I don't have to tell you that people rightly regard me as the 'hardest man' in the French government with regard to our relations with Germany. You remember that when we talked in September, 1938, I told you that France should declare war upon Germany in order to save Czechoslovakia. You know I was right. You know that if France had done so at that time England could not have avoided coming into the war on the side of France. Munich has been the cardinal error of French and British policy." But that, he went on to say, was now past history. His well known sentiments on this subject, and on the general subject of Franco-German relations, made it easier for him now to follow an objective policy.

France could never obtain security and insure herself against a repetition of German aggression unless some international organization could be created capable of keeping peace. In his judgment no such organization could be effective unless precise arrangements were made for the establishment of an international police force, and the abolition, outside of that force, of all categories of offensive armaments.

The other interview which stands out is the conversation which I had with Léon Blum. Blum was no longer in office at that time, and he was living in almost complete retirement in his small apartment on the Left Bank of the Seine, overlooking the quais beyond Notre Dame.

In his crowded and charming study we talked for a long time of the events of the two years since I had last seen him, and of the tragically swift collapse of the cardboard structure of international security.

There was no change in his always astonishing ability to take delight in the amenities of life, like the good Parisian that he was; in his interest in so many widely different things, nor in the rapidity and lucidity of his mental processes. But, as an undercurrent to every word that he said, there was only too evident a profound sadness and an almost corroding discouragement. From Léon Blum, as from Edouard Herriot, one could only derive the feeling that for their country the hours were numbered, and time was passing very swiftly.

I think that of all of the experiences which I had in Paris in those March days of 1940, the experience which came with the greatest shock, and which made me realize for the first time how far the penetration of Nazi ideas had already proceeded in perverting the mentality of at least a portion of the French people, was that resulting from my visit to Léon Blum.

The following day I left for London. During my absence the French press published the fact that I had called upon the former Prime Minister, Léon Blum. When I returned to Paris four days later my secretaries estimated that while I was in England almost three thousand letters had been received addressed to me by Frenchmen, and in no stereotyped form, protesting against my visit. The vast majority of these letters were written in the most violent and insulting terms. A few of them were couched in moderate words of reproach. They were all written, however, solely because, as a representative of the President of the United States, I had dared to call upon a Jew. I have lived in France, and I have known France since the time of my earliest childhood. In all of those many years, except during the period of the Dreyfus case, I had never found that anti-Semitism existed in France. Now, for the first time, I realized how widely the poison engendered by the Nazis had already seeped into Western Europe.

It was on the morning of March 11 that I left Le Bourget for London on a plane offered me by the French government, accompanied by French combat planes. It was a bright and sunny morning, and as we crossed the Channel to England I could see an amount of shipping surprising in war time. Our course took us over the red brick houses of Brighton. From there to London we flew so low that one could plainly see the preparations already being made for the spring planting in the green English countryside.

Our Ambassador, Joseph P. Kennedy, who had been tireless in making all the arrangements for my visit, had arranged that I was first to call upon Lord Halifax, then the Secretary of State for Foreign Affairs, and from there proceed immediately to Buckingham Palace, where the King and Queen had indicated their desire to receive me.

As I have always found him on the innumerable times I have talked with him, Lord Halifax proved to be moderate, liberal minded and, above all, constructive, in his point of view on the present bitter crisis.

The key to his approach to the European problem was his conviction that no lasting peace could be made in Europe so long as the Nazi regime dominated Germany and dictated German policy. Peace was impossible except on the basis of confidence, and what confidence could be placed in the pledged word of a government that was pursuing a policy of open and brutal aggression, and that had repeatedly and openly violated its most solemn contractual obligations?

The King and Queen were living in a wing of Buckingham Palace, with the remainder of the great edifice closed for the war period. They were as charming and gracious as they had been during their trip to the United States, and they both spoke with enthusiasm of their American visit. To them it already seemed a long time ago and a bright recollection of another world which had now passed. The King was far graver in his manner than he had been in the preceding summer in Washington, and he spoke with great force of his convictions about the course of events to come.

When I went with Ambassador Kennedy for my first interview with Neville Chamberlain, the Prime Minister, at 10 Downing Street, we were shown immediately into the historic Cabinet room which occupies the back of the ground floor of the Prime Minister's official residence. A green baize table almost fills it. The windows look out upon the park.

Mr. Chamberlain was seated alone at his place at the Cabinet table when we were shown in. He was spare, but gave the impression both of physical strength and energy. He appeared to be much younger than his seventy-one years. His hair was still dark, except for a white strand across his forehead. His dominating features were a pair of large, very dark, piercing eyes. His voice was low, but incisive.

I gave the Prime Minister a personal letter which the President had asked me to hand him and, after he had read it, we talked informally for a few minutes until Lord Halifax joined us.

No fair and impartial estimate can be made of Neville Chamberlain's conduct of affairs as British Prime Minister until after the close of the present war, when a better perspective can be obtained. Until that time has come, it would be impossible for me to give even a personal appraisal of a man whose fate it was to be charged with chief authority at the moment when his country was paying for the accumulated errors of many preceding British governments, and, in particular, for the lack of understanding and vision for which Stanley Baldwin was primarily responsible.

In all the conversations which I had with Mr. Chamberlain neither courage nor determination were lacking, nor the frankest admission of his own mistakes.

He referred in full detail to his own efforts to maintain peace by making every possible concession to Germany during the preceding two years. He had been deceived, he had been lied to. There was now no question that Hitler did not desire a peaceful Europe founded upon justice, reason and security, as against a Europe dominated by Hitlerism. England had been forced into war as a last resort in order to preserve liberty and democracy which were threatened with extinction. So long as the Nazi government existed there could be no hope of any real peace, for no nation of the world could place any faith in the pledges of the Nazi government. Throughout his discussion of Nazi policy, Mr. Chamberlain spoke with white hot anger.

One of the points he made, which has lingered vividly in my mind, was his reference to the total inability of the Western democracies to procure any real understanding on the part of the German people themselves of what the facts were. He said to me, "It makes more than ever clear in my own mind the truth of what your President has said, that one of the essentials to a lasting peace is freedom of information."

Even in those early months of the war the life of London had completely changed. Not only was there a total blackout, but most of the private houses had already been closed. The members of the government who were obliged to live in London had moved from their own homes to flats, or to apartments and hotels. Lord Halifax himself had moved to an apartment in the Dorchester Hotel, and it was there that I later dined with him. There were at dinner the Marquess of Crewe; Lord Snell, the leader of the Labor Party in the House of Lords; Anthony Eden, then Secretary of State for the Dominions; Oliver Stanley, at that time Secretary of State for War; Sir John Anderson, Minister for Civilian Defense; Sir Dudley Pound, First Sea Lord; and Sir Alexander Cadogan, Permanent Under Secretary at the Foreign Office. After dinner Lord Halifax gave me the opportunity of hearing the views of all the members of the government on the existing situation.

One of my most vivid memories of that evening was the brief statement made to me by Lord Snell as to the basic reason why the Labor Party supported the Chamberlain Cabinet in its war policy. He said that he and his colleagues in the Labor Party felt that if Hitler were to triumph, all of those human values on which British freedom was based, and which alone made life worth living—liberty of conscience, of speech, and of information—would inevitably be destroyed, and that free British men and women would become no better than slaves. Deeply opposed as Labor had been to war and hard as it had fought to avert it, Labor today had no other recourse.

During my stay in London I had a chance to talk at length with Major Clement Attlee and Arthur Greenwood, the leader and deputy leader of the Labor Party; Sir Archibald Sinclair, leader of the Liberal Party and Minister for Air; all of the members of the Cabinet whom I had not met upon the evening of my arrival, and with many old friends, some of them foreign diplomatic representatives then stationed in London.

Among these conversations, one which to me will always be of outstanding historic interest was that which I had with David Lloyd George. The Prime Minister who had done so much to bring about British victory in the first World War, and who had played so preponderant a part in the peace settlements, had no hesitation in speaking with the utmost precision, placing the blame where he felt it should lie, of the errors in British and French policy during the twenty years which had ended in the second great war.

Another memorable conversation was the talk I had at the Admiralty with Winston Churchill, who was still destined for a brief time to serve as First Lord. His fierce energy and his amazingly comprehensive executive ability, his grasp of facts and his initiative, have surely never been better demonstrated than during the periods when he has been recurrently called upon over more than thirty years to guide the destinies of the British Navy.

Much of what Mr. Churchill said had to do with the technical questions then confronting the Admiralty, the need to find new devices to combat submarines and mines, and the supreme problem of aviation.

But now, after four years have passed, I may be permitted to refer more specifically to one point which Mr. Churchill stressed, because of its value as a convincing indication of the accuracy of his foresight for more than a quarter of a century.

He said to me that he was now sitting in the same office in which he had sat twenty-five years before, confronted by exactly the same situation. This was because British governments during the past twenty years had refused to follow a realistic policy towards Germany. The objectives of the German people had not changed and would not change. These were world supremacy and military conquest; objectives which endangered the security of the United States as much as they imperiled the safety of the British Empire. He had foreseen the present crisis; time and again he had pointed out to previous British governments the dangers they were incurring, but he had not been listened to and now the crisis once more was upon them.

There could be no solution other than outright and complete defeat of Germany, the destruction of National Socialism, and the inclusion, in the new peace treaties, of provisions which would control Germany's course in the future in such a way as to give Europe and the world peace and security in the days to come, at least for a hundred years.

There was no resemblance between the impressions which I obtained in London and those which had been forced upon me in Paris. In England there was no evidence that I could see that German propaganda, which had so fatally undermined French morale, had made any headway. One could only get a feeling that the British people bitterly resented being in the war, and loathed the prospects of what in all probability they would be called upon to endure. But beneath it all one could sense a determination that they would fight to the last ditch to make it impossible for Hitler to force them to do his bidding. There appeared to be a relentless determination that rather than live once more through the experiences that they had suffered since the autumn of 1938, they would see it through to the end no matter how far off that end might be, nor how bitter the progress towards it might prove.

I left London by airplane on March 14 in a morning of blinding snow when all other planes had been grounded. On this trip there was no sight of land or of the Channel, and it was not until we reached Le Bourget once more that the sky commenced to clear.

During the few hours I remained in Paris before starting on my return journey to Rome, I had final talks with Daladier and with Paul Reynaud, who came to my hotel to talk with me just before I had to leave for the station.

The last words which Reynaud said to me as I left were that what the world today needed above all else was "daring statesmanship."

I have often thought since that time that of the French leaders of the period of the second World War whom I have personally known, only Paul Reynaud and Georges Mandel possessed the quality of which "daring statesmanship" is made. But when Reynaud's great opportunity was offered him, he lacked the essential conditions without which no amount of daring statesmanship in a democracy can conceivably succeed, and which the President and Mr. Churchill fortunately possessed in abundance. For to Paul Reynaud were given neither the confidence of his fellow citizens, the support of the legislative branch of his government, nor, what was even more essential in the shattering crisis with which France was faced, a country whole-heartedly determined to fight, to keep on resisting, and to triumph.

Spring had already commenced when I returned to Rome on March 16. The sun was shining brightly, and the Piazza di Spagna was filled with flowers as I drove to the Chigi Palace to see Count Ciano on the morning of my return.

I reminded the Minister that when I had left Rome Mussolini had told me that I would find far greater intransigence in London and in Paris than I would in Berlin. I said that, on the contrary, I had found no intransigence in either London or Paris. I had, however, found a thorough determination on the part of those two governments to continue the war to its bitter end unless they could obtain practical and complete assurance that they would not again be plunged into a war of this kind.

Ciano broke in to say that he himself knew that that was the case. He said that he would tell me immediately and frankly that Ribbentrop, who had visited Rome during the days I was in London, had told both Mussolini and himself, and he believed the Pope as well, that Germany was determined to undertake an all-out military offensive in the near future; that she was not considering any peace solution short of a military victory, and that after German victory peace would be laid down by German "diktat." He said that Ribbentrop seemed to be convinced that the German Army could achieve a military victory within five months, and that the German government believed France would crumble first and England shortly after. He said that he had again attempted, as he had at Berchtesgaden, to persuade Ribbentrop that any reasonable objectives of Germany could be achieved by negotiation. Ribbentrop, however, had brushed to one side all references of this character, and had talked in very loud and violent terms of German power and of German military strength.

Ciano added that he himself was by no means convinced of Germany's ability to win such a victory. He said it might well be that the present German regime was like a man suffering from tuberculosis, who looked strong and healthy, but who had within him the germ of a fatal disease which might lay him low at the most unexpected moment. He believed that if the Allied Powers maintained a defensive position, and prevented Germany from breaking through, that alone would result in Allied victory. Germany could be victorious only by breaking through, whereas the Allied Powers could conquer eventually either by preventing Germany from breaking through or by breaking through themselves.

Count Ciano went on to say that in his own judgment Hitler was completely under the domination of Ribbentrop who, he said, possessed a fatally malignant influence. The formerly close and pleasant relations which he himself used to enjoy with Goering no longer existed, presumably because Goering felt that Ciano was responsible for Italy's policy of non-belligerency. When he went to Berlin in the preceding month of October, Goering had not seen him, nor had he made any attempt to communicate with him. Count Ciano then stated that he wanted to remind me that Mussolini was definitely "pro-German." He believed that, notwithstanding this fact, Mussolini would never endanger the position of Italy, nor would he in any way change the present policy of Italy so as to add to the complexities of the present European situation. He wished to assure me that no new agreements of any kind had been entered into as a result of Ribbentrop's visit to Rome, nor would Italy deviate one inch from the course which she had set for herself.

With regard to the Balkans, Ciano knew quite well that stories were current that Italy was stirring up trouble in Croatia. He wished to assure me that was not the case. Italy and Germany had entered into an agreement to guard against any intervention by either one of them in Yugoslavia, and Italy's Balkan policy remained as he had told me two weeks before—the maintenance of peace and the status quo in that area.

He then returned to the subject of security in Europe. He said he did not know any practical way in which that could be achieved except through the creation of a four-power pact between Great Britain, France, Italy and Germany, with a guarantee that if any one of the four powers undertook to commit any new act of aggression, the other three powers would immediately combine to take action against the offending power.

I answered that in the event such negotiations were undertaken, I wondered whether he would not find that far more than that was required. By this statement, I said, I meant an agreement upon measures of real disarmament, and a satisfactory measure of international control over all offensive types of armament, particularly aviation, as well as international control over armament production. Ciano immediately replied that he quite agreed that such a step could and should be taken.

Ciano spoke with bitter sarcasm of Ribbentrop, particularly of the efforts which Ribbentrop was now making to force the Italian government to believe that the relations between the Soviet Union and Germany were inviolable and based upon some permanent and lasting understanding. As an indication of Ribbentrop's mendacity and insincerity, he told me that only shortly before the agreement of August 1939 had been concluded between Berlin and Moscow, Ribbentrop, in talking with Ciano, had referred to Stalin as "that most perverted of all damned Communists." He went on to say that, as a result of his past experiences with Ribbentrop, he realized what the latter said one day would be completely reversed the next.

Before the conversation ended Ciano said that he wished me to know that Mussolini and he were now in contact with Berlin and he suggested that I postpone my departure from Rome from March 18 until the following day. He wished to give me confidentially, before I left, some last word information which he expected to obtain from the Nazi government.

That evening at six o'clock Mussolini received me again at the

Palazzo Venezia. Count Ciano again served as interpreter, and Ambassador Phillips was present at the interview.

I found Mussolini looking far better physically than he had when I had seen him two weeks before. He did not seem to be laboring under the physical or mental oppression which had been so obvious during my first conversation with him. The conversation was on a decidedly more personal basis than the first talk I had had with him. He seemed to have thrown off some great weight. Since that time I have often wondered whether, during the two weeks which had elapsed since my first visit to Rome, he had not determined to cross the Rubicon, and during Ribbentrop's visit had not decided to force Italy into the war after Germany's all-out offensive commenced. Of one thing, however, I am convinced, that if he had in fact reached this decision, he had not as yet informed the members of his government of it.

At the outset of our conversation Mussolini said he would be glad to answer any questions which I cared to put to him, but that he would appreciate it if I would give him my impressions of my recent visits to Berlin, Paris and London.

I countered by saying that, as he knew, the views expressed to me by heads of governments, or by other prominent officials in the countries which I had visited must be regarded as strictly confidential and for the sole information of my own government. I said that I had so regarded the earlier conversations which I had had with him, and that in my visits to the other European capitals I had limited myself to saying that I had gained the impression in Rome that the Chief of the Italian government believed that the establishment of a lasting peace was still possible. Mussolini interjected to say that that was entirely correct. He said that he had done everything possible to avert the present war and that, if he had not in fact desired to bring about the re-establishment of a "good" peace, two hundred millions of additional human beings in the Mediterranean and in Africa would now be engaged in the present hostilities.

He told me that approximately twelve hours before my return to Rome he had received word from Berlin that Hitler wished to confer with him. The meeting had been arranged for 10:00 a. m., on Monday, March 18, at the Brenner Pass. Throughout the course of Ribbentrop's recent visit to Rome, Ribbentrop had insisted that Germany would consider no solution other than a military victory, and that any peace negotiations were impossible. He stated that Ribbentrop had informed him that Germany would undertake an immediate offensive; that she would conquer France within three or four months, and that thereafter Great Britain would be forced to her knees. Mussolini believed the German military offensive was in fact very close and that it would be undertaken within a number of days rather than within a number of weeks. As he phrased it, "The minute hand is pointing to one minute before midnight."

He continued that, if he was to have any success at all in persuading Hitler to postpone his military offensive, he must have some hope to offer him that the Allied governments would not prove completely intransigent if negotiations were undertaken to provide Germany with her "lebensraum." He wished to know whether I would authorize him to communicate to Hitler the impressions I had formed with regard to the possibility of a negotiated solution of territorial and political questions in Europe.

I replied that I was not empowered to give him such authorization, and that I would require specific instruction from the President of the United States before I could make a reply. I said that I would be glad to telephone the President, and communicate the President's decision to Mussolini through Count Ciano later in the evening.

Mussolini then went on to say that, while he felt the question of security was paramount, in his judgment no agreement in regard to security could be settled prior to an agreement on political and territorial readjustments. He said that he felt that the two things must be handled simultaneously, and that if that were done the economic problems should likewise be considered simultaneously. With regard to the independence of the Polish people, he believed it imperative that the new Poland should no longer contain within its boundaries people who were not Polish, and that in any determination of new boundaries for Poland the transfer of populations recently carried out by the Germans must be regarded as definitive. He said that, for example, one million Poles had been removed from German Poland to Warsaw, and to other purely Polish areas. It would be impossible for such adjustments not to be taken into account, as a basis for agreement.

With regard to a new Czech state, he said he believed that not only must the new Czech state be neutralized but that it also should have special economic relations with the German Reich.

In any new general settlement the just claims of Hungary for fair treatment of her minorities and for the readjustment of her frontiers must be taken into account.

All of the claims of Italy must be given a satisfactory solution.

He expressed the positive belief that, if a settlement could be found, the curse of the minority problem must be removed once and for all from the European scene. Steps which might appear cruel, such as those he himself had taken in the Upper Adige, must be taken because the ultimate good was far greater than the immediate hardships which certain peoples might be forced to undergo.

He did not believe that Europe could ever go back to the kind of illusory security which had been promised, but never afforded, by the League of Nations. He envisioned a new kind of Europe resulting from a federation of the major powers, guaranteeing the integrity and independent life of those smaller powers which were logically and justly entitled to independent existence as proven nationalities. He felt that only through the creation of such a system could real disarmament be obtained and the peoples of Europe be freed from the intolerable burden of armaments and from the equally intolerable fear of constant aggression.

He said that Europe could not today stand the outbreak of a "real" war. Europe could not undergo recurrent great wars every twenty years.

He then brought the conversation back to the question of an immediate agreement upon territorial and political readjustments of the nature he had indicated, and stated that he believed that in any agreement which might be reached, what he repeatedly termed a "just political peace" was the indispensable *first point*.

I asked him if he would not tell me how he felt the Allied Powers could conceivably undertake to reach such an agreement as a first step, unless they first had a concrete guarantee of security, when during the course of the last four years Germany had within a few months flagrantly violated each agreement she made with them. I said, "What assurance could the Allied governments obtain that an agreement of the kind you describe into which they might now enter would not be as quickly violated as the agreement reached at Munich in which you yourself played so great a part?"

To this enquiry, he made no direct reply, but limited himself to saying that he felt the problem of security could be dealt with simultaneously with the problem of political peace.

As I started to leave, Mussolini made one final remark which appeared to me to be of particular significance. He said, "You may wish to remember that, while the German-Italian Pact exists, *I* nevertheless retain complete liberty of action."

As I was leaving, Mussolini said in English, "I am most grateful to you for having come to see me. I will communicate with you again on Tuesday before you leave Rome."

When I dined informally with Count Ciano that night he said he fully agreed that the problem of security was the key problem, and, while he believed with Mussolini that no security could be achieved unless an agreement in principle were reached upon a "just political peace," he nevertheless felt strongly that the two problems could and should be treated simultaneously.

He reiterated his own belief that a four-power pact between Germany, Italy, France and Great Britain might prove the basis of a plan for real security, with the all-important stipulation that, if any one of the four powers undertook an act of aggression, the other three powers would immediately join together in declaring war upon the aggressor. He felt that upon this foundation an effective disarmament plan could be worked out, which would result in the abolition of offensive aviation and of other offensive armaments, and in an international control (which might later be enlarged to include the smaller European states) to supervise the destruction of all such types of armaments, including the razing of the factories where they were manufactured.

Count Ciano expressed complete pessimism as to the scheduled meeting at the Brenner Pass. He said that since Ribbentrop would be present at the interview, Mussolini would not have an opportunity to persuade Hitler to follow a more reasonable course. He himself had many times had interviews with Hitler, and had seen him reach the point where he indicated some willingness to adopt a reasonable attitude, only to have Ribbentrop interject and change Hitler's point of view.

He knew that the all-out offensive was imminent and that Germany would pursue exactly the same policy that she had pursued in Poland, namely, the unrestricted bombardment of cities, including London and Paris, and the creation of the same kind of reign of terror as that which lasted during the eighteen days of the Polish war. He believed, however, that the Allies would ultimately win. He said again that the only way, in his own judgment, in which Germany could win would be by breaking through France, whereas, if the Allies successfully remained on the defensive, they themselves would ultimately achieve victory.

During the following two days, while I was awaiting such final word of the outcome of the meeting at the Brenner Pass as the Italian government was disposed to give me, I was received by Pope Pius XII at the Vatican. Subsequently, I was afforded the opportunity of talking with Cardinal Maglione, the Cardinal Secretary of State. The detailed and accurate knowledge of the Holy See of conditions in every part of the world, particularly in the countries of Europe, is proverbial. What is perhaps not so well recognized is the quality of statesmanship which, at least in recent years, has distinguished the Vatican's policy.

Pope Pius XII possesses that quality in high degree. I found him profoundly saddened by the future he saw shaping so inevitably, and profoundly grieved by the barbarous inhumanity in so many regions of the world. It is, of course, impossible for me to give any indication of the nature of these conversations or of the views expressed to me. I can, however, state that I left the Vatican with the conviction that one of the constructive forces working for the regeneration of mankind will be the present Pope and many of those about him.

I also saw many Italians, both those in official positions and those who played some part in the business and intellectual life of the country. Without a single exception they not only expressed their bitter opposition to Italy's involvement in the war, but pled almost hysterically that the President of the United States exercise his influence to prevent that from happening. They appeared to possess the belief that President Roosevelt, by some magic power, could prevent Mussolini from forcing the Italian people into hostilities to which they were utterly opposed. When I ventured the suggestion, particularly to members of the Italian government, that if, as they told me, all Italians except for a handful of Fascists now under German influence were unwilling to go to war, it was incredible that an entire nation of forty millions of people could be forced to fight against its will, the only reply that was vouchsafed to me was the reiterated statement, "The Duce controls everything."

Early in the morning of March 19 Ciano returned to Rome. In order to avoid publicity with regard to our meeting, he asked me to lunch privately with him at the golf club outside of Rome so that he might inform me of the meeting at the Brenner Pass.

He commenced the conversation by stating that he would tell me what had transpired at the meeting with the exception of such questions as had to do with the Axis relationship. He made it clear that, notwithstanding a German official announcement, the meeting at the Brenner Pass had not been arranged at the time Ribbentrop was in Rome the week before, but had been arranged by telephone from Berlin, upon the initiative of Hitler, the day of my return to Rome. He added, somewhat acidly, that he believed Ribbentrop's inability to make any progress when he had visited Rome the week before, and Hitler's knowledge that he, Ciano, was determined to do everything within his power to keep Italy from getting into the war, were additional reasons for the meeting. He went on to say that Hitler had seemed in far better physical and mental condition than when he had seen him the preceding autumn. Hitler had done practically all of the talking and Mussolini had done little.

He assured me that no change in Italy's attitude of non-belligerency had been decided upon as a result of the meeting. He had gained the positive belief that Hitler was using the German-Soviet arrangement to his own interest, with the expectation that the time would come when he could turn against Russia and recover the positions which Germany had given away to the Soviet government in the Baltic States and Finland.

No special proposals had been made by Hitler, nor had he requested Mussolini to present any suggestions for peace proposals to the Allied governments.

Ciano emphasized repeatedly his own belief that the maintenance of relations between the United States and Italy was to the advantage of the whole of Europe in case any opportunity for peace arose. In such event he thought that only the President of the United States could undertake any initiative, and that Italy would support it.

At the Brenner Pass meeting Italy had made it clear that she would not agree to any German penetration of Yugoslavia. Italy intended to do all that she could to maintain the Balkan status quo, leaving the question of territorial revision in abeyance until the time came for a general peace settlement.

He went on to tell me that, notwithstanding Ribbentrop's assurance that Germany would immediately begin a military offensive, Hitler had stated that the long threatened offensive on the western front would be postponed momentarily. Hitler had, however, indicated immediate aviation activity, including the bombing of British ports and inland cities, particularly London. As an explanation of this delay of the big offensive, Hitler had referred to weather conditions, and certain "momentary obstacles." Ciano did not say whether he knew what the actual reasons for this change of plan might be. He said, however, that some of the Italian military officers who had accompanied Mussolini had talked with General Bodenschatz, of the German General Staff, and had gained the impression that the German General Staff itself was resolutely opposed to any immediate military offensive along the western frontiers.

When I said good-bye to him, Count Ciano said, "Please give this message to President Roosevelt. Tell him that I personally have the utmost admiration for him, and great confidence in what he himself can do to be of service to the cause of civilization in Europe. Tell him further that so long as I remain Foreign Minister, Italy will not enter the war on the side of Germany, and that I will do everything within my power to influence Mussolini in that same direction. Tell him that I will appreciate nothing more than the opportunity to co-operate in the name of Italy with the United States for the re-establishment of that kind of peace in which the President believes. You may add that I believe alliances at times are necessary in Europe, and that I do not believe that under present conditions peace can be established or maintained without an equilibrium of force and a balance of power, but I am sure that the President will realize that while the safety of Italy itself depends upon the maintenance of such an equilibrium, Italy also requires the safety of the smaller neutral powers, as well as rapid disarmament and the security which only the abolition of offensive armaments can ever bring."

When I finally left Rome that night of March 19 to sail for the United States the following day from Naples, I remember that these considerations concerning Italy were uppermost in my mind.

Italy would unquestionably move as Mussolini alone determined. It should never be forgotten that Mussolini remained at heart and in instinct an Italian peasant. He was vindictive and would never forget an injury or a blow to his personal or national prestige. He admired nothing except force and power. His own obsession was the re-creation of the Roman Empire. His conscience would never trouble him as to the way or means, providing his instinct told him that the method of accomplishment would serve to further the desired end.

He would never forget nor forgive the sanctions episode of 1935 and the policy pursued by Great Britain towards Italy at that time. Up to that moment strongly anti-German, he then determined to seek an understanding with Hitler in order to prevent Italian isolation. He believed he had found a successful answer to that problem, and that it would help him to secure at an eventual peace conference, if necessary by throwing his weight on the winning side in the war, the territorial and political advantages which he was seeking. He could at any moment during the preceding two years have obtained the concessions he sought from France, short of the cession of political jurisdiction in Tunisia. He had deliberately re-fused these concessions because he knew that if he reached such an agreement with France, he could not readily obtain the additional concessions he desired from Great Britain, namely, the demilitarization of Gibraltar and Malta, the neutralization of the Mediterranean and (as a minimum) British Somaliland. He intended to retain his great nuisance value until he could get what he wanted at the same moment from both the Allied Powers.

A highly intelligent Italian, holding a very important post in the Fascist government, had said to me, "It was a great tragedy for Italy when Mussolini visited Berlin two years ago." What this Italian meant was that, when Mussolini went to Berlin, he became so enormously impressed with German military strength and with the ruthless efficiency of German organization, that he came back convinced that nothing could defeat Germany's power.

The new Italian fortifications along the Austrian boundary seemed to indicate that Mussolini had fears regarding his own northern frontiers. But I could not help but feel that his hatred for Great Britain and France was so powerful, and his faith in Germany's military supremacy so strong, that he would never modify his policy of supporting Hitler unless an Allied victory became overwhelmingly clear.

If, on the other hand, Germany obtained some rapid victories, such as the occupation of Holland and Belgium, I feared that Mussolini would then force Italy into the war on the side of Germany.

No one in the Italian government with whom I spoke wanted Italy to enter the war. Count Ciano was violently against it, as well as a great majority of the other officials in the Fascist government. The Italian General Staff was wholly antagonistic, and I was told in many quarters that feeling in the Italian Army against Italy's entrance into the war was formidable. The newer and apparently increasingly strong element in the Fascios, led by Ciano, Grandi, and Balbo, was strongly opposed. So was the Royal Family. The Church was openly against it. So were the financial and commercial interests, and every man and woman with whom one could talk. Popular feeling was not pro-Ally, but it was anti-German.

The economic situation was constantly deteriorating; the price of living was rapidly rising, and salaries were not. Taxes were skyrocketing, and public complaint could no longer be wholly stifled. Everywhere one could hear the same phrase: "Italy cannot stand a new war." And yet there was no doubt in anyone's mind that, if

Mussolini gave the word, the Italian Army and the Italian people would enter the war on the German side.

If there was ever a case in modern history when a dictator plunged a great nation into a wholly unjustified and wholly unpopular military adventure, it was when Mussolini forced the Italian people into a war against their traditional friends, solely to serve the interests of a country which for generations they had both feared and hated.

# CHAPTER IV

## From Defensive to Offensive

I CAME back to a Washington which, except in the White House and in the circles closest to it, and in a few sectors of the Congress and of the press, appeared to be still amused by wisecracks about the "phony war." The ominous signs of the catastrophic summer of 1940 were already so overpowering as to be suffocating. But when the Nazi occupation of Denmark and the invasion of Norway were under way many people seemed to find an almost hysterical satisfaction in taunting Neville Chamberlain for the use of his fatal phrase at the outset of the Norwegian campaign that Hitler had "missed the bus." Neither the tragedy itself nor the peril to ourselves seemed to sink very deep. Then came, on May 10, the attack upon the Low Countries.

Now the democracies could estimate the devastating impact of the "blitzkrieg" which Goering and Ciano had forecast in talking to me. Germany was able to demonstrate for the first time the full measure of her striking power and the hideous effectiveness of the new technique devised by her General Staff. Those weeks of May and June will represent to some of us as long as we live a nightmare of frustration. For the United States government had no means whatever, short of going to war, to which American public opinion was overwhelmingly opposed, of diverting or checking the world cataclysm and the threat to the very survival of this country.

In the crowded and yet at times curiously detailed recollections of those days I recall the initial shock at the rapidity of the German sweep over Holland and at the inability of the Dutch infantry or artillery to resist for more than a few hours the striking power of the Luftwaffe; my long-distance telephone conversations with our able Minister in The Hague, George Gordon, and the actual sound of the bombardment of the Dutch capital which came over the telephone; the horror of receiving detailed accounts of the terrible destruction of life and property wrought by the German bombers to Rotterdam. I remember the dismay with which we heard of the crumbling of the fortresses along the Belgian eastern frontier, and our realization for the first time of the extent of the assistance rendered the German Armies by its hidden accomplices within countries destined for invasion. Worst of all was the increasing apprehension that the German war machine was so overwhelmingly superior in might, quality, strategy, matériel, and morale, to the available forces of the Western European powers, that Germany might well become the supreme master of all Europe before the summer had passed. But it was the collapse of France that finally shocked American public opinion into the full realization of the danger confronting the United States itself.

Those were the days in Washington when maps of the European front appeared in all governmental offices. Every morning an officer of the G-2 of the War Department would bring to the Department of State a map of France, with the latest progress of the German Armies marked upon it. As day by day the German lines advanced with stupendous speed over the well-remembered regions of northern and central France, it became plain that this was not the France of the heroic resistance of 1914 and 1918—not the French Army which had so gallantly defended every inch of the road to the Marne and which had stemmed the tide before the gates of Paris. It was now all too clear that the German sappers had succeeded in their efforts to destroy not only French military capacity but the very will to resist of the majority of the French leaders, and that the defeat of France was a foregone conclusion.

No pages in French history can ever be sadder than those that tell of the weeks between the last days of May, when it became plain to all that France would be defeated, and June 22, when French resistance ceased. It is not only a tragic history. It is also fantastic.

There flash through the memory of those surcharged weeks such magnificent examples of human courage and endurance as the evacuation from Dunkirk; such pitiful tragedies as the exodus from Belgium and northern France of hundreds of thousands of refugees, constantly bombed and machine-gunned by the German aviators; which, as the Germans had planned, blocked the very roads the

French Army so desperately needed for its transport requirements. One recalls the efforts of President Roosevelt to find some way by which the British and French governments could obtain munitions, and his final success; the desperate appeal of the French Prime Minister to the President for outright help, and the drafting of the only reply that the President could make; the shuttling back and forth between London and France of the new British Prime Minister, Winston Churchill, and his febrile last moment attempt to forestall a French surrender by his proposal of joint nationality for British and French citizens; the German occupation of Paris on June 14, and its crushing effect on all those who still dared to hope; the daily flight ever farther to the south of the members of the French government; the bitter recriminations between the British and French which now became public, and always, throughout it all, the inexorable forward sweep of the German war machine.

From the standpoint of the immediate security of this country, however, there were two points uppermost in our minds. What assurance could we receive that the French fleet would not be surrendered by a defeated France to Germany; and what possibility was there that the French government would continue to fight even if it had to flee from Europe?

To the President the question of the French fleet was basic. Were France's naval vessels to fall into German hands, a greatly weakened England could not only be more readily invaded but even more readily starved. The control of the Atlantic would be endangered at once.

During the last half of June assurance after assurance was given by the French government—by the Prime Minister, by his colleagues in the Cabinet, by Admiral Darlan—that the French Navy would be scuttled sooner than surrendered to Germany. And from the Prime Minister came the additional hope, which the President had urged, that even if all of metropolitan France were occupied by the German invader, the French government would move to North Africa, to West Africa, or if need be, to its colonies in the New World, to carry on the fight.

The substitution for the Daladier Cabinet in March of 1940 of a Cabinet headed by Paul Reynaud, approved by a precarious majority of only one vote in the Chamber of Deputies, had brought to the head of the French government a man who had not faltered in his bitter opposition to any form of appeasement of Germany. Reynaud was a man of unusual intellectual capacity and high courage. His fatal weakness, we now know, lay in the influence which Madame de Portes had secured over him, and in her subservience, in turn, to many accomplices of Germany. (As one example among countless instances showing the nature of her influence, there may be cited the following: During the final days before Reynaud was forced to flee Paris, Madame de Portes strongly supported the efforts of Madame Huntzinger to persuade Reynaud to appoint her husband, General Huntzinger—believed by the French secret service to be a direct accomplice of the Germans—in the place of General Weygand. The insistence of the latter lady was so strong that Reynaud was finally obliged to order the Prefect of Police in Paris to remove her by force from the French capital should she not immediately leave voluntarily.) Reynaud was also wholly erratic in his judgment. While he leant upon such patriots as Georges Mandel and General Charles de Gaulle, he nevertheless dismissed from office an indispensable public servant like Alexis Léger and appointed to high positions officials already notoriously subject to German pressure, who later from Vichy served openly as German tools.

The personal friendship between Winston Churchill and Paul Reynaud was close and of long standing. But neither this personal tie nor Reynaud's sincere loyalty to the British Alliance could withstand the corroding effects of those closest to Madame de Portes, who sought tirelessly day and night to counteract the appeals and the arguments advanced by Mr. Churchill that the French government live up to its solemn commitment to make no separate peace with the invader. The termites within Reynaud's own Cabinet continued to assert that the British government was neither able nor willing to render any further material assistance to France; that it was playing the game solely to sell out France; and that France could save what was left to save only by making peace with Germany before Great Britain had time to do so.

Reynaud had believed, when in the latter days of May he forced the replacement of General Gamelin as head of the French Armies by General Weygand, that the latter, brilliant and loyal disciple of Marshal Foch, would be able even at that last moment to accomplish the miracle of breathing a new spirit of loyalty and of discipline into the French military forces. He was confident that he could stamp out the corrupting plague of defeatism so shattering to French morale. But he found in General Weygand a broken reed.

The explanation of the change which had come over Weygand is not easy to find. For Maxime Weygand had not only been Foch's closest adviser in the French military hierarchy but had also been throughout his long and distinguished career a great soldier, a great administrator and a patriotic, if reactionary, Frenchman. He was called back from his post as High Commissioner in Syria to assume supreme command of an already disintegrated army. He was forced to realize after only a few days that French air strength, mechanical equipment, and above all else, morale, were so deficient that France herself could not long escape total German occupation. The Weygand of the earlier days would have carried on the fight to the beaches of the Mediterranean and, when they were in enemy hands, to the coasts of North Africa. General Weygand in 1940, however, was already an old man. He no longer possessed either the physical strength or the moral stamina to withstand the annihilating strain of the supreme responsibility with which he was so suddenly burdened. He foresaw the defeat of his own country. He could no longer conceive that Germany might eventually be crushed if France herself were defeated. He could foresee only a world ruled by Hitler. At the final moment of crisis, when Reynaud needed the support of Weygand more than that of any other member of the French government for a decision to keep on fighting, he obtained from Weygand only the recommendation for abject surrender.

The horde of famishing and hysterical refugees from northern and central France piled pell-mell into Bordeaux during the third week of June. With them came the President of the Republic, the Prime Minister and the members of his Cabinet, a great number of the members of the two Houses of Parliament, and many military and naval officers. By this time the defeat of the French Armies had become a rout.

There was only one issue before the French Cabinet for immediate decision: whether to continue to resist or to ask an armistice.

Resistance could take only one form, given the military situation within continental France. The French government could take refuge in Algiers. There it could continue constitutionally to govern, inasmuch as Algeria is an integral part of the French Republic. There it could rally such remnants of the French armies as might escape from France, and with the French armies in North Africa attempt to stave off any immediate attempts at German invasion. It is true that the North African armies were depleted of military equipment, since much had been rushed to the battle lines from North Africa in the preceding weeks. But the arrangements made by President Roosevelt to enable the French government to obtain airplanes and munitions from the United States promised some measure of relief. And the French fleet was intact and would have provided considerable support against any early German invasion attempts.

Reynaud demanded the opinion of the members of the Cabinet as to the course to be pursued by the French government. The Cabinet divided into two parts, with a majority in favor of an immediate request for armistice. The views of the majority were expressed by Marshal Pétain, abetted from behind the scenes by Laval and his collaborationists and fortified by the opinions advanced by General Weygand and many of the leading military and naval authorities. Weygand and Admiral Darlan expressed the conviction not only that Great Britain was unable and unwilling to lend any real assistance but that, if France continued to resist, both France and Great Britain would be inevitably defeated by Germany within a few brief weeks. They insisted that if France now sought armistice terms she would receive far better treatment than if she continued to wage a hopeless struggle. The argument was further advanced that any hope of American help was illusory and that the American government (and this, strangely enough, with reference to the Roosevelt Administration) was subject to the influence of the great financial and commercial interests which were insistent not only that the United States remain out of the war but that arrangements be made with the Nazi government for a division of economic and financial spoils. They maintained that no French government having regard to its responsibility to the people would consider fleeing from the territory of metropolitan France and leaving the French inhabitants to the cruel exactions which Germany would make of them should resistance be continued in North Africa.

The views of the other group in the Cabinet were expounded, with trenchant clarity, by Georges Mandel. They were eloquently supplemented from without the Cabinet by that sturdy old friend of Clemenceau, the President of the Senate, Jules Jeanneney, and by the President of the Chamber of Deputies, Edouard Herriot. They declared that resistance must be continued from North Africa; that France had everything to lose and nothing to gain by an immediate surrender; that no French government could dishonor its solemn commitments to its ally, Great Britain, by seeking a separate peace; and that if resistance were continued, sooner or later the United States, in its own interest, must make available some greater measure of assistance to France.

Because of French constitutional procedure and because under those chaotic conditions no sessions of the Senate or of the Chamber of Deputies could be held, the Prime Minister was forced to tender his resignation and that of his Cabinet to the President of the Republic. Without the support of at least a majority of his Cabinet, Reynaud could not have removed the seat of government to Algiers, particularly when such a step would have been taken counter to the official recommendations of his chief military and naval advisers.

The partiality of French National Assemblies for electing a nonentity to the Presidency of the Republic has never proved more unfortunate than in the case of Albert Lebrun. When Reynaud presented the resignation of his Cabinet to President Lebrun, he informed the President that he was doing so because a majority of the Cabinet was opposed to a policy of continued resistance. He stated that if the President would entrust him with the task of selecting a new Cabinet, he would be able within a few hours to designate Ministers unanimously determined to continue resistance. President Lebrun agreed to this proposal. During the brief period, however, in which the Prime Minister was attempting to constitute his new Cabinet, the President was besieged by members of the group who were opposed to a resistance policy. He was persuaded to call upon

Marshal Pétain to replace Reynaud. As a result of this decision of
June 16, which Lebrun, as President of the Republic, alone could
make, the die was cast. The Pétain Cabinet sent emissaries to the
German High Command. The armistice was signed on June 22.

Disastrous as the armistice proved to the French people, crushing
as the collapse of French resistance was to British and American
hopes, it at least contained the desired provisions by which control
of the major part of the fleet remained in French hands. The concern of President Roosevelt about the French Navy increased hourly
during the last days prior to the signing of the armistice. Our ad hoc
Ambassador at Bordeaux, Anthony Biddle, did yeoman service
during those chaotic and despairing days while the glory of France
was departing. Time after time he repeated to Pétain and to Admiral
Darlan insistent messages from the President that in the interest of
the future of the French people not only must the fleet never be
surrendered, but also the warships must be safely out of French ports
before German forces could seize them. In these urgent pleas Mr.
Churchill joined. In the discussions which he had had with Reynaud
before the latter's resignation, when the French Cabinet was urging
the British government to release them from their alliance commitments, Mr. Churchill, on behalf of the British Cabinet, had consented to the French request solely on condition that the French fleet
be in British hands before any armistice with Germany was concluded. When French resistance ceased, the bulk of the French Navy
had safely escaped the danger of German seizure. A few vessels had
gone to British ports; more had accepted internment in Alexandria;
most of the remainder were in North African or West African
French bases, and of these several were soon to be immobilized as a
result of the sad incident of Mers-el-Kébir.

The future of these warships, still in French hands, was to be the
dominating issue in deciding United States policy toward the French
people throughout the succeeding three years. For not only did the
ability of the French government to keep the Germans out of Africa
and out of their Near Eastern mandates and colonies depend in great
part upon their retention of their fleet, but the ability of the British
to defend Egypt and the Suez Canal would have ended instantly
had the Germans or the Italians been able to use the French Navy

for their own ends. In any evaluation of American policy toward France during that period, it is important to estimate fairly the value to this country of keeping the French Navy out of Axis hands, and the Germans out of French overseas possessions. Had these aims not been realized, Axis control of the Atlantic before the United States entered the war would have been far more likely.

It has often been asserted that this government should have refused to recognize the government established by Marshal Pétain at Vichy, and should have awaited the creation outside of France of a French provisional government-in-exile composed of representatives of the forces of resistance. But the Pétain Cabinet which succeeded the Cabinet headed by Paul Reynaud had been appointed in strict conformity with French constitutional procedure. The United States could have refused to recognize the Pétain government, it is true—but only on some ground other than legitimacy. And at that time there were not in existence outside of France any of the "forces of resistance" which later coalesced. Although General de Gaulle was in London and had been recognized by the British government even before the armistice as leader of the "Free French," he was almost alone. A policy of nonrecognition would have deprived this government of any official contact with events in France; of any means of obtaining direct information as to the policies and intentions of the new French authorities; and of any method of exercising its influence in its own direct interests.

I do not recall that during the weeks after the signing of the armistice there was even any difference of opinion within the Administration in Washington regarding the expediency of dealing with the Pétain Cabinet. It must be remembered that the divergent course pursued by the British government was due primarily to the rupture of relations between France and Great Britain resulting from the British attack at Mers-el-Kébir. The policy of this government in maintaining relations with the Pétain government, even after it had established itself in its new and pitiful guise at Vichy, was adopted by the Canadian government as well. From the outset the expediency and practical value of this course in combating Axis activities was recognized on innumerable occasions by the British Cabinet. From the strictly humanitarian standpoint the lives of many thousands of refugees were saved by a policy which was later bitterly criticized by the closest friends of these very refugees.

Furthermore, at that moment there was no means of foretelling what the trend within France would be; how controlling the forces of defeatism might prove; and whether French popular or military reaction might still provoke a renewal of French resistance in North Africa.

It was becoming constantly clearer that our vital interests in the Pacific were in grave danger. It was well within the bounds of possibility that the preponderance of American naval strength might be required at any moment to protect our Pacific possessions, the western coast of the United States, and the strategic approaches to the Panama Canal. The entrance into the service of the Axis of the Italian fleet jeopardized the ability of the British Navy to control the Atlantic and at the same time to keep open the urgently needed means of communication between the Suez Canal and the British Isles by way of Gibraltar. Consequently, it was essential that the United States government continue its attempts to influence the French authorities to keep the fleet out of German hands. But this it could not do were official relations between the Pétain government and the government of Washington to be severed.

The practical value of the United States policy was emphasized after the British naval engagement with French naval units at Mers-el-Kébir and the singularly ill-prepared and ill-advised British venture in attempting to seize Dakar. These acts not only brought about a rupture between Great Britain and the French government at Vichy but likewise brought to a climax the long-smoldering hatred of the French military and naval forces in North Africa for Great Britain, which had been carefully incited and fostered by German propaganda. After that, our ability to counteract the effects of German propaganda on the authorities at Vichy and to assuage the resentment of high-ranking French military and naval officers was of particular importance, later to be fully demonstrated.

Finally, our policy made it far easier to deal with the questions arising from the continuation of a tenuous French sovereignty in French Guiana and in the French West Indies. Notwithstanding the efforts of the German government and a gradual breakdown of

French discipline and morale in those colonies, the insistence of the government at Washington in maintaining daily, almost hourly, contact with the French authorities there prevented the development of any situation which imperiled the interests of the United States or the security of the Western Hemisphere.

In the autumn of 1940 the President appointed Admiral William D. Leahy, who had retired as Chief of Naval Operations and had meanwhile served briefly as Governor of Puerto Rico, as the American Ambassador to the government of Marshal Pétain at Vichy. By this time the Vichy government had undergone the first stages of its transformation. After the suicide of the French Parliament, France had become an authoritarian state with Marshal Pétain as its figurehead and with Pierre Laval as the real power. The new French government adopted at German behest all the most vicious aspects of totalitarian rule. Decrees were promulgated providing for the registration and sequestration not only of the unfortunate refugees of the Jewish faith who had already obtained sanctuary in France but eventually of all French Jews as well. The land which for generations had opened its hospitable doors to men persecuted for their political or religious beliefs, which had never permitted human discriminations within its own borders, was now the scene of the same shameful crimes against humanity and against the very spirit of democracy that were inflicted by the German Gestapo upon the people of the occupied countries.

The revulsion of feeling within the United States which the adoption of such measures caused was not only violent but legitimate and salutary. The contempt felt for the craven submission of Marshal Pétain and his advisers was a strong factor in the mounting enthusiasm for the French Committee of Resistance headed by de Gaulle. By then, de Gaulle had assumed the leadership of all those elements outside of continental France which were willing to defy the authority of the Pétain government and to continue French resistance against the German invaders. The value of the courage and indomitable spirit which he displayed during those first months after the collapse of France can never be exaggerated. His determination quickened the regeneration of French morale. For the French people, after the breakdown of resistance to Germany, were sick—

sick at heart and sick in spirit. Their recovery was halting and support for General de Gaulle and his associates in French colonies and
in territories under French jurisdiction was at first slow in its
development. The ability of the Free French Committee in London,
even with the support given it by the British government, to maintain
a nucleus of patriotic resistance and gradually to increase its scope
and its authority seemed for more than a year to be very doubtful.
But the Committee succeeded and later proved to be of outstanding
value in the war effort of the United Nations.

It must be admitted, however, that the more vehement and
fanatical adherents of General de Gaulle's Committee, both in England and in the United States, as well as his propaganda services,
made the task of the United States government and its Ambassador
to Vichy a difficult one. American public opinion was uneasy as a
result of the reiterated charges that its government was following
a humiliating and unworkable policy of "appeasement." Certain of
the more extreme forms of propaganda even persuaded a few French
colonial authorities, who were not German collaborationists but
remained loyal to the Marshal and his government, that this country
intended to supplant French sovereignty over French overseas territories and partition the colonies between the British Empire and the
United States.

Within a very brief period Admiral Leahy was able to establish
a personal relationship with Marshal Pétain which was to prove
extremely useful. Already approaching the end of his eighth decade,
harassed and worn by the continuous pressure of the German government, and betrayed hourly by his associates who had prostituted
themselves to Hitler, Marshal Pétain remembered the worth of his
close association with the United States in earlier years. He did not
suspect this country of having any ulterior purposes. He felt that it
was the one element remaining from which he could derive either
hope or encouragement. The friendly arguments of Admiral Leahy
were sufficient upon several occasions to cause the Marshal to react
sharply against steps that he was counseled to take by his immediate
associates, steps which would have endangered both the safety of the
French fleet and the continued ability of French authorities in North
Africa to stave off total German control. I recall in particular the

success which finally marked Admiral Leahy's repeated protests against sending units of the French Navy from Oran and Casablanca to Toulon for what a few of Pétain's advisers alleged were in- dispensable repairs. Marshal Pétain himself finally realized that French naval vessels sent to French continental ports would be at once liable either to seizure or to temporary immobilization by Ger- man demand.

If the Ambassador's influence was thus of demonstrated value, the maintenance of official relations with Vichy was even more justified by the opportunity that it gave the United States to retain American consular officers and their staffs in unoccupied France, in Tunisia, Algeria, and Morocco. The American consular establish- ments in those places not only provided invaluable information on Axis activities and French trends and policies in that area, but they were also useful in counteracting German and Italian propaganda. Through their personal relationships with members of the French North African administrations, our representatives were often able to thwart the plans of the Axis.

Eventually this government permitted French merchant vessels again to sail between the North African ports and the United States so that supplies for civilian use in North Africa might be exchanged for various products of the area. This arrangement was concluded on the understanding that all civilian supplies sent from the United States would be distributed under the control of American observers sent as attachés to our Consulates. The importance of the informa- tion sent and the contacts established by this corps of additional American representatives cannot be overestimated. These agents sent constantly detailed information covering the nature of the machinations undertaken by German spies and saboteurs and attempts on the part of the latter to send clandestine shipments of strategic materials from North Africa to continental France. But what was more important, they were able to report upon French officers in North Africa who were disposed to assist the United States should their help be required, and also upon many occasions to block the shipment to Germany of material which Germany urgently needed in her war industries. Although this policy was derided and decried by the more fanatical sympathizers of the Free French Committee, it is

not too much to say that the subsequent astoundingly successful invasion of North Africa could never have been carried out without a
far greater loss of life and without infinitely greater hazards had it
not been for the careful, detailed, and efficient preparatory work
accomplished by our representatives. That work could not have been
done had we broken relations with Vichy.

Local control over American consular officers and special observers
throughout North Africa was placed in 1941 in the hands of Robert
Murphy, who had served previously as counselor of the American
Embassy in France. He was instructed to establish as close a relationship as possible with the highest French military and civilian officials
for the immediate purpose of counteracting any increase in German
influence. Through these contacts he was to ensure, in any way that
subsequently might become necessary, the success of whatever policy
in North Africa our government might be forced to adopt.

Soon after the armistice with Germany, General Weygand had
accepted from Marshal Pétain command of French forces in North
Africa. Until the autumn of 1941 he continued firm in the belief that
Germany would win and that, precarious as the situation of France
would become after a German victory, acceptance of the German
terms was the wisest decision France could make at a desperate
moment. With the entrance of the United States into the war his
opinions underwent a rapid change. Persuaded at times that the
United States could not complete its war preparations soon enough to
prevent Germany and Japan from crushing British resistance, he
nevertheless began to hope that the Axis would perhaps not be able
to win an outright victory. He now became inclined to the belief that
as the result of a possible compromise peace, the situation in France
might be improved. Loyal to the authority of Marshal Pétain, he
unfortunately reported to him the fact that he was being confidentially sounded by American authorities regarding the possibility
of the French forces under his command lending active aid to the
United States should the latter furnish the French North African
armies with arms and ammunition. The inability of Pétain, through
the treachery of those around him, to keep any confidential reports
from the German authorities in France brought about the German
demand in 1942 that General Weygand be recalled from North

Africa and replaced with a notorious collaborationist. (It is now definitely known that the airplane "accident" in which his successor, General Huntzinger, was killed had been deliberately brought about by an act of sabotage committed by a high officer in the French military secret service.)

For a long time before this, however, Washington had been establishing contacts with French leaders still in metropolitan France. President Roosevelt himself had sent personal messages through secret channels to many of them insisting that they could be of far greater service in hastening the restoration of independence in their country if they were to leave France and work for her freedom from outside. Most of these French leaders replied that they would not "desert," as they called it, their fellow countrymen. This attitude showed a high degree of self-sacrifice. But from the practical standpoint, they would have been able to serve their nation's best interests much more effectively had they been willing to leave the country at that time. The majority of them were thrown into prison when the Germans later occupied the whole of France. Moreover, the prestige and the effectiveness of the French Committee of National Liberation would have been vastly enhanced had some of these leaders been able to participate in it.

By January of 1942 the French Committee in London had already become a problem to the British and United States governments. The sudden occupation by Free French forces of the French islands of St. Pierre and Miquelon off the Canadian coast, of which Washington had had no prior warning, counter to assurances given to the Canadian authorities by the Free French agent, Admiral Muselier, created a serious difficulty for the United States government. For at that moment it was doing its utmost to maintain a workable relationship with Admiral Robert, chief Vichy authority in the French colonies in the New World. The latter insisted that his control over these two tiny islands be re-established.

It will be readily understood that only a few weeks after Pearl Harbor this government was little disposed to face a situation where our military or naval force might have to be employed in the West Indies. The flare-up occasioned by an unfortunately worded communiqué issued by the Department of State, which referred to the

Free French movement as "so-called," added fuel to the fire. In fact the determination of President Roosevelt and of Prime Minister Churchill, who at that moment was visiting Washington, that the two governments should reach some understanding regarding the practical advantages derived by Great Britain as well as the United States from the policy pursued by this country toward France and all other aspects of the French situation was frequently impeded and rendered difficult of realization by the American public's failure to comprehend the basic causes for that policy and the consequent effect of this attitude on British public opinion.

It was, of course, impossible for the public to be informed that plans were already being laid for an invasion of North Africa, and that under these conditions any break with the government at Vichy would nullify all our efforts to obtain support among the French military forces. It was equally impossible to explain the peculiar untimeliness of the public attacks upon the authorities loyal to Marshal Pétain, which greatly facilitated the efforts of the German High Command to persuade French military leaders that all American sympathy for France had vanished, and that consequently cooperation with Germany was the only alternative.

The most damaging feature of the St. Pierre-Miquelon incident was that it greatly hampered the American government in continuing its relations with Vichy and in carrying out its policies in North Africa. But neither course could be abandoned if the American and British plans for the invasion of North Africa were to be carried out successfully.

To President Roosevelt himself was due both the conception of, and the decision to undertake, the invasion of North Africa. As far back as the first months of 1942, after weighing the advantages and disadvantages of all the alternative means by which United States assistance could be made most effective toward hastening the defeat of Germany and Italy, he had reached the conclusion that North African operations were those best calculated to ensure the achievement of the desired results. In reaching this determination he had, of course, discussed the pros and cons during innumerable conferences with his chief military and naval advisers as well as with the best qualified experts of the British government. Robert Murphy, with a handful of assistants from the American Foreign Service, under the direct orders of the President, carried out the final steps in the preparatory arrangements which covered French co-operation in the enterprise. They made possible the successful conclusion of one of the most difficult combined naval and military operations ever undertaken. In view of the scale of the effort, the immense transport problem, and the large number of individuals who necessarily had to take part in the formulation of the plans, the secrecy maintained was altogether remarkable. The Germans' complete lack of knowledge at this stage of our preparations was decidedly a contributing factor to the success achieved.

There has not perhaps been sufficient recognition of the service of the handful of American civilians who directed the clandestine preparations in North Africa and who, with the assistance of a few brave French officers, arranged for the arrival of the landing forces. It was also owing to them that General Giraud's dramatic escape from France by submarine was carried out successfully. After many discouragements and worrying negotiations with certain French leaders it had finally been determined that General Giraud, who had shortly before fled from a German prison, was the French military leader most capable of taking over control of the French armies of North Africa, and of reviving their spirit and their will to fight when the American forces reached North African territory.

Here again the more vociferous supporters of General de Gaulle have given a wholly unwarranted political interpretation to the complicated series of events which accompanied the landing of American troops in Algeria and in Morocco.

Two main points must be emphasized. The American General Staff quite properly insisted that every political decision should be made with a primary regard for the success of the military operations, and that consequently the chief purpose of our policy should be to reduce the opposition of the French military and naval establishments in North Africa to the barest possible minimum. To carry out this logical and wise decision, we had to make every effort to assure ourselves that the French authorities with whom we dealt would be obeyed by the forces whom they undertook to command. The officers of the French North African Army, like the officers of the

French Navy, had without exception pledged their loyalty to Marshal Pétain. At that time not only would they have no traffic with General de Gaulle, but from a variety of motives, some material and some ideological, they were personally hostile to him. If we had invaded North Africa and simultaneously demanded that the French military and naval forces in that region carry out the orders of General de Gaulle, the American landings would have met with concerted French resistance. Moreover, this would have come at a moment when any prolonged interruption of railroad or highway communications between Casablanca and the Mediterranean ports of Oran and Algiers would have gravely endangered the safety of our first invasion forces. In the light of such a development the German forces of occupation in France very probably would have risked an immediate move through Spain, or from Marseille, into French North Africa. As President Roosevelt has concisely phrased it, the policy pursued by this government in North Africa in the autumn of 1942 was one of expediency.

At that time General Weygand was living in complete retirement in Cannes and was refusing to have any outside contacts except with three or four French officers in whom he had complete confidence. Through one of them, he urged General Giraud to co-operate in the plans for the invasion of North Africa and urged him to proceed there.

During the three weeks preceding the invasion, Admiral Darlan had personally assumed charge of the appointment of officers of the French Army to ensure the defense of strategic portions of unoccupied France "against any alien invasion." It was not without significance that Admiral Darlan himself appointed General de Lattre de Tassigny as Commander of the district running from Marseille to the Italian coast, although it was well-known that the General was an open supporter of the United States.

There were many pro-Allied agents among Darlan's closest associates. There can be no question that Darlan was informed of the secret plans made by certain French officers to assist in the American invasion of North Africa.

In the final days prior to the invasion the German military authorities unquestionably had wind of what was under way. The German radio interference put out of commission practically all of the clandestine radio sets in the hands of those members of the French secret service who were co-operating, and almost prevented the final carrying out of the arrangements which had been made for removing General Giraud from a southern French port by submarine.

As it turned out, even General Giraud, whose popularity and high standing with the French officers in North Africa was unquestioned, was unable to gain their immediate agreement to carry out his orders. Upon his arrival in Algiers, he was forced frankly to inform General Eisenhower that he could not secure obedience to his authority.

It is for that reason, and for that reason alone, that we turned to Admiral Darlan because of his willingness and ability to help us. The Vichy government had granted the Admiral supreme control of the military and naval forces still subject to French authority. He had arrived in Algiers to visit his sick son after a visit of inspection which had taken him as far as Dakar. Like General Weygand, he had come to realize that the United States' entrance into the war made an ultimate German victory improbable, and he had at length reached the conclusion that the liberation of France could be assured only through American help. He was willing to order all the forces under his command to assist, rather than to resist, the American armies. The utilization of his services was urgently recommended to General Eisenhower by General Giraud as the one solution of the desperate crisis with which the former was confronted. There was no other authority prepared to help us whom the French troops would obey. In that critical moment, when there was not a minute to be lost and the success of the entire military operation hung in the balance, what other decision could have been taken?

The identification of Darlan with many of the most objectionable features of Vichy policy and his willingness during the earlier stages of the Vichy government to carry out German orders could not be permitted to outweigh the practical fact that, if the American landing forces were to be saved from a serious danger, orders to the French troops to co-operate with them must be issued, and that Darlan was the only authority in French North Africa who momentarily was both able and willing to issue such orders.

The assassination of Darlan soon afterward removed that element of controversy. In the months which have subsequently elapsed, political and military conditions in French Africa and in France itself, after many difficulties and by slow degrees, have changed radically for the better. Today the French Consultative Assembly and the French Committee of National Liberation, headed by General de Gaulle, have taken over control in the political field in French Africa.

Time alone will show how permanent this change may be. But it is difficult to see how our occupation of North Africa, the keystone in the strategic design for the defeat of Germany, could have been successfully carried out if the United States government had based its plans at the time of the landing operations on questions of ideology rather than of military and naval strategy.

Any decision as to the wisdom of our course in relation to the people of France depends upon the answer to this question: Since the United States government has assured the French people that after the war they will be free to choose the government they want, was it more to their interest to hasten that day by concentrating upon the defeat of Germany or would it have been preferable, by putting purely political considerations first, knowingly to have risked the victory which alone will give them the freedom to make that choice?

Another question, involving primarily strategic considerations, which aroused controversy, came up in the spring of 1941 when the Greek armies defeated Mussolini's forces of invasion, and Hitler ordered a German blitzkrieg against Greece. At that moment the ebb and flow of the British battle in Eastern North Africa against Rommel's Africa Corps was at a precarious stage. The British forces, both in numbers and in matériel, were sadly deficient. Their leadership was still defective. It was only too plain that in order to make Egypt and the whole of the Near East secure against invasion, the British government desperately needed all the troops and war matériel it could collect for its military campaign in Libya. At this critical moment the Greek government, now confronted with a vastly superior German force, made a despairing plea to the British War Cabinet for immediate assistance, and the British government determined to send an expeditionary force, which it could so ill-afford to spare, to fight with the Greek Army.

I remember that many officials in Washington at that time solemnly deplored this move and inveighed against the lack of intelligent strategy on the part of the British Cabinet. It seemed to me then, as it does now, that this decision, for which I believe Anthony Eden was largely responsible, was one of the wisest taken during the war. In the first place, if Great Britain had not lived up to its obligation to give this assistance to her allies in their moment of desperate peril, particularly after they had made so gallant and successful a resistance against Italy, she would have incurred the justifiable resentment not only of Greece but of all the smaller powers of Europe as well. Moreover, the assistance given by the British held up the German advance through Greece into the islands of the Eastern Mediterranean long enough for the British to overcome the German-engineered uprisings which had broken out in Iraq. It thus forestalled the drive to the Red Sea and the Persian Gulf through Turkey or through Syria which Hitler would inevitably have undertaken had he been able to occupy Greece quickly, and had the revolution in Iraq proved successful.

It is true that sending aid to Greece made possible the subsequent advance of Rommel's armies and put Alexandria in imminent danger of Axis occupation. But the issues involved warranted the gamble taken.

The Russian problem was causing considerable apprehension to officials of our government when I returned from abroad.

The Soviet-German Agreement of August, 1939, had greatly chilled the friendly interest in the Soviet Union which the American public had gradually been acquiring since the two countries had resumed official relations in 1933. During that period, notwithstanding features of Soviet foreign and internal policy which had at times confused and at other times disturbed them, the people in the United States had begun to take a more realistic point of view of the position which the Soviet Union occupied in the world. The feeling had grown that Russian world power could not be disregarded, and that consequently it would be to the interest of this country to try to place our relations on a firmer basis. Therefore, the Soviet government's apparent decision to permit Hitler to carry out his plans for the conquest of Western Europe disillusioned all those who had been

anxious to establish closer relations between the two countries, and
who had been impressed by many of the social achievements of the
Russian people during the preceding twenty years. It must be said
that the disillusionment was sharpened by the extraordinary volte-
face of the Communist press both in the United States and in Great
Britain, which changed overnight from a policy of violent attack
upon Hitlerism and all that it stood for to a policy of almost incoher-
ent abuse of the Western powers because of the "capitalistic and
imperialistic war" it alleged they had undertaken. It must further be
frankly admitted that the action of the Soviet Union in dividing the
Polish spoils with Germany, certain aspects of the method by which
it assimilated the Baltic Republics, and, even more, the Soviet war of
1940 upon Finland, all helped to dispel rapidly whatever improvement in United States-Soviet understanding had taken place. Except
among the members of the Communist party itself, there now
developed a strong feeling of antagonism and, in fact, of extreme
suspicion with regard to all features of Soviet policy.

In this case the attitude of the United States government was, at
least at first, in entire harmony with public opinion. Restrictions of
every kind were imposed upon imports from the Soviet Union. To
an even greater degree exports from the United States to Russia
were cut off. By the spring of 1940 official relations between the two
countries were only nominal.

I began to wonder whether some change in this situation could
not be brought about. It seemed to me obvious that, granted the
essential nature of Hitlerism, any agreement between Germany and
the Soviet Union could only be one of sheer expediency and of a
relatively short duration. The shorter the duration the less disadvantageous to the United States, since under the terms of the arrangement Germany was to obtain from Russia many vitally needed commodities, including oil, which would make it just so much easier
for her to carry on a successful war against the Western powers.

I consulted the President and the Secretary of State about this
situation, suggesting that an effort be made to ameliorate the de
facto embargo then existing upon all exports to Russia, even among
materials previously ordered and paid for by Amtorg. With their
approval, I began a series of conferences—twenty-seven in all—with

the then Soviet Ambassador, Constantin Oumansky. A careful investigation was made of the imports which the Soviet Union wanted from the United States and of the new orders it wanted to place in this country. In many cases the restrictions were relaxed. The Soviet government was able at once to obtain some machine tools. When the Soviet Union in the following summer found itself at war with Germany, the fact that these restrictions had been lifted the year before and certain standards and specifications established, made it possible to increase immediately the volume of commercial supplies which could then be sent to Russia. It greatly assisted in speeding the output of munitions. The ability of the Lend-Lease Administration to give rapid assistance also was increased for the same reasons.

While there was nothing at all spectacular about these negotiations, they offered the Soviet government concrete evidence of our willingness to give reasonable consideration to their point of view and to bring about an improvement in Soviet-American relations.

Throughout the last months of 1940 evidence from reliable sources commenced to reach the Department of State that a German attack upon the Soviet Union was imminent. In the first days of January, 1941, information was handed to me which in my judgment proved beyond the shadow of a doubt that the German General Staff had agreed with Hitler that an attack should suddenly be launched by the German Armies upon the Soviet Union the coming spring. The information was detailed and came from sources which were unquestionably authentic. It appeared to me to be in complete harmony with the policy which this government had already adopted— a policy which was to convince the Soviet Union of American good will—and very much to the interest of the United States and the other democracies, that the Soviet government be secretly advised of the information that had reached Washington. While it is true that the Soviet government is probably better informed with regard to European and Near Eastern affairs than any other government, nevertheless, in this particular instance the source of our information was such that I had no reason to believe that the Soviet government necessarily had any knowledge of it.

I expressed to the President and the Secretary of State my belief that the Soviet government should be informed at the earliest possible moment. With their hearty approval, I asked Ambassador Oumansky to come to see me and in a very brief interview gave him the information. I told him that in our judgment it was completely authentic and we consequently believed that it should be communicated to Moscow immediately.

Because of its nature I remember our conversation clearly. After I had communicated my message, Mr. Oumansky turned very white. He was silent for a moment and then merely said, "I fully realize the gravity of the message you have given me. My government will be grateful for your confidence and I will inform it immediately of our conversation." Some five weeks later I took occasion to tell the Ambassador once more that I had further confirmation of the accuracy of the news I had given him. By that time, however, any informed observer of events in Eastern Europe could have seen many indications that the German High Command was basing its strategy upon an offensive campaign on the Eastern Front.

When the anticipated German assault upon the Soviet Union finally took place, I was serving as Acting Secretary of State. It seemed to me imperative that the government itself make plain the vital importance of this tremendous event to the people of this country. Through an immediate official and public appraisal of the basic elements involved, they could learn the point of view of their government before other quarters deliberately confused or beclouded the issues. I consequently wrote a suggested statement and took it to the President, who received me in his bedroom early the following morning so that I might give it to the press at the regular State Department press conference. The President approved the text as prepared, but added what is perhaps the most salient point in it, the final sentence, in his own handwriting.

Although the statement made in London by Prime Minister Churchill struck exactly the same note, and although it was released previously, neither the President nor I had seen the British text before the American statement was given out.

As time went on and the German Armies failed to reach their Russian objectives quite as rapidly as had been anticipated, public enthusiasm mounted. The popular demand became overwhelming

that the Soviet Union be given every form of assistance which could
be spared from the war production of this country.

The President, however, had already acted the moment the Soviet
Union was attacked. He sent the Lend-Lease Administrator, then
Harry Hopkins, and a number of American experts to Moscow in
the company of Lord Beaverbrook, who had been appointed by
Churchill to head a British Mission of the same character. Their
purpose was to reach a tripartite agreement and to arrange for the
Soviet government to obtain at once from this country whatever it
needed that was not required in American defense preparations or
pledged to supply the increasingly urgent needs of the British.

The political courage, the vision, and the constructive statesmanship of the President were never more dramatically demonstrated
than in the darkening years of 1940-1941. When, after the war, an
impartial estimate is made of the major factors responsible for the
victory of the United Nations, among them I believe will be three
great achievements realized in the months before our own entrance
into the war, each of them due to the personal initiative of the President. These are the Destroyers-Bases Agreement, the Lend-Lease
Act, and the Proclamation of the Atlantic Charter.

By midsummer of 1940 the German submarine menace in the
North Atlantic had reached a desperately dangerous point. The in-
roads made on British convoys were disastrous and it was far from
certain that the British government could maintain even the food
stocks needed for civilian and military consumption at the minimum
basis required for security. British armaments were almost at zero
level. British destroyers, which were the key to the convoy problem,
were being sunk at an alarming rate. The prospects during July for a
German victory appeared to be almost conclusive.

Had the Destroyers-Bases Agreement not been concluded in
September of that year and had the British Navy not been enabled
at once to use the fifty American destroyers for escort protection,
England might well have been beaten down before the winter months
had gone by. At the same time, owing to an offer unique in British
history, this country was given the chance to secure naval bases and
airfields within British territory which would vastly assist in the
defense of our Atlantic coast line no matter what might happen in

Europe. The actual agreement represented a combination of suggestions and projects developed as a result of direct communication between the President and the British Prime Minister. Mr. Churchill was insistent that the offer of British-held bases to the United States be made spontaneously without quid pro quo. The logical outcome of that plan, however, would have been for the government of the United States likewise to offer spontaneously to the British government the fifty destroyers, which the latter so desperately needed. The President, however, realized fully that the constitutional difficulties involved, as well as their effect upon public opinion in the United States, rendered such a procedure impracticable. The agreement as finally consummated contained, however, the essence of the plans which both leaders had had in mind.

Nor should the American people ever forget that, by the insistence of Winston Churchill, three of the bases—those in the Avalon Peninsula, in Newfoundland, and in Bermuda—were granted to the United States "freely, and without consideration." The whole transaction was an arrangement between friends, both of them in sore straits. It is due to the wisdom of the President and Mr. Churchill that it was concluded in such a manner that it need not cause friction and misunderstanding when the two peoples may have forgotten the war perils which brought it into being.

The passage of the Lend-Lease Act early in 1941 made it possible for the British government to secure armaments and airplanes at the most critical moment in its war production effort. Through its effect in stimulating American armament production the Act greatly facilitated and supplemented our own defense preparations after Pearl Harbor. It continues today to be one of the methods by which we are making our most effective contributions toward winning the war.

Early in August, during a period when I was again serving as Acting Secretary of State, the President sent for me to come to his study in the White House one afternoon. He told me that he had determined to hold a personal conference with the British Prime Minister. For reasons of security, the meeting was to be kept secret until after it was over. Mr. Churchill and he were to meet on warships of the two navies in the harbor of one of the bases recently secured by the United States in Newfoundland.

The President told me that, while a large part of the meeting would be devoted to a discussion of defense questions and that consequently all our top-ranking military, naval, and air officers would go with him, he felt it was imperative for him to take up for consideration certain major political problems. Mr. Churchill would be accompanied by the Permanent Undersecretary of State for Foreign Affairs, Sir Alexander Cadogan, and the President felt that it would be helpful for me to attend the meeting as well. In order that the plans might be kept completely quiet the President ostensibly would leave for a fishing trip along the Atlantic coast within the next few days. Arrangements would be made for me to be flown up to Newfoundland in a navy plane so that I could join the President at his meeting place upon the day of his arrival.

Most important among the political problems which he desired to discuss with Mr. Churchill was the need for a general agreement between the two governments, while the United States was still at peace and the European war was still in its earlier stages, covering the major bases upon which a new world structure should be set up when peace finally came.

The President had felt since the conclusion of the first World War that one of the chief factors in the ultimate breakdown of organized world society had been the lack of any over-all agreement between the Allied powers at the time of the Armistice in November, 1918. He was foresighted enough to recognize that the United States could best prevent a recurrence of these conditions by insisting that Great Britain and the United States reach such an agreement without further delay. Subsequently, the effort could be made to obtain the support of all other nations fighting the Axis powers. The President rightly believed that the mere announcement of such an agreement would prove invaluable in giving encouragement and hope to the peoples now fighting for survival.

Early in the morning of August 9, I left the Naval Air Base outside of Boston accompanied by Averell Harriman, reaching Argentina early the same evening. The President had already arrived on the U.S.S. *Augusta*. With him were Generals Marshall and Arnold,

Admirals Stark and King, as well as a large group of other representatives of the three branches of our armed services. A number of American battleships and destroyers were already anchored in the harbor. In the distance along the shoreline covered with stunted northern spruce could be seen the United States barracks, constructed with fantastic rapidity during the previous two months.

In the afternoon of the following day the British battle cruiser, *Prince of Wales*, which was bringing the Prime Minister to the meeting place, with its escorting destroyers, glided through the gray North Atlantic waters into the sunny harbor and dropped anchor.

Almost immediately, Mr. Churchill and his party came aboard the President's flagship. Harry Hopkins, who had flown to England on his return from Moscow, came with the Prime Minister.

After the official dinner given the first night to the Prime Minister and the members of his staff by the President on the *Augusta*, the British and Americans broke up into groups in order to reach preliminary agreements upon the specific matters coming within their particular jurisdictions.

As the President had previously predicted, a great number of his conversations with Mr. Churchill were devoted solely to questions of naval and military strategy. Upon the first morning after Mr. Churchill's arrival, however, at a meeting held in the President's quarters, consisting of the President, the Prime Minister, Sir Alexander Cadogan, Harry Hopkins, and myself, Mr. Churchill told the President that he hoped the President and he might issue, at the conclusion of their meeting, a joint declaration of the aims and desires of the two governments regarding the kind of world that should be constituted after the war. It was to be regarded as a summary of the objectives of those nations opposed to the domination of the world by the Axis powers.

The President expressed his enthusiastic approval of the proposal, since it entirely coincided with his own plans. He stated, however, that he would like to consider the precise text very fully in order to be certain that all the points which he himself had already formulated, and which he regarded as essential, were amply covered. He therefore asked me to determine upon a draft text at a meeting I was scheduled to have that same afternoon with Sir Alexander Cadogan.

I was impressed with the unhappy effects which the Ottawa Agreements, providing for Imperial tariff preferences, had had on the economy of all nations, and particularly on that of the United States. It was my strong hope that the British Prime Minister would be willing in this document to indicate the intention of Great Britain to co-operate fully with the United States in holding out to peoples everywhere the hope that the two governments would jointly assume leadership in the postwar world in bringing about the elimination of autarchic trade systems, and in abolishing such examples of discriminatory commercial arrangements as the Imperial preferences themselves.

This was of course the view of the President. Mr. Churchill stated quite frankly that, while he himself throughout his political career had vigorously opposed Imperial preferences, and had consistently favored the liberal trade principles of the latter part of the nineteenth century, he was not empowered constitutionally to enter into any commitments of this character without the consent of the other members of the British Commonwealth of Nations. In view of this insistence of Mr. Churchill, the fourth article of the Declaration, when it was finally drafted, contained the well-known reservation "with due regard for their existing obligations." It was fully understood, however, that this reservation was inserted solely to take care of what it was hoped would be merely temporary impediments to the more far-reaching commitment originally envisaged in that article.

The final version of the Joint Declaration was not in fact agreed upon by President Roosevelt and Mr. Churchill until after lunch on the last day of the meeting. By this time Lord Beaverbrook had flown from England to join the Prime Minister, and took part in this final conference.

The text of the Joint Declaration as finally established, later to be known as the Atlantic Charter, was as follows:

The President of the United States of America and the Prime Minister, Mr. Churchill, representing His Majesty's Government in the United Kingdom, being met together, deem it right to make known certain principles in the national policies of their respective countries on which they base their hopes for a better future for the world.

First, their countries seek no aggrandizement, territorial or other;

Second, they desire to see no territorial changes that do not accord with the freely expressed wishes of the peoples concerned;

Third, they respect the right of all peoples to choose the form of government under which they will live and they wish to see sovereign rights and self-government restored to those who have been forcibly deprived of them;

Fourth, they will endeavor with due respect for their existing obligations, to further the enjoyment by all States, great or small, victor or vanquished, of access, on equal terms, to the trade and to the raw materials of the world which are needed for their economic prosperity;

Fifth, they desire to bring about the fullest collaborations between all nations in the economic field with the object of securing, for all, improved labor standards, economic adjustment and social security;

Sixth, after the final destruction of the Nazi tyranny, they hope to see established a peace which will afford to all nations, the means of dwelling in safety within their own boundaries, and which will afford assurance that all the men in all the lands may live out their lives in freedom from fear and want;

Seventh, such a peace should enable all men to traverse the high seas and oceans without hindrance;

Eighth, they believe that all of the nations of the world, for realistic as well as spiritual reasons, must come to the abandonment of the use of force. Since no future peace can be maintained if land, sea or air armaments continue to be employed by nations which threaten, or may threaten, aggression outside of their frontiers, they believe, pending the establishment of a wider and permanent system of general security, that the disarmament of such nations is essential. They will likewise aid and encourage all other practicable measures which will lighten for peace-loving peoples the crushing burden of armaments.

Franklin D. Roosevelt
Winston S. Churchill

Since that time the President and the Prime Minister have met frequently, not only in Washington, but in many distant parts of the world. Their working understanding and the cordiality of their personal relationship have constantly developed in their many subsequent meetings. But for many reasons this first meeting between them will always bear a special significance. While the United States had broken all relations with Germany, it was not at war. With the overwhelming approval of the country, the President had concluded the Destroyers-Bases Agreement with Mr. Churchill and had undertaken essential measures of preparation for the defense of the United States, without which we would have been in a sorry plight when Japan attacked Pearl Harbor. Yet so little did public opinion in the United States really seem to comprehend the extent of the danger that during the very days when the President was meeting Mr. Churchill we received the radio news from Washington that the House of Representatives had approved the continuation of oblig-atory military service, without which American defense preparations would have been wholly ineffective, by a majority of only one vote.

The President showed a measure of political courage which cannot be overemphasized. The implications of the meeting in the waters of Newfoundland were overwhelming. Yet nothing was more desirable from the standpoint of our own safety if, as already seemed to so many of us inevitable, we were to be drawn into the war in defense of our own survival.

When the United States was forced into war less than four months later, the Atlantic Charter became the agreement that was to bind together the United Nations. It linked them as allies during the war, and it pledged them to continue their association after victory had been won. In January, 1942, the United Nations Declaration, adhered to by all the governments at war with the Axis powers, and later signed by additional governments as they also entered the war for liberty, bound them all to support the principles set forth in the Atlantic Charter and committed each of them to make no separate peace with the Axis nations so long as the war continued.

Since this country entered the war, there has been a considerable measure of criticism not only of American policy toward France, but also of our policy toward Spain. As I pointed out in the dis-cussion of the events leading up to the American invasion of North Africa, the position of Spain as a buffer between our forces of occupation in North Africa and the German troops entrenched in France has necessarily been a matter of vital military importance to this government. Here again policy has been based primarily upon questions of military expediency, and questions of ideology have had to take second place.

Those who believe, as I do, that democracy must be able to function freely and without threat from any quarter if a decent and orderly world is to be created, and that it cannot function freely or without grave danger so long as Nazi and Fascist governments can impose their kind of rule upon peoples anywhere in the world, must view the policies of the present Spanish government with disquiet and suspicion. During the first years of the war nothing could have been plainer than that General Franco, his flamboyant Foreign Minister, Serrano Suñer, and the Falange party, which had become the keystone in the structure of the Franco government, were convinced not only that the triumph of Fascism and Hitlerism was inevitable, but that such a triumph was in the interest of Spain. It was equally apparent that German agents were omnipresent and in fact all-powerful in Spain. What made the situation so difficult was that Germany's continued ascendancy in the Iberian Peninsula constituted the gravest possible threat to the United Nations. Not only did it endanger British control in Gibraltar but, particularly during the last months of 1942, it also threatened the vital lines of communication now in American hands in North Africa. Were Germany actually to occupy Spain and Portugal, the Azores would in all probability fall into German hands. If that happened Great Britain would be shut off from the eastern South Atlantic and our life line to North Africa would be in hourly danger from the Axis outpost on our flank.

It has always seemed to me that the President's policy toward Spain, once we had entered the war, was both wise and realistic. From the standpoint of our aim to prosecute effectively a European war of invasion it was hardly open to question. The successful results of this policy have now been clearly demonstrated. We have shown a friendly attitude toward the Spanish people themselves, and we made available at a moment of great distress the supplies without which their suffering and starvation, already widespread as a result of the civil war, would have been greatly increased. Through our preclusive buying activities we have prevented the Germans from obtaining in Spain more than a fraction of the strategic materials they need. We have succeeded today in greatly diminishing German influence, and we discouraged the Spanish government from giving

overt assistance to the Axis powers at a time when its open align-
ment at the side of the Axis would have crippled our operations in
North Africa and probably gravely delayed our invasion of Italy.
Moreover, not all the members of the Spanish government have
sympathized with General Franco's strongly pro-Axis proclivities,
even during Serrano Suñer's heyday. Had it not been for the help
of high officials of the government, our progress in checking the
spread of German influence and infiltration in Spain would not have
been possible.

Today we are firmly established in North Africa, and the French
armies of resistance are fighting at our side with renewed courage
and energy. Italy has fallen out of the war, and the armies of the
United Nations are in occupation of the strategically important
Italian regions. The government of Portugal has revalidated its
ancient alliance with the United Kingdom, and the Azores are in safe
hands. Spain has, to a very great extent, lost its value to Hitler as a
means of jeopardizing the Allied invasion of Europe.

The United States and Great Britain are now quite properly demanding that the Franco government no longer permit Hitler to
obtain any strategic materials within Spain and thus prolong the
war. The Spanish people themselves have to a great extent been able
to relieve their condition of near-starvation. Consequently, a decision
to cut off supplies of petroleum and other raw materials, which the
Spanish government had previously obtained from the Western powers, could no longer result in the acute human suffering that would
have occurred had this policy been adopted two years ago. The time
has come when the Western powers are obligated to insist that General Franco's government refrain from giving material assistance to
our enemies. Were foreign policy solely a question of political sympathies or antipathies, the United States could never have maintained official relations with Spain during the past five years. At times
the Spanish government, by the notorious pro-Axis activities of
certain of its agents and representatives in the Western Hemisphere,
its willingness to serve Axis interests, and the military support
rendered to the German offensive against Russia, has given more
than sufficient cause for a severance of all official relations.

Nevertheless, had the American government seized upon these

legitimate grounds for breaking with General Franco, we would have gravely handicapped our war effort in the Mediterranean. Instead, we have not only averted that danger but have brought about a noteworthy change in the feeling of the Spanish people toward the United States notwithstanding the widespread bitter resentment occasioned by official American policy during the period of their civil war. Foundations have been laid for a sound relationship with a representative government, should the Spanish people set one up after the war, as we hope they will.

# THE TIME FOR DECISION

## PART TWO

# CHAPTER V

# The Good Neighbor Policy

## I. ITS ESTABLISHMENT

THE conception of the nations of the New World as a hemispheric group of sovereign states making up a regional system of free democracies is by no means new. It is, in fact, considerably more than a century old.

Early in the nineteenth century, Simón Bolívar and Henry Clay emphasized this ideal as the strongest weapon of defense which could be forged to ensure continued liberty and democracy in the Western Hemisphere. In 1826 a Pan-American Congress was held at Panama which it was hoped would lay the foundations for some practical form of union between the Americas. Had the United States taken full part in those early deliberations, the history of inter-American relations might well have been far different and far better. As it was, the fantastic material growth of the United States during the latter half of the past century, its bullying and domineering policy in its relations with the other nations of the hemisphere, the lack of communications and of a common language, and the disorders of adolescence which affected many of the Ibero-American republics during succeeding generations, all contributed to a total lack of any real understanding between the people of the United States and the peoples of the republics to the south.

The vision of Blaine engendered an initial growing together of the peoples of the Americas in the nineties. The repercussions of our age of imperialism drew them once more sharply apart. It was not until Elihu Root became Secretary of State that an official spokesman for the United States again presented the concept of a Western Hemisphere governed by reciprocal respect for the rights of others, in which the sovereign equality of all the component states would be recognized, whether they were large or small.

Woodrow Wilson, in his first years in the Presidency, moved still further. He denounced not only all semblance of official imperialism but, equally important, imperialistic domination by financial or commercial interests. He had been incensed by the charges brought to him that the United Fruit Company was continually intervening in the political life of several republics of Central America and by the highhanded attempts of British and American oil companies to control governmental policy in Mexico. Public opinion in the other American republics reacted immediately to his enlightened declarations. Sentiment shifted rapidly to favor a renewal of efforts to seek equitable adjustments of the controversies which had for so many years prevented any true understanding or co-operation between the United States and the republics of the other Americas.

More than that, Wilson first put forward the idea of a League of Nations in 1914. The plan which he then partially drafted provided for an inter-American league very similar in general scope and intent to the provisions later contained in the Covenant of the League of Nations. He likewise made the first concrete move in the direction of collective inter-American responsibility if a breakdown of constitutional government in any part of the Americas should endanger the security of the other republics. This was undertaken in his imperfectly envisaged and faultily executed plan to obtain Argentine, Brazilian, and Chilean co-operation in solving the difficulties which had arisen in 1914 between Mexico and the United States. But here in any event were the germs of a new policy for the Americas. It contained, in its conception at least, the essential requirements of a comprehensive regional understanding.

It has always seemed to me most tragic that Wilson, in spite of his enlightened views, should have authorized the military occupation of both Haiti and the Dominican Republic. These unjustifiable interventions, carried out in the years prior to 1917, when Wilson was gravely preoccupied with the problems arising from the first World War, at once alienated the sympathies of the other American nations and fatally undermined their confidence in the sincerity of Wilson himself.

Furthermore, in 1919 the United States government studiedly avoided anything which approached consultation with the allied

American republics as to the peace settlement. In fact, their delegations at the Peace Conference were virtually ignored. Not unnaturally this strengthened their resentment against the United States and checked any trend on their part toward a more co-operative relationship.

In the Harding Administration but one outstanding figure strove to correct these conditions. Except for Secretary of State Hughes, those members of the Harding Cabinet who displayed any interest in inter-American affairs were primarily intent upon what to them were practical considerations. These considerations had to do very largely with oil. On the other hand, Mr. Hughes undertook from the very first to remove the more salient causes for ill will. In a task, however, which required a long period of remedial adjustment, his term of office was too short for him to do more than correct, at least in part, our basic errors in policy. Unfortunately, neither his successor, Secretary Kellogg, nor President Coolidge possessed the ideals and the vision required were the policies which he inaugurated to continue.

Mr. Coolidge lacked both knowledge of and interest in inter-American affairs. The question, in his opinion, was one that involved relations with insignificant peoples whose good will was of no real importance to the United States. Secretary Kellogg, while serving as United States Senator, had attended the Pan-American Conference of 1923 in Santiago as a delegate of this government. In the long history of Pan-American conferences, the United States was never more completely at odds with its American neighbors than during those sessions. Nervous and irritable in temperament, Secretary Kellogg gained impressions at that meeting which lingered with him and apparently colored his thought later when, as Secretary of State, he had to make important decisions affecting inter-American policy.

The attitude of President Coolidge himself has always been most vividly exemplified to me by a personal experience. In 1924, as American Commissioner to the Dominican Republic, I had assisted in preparing for the termination of the American military occupation. Our purpose was to ensure that after national elections had been held a freely elected Dominican government might resume its rightful place at the helm of Dominican affairs. General Horacio

Vasquez was elected President by a large majority, and at the instance of Secretary Hughes was invited to visit Washington before assuming office. I accompanied General Vasquez to Washington and attended a luncheon which President Coolidge was induced to give in his honor at the White House.

General Vasquez had figured prominently in the political life of his own country for more than a quarter of a century. Of imposing and somewhat reserved presence, he possessed an old-time courtesy modeled on those gracious Spanish traditions which unfortunately today are fast disappearing. Above all else he was highly susceptible to any slight upon the national dignity or prestige of his native land.

The State Department protocol officials had taken the precaution to see that a Spanish-speaking American official was placed at the side of the Dominican President-elect to act as interpreter, inasmuch as neither Mr. Coolidge nor General Vasquez was able to speak the other's language. Throughout the entire luncheon Mr. Coolidge, who apparently was in one of those petulant moods from which he frequently suffered, not only never conversed with his guest, but replied solely in monosyllables to the frequent attempts which General Vasquez, through the interpreter, made to talk with him. After lunch, the President led the way, since it was a warm summer day, to the porch on the south front of the White House. After a few minutes spent in conversation with some of the American officials who had been invited, he sent word to his guest that he was obliged to leave, presumably to take his postprandial nap, and forthwith departed. The effect which this neglect of even the elementary requirements of hospitality had upon the Dominican President-elect may readily be imagined.

Throughout his term of office Mr. Coolidge's disregard of the very acute and very human susceptibilities of our American neighbors was entirely on a par with his conduct in this instance. Everything that had to do with inter-American affairs was a bore to him.

During those unhappy four years after Mr. Hughes retired as Secretary of State our inter-American relations continued to deteriorate. It is true that the action taken by Secretary Kellogg to assist in the settlement of the Tacna-Arica dispute between Chile and Peru was a step in the right direction, but the dictatorial attitude and methods adopted by this government created an unfortunate impression throughout South America.

Likewise, our general attitude toward Mexico during this period was one of hectoring and domineering admonition, similar to that of a choleric corporation lawyer toward an inferior whom he suspects of shady practice.

The one bright spot in the conduct of inter-American foreign policy by Mr. Coolidge was his appointment in the latter years of his Presidency of Dwight Morrow as Ambassador to Mexico. Mr. Morrow, instead of browbeating and recriminating, immediately sought the roots of difficulties and endeavored in friendship and good faith to find the best means for their solution. But in his case, as in the case of Mr. Hughes, the time of his service was too short for him to do more than reverse the trend, successfully continued by Josephus Daniels and George Messersmith, which helped to create the comprehensive ties existing today between Mexico and the United States.

In short, the policy of the Coolidge Administration in inter-American affairs can most readily be summarized in the words of an address which Mr. Coolidge made in New York on April 25, 1927. They read as follows:

> The person and property of a citizen are a part of the general domain of the nation, even when abroad . . . there is a distinct and binding obligation on the part of self-respecting governments to afford protection to the persons and property of their citizens, wherever they may be.

In a United States policy which proclaimed that the American flag followed the American dollar the nations of Central and South America found ample confirmation of their suspicions. To them this pronouncement implied that American imperialism and the policy of armed intervention were once more, and this time blatantly, on the march.

President Hoover was far too able a man not to appreciate fully the significance to the security of the United States, both political and material, of the good will and understanding of our American neighbors. He likewise could not fail to see the damage which had resulted from the policies carried on by his predecessor. Prior to his inauguration, therefore, he undertook his well-remembered tour around Central and South America. His intentions were admirable and should have resulted in much good. But he failed lamentably in his purpose.

He failed primarily because it was scarcely possible for people in the other American republics to believe that the policy of a President of the United States, who had served for eight years in the preceding Cabinets, would be different from the policies of his predecessors. Moreover—and this is something for which Mr. Hoover clearly cannot be blamed—neither his personality nor his tact and human understanding are such as to endear him to the Spanish-American or to the Portuguese-American public at large. Throughout the course of his visits in South America, while he was received with a full measure of official courtesy, except perhaps in Argentina, his reception by the people themselves could not have been less enthusiastic. Only one thing might have changed their reaction: his assurance that his administration would give at least a reasonable measure of friendly consideration to their economic interests. But such an assurance was not forthcoming.

In various statements which the former President has issued, and in particular in the statement made public on December 13, 1943, he has claimed the credit for the paternity of the good neighbor policy. He has made it clear that, in his judgment, the achievements of the Roosevelt Administration are to be regarded solely as an outgrowth of what he himself initiated. Mr. Hoover refers to his preinauguration visit to the other American republics as a chief factor in the creation of the good neighbor policy, and asserts that the principle of nonintervention and the termination of our military occupation in other American republics were originally sponsored by his administration.

In foreign policy, as well as in many other forms of human enterprise, the proof of the pudding is in the eating. Mr. Hoover undoubtedly desired to reverse the Coolidge inter-American policy and to promote good feeling between this country and its neighbors. Unfortunately, it is an obvious fact that after four years of the Hoover Administration there was no country of the Western Hemisphere where the United States was, in even the most superficial sense of the word, regarded as a good neighbor. The reason for this was that only a year after Mr. Hoover assumed office he signed the Smoot-Hawley Tariff Act. This act automatically deprived our American neighbors of a major part of the market which they had previously enjoyed in this country. Coming at a time of world-wide depression, which had already hit them very hard, it brought some of these countries to the edge of national ruin, with resultant unemployment and starvation for many millions of their peoples. This situation I saw at first hand in Cuba.

Nevertheless, in many ways the inter-American policies of the Hoover administration were both enlightened and constructive. Hoover dispatched a commission to Haiti to prepare the way for the termination of our military control in that republic. He also reversed the previous American policy of refusing to recognize revolutionary changes of government in the other American republics, which had inevitably implied a measure of intervention in the free determination by those peoples of their own destinies. In both these policies the influence of his Secretary of State, Henry L. Stimson, was predominant. However, the effort of the United States to play a helpful part in composing the sharp controversy between Colombia and Peru over the territory of Leticia was considerably weakened by an attitude which could more properly be adopted by a schoolteacher admonishing his pupils.

When Franklin Roosevelt became President he had for a long time taken a deep and constructive interest in inter-American affairs. He believed that in its own interest this country should put its relations with its American neighbors upon a new and completely different foundation. He believed primarily that it must abandon its long-standing policy of interference, and above all of military intervention. He was convinced that the juridical equality of all the American nations must be recognized in practice as well as in words. Furthermore, he was persuaded of the necessity for inter-American consultation whenever trouble within one republic threatened to become a source of danger to the others. This would ensure that mediation or any protective measure would be undertaken only by concerted action.

Moreover, President Roosevelt, unlike all of his predecessors, had been long familiar with the nations of Central and South America, from both personal knowledge and experience. He had, long before he assumed office, visited Venezuela and Colombia. During his eight years as Assistant Secretary of the Navy, he had had occasion to visit Panama and Cuba, and he had not only visited, but voyaged extensively through, the Dominican Republic and Haiti, for whose peoples he had developed a peculiar regard. Finally, while not fluent in the Spanish language, he could understand it and read it with ease. All this facilitated his grasp of the underlying problems of inter-American relations and made it easier for him to determine the most effective methods of remedying the mistakes of the past.

He was constantly anxious to obtain the fullest possible information on developments in the Western Hemisphere, and to learn every aspect of the problems, both political and economic, which were affecting the welfare of the other American peoples. He was particularly interested in finding markets in the United States for new exports from the countries to the south as the most practical way to relieve their growing economic distress. During the months prior to his inauguration, inter-American relations formed an important part of his study of national problems. As one of the basic objectives in his foreign policy, he set the creation of hemispheric unity.

This new inter-American policy came to be known as the "good neighbor policy" more by chance than by deliberate intent. In his first inaugural message, President Roosevelt announced that the United States would pursue in its dealings with all the nations of the world the policy of the good neighbor. The phrase was not intended to apply solely to the other American republics. But in an address on Pan-American Day, the first April 14 after he took office, the President laid special emphasis upon this aspect of his foreign policy as the course which his government would follow in its dealings with the peoples of the New World. Inasmuch as his words were immediately backed by practical action in this hemisphere, it was not many months before the people of Central and South America, and subsequently of the United States, seized upon the "good neighbor" phrase as particularly applicable to the policy pursued by this government in its dealings with the twenty other republics. It has now so definitely become associated with inter-American relations that its broader meaning, as used in the President's first inaugural message, has been lost.

It happened that I had the opportunity of carrying out the policy of the good neighbor in its first major application to inter-American relations. For some time prior to 1933 the situation which had arisen in Cuba had created a maximum amount of embarrassment to the government in Washington. General Machado, the President of Cuba, had been elected in 1925 for the constitutional four-year term. In 1928, by methods which were generally regarded as questionable, and unconstitutional, he had secured a revision of the Cuban Constitution which not only extended the term of office for which he had been elected, but likewise provided for a second term of six years rather than of the original four.

The world depression had hit Cuba very hard indeed. Eighty-five per cent of her national income was derived from the sale of sugar in the world market, and her ability to prosper depended on her ability to sell to the United States with some reasonable margin of profit. Consequently, the material increase in the tariff on sugar, imposed by the Smoot-Hawley Tariff Act, had rapidly brought the Cuban people to a condition of abject destitution which had never previously been equaled in the history of their independence.

President Machado had secured tremendous loans in the United States for the construction of a series of public works. As a result, the Cuban national debt had been vastly increased, and in the expenditure of the sums obtained by these loans there had notoriously existed much graft and corruption. All these facts had raised up against the Machado government a bitter feeling of hostility throughout Cuba.

Like many others of his domineering type in positions of authority, President Machado had deluded himself into the conviction that his government still had popular support. He was sure that the opposition to him, now daily becoming more vocal and more violent, was stimulated by what he termed "communistic" agitators and professional oppositionists, who would soon cease to give trouble if they were repressed with a strong hand. The violence and cold-blooded cruelty of the repressive measures which he undertook were immediately answered by equally violent outbursts on the part of the opposition.

By the winter of 1933 the situation had reached such a point that the processes of constitutional government were halted, business was at a standstill, the universities and high schools could no longer function. The atrocities perpetrated by the federal police employed by the Machado government—atrocities quite similar to those later carried on by the Nazi Gestapo—had aroused indignation throughout the Americas.

The secret Cuban political society, known as the A B C, and comprising many of the ablest and most patriotic of the younger professional men of Cuba, had for some time been using bombs and other weapons of assassination against the members of the Machado government. Scarcely a night passed in Havana without some attempt at assassination, or some cruel measure of reprisal by the secret police.

The original treaty between the United States and Cuba, granting the United States the right to intervene by force if in its judgment the Cuban authorities were unable to render due protection to life and property, was still in existence. The Hoover Administration closed its eyes to a situation which was fast degenerating into anarchy, and was shocking the conscience of the Western world. It limited itself to asserting that, inasmuch as the government of President Machado had been recognized by the United States as the constitutional government of the republic, no steps would be taken by the United States that could in any sense interfere with the free right of the Machado government to put down disorders by any means which it might deem fit.

With the inauguration of President Roosevelt, a slight lull occurred; both sides were waiting to see what course the new United States government would pursue. To President Roosevelt two facts were clear. First, that, while the existing treaty with Cuba gave this country the right to intervene, any such intervention would be entirely contrary to the general line of inter-American policy which he had set for himself. Second, that a state of affairs where governmental murder and clandestine assassination had become matters of daily occurrence must be ended. Such a condition at the front door of the

United States could not be allowed to continue indefinitely, particularly in a country bound to this nation by peculiarly close treaty ties, and for which the people of this country had a very special regard.

The obvious solution was for our government to try to solve the difficulties by negotiation and friendly mediation, while fully respecting the sovereign rights of the Cuban people and avoiding any act of official intervention.

I was appointed United States Ambassador to Cuba in April of 1933. I remember the final conversation I had with the President in his study in the White House the night before my departure. His sympathy for the Cuban people was deep and real. He hoped that the government and the leaders of the opposition parties and groups might be persuaded to reach an agreement upon a course of procedure which would make it possible, through the methods afforded by the Cuban Constitution, for a change of administration to take place. This would give the people of Cuba the opportunity to start afresh under new auspices.

It is impossible here to do more than touch briefly upon the salient events of that dramatic summer of 1933 in Cuba. President Machado was undoubtedly a type which would have been of interest to a psychiatrist. He was a man of vigor and of force, utterly autocratic and reactionary in his beliefs, and motivated, I think, primarily by a feeling of burning resentment that the early popularity which he had enjoyed should have turned into violent popular hatred. His life was in constant danger. His movements from the palace in Havana to his country place in the outskirts of the capital had to be surreptitious. In the frequent conversations I had with him, in which time and again there came up for discussion the revolting details of the murders committed by his secret police, particularly those of young patriots hardly more than boys, he never gave the slightest indication that these acts of barbaric cruelty were anything but justified. In the last days of his tenure of office a shocking incident occurred. The police of Havana fired upon a completely disarmed and orderly crowd marching in demonstration on one of the main avenues of Havana, killing many innocent persons. I remember particularly how General Machado brushed aside the incident as of no importance.

He added: "As a matter of fact more than half of those killed were not even Cubans, they were foreigners." And yet I myself saw the tears roll down his cheeks when, walking one afternoon through the menagerie he had established in his country villa, he came upon one of the doves in his aviary which had broken its neck by flying against the cage.

After many weeks of negotiation, President Machado and the leaders of the majority of the opposition parties and groups agreed to accept my mediation, as United States Ambassador, in finding a solution of the political problem, and thus make it possible for the United States to co-operate with the Cuban government to relieve the rapidly mounting distress of the Cuban people.

The only practicable solution, as afforded by the terms of the Cuban Constitution, was for the Cuban President to resign and permit the ranking member of his Cabinet to act as his successor until national elections could be held and a new government installed. The mediation proceedings progressed satisfactorily for a brief period, although it was clear to me from the outset that President Machado would put every possible obstacle in the way of a solution that would result in his resignation. But in the early days of August a spontaneous mutiny of the Cuban Army took the matter out of his hands and he was forced to flee from Cuba on August 12. Mob rule prevailed in Havana and in many other regions for several days before order could once more be restored.

In the meantime, however, by the free designation of the heads of the opposition parties, Dr. Carlos Manuel de Cespedes, only son of the great Cuban patriot of the same name, became Provisional President. He appointed a Provisional Cabinet composed of representatives of all the groups by which he had been selected.

During the brief anarchic period through which Cuba passed in August of 1933, there were, of course, innumerable demands for American armed intervention, especially from certain people representing commercial interests. Every request was rejected flatly. As a precautionary measure, however, President Roosevelt directed that certain vessels of the United States Navy be sent to Cuban waters, to take away any American citizens or other foreigners whose lives might be endangered and who were unable to find any other safe means of avoiding mob violence. At the same time the President created the precedent for what was to become the studied policy of his Administration: consultation with the other American republics whenever the United States should find itself in a position where it might be obliged to take action affecting any other people of the Americas. The President summoned to the White House all the diplomatic representatives of the other American republics then in Washington, informed them frankly and in the fullest detail of the situation which had arisen in Cuba. He told them that, while the United States would not avail itself of its treaty rights to intervene, a situation threatened to develop which might give rise to a breakdown of orderly government, with a consequent state of affairs which must necessarily be of concern to all the other American nations. The President did not request or suggest any action on the part of the inter-American family, but limited himself to a frank exposition of the circumstances in order that the other American governments might be fully and officially informed of what had taken place, and of the reasons why American men-of-war had been sent to Cuban ports.

Not an American sailor was landed on Cuban territory. By the latter part of August the situation had quieted to such an extent that the few American naval vessels which had been dispatched to Cuba were withdrawn.

At the beginning of September, however, the constructive efforts of the Cespedes government to relieve the appalling distress of the Cuban people were suddenly arrested by a second mutiny in the Cuban Army. This time it was a mutiny led by noncommissioned officers against the commissioned officers, the great majority of whom were regarded as having been directly responsible for the excesses of the Machado government. This second mutiny, which was led, and to a very considerable extent planned, by that extraordinarily brilliant and able figure, Fulgencio Batista, now President of Cuba, was not intended primarily to overthrow the Cespedes government. It was only in the last stages of the conspiracy that a handful of political figures of secondary importance associated themselves with the movement, and brought about a state of affairs which compelled Dr. Cespedes and the members of his Cabinet to resign.

For a brief period the direction of Cuban affairs was undertaken by a committee, largely inspired and controlled by the student council of the University of Havana. After some disorderly and sterile weeks, one of the members of the original committee, a well-known Havana physician, Dr. Ramón Grau San Martín, emerged as the sole head of the civilian branch of what was then termed a new provisional government.

Unfortunately, disorders increased both in number and in gravity. The new provisional government, while proclaiming its intention of helping the common man and while promulgating a series of decrees providing for better conditions for the working classes, appeared to be completely incapable of maintaining even a semblance of public order. Property after property was seized by groups of workers, and industry generally was forced to close down. Opportunity for employment naturally ceased. The government seemed to overlook the fact that the bettered conditions for Cuban labor which it had decreed necessarily would remain theoretical while plantations and industries remained in the control of the workers and no opportunity for actual employment existed. Sporadic minor rebellions broke out in various parts of the republic. By the end of November a seriously anarchic condition had once more arisen.

The open-minded expectation with which the majority of the Cuban public had at first regarded the new government soon crystallized into a studied opposition. None of the established political parties, none of the commercial or business interests, no responsible labor organization, and only a few of the members of the professional classes supported the government.

The failure of this government to recognize the provisional Cuban regime headed by Dr. Grau San Martín called forth the most violent complaints from his adherents, directed in particular against myself. I have always felt that, in view of the existence at that time of the Treaty of 1901, which granted this government the right of intervention in Cuba, and only because of that fact, the United States would have been derelict in its obligations to the Cuban people themselves had it given official support to a de facto regime which, in its considered judgment, was not approved by the great majority of the Cuban people, and which had shown itself so disastrously incompetent in every branch of public administration. For so long as the treaty containing the so-called "Platt Amendment" continued in force, the Cuban people were persuaded that recognition of a government by the United States was tantamount to official United States support for that government. The overthrow of the Grau San Martín government the following winter as a result of the determined attitude displayed by Colonel Batista, and the selection of an honored Cuban patriot, Colonel Carlos Mendieta, as Provisional President, was unquestionably welcomed by an overwhelming majority of the people. It was the first step in the long process of Cuba's return to constitutional government, economic prosperity, and normal social stability.

I believe, however, that now that the United States government no longer possesses any treaty right of intervention in any American republic, the wisest inter-American policy in respect to recognition is embodied in the so-called Estrada Doctrine. This provides that recognition will be automatically accorded to any government as it comes into power. As expressed by the Mexican Minister for Foreign Affairs in 1934, the procedure envisaged by the Estrada Doctrine does not "give place to diplomatic haggling for recognition, nor does it involve a wound of any kind to the dignity and independence of a state."

The United States recognition of a new government which comes into being through extraconstitutional methods in some other American republic is generally interpreted in the rest of the hemisphere as an indication of approval of the policies and composition of the regime. There is consequently implicit in the act itself under existing conditions at least a suggestion of intervention. By the adoption of the Estrada Doctrine this would be avoided, and recognition would become what it should be: merely the official recognition of a fact— the fact that the supreme executive authority in another American state is lodged at that moment in the hands of certain individuals or groups. It would also prevent the interruption of all official channels of communication, frequently a grave inconvenience. It is far easier to maintain understanding between peoples when governments remain on speaking terms.

The Cuban revolutions had their repercussions at the Seventh Pan-

American Conference, which assembled in Montevideo in the autumn of 1933. At the time of the conference, the Roosevelt Administration had been in office only six months and, except in the case of Cuba, had had little opportunity to put the good neighbor policy into practice. Consequently, the majority of the other American governments were by no means convinced of the real intentions or the ultimate policy of this government. The sincerity of President Roosevelt's declarations with regard to nonintervention had yet to be demonstrated in actual fact. It was not unnatural that the highly vocal but inexperienced delegation sent to the conference by the Cuban government of Dr. Grau San Martín should inveigh against the refusal of the United States, and the great majority of the other American republics, to accord official recognition to the provisional Cuban regime. It was very naturally asserted by the Cuban delegates that the course followed smacked of interference in Cuba's domestic affairs.

The United States delegation undertook to allay all fears. The Secretary of State, as chief of the delegation, signed the Convention on the Rights and Duties of States which, in its eighth article, prohibits the intervention by any state "in the internal or external affairs of another."

After the passage of ten years it already seems strange that any such inter-American commitment could have been necessary. Yet at the time, the United States could have taken no one step that would have more completely allayed the suspicions and antagonisms of its American neighbors. It was the first great step toward the construction of the new inter-American relationship.

In December of 1933 I had been recalled as Ambassador to Cuba and appointed Assistant Secretary of State, a position which I had occupied for a few brief weeks the preceding spring. I was assigned general jurisdiction within the Department over inter-American affairs. There were manifold problems which urgently called for remedial action. Some of them obviously could be rapidly solved. Others inevitably required patience, considerable time, and a measure of co-operative good will on the part of the other governments involved before any solution could be hoped for.

In the first category lay such matters as the failure of the United

States to maintain any official relations with the government of El Salvador. This question was immediately adjusted through the decision on the part of both governments to renew the relations which had been interrupted.

In the second category were such problems as the imperative need to revise the whole structure of our relationship with the government and people of Panama. In 1903 the United States entered into a treaty with Panama, immediately after recognizing its independence. The treaty, which dealt primarily with the problems involved in the construction and maintenance of the Canal, contained many features that constituted a major restriction of Panamanian rights and privileges.

In the first place, like the Cuban treaty, it gave this government the right to intervene by force. The treaty likewise gave the United States an unlimited right to take over all lands and waters within the republic of Panama which at any time in our judgment might be regarded as necessary for the maintenance or security of the Canal. In addition, there was a further mortifying inconvenience in the fact that the Canal Zone divided the republic into two parts, and that no Panamanian, even a high official of the government, was allowed to pass from one part to the other without the consent of the Canal Zone authorities. Another serious complaint arose from the fact that the Canal Zone commissaries, because their goods were imported duty-free, could undersell Panamanian merchants and deprive them of the tourist trade created by the Canal.

For many long years previous United States administrations had taken the attitude that the construction of the Canal had afforded the people of Panama opportunities and rights which they never would have possessed otherwise, and that it was unreasonable and ungrateful of them to complain.

In 1926, during the Coolidge Administration, an effort had been made to modify in some slight degree the burdensome provisions of the original treaty, and a new treaty had, in fact, been negotiated. However, the Panamanian National Assembly had failed to ratify it because of the belief of the people of Panama that it afforded far too little relief for their difficulties.

The resentment of the Panamanian people had become so acute by the summer of 1933 that President Roosevelt took the opportunity offered by the visit to Washington of Dr. Harmodio Arias, the President-elect of Panama, to issue a joint statement in the names of the two Presidents. The Panamanian people were assured that the most sympathetic consideration would be given to the removal of their just grievances.

Soon after my return to Washington in the winter of 1934, with the approval of the President and with his personal knowledge of every stage of the negotiations, I began to arrange for a new treaty to replace the instrument of 1903.

Negotiations with the three commissioners appointed by the government of Panama continued for well over a year and a half. All of us tried to find a formula which, while in no way hampering the necessary right of the United States to protect, operate, and maintain the Canal, and to enlarge its capacity should that at any time become necessary, would nevertheless abrogate the treaty provisions which impaired the sovereignty of the republic and placed inequitable burdens upon her citizens. In the new treaty which finally emerged, Panama agreed, as a partner with the United States, to take whatever measures might be necessary for the protection of the Canal and for its efficient maintenance and operation. All provisions permitting any intervention by the United States were abolished. In a long series of supplementary agreements, arrangements were made which have since greatly stimulated the economic interests of Panama and removed the grounds for legitimate complaint on the part of Panamanian commercial interests. The treaty was finally signed in 1936 and thereafter ratified by both governments.

When the world crisis of 1939 occurred, the government of Panama immediately took every step which could conceivably be regarded as required of her under the Treaty of 1936 to provide for the security of the Canal. Two years later, when the United States was forced into the war, Panama without a moment's hesitation declared war upon the enemies of the United States and placed herself in every sense at the side of the American nation. A few minor agreements have subsequently been entered into to provide for the adjustment of questions arising from the war.

The Mexican situation likewise provided an almost unlimited field for remedial action on the part of both countries. Many of the controversies between the two countries have arisen as the result of action taken by the United States—action which occasionally was in flagrant violation of equity and of comity, and in other instances at least singularly ill-advised. One such case is afforded by the notorious "Chamizal" dispute, involving the determination of sovereignty over a small area along the boundary between the two republics. The dispute was submitted to arbitration, and the United States government refused to abide by the arbitral award.

There were other cases in which the Mexican government, for its part, was wrong or ill-advised. Such an instance occurred when the Mexican government expropriated properties belonging to American nationals, in order to distribute them among the Mexican agricultural workers, without making fair or equitable compensation.

There were other cases where it could not be claimed that either government was at fault, and yet where an adjustment of the question was extremely difficult because of the domestic interests involved in one or the other of the two countries. One example was the excessively difficult problem of the distribution of the waters of the Rio Grande and Lower Colorado rivers between the two countries.

I have mentioned but these three Mexican instances as typical of a great number of problems of the same character. I am glad to say that during the Presidencies of both General Cardenas and his successor, General Avila Camacho, the Mexican government has shown itself as sincerely eager as the United States to find a fair solution for all these problems.

Well after the effort to settle this long list of disputes had begun, a serious difficulty arose when the Mexican government suddenly expropriated the foreign-owned oil properties in the country. Here again, however, at the personal insistence of President Roosevelt, the issue was not permitted to occasion any such highhanded and domineering attitude on the part of the United States as would undoubtedly have been adopted in earlier years. While grave questions of international law and of international comity were involved, they have gradually been solved. The appointment of a joint commission by the two governments to evaluate the properties and provide for fair compensation to the American investors terminated what at first bade fair to become an insoluble difference.

The cordial and co-operative policy consistently followed by this government in all its relations with Mexico during the past eleven years has borne fruit. There exists today a foundation for Mexican-American friendship which seemed inconceivable only a short time ago.

In fact, it is difficult today to believe that only twenty-five years ago, during the time of the first World War, this same neighbor of ours which co-operates so whole-heartedly in the United Nations war effort, was responsible for a considerable measure of concern about our own security.

When President Roosevelt and President Avila Camacho exchanged visits in April of 1943, it was more than obvious that the remembrance of our long and turbulent relationship had already been largely erased. A great part of the credit for this happy situation can justly be ascribed to President Avila Camacho himself.

When future historians appraise the President's grasp of international affairs, and his vision in the field of inter-American relations, they will perhaps give him greatest credit for his initiative in suggesting, in 1936, that a special inter-American conference be held for the sole purpose of determining the best way of maintaining the peace of the New World and safeguarding its future security. In the early winter of 1936 the President was already sharply aware of the dangers to world peace. He further saw that, if a general world conflict broke out, the structure of inter-American relations, materially improved though it already had become, was not sufficiently strong to bear the strain which a second and greater World War would inevitably create. It seemed to him imperative that every effort be made to secure a firmer and a more detailed implementation of existing inter-American agreements.

As is customary in diplomatic soundings, this government, prior to making any official move, undertook to learn confidentially of the other American governments what their reaction would be to the idea which the President had in mind. The United States Ambassadors in the capitals of the other republics were instructed to talk over the plans with the Foreign Ministers in confidence. The reaction was, in general, more than satisfactory. The governments of the other American republics, with some few exceptions, were already apprehensive about the world situation, and were fully agreed that some further step should be taken by all of them to prepare themselves to meet the mounting crisis. I remember, however, that when we sounded the Argentine government, they made it very clear that they would accede to the proposal much more willingly if the President were to suggest the conference be held at Buenos Aires. This suggestion was entirely acceptable to this government, although perhaps less satisfactory to certain other of the American republics.

After the preliminary and confidential negotiations had been concluded, the President addressed personal letters to all the Presidents of the other American republics, inviting them to send delegates to an extraordinary conference to determine how the maintenance of peace between the American republics might best be safeguarded.

Acceptances were immediately received and the date of the conference was set for December, 1936.

In November of that year President Roosevelt was elected for a second term, but long before the results of the elections were known, he decided that he would go himself to Buenos Aires in order to attend the inaugural session. I shall never forget the amazing reception which was accorded him in his state drive through the Argentine capital. The enthusiasm of the Argentine public was neither artificial nor superficial. Anyone with some experience in the psychology of crowds could tell that this welcome accorded to the President of the United States came from the heart and was in no small measure due to the fact that the Argentine masses, in their almost continuous shout of "Viva la democracia," were applauding the man whom they regarded as the leading exponent of real democracy of that day. There could not have been a better demonstration of the change in popular sentiment created by the policies of the three previous years.

To the conference at Buenos Aires the American republics sent their outstanding statesmen. As I look today through the long list of delegates I see the names of innumerable men who have been shaping the destinies of their own countries, and for that matter of all of the Americas, in the eight years which have since elapsed.

In my judgment the conference at Buenos Aires was intrinsically the most important inter-American gathering that has ever taken place. The consultative meeting of the American Foreign Ministers at Rio de Janeiro in 1942 was in every sense more dramatic, and the immediate practical results were more far-reaching, but it could never have accomplished what was there so greatly achieved had not the Buenos Aires conference firmly placed the keystone in the future arch of real Pan-Americanism.

There were two real issues at Buenos Aires. The first was whether the American republics would agree to create some workable machinery to operate promptly whenever intracontinental disputes threatened a breach of the peace or whenever the security of the hemisphere was menaced from abroad. The second was whether they would jointly recognize that a threat to the safety of any one of them involved the security of the remainder. Unless these two principles could be established, no regional system could be developed, and no hemispheric unity could be achieved which could be depended upon as a protection in time of imminent danger.

I learned soon after the delegations had assembled that the vast majority of them favored the establishment of these two principles. I learned quite as quickly that the Argentine delegation, of which the then Foreign Minister, Dr. Carlos Saavedra Lamas, was chairman, was opposed to the establishment of either principle.

Argentina had for many years opposed the formation of any inter-American organization that would have legitimate authority to pass upon political questions, and in which the United States and Brazil could conceivably develop sufficient influence to check Argentina's traditional attempt to assert the right to speak for the other Spanish-American republics of South America. The Argentine government at the conference at Buenos Aires had, of course, been fully informed that this government was proposing the establishment of an inter-American system providing for immediate consultation through the Ministers for Foreign Affairs in the event of any threat to the peace of the hemisphere.

Three years previously, or for that matter even one year previously, the ulterior purposes of this country were still so suspect that any such proposal would have fallen upon barren ground. But the practical application of the good neighbor policy had worked a material change in the sentiments of the other American republics toward the United States. Proposals which earlier would have been regarded with antagonism, even though they might have seemed inherently desirable and in the common interest, would now meet with objective and unprejudiced consideration by all the other American governments. These were facts that Dr. Saavedra Lamas did not sufficiently appreciate.

Carlos Saavedra Lamas is one of the ablest statesmen produced in the Western Hemisphere in our generation. A son-in-law of one of Argentina's greatest Presidents, Roque Saenz Peña, he has been steeped from his early manhood in the study of foreign policy. As Foreign Minister he was astute, forceful, tireless, and intolerant. He was the foremost exponent of the Argentine school of thought that insists Argentina's ties with Europe are paramount and that her relations with the other American republics, with the exception of Brazil, are altogether secondary. He was firm in his determination, however, that Argentine supremacy as the leader of the Spanish-American nations must be maintained, and that any attempt on the part of the United States to increase its political influence in the hemisphere must be thwarted. Eloquent, brilliant, and dictatorial, he was a dominating figure in any meeting in which he took part.

Owing perhaps to the part he had played in Geneva, and to his convictions regarding the unimportance of inter-American affairs, Dr. Saavedra Lamas had developed a contemptuous disregard for the susceptibilities of the smaller American republics which he took little care to conceal. Only a few days after the opening of the conference the Argentine Foreign Minister summoned the chiefs of the five delegations from Central America to his private residence and, treating them in a cavalier manner, informed them flatly that they should immediately reject the proposals favored by the United States, inasmuch as they contained traps set for the unwary and were nothing more nor less than a means by which the United States hoped to extend its power and influence over the smaller nations of the hemisphere. The senior member of the Central American delegations, that admirable and universally respected statesman, Dr. Carlos Salazar, Minister for Foreign Affairs of Guatemala, speaking for all

his associates, ended the interview abruptly. He made it clear that
the Central American governments were in no need of advice as to
the course they should follow.

Argentina's attitude gave rise to a considerable amount of tension
and personal friction throughout the meetings of the conference.
However, her delegation soon realized clearly that it was fighting a
defensive battle, and that practically all the American delegations,
with the possible exception of two, were strongly in favor of the principles supported by the United States. The Brazilian delegation,
headed by their Foreign Minister, Dr. José Carlos de Macedo Soares,
in which Dr. Oswaldo Aranha, the present Brazilian Foreign Minister, played so brilliant a part, contributed greatly to the eventual
acceptance of these two principles.

The final showdown occurred in a night session of a conference
subcommittee, when the Argentine delegate, Dr. José Maria Cantilo,
subsequently himself Argentine Foreign Minister but speaking at
the time for the chief of his delegation, accepted a compromise with
regard to the principle of consultation, which the other delegations
also found satisfactory. This compromise is found in the first article
of the Convention for the Maintenance, Preservation and Re-establishment of Peace, which provides that, whenever the peace of the
American republics is menaced, inter-American consultation shall
take place.

But the great accomplishment of the conference at Buenos Aires is
the second article of the Declaration introduced by the delegations
of the Central American republics, and finally unanimously adopted.
It stipulates "that every act susceptible of disturbing the peace of
America affects each and every American republic and justifies the
initiation of the procedural consultation provided for in the Convention for the Maintenance, Preservation and Re-establishment of
Peace."

On these two principles, unanimously agreed upon, there has since
been erected the whole structure of the inter-American system, which
preserved the unity of the hemisphere at the outbreak of the second
World War.

By contrast, the Inter-American Conference held in Lima in 1938
(which also was almost disrupted by the Argentine delegation),

while adopting a vast number of resolutions, accomplished little beyond implementing the basic principles adopted at Buenos Aires. The Declaration of Lima provided the machinery necessary for inter-American consultation by specifically stating that the Ministers for Foreign Affairs of the American republics should meet for that purpose. At Buenos Aires, Dr. Saavedra Lamas had successfully prevented the adoption of this wholly necessary and desirable implementation. He had called any such consultative system an "ambulatory Pan-American Union."

Throughout the period between the inauguration of the good neighbor policy and the outbreak of war in 1939, a large part of the work of creating the new inter-American relationship had been taken up with economic and financial considerations. The trade agreements program, which stimulated the exportation of our products to the other American republics and enlarged the market within the United States for the exports of our American neighbors, had produced a highly beneficial two-way trade relationship and had already done much to erase the harmful effects of the tariff act of 1930. More than that, the establishment of the United States government Export-Import Bank had facilitated the extension of credits by the United States in many constructive ways when private capital in this country was hesitant. Time and again I have seen new industries brought into being which it would have taken generations to create had it been necessary to depend upon private capital. In my belief, the investments in themselves have been sound, and the money lent will be repaid. Even if this were not the case, I am convinced that the operations of the bank have been highly effective in counteracting Germany's efforts to exercise financial and commercial control over the national economies of many of the other American republics.

Throughout these years German activities in Central and South America were by no means limited to the economic or financial field. German agents and, to a minor extent, Italian agents were active in every American republic, as they were in the United States itself. The Japanese government also had agents in all parts of the hemisphere. However, the Japanese government has always been singularly ineffective in its dealings with the peoples of Spanish or Portuguese America. The Japanese immigrants cannot be assimilated, and, as in the United States, their lower standard of living and their willingness to work longer hours for lower pay provide a ready ground for friction. It is consequently only where they are established in large numbers, as in Brazil or Peru, that they could conceivably become a real danger. The Japanese Ambassadors and Ministers met frequently in one or the other of the American republics, usually in Brazil. Their meetings were closely watched by the governments involved, and what was learned of the proceedings made it more than obvious that the threat arising from their activities in the hemisphere was slight.

When the war broke out in Europe on September 1, 1939, the American republics were prepared for the impact. Nearly all of them had been made sharply aware of how the impending struggle would affect their security, internal stability, and national economy. Inter-American co-operation was now to be put to the test.

With one accord the American republics, pursuant to the great principles established at Buenos Aires, requested an immediate inter-governmental consultation. The first Consultative Meeting of the American Foreign Ministers was, therefore, held in September, 1939, at Panama.

## 2. THE INTER-AMERICAN SYSTEM STANDS THE STRAIN

Intense expectation was created throughout the hemisphere by the announcement of the First Consultative Meeting of the American Foreign Ministers.

The mounting apprehension over the ultimate effects of the European war upon the New World's security was increased by the threatening attitude of the Axis powers. The Japanese government addressed several insulting official communications to the government of Panama with regard to the treatment of Japanese nationals in that republic, and the German Minister accredited to the Central American republics, with much offensive publicity, proceeded to Panama in order to be present during the sessions of the conference. Not unnaturally the governments of the republics bordering upon the Caribbean were in a high state of irritation. Once more the Japanese and German governments had displayed their inability to appreciate the psychology of the peoples of the Americas.

Panama had been selected as the place for the First Consultative Meeting because of its convenient central location, an important factor at a time when every day counted. The conference opened on September 23. The President had selected me as the American representative, and I had arrived at Panama a few days before the date set for the opening of the meeting. I spent those days in visiting the delegates of the other American republics and was immediately impressed by the extraordinary feeling of inter-American unity displayed by all of them. It was so strong as to be palpable. There was not the slightest divergence of views as to the moral issues involved in the European contest; nor was there other than a deep-seated feeling that the triumph of the Axis powers would result in a curtailment of the liberties of the American peoples and inevitable peril to the integrity of the hemisphere. The well-known designs of the Second Reich upon the New World were to all American statesmen but an indication of what must inevitably be the far more ambitious designs of the Third Reich.

In this precedent-creating meeting the practical accomplishments were far greater in scope than has been fully realized. The position of the American republics was clearly defined and clearly established in the Joint Declaration of Continental Solidarity. While emphasizing their general neutrality, and proclaiming their determination to do what lay within their power to maintain the peace of the New World, the Declaration also asserted that this position was "free from any selfish purpose of isolation." It likewise bespoke the re-establishment of a peace in the world "not based on violence but on justice and law."

The neutral position of the American republics was reinforced by the creation of a maritime security zone proclaimed in the Declaration of Panama. The belligerents were warned to take no hostile action within this zone, and the republics themselves undertook to maintain such patrols as in their individual judgment might be required to preserve peace within those waters. In this Declaration it was asserted that so long as the American republics maintain their neutrality they are "of inherent right" entitled to have the waters adjacent to the American continent kept free from hostile acts by the belligerent nations.

The principle which the American republics sought to establish in the Declaration of Panama, seemed to be based on equity and reason. The guiding thought which lay behind the Declaration, which was certainly shared by all the delegations, was that, inasmuch as Germany and her Axis partners had brought war upon Europe and the Far East, inasmuch as the entire Western Hemisphere was remote from the scenes of the conflict, and inasmuch as the American republics had no part in the genesis of the conflict, there was no justification for the war being forced upon them in such a manner as to jeopardize their security, imperil their trade and their commerce, and interfere with purely inter-American communications.

I am frank to confess that at the time the Declaration seemed to me not only justified but desirable. But all of us then present at Panama, I think, believed, perhaps blindly, that the war both in Europe and in Asia might in some manner be won by the forces of freedom without becoming universal. The legitimate right of the American republics as neutral powers to make every effort to keep clear of the war could hardly be questioned. What we did not then see sufficiently clearly was that a war having its origin in the causes which brought about the war in Europe in 1939 could hardly become anything other than world-wide—a war between free men and the powers intent upon creating universal tyranny and oppression.

The Declaration of Panama, communicated officially to all the belligerent powers, probably marks the end of a period in human history. It was, I trust, the last official expression of the belief in this modern world that the responsibility for the repression of war can be other than universal.

The most practical and useful accomplishments of the Panama meeting lay, however, in the creation, by unanimous accord, of two permanent standing inter-American committees.

The first committee, which has ever since labored efficiently and unceasingly in Washington, was the Inter-American Financial and Economic Advisory Committee. Composed of representatives of each of the American republics, it was charged with the study of all financial and economic questions affecting the interests of the American nations. In the whole field of inter-American relationships during the war period, no work has resulted in more concrete and direct advantage to all of them. Among the vast number of problems with which the committee has successfully dealt has been the question of what to do with the Axis or Axis satellite ships immobilized in American ports. They have all been taken over by the republics under the right of angary, and put to use in maintaining maritime communication between the Americas at a time when, because of sinkings and war requirements, normal shipping had become very scarce indeed.

Had it not been for the committee, inter-American communication and trade would have been seriously handicapped, and in many cases altogether interrupted.

The other permanent inter-American body set up at Panama was the committee established at Rio de Janeiro, first known as the Inter-American Neutrality Committee and later as the Inter-American Juridical Committee. This organization was at first intended to formulate general standards of conduct appropriate to the neutral status of the American republics. More recently, as a result of the Third Consultative Meeting at Rio de Janeiro, the work of this committee has been greatly enlarged in scope. Its original functions having ceased when most American republics lost their neutral status, there was a general feeling that this body should reach some agreement as to the most desirable form of international organization to be established upon the conclusion of the war. The Committee has already formulated many recommendations which should be of great practical value to the American governments when they are called upon to take part in peace deliberations.

While these two committees were originally set up to deal with the urgent problems arising from the war, they have proved to be of such positive benefit to the New World as a whole that their continued existence after the war is most desirable. The problems of the reconstruction period will call for the co-operative measures which these two inter-American bodies can so efficiently formulate and recommend.

Because much has been written and said in recent years of the difficulties created for the cause of inter-American unity by the policies pursued by the Argentine government, I must emphasize the altogether co-operative, helpful, and able services rendered during the meeting at Panama by the Argentine delegation, headed by Dr. Leopoldo Melo. Dr. Melo's long experience in the public life of his own country has caused him to be generally regarded as one of the elder statesmen of the Western Hemisphere, and at the meeting he consistently exercised his great ability to achieve practical and successful results. In fact, throughout the meeting there was not the slightest cloud upon the horizon of inter-American unity. The delegations were animated by only one ideal, and the realization of a workable inter-American system was greatly advanced by the Panama Conference.

Six months after the opening of the First Consultative Meeting the apparent stalemate in Europe was suddenly broken, and the war passed into the kaleidoscopic stage of the months of May and June of 1940. Admiration for France, for French institutions, and for French culture has always been stronger in the American republics, particularly in those of South America, than the regard felt for any other European nation. France's tragically rapid collapse and the terms of the armistice accepted by the French Cabinet created a violent wave of feeling in all parts of the American continent.

This reaction had two aspects. First, there were consternation and panic that the cause of human liberty in the Old World, which had become identified with the fate of the democracies of Western Europe, seemed to be in its death throes. Among the majority of the younger generation in all the American republics and among the liberal political groups, it created a more outspoken hostility against Hitlerism and Fascism and a more determined resolve to do what they could to show their support for Great Britain, the sole power of Europe which still resisted Hitler. The other reaction, less agreeable, likewise existed among many classes in the United States. It sprang from the belief that, with the collapse of France, the invasion and downfall of England could be only a question of weeks, that the complete triumph of Hitler was, therefore, imminent, and that it behooved the American nations to speak softly and to take no overt action which might invoke reprisals from the Axis partners.

The invasion and occupation by Germany of the Netherlands and France involved a problem that was of immediate importance to all the American nations: the status of the Dutch and French colonies in the New World. In the case of the Dutch colonies, the local authorities maintained an attitude of unyielding resistance to German influence and were unswerving in their allegiance to the Netherlands government, which had by then taken refuge in London. The attitude of the French authorities in French Guiana and in the French West Indies, however, was far less satisfactory. Technically they maintained allegiance to the government which Marshal Pétain had set up in Vichy, but, inasmuch as it was already notorious that a considerable number of those Frenchmen who surrounded the Marshal had delivered themselves body and soul to Hitlerism, there was little assurance that they might not any day be found to be dominant in the French possessions in the Western world: that the American republics might not suddenly awaken to find themselves confronted with actual Nazi rule in South America or in the Caribbean.

This sinister possibility was the chief cause for the decision to hold, without delay, the Second Consultative Meeting of the American Foreign Ministers, which was summoned to meet at Havana on July 21, 1940.

The practical accomplishments of that meeting are to be found in "The Act of Havana Concerning the Provisional Administration of European Colonies and Possessions in the Americas," and in the "Convention on the Provisional Administration of European Colonies in the Americas." The Convention provided that "If a non-American state shall directly or indirectly attempt to replace another non-American state in the sovereignty or control which it exercised over any territory located in the Americas, thus threatening the peace of the continent, such territory shall automatically come under the provisions of this Convention and shall be submitted to a provisional administrative regime. The administration shall be exercised, as may be considered feasible in each case, by one or more American states, with their previous approval." And, inasmuch as the Convention could not become effective until two-thirds of the American republics had ratified it, the Act of Havana, designed to deal with such emergencies as might arise prior to ratification of the Convention, created an Emergency Committee which was to administer any of the regions comprehended within the terms of the Convention, if any one of these regions was either threatened or attacked. The act furthermore provided that, should the emergency be so urgent that action by the Emergency Committee could not be awaited, any one of the republics individually, or acting jointly with others, should have the right to act in any manner which its own defense or that of the continent required, with the stipulation that it should immediately place the matter before the Emergency Committee.

Circumstances have fortunately not made it necessary for either the provisions of the Convention of Havana, which was subsequently ratified, or of the Act of Havana to be invoked. The provisions of both instruments constituted an essential precaution in the interest of hemispheric security.

From the outbreak of the war in Europe until the United States itself entered the war, this government did what it could to co-operate with the other American republics to relieve the economic distress which had resulted from the loss of so many of their normal markets. The Inter-American Financial and Economic Advisory Committee proved to be invaluable in this emergency. While the members of that body could only make recommendations to be presented to the several governments concerned, and although these recommendations envisaged co-operative and joint action, so far as I can recall they were adopted in every instance.

Because of our material resources, it was obvious that the main brunt of the hemisphere effort to maintain the inter-American economic and commercial structure would have to be borne by this country. For that purpose, particularly during the first twelve months after the outbreak of the European war, the facilities of the Export-Import Bank in Washington were called upon to tide over several American governments that were under a severe financial or commercial strain.

The President likewise created the Office of the Co-ordinator of Inter-American Affairs. Originally it had been intended that, as the title implied, it should co-ordinate the efforts of the various agencies of the United States government with a view to achieving effective co-operation with the other American republics. As the months passed the Office of the Co-ordinator devoted itself more and more to administration rather than to co-ordination. However, a great amount of useful and desirable work in the field of cultural relations and in the fields of information, education, and public health has been undertaken, and successfully carried out, by the Co-ordinator's Office.

Later, after the United States became a belligerent, the entrance of the Board of Economic Warfare into the field of inter-American activities gave rise to a conflict of jurisdiction, and the creation of other agencies, all engaged in activities which were of vital importance to the American war effort, heightened the jurisdictional dispute. I have never had the slightest reason to doubt the sincerity or to question the ability of the Directors of all these agencies. However, extradepartmental agencies, which have to be thrown together at a moment's notice to serve in an emergency program, can scarcely be expected to acquire speedily either a wholly competent or a disciplined administrative personnel. The chief cause for the internecine warfare which so long afflicted these various agencies and which occasionally gravely embarrassed the Department of State was precisely that lack of efficient organization and properly qualified personnel.

Such difficulties appear to be inherent in our governmental system when it has to establish administrative agencies to cope with an emergency program, and will continue so long as the United States possesses no permanent Civil Service superior administrative personnel. Nevertheless, the assistance rendered by agencies of this government to the other American governments since the autumn of 1939 produced extremely beneficial results. It helped to stabilize the national economies of our neighbors and enabled them to pass through the most serious crisis they had ever faced. It likewise proved of value to the United States itself by thus preventing the growth of the chaotic social conditions which must inevitably have followed the collapse of the economic structure of any one of the republics of the New World. Indeed, much of the help which we were in this way able to give our neighbors was at the same time of incalculable value in the furtherance of our own war effort, for by far the largest part of our increased purchases in the other American republics during the past few years has provided us with strategic materials, such as tin, tungsten and rubber, without which our war production would have been greatly handicapped.

In Chile, dependent for its national income largely upon the sale abroad of its copper and nitrates, the outbreak of war had desperately serious repercussions.

The republic of Ecuador was not only involved in an increasingly serious boundary controversy with Peru but also suffered from internal political troubles which had resulted, in the last few years, in frequent changes of government. As a result of the war, Ecuador was unable to export to her normal markets, and, since domestic agricultural production had been seriously curtailed by the recent armed clash with Peru, she was also unable to obtain those staple food supplies most needed by the population. A continuation of such economic stress would have created a political and social collapse from which Axis interests would have been quick to draw their own advantage.

In Central America, the shortage of shipping created an impossible situation for certain of the republics dependent chiefly upon their markets in the United States for the sale of their principal exports, bananas and coffee. Failure on the part of the United States government to lend a helping hand would have resulted here also in economic and social collapse.

In Venezuela, a lack of shipping resulted in a serious shortage of food. In Brazil, where many cities are dependent entirely upon maritime communication for their imports, the lack of shipping created shortages in fuel, both coal and oil, without which neither transportation systems nor industries could have continued to function. In the regions where strategic materials for the American war effort were obtained, as in the Amazon Valley, food shortages would have blocked the production of essential supplies.

In Colombia, time and again the shortage of shipping came near to creating economic paralysis. In Uruguay, dependent upon imports for all its fuel supplies and unable to obtain any assistance from its neighbor, Argentina, the lack of tankers repeatedly threatened a paralysis of all normal industrial enterprise. In Paraguay, both exports and imports were dependent upon shipping.

In all these cases the agencies of the United States government were able to afford a measure of assistance which made it possible for every crisis to be overcome, and for the normal life of each republic—so far as war conditions made any normal life possible—to continue. Even in Mexico, where natural resources provide the fuel necessary to run the industries and where rail connections with the United States prevented any serious breakdown of exports or imports, one economic difficulty after another cropped up, only to be solved by co-operative measure between the two neighboring countries.

I think it accurate to say that in the conduct of relations between the United States and the other American republics during the war years, our purely political relations have been supplemented in every essential feature by economic and financial measures. One aspect would not have been complete without the other. The assistance we have given to the other American nations has required sacrifices by the people of the United States. But from a purely selfish standpoint, these sacrifices have been more than justified by the fact that, had they not been made, the material breakdown in the political and social structure of the Western Hemisphere would have jeopardized the security of the United States and the successful prosecution of the war effort.

The news of the Japanese attack upon Pearl Harbor swept the peoples of Central and South America like a tornado. Public opinion in the other American republics was even less prepared for the attack than in the United States. The overwhelming reaction after the first period of complete consternation was one of deep anger. The most powerful country of the New World had been drawn into the war. The safety of every American nation was thereby clearly and immediately imperiled; and the high standard of honor and chivalry which the peoples of Latin America have inherited from the Spain and Portugal of the past was utterly outraged by the cowardly nature of the Japanese attack.

Official and popular sentiment was immediately translated into action. The government of Costa Rica at once declared war upon the Axis powers, and was closely followed by the governments of the other Central American republics, by those of the Caribbean, and by

Panama. By the beginning of January, 1942, the governments of Mexico, of Colombia, and of Venezuela had broken diplomatic relations.

Throughout those weeks most of the American republics made more and more evident their desire to utilize the consultative machinery first agreed upon in 1936. The question uppermost in the minds of all the American peoples was whether the newly forged continental solidarity would prove strong enough to resist the strain of the sudden crisis.

Because of the fact that the United States was the nation attacked, it was felt at first in Washington that the initiative for inter-American consultation might more appropriately be taken by some other American power. As time passed, however, it became clear that certain of the larger American states were waiting for the first step to be taken by this country. The request for joint consultation was therefore sent out by the government at Washington to the other American nations at the end of December, 1941. Simultaneously, a like request was dispatched by the government of Chile.

There is an element of humor in the recollection that that calamitous figure, Argentina's Foreign Minister, Dr. Enrique Ruiz Guiñazú, in discussing the request for a consultative meeting with certain South American ambassadors, is alleged to have insisted that, inasmuch as the Japanese attack had been made upon Hawaii rather than upon the American continent itself, no act of aggression had been committed upon the New World and consequently no legitimate reason could be adduced for a consultative meeting. The demand for immediate consultation from every other part of the hemisphere was so insistent and so nearly unanimous that the casuistry of the Argentine government met with no support and it consequently announced its intention of being represented at the meeting by its Foreign Minister.

From many points of view, the capital selected as the seat of the conference, Rio de Janeiro, could not have been more wisely chosen. Those who have taken part in international conferences, particularly conferences of crucial significance, can appreciate the psychological importance of the prevailing atmosphere in the country where the conference is held. Had the Consultative Meeting of 1942 taken

place in a country where public opinion was sharply divided as to
the wisdom of taking overt action against the Axis, or where Axis
influence held any appreciable measure of control over the government, the press, or public opinion in general, the situation would
have proved a formidable obstacle to the realization of the objectives
upon which the majority of the delegates were already determined.
But in Brazil there was never any question as to where the sympathies of the people lay. Public opinion in the United States has exaggerated the influence upon Brazilian foreign policy and sentiment
of the considerable numbers of Italians, Germans, and Japanese who
emigrated there during the past century. The practical truth of this
assertion is found in the fact that the protracted and highly efficient
efforts of Nazi agents and the cruder attempts of Japanese emissaries to bring pressure to bear upon their fellow countrymen of
Brazil proved abortive. Unquestionably, however, the largely un-
assimilated masses of Germans in Brazil sympathized strongly with
the land of their origin and were hysterically antagonistic to the
cause of the United Nations. German espionage systems were omnipresent, and clandestine radio stations were active. But for some
time past the Brazilian government, with the knowledge of the
United States, had maintained close surveillance over these operations, and as a result the German government was disappointed in
its hope that its subversive activities would have any effect on
Brazilian policy. The Brazilian government, the Brazilian armed
services, and the Brazilian people held unswervingly to their own
independent course.

Japanese immigrants in Brazil have always been an extraneous
mass in the Brazilian body politic. The very large Italian element,
on the contrary, has been rapidly assimilated. There was scant evidence in 1942 that Fascism possessed any real attraction for first- or
second-generation Italians in Brazil. Whatever their love for Italy,
they had little love for the Italy of Mussolini. In general, they remained as loyal to the country of their adoption as the Italians in
the United States have proved to be.

No New World nation has throughout its history been a closer
friend to its neighbor of North America than Brazil. Always jealous
of its own independent position and never at any time subject to

United States influence, Brazil, because it is the sole South American
nation of Portuguese rather than Spanish origin, has felt that its
situation with regard to the Spanish-American republics is not
unlike our own. For many reasons and in many ways, Brazilian and
American interests have tended to coincide during the respective his-
tories of the two peoples. Brazilian sentiment for the United States
is a healthy reality.

Most important, however, in determining the success of the
conference was the decisive attitude assumed by the Brazilian government itself. Outstanding in the government, and in all Brazil,
is the figure of Getulio Vargas. President since 1930, and Chief
Executive during a period of many national vicissitudes, President
Vargas had, in 1942, attained a position of complete supremacy.
When he took office, Brazil was a vast country of loosely linked,
almost autonomous states, most of them unconnected by rapid or
convenient communication, governed from the federal capital at
Rio de Janeiro by executive authorities responsive traditionally to
political forces centered in only two or three of the states. In but
few instances, prior to the commencement of Vargas's term of
office, had the national government done anything to benefit the
working classes, develop the country's unlimited natural resources,
or stimulate the industry upon which the future prosperity of the
Brazilian people depends.

In my judgment Getulio Vargas, in the qualities which make for
real statesmanship, should be ranked high among the world leaders
of today. He is taciturn and shrewd. He has an extraordinary
capacity for judging men, and the warmth of his friendship for
those whom he has selected as collaborators in his government does
not blind him to their weaknesses. He has an unerring instinct in
gauging public opinion in his own country. And I believe that this
all-important quality is derived primarily from his wholly sincere
devotion to his fellow citizens and to his never-failing desire that
his administration be remembered chiefly by the benefits which it
has conferred upon the masses of the Brazilian people. No Brazilian
has ever even attempted to maintain that President Vargas or the
members of his family have benefited personally by his occupancy
of the Presidency. A large measure of the unquestioned personal

popularity which he possesses is due to the general recognition of the fact that the Brazilian government under his leadership has worked for the well-being of the Brazilian people and particularly for the improvement of the conditions of the underprivileged.

Constitutional government has, of course, been suspended. So far the length of the tenure of office of President Vargas has not been fixed. President Vargas has, however, publicly assured the Brazilian people that as soon as the war is won they will be given the opportunity freely to return to the enjoyment of constitutional and representative democracy.

After twelve years of power, President Vargas had transformed what might well have proved to be a disintegrating federation into a closely knit, unified nation. Communications of every kind had been rapidly developed; basic and essential industries, whose creation European commercial interests had previously successfully thwarted, had been put in operation; and most important of all, the President had dedicated a large part of the energies of his government to the amelioration of labor conditions. Legislation providing for enlightened minimum-wage standards, old-age and accident insurance, and the construction of modern housing of an advanced type had produced a higher standard of living for Brazilian labor than had ever previously been envisioned.

Some years ago, it became the fashion among a few groups in this country to inveigh against what was termed the Brazilian "dictatorship." Charges have been repeatedly advanced that the Brazilian masses were downtrodden; that they were yearning to throw off the yoke of oppression; and that there was no visible distinction between the philosophy of the Brazilian government and that of the Nazi or Fascist leaders. Nothing could be further from the truth. It is not incumbent upon me as a citizen of another American republic to pass upon the intrinsic merits or demerits of the present Brazilian system of government, but it would be impossible for me to acquiesce in the claim that there is, or has been, the slightest similarity between the Nazi or Fascist concept of government and the governmental philosophy of the present Brazilian regime.

In such an atmosphere and under such circumstances the Third Consultative Meeting of the American Foreign Ministers assembled at Rio de Janeiro on January 15, 1942. No graver, no more menacing situation had ever previously confronted the nations of the New World.

It is necessary at this stage to emphasize the precise circumstances under which the American governments then met. Up to that point, the war in Europe had gone altogether in favor of the Axis powers. Germany and Italy had declared war upon the United States immediately after Pearl Harbor. Furthermore, the satellite countries of Eastern Europe had also proceeded to declare war, which was generally regarded in South America as an indication of the certainty with which they viewed the outcome of the contest. The Franco government of Spain had openly aligned itself with Nazi Germany, an attitude which necessarily had had a considerable effect upon some of the more reactionary elements in certain of the Spanish-American countries. While no details of the attack were known to the general public, it was widely feared that the damage which the Japanese had inflicted upon the American Navy in Pearl Harbor had seriously crippled the fighting strength of the United States fleet for some time to come. Finally, German propaganda in the other American republics had lost no opportunity of proclaiming jubilantly that the United States had been taken completely by surprise. The consternation created within this country by the attack, the propagandists claimed, and the internal dissensions (particularly labor disputes) with which, they alleged, the country was beset, would make it impossible for the United States to get into fighting array for a long period of time. Consequently, they said, her final defeat was a foregone conclusion. Such propaganda was not without its effect, particularly among the armed forces of several of the American republics.

While decisive action had already been taken by the republics of the Caribbean, of Central America, and in northern South America, internal complexities existed in some of the other South American republics which seemed to make any decisive action on their part most unlikely. The sudden death of President Aguirre Cerda of Chile a short time before had made Presidential elections in Chile obligatory. The Chilean government was consequently of a provisional nature and perhaps would not feel able to take the responsibility for a clear-cut policy which might, theoretically at least, involve the nation in war. There was also widespread anxiety in Chile as to the ability of their armed forces, with the resources which they then possessed, to protect the very long Chilean coast line against a possible Japanese attack.

In Bolivia and in Paraguay, both but recently recovered from the long protracted war of the Chaco, much popular opposition existed to any national policy which might again involve their respective peoples in hostilities.

Finally, in Argentina, the resignation and subsequent death of President Ortiz, who sympathized with the cause of the United Nations, had placed the control of the government in the hands of the Vice-President, Dr. Ramón Castillo. Not only were his views wholly different from those of his predecessor, but he permitted his Foreign Minister, Dr. Ruiz Guiñazú, to determine more and more the foreign policy of the nation. The lines followed by the Minister were in great part determined for him by the ultranationalist groups, by the elements in the Argentine Army that were openly pro-Nazi, and by other reactionary influences in the republic.

President Roosevelt appointed me representative of the United States at the conference, and I had the opportunity of flying to Rio de Janeiro with the Foreign Ministers of Mexico and Venezuela and with the delegates of Colombia, Cuba, El Salvador, and Costa Rica.

The objectives which the United States sought to obtain at the conference were quite simple and had been laid down by the President. First, they were to seek to persuade all the other American governments that it was essential to sever diplomatic relations and all commercial and financial intercourse with the Axis nations, in order to end Axis espionage and subversive activities in this hemisphere. Second, to try to find the basis for agreement upon such co-operative steps of a military and naval character as might be necessary for the security of the American republics, as well as upon such measures of collaboration as were required to enable the Americas to withstand the economic strain resulting from war conditions.

The United States did not seek to influence the decision of any American nation as to whether it should or should not declare war.

That was considered a matter solely for the sovereign people of each republic to determine. Furthermore, in conferences which I had had with the responsible authorities of the American Army and Navy before leaving Washington, I had learned that, from the point of view of our own armed services, declarations of war by the other American nations at that particular moment might well place upon the United States Army and Navy greater responsibilities than they were at that stage fully prepared to meet.

In the address to the conference which I delivered at the opening session I stated with complete frankness the position of the government of the United States in these words:

> The greatest assurance that our great association of sovereign and independent peoples—the American family of nations—can survive this world upheaval safely, lies in the unity with which we face the common peril.
>
> Some of us by our own power, by our own resources, by the extent of our population, are able successfully beyond the shadow of a doubt to defend ourselves. Others of us who do not possess these material advantages, equal though they be in their courage and in their determination to resist aggression, must depend for their continued security upon the co-operation which other members of the American family may give them. The only assured safety which this continent possesses lies in full co-operation between us all in the common defense; equal and sovereign partners in times of aggression as in times of peace.

. . . . . . . .

> As each one of you knows, my Government has made no suggestion, and no request, as to the course which any of the governments of the other American Republics should pursue subsequent to the Japanese attack upon the United States and the Declaration of War upon it by the other Axis powers.
>
> We do not function in that way in the American family of nations.
>
> Each one of the American Governments has determined, and will continue to determine, in its own wisdom, the course which it will pursue to the best interest of its people in this world struggle. But of one thing I feel sure we are all convinced. In accordance with the obligations we have all undertaken under the provisions of our

inter-American agreements, and in accordance with the spirit of that continental solidarity unanimously proclaimed, those nations of the Americas which are not engaged in war will never permit their territory to be used by agents of the Axis powers in order that these may conspire against, or prepare attacks upon, those Republics which are fighting for their own liberties and for those of the entire continent.

The shibboleth of classic neutrality in its narrow sense can, in this tragic modern world, no longer be the ideal of any freedom-loving people of the Americas.

There can no longer be any real neutrality as between the Powers of Evil and the forces that are struggling to preserve the rights and the independence of free peoples.

I urge upon you all the imperative need for unity between us, not only in the measures which must presently be taken in the defense of our Western World, but also in order that the American Republics, joined as one, may prove to be the potent factor which they should be of right in the determination of the nature of the world of the future, after the victory is won.

The conduct of the proceedings at the meeting at Rio de Janeiro was rapid and efficient, largely because of the admirable preparations made by the Brazilian government. From the first day to the last I could feel the strength of the spirit animating all but one or two of the delegates. The force which moved them was not only a determination to achieve unity, but a realization that Pan-Americanism had at last become a real, a vital, and a living thing. Above everything else, as was once said publicly by the Brazilian Foreign Minister, Dr. Oswaldo Aranha, Chairman of the Conference, the conference of Rio de Janeiro was a conference of acts and not of words.

Moreover, at no inter-American gathering have the delegates themselves been more able—more outstanding in their competence.*

* The contribution made by the delegates at this conference was such that readers in this country should know the leading figures who participated. Accordingly I have included in an appendix a brief mention of the representatives of the American governments who attended the historic meeting.

Many of them were orators of rare eloquence; almost without exception they were profound students of international affairs. Sincerely devoted to the interests of their own countries, they all nevertheless were animated by a common belief in the importance of inter-American unity, and throughout the conference labored tirelessly to bring about a united front.

The case of the Argentine Foreign Minister, Dr. Enrique Ruiz Guiñazú, presents an exception. His almost incredible lack of comprehension of the salient points in the field of foreign relations, which he had been called upon to conduct on behalf of his government, can best be illustrated by a personal encounter which I had with him during the course of the conference.

Immediately after the adoption of the compromise resolution for the inter-American break of relations with the Axis, when Argentina's course had been so deeply resented by the other American governments, Dr. Ruiz Guiñazú sat down beside me in the office of the Brazilian Minister for Foreign Affairs. Without any further preliminaries, Dr. Ruiz Guiñazú informed me that his government, and particularly his War and Navy Departments, desired him to conclude, while we were both in the Brazilian capital, an arrangement providing for the transfer to the Argentine government, under the Lend-Lease Act, of airplanes, warships, and arms and ammunition. In view of the reiterated statements already made to the Argentine government that, under the terms of the Act, assistance of this character could only be granted when such measures were regarded as contributory to the defense of the United States, I replied that, until the Argentine government had at least taken steps to comply with the terms of the resolution adopted the day before, had broken relations of every character with the Axis, and was actually contributing what it could in defending the Western Hemisphere from Axis attacks, it was useless to enter into any conversation on this subject.

After some indications of pained surprise, Dr. Ruiz Guiñazú then remarked: "I must confess to very great disappointment in listening to this statement from you, since I have always been told that you were an outstanding exponent of the policy that no discrimination should be practiced by the United States in its relations with the other American republics."

The answer to this, of course, was obvious. I said that in my belief it was only Argentina herself who was responsible for the discrimination against which he complained. The Argentine government had not only refused to join the other American republics in forceful measures to safeguard the New World, but had even refused to permit the Argentine Navy to patrol the waters of the South Atlantic so that the other American nations might maintain safe communications with his own nation. So long as Argentina refused to lift a finger in the common defense of the Americas, she alone was responsible for the position in which she found herself.

I am convinced today that these self-evident truths were wholly incomprehensible to the Argentine Foreign Minister.

If one can presume to attempt to define the mental processes by which Dr. Ruiz Guiñazú was guided when he reached Rio de Janeiro, one might venture to set them down as follows: he had a strong prejudice against the United States and a barely concealed belief that the civilization of this country was so decadent and inefficient, because of its democratic institutions, that it would not conceivably be able to stand up against the power and might of the Axis nations.

While strongly deprecating the attitude taken by the Nazi regime toward the Catholics of Germany, and deploring the brutality displayed by the German government toward Catholic Poland, he nevertheless believed that only through the triumph of the authoritarian regimes, primarily of Italy and secondarily of Germany and Japan, could authority, discipline, and order be maintained and those conservative doctrines to which he so firmly adhered be preserved.

Like not a few other Argentine statesmen, he was obsessed with the belief that it was beneath the dignity of the Argentine Republic ever to follow the course upon which the United States had embarked.

He considered Madrid the center of the civilized world: the Hispanic tradition to him was the ultimate, from the moral and cultural as well as the political point of view. The fact that the Spain of General Franco had proclaimed its sympathy with the Axis cause was to him an added proof of the validity of his own judgment.

Finally, and by no means least, he was to a large extent dominated

by a group of very young men (among them his own son), representative of the retrograde ultranationalism which had recently been
shaping in the Argentine Republic. Denouncing democracy as a
failure, they were proclaiming that a purely nationalistic authoritarian regime was the only form of government that could save
Argentina. These elements, with the zeal of fanatics, were clamoring for a return to the days of the Argentine dictator Rosas. They
regarded Hitler, Mussolini, and Franco as inspired exponents of
their own beliefs.

I had previously known Dr. Ruiz Guiñazú during a brief official
visit which he made in Washington the preceding year, before assuming the duties of Foreign Minister. When I called upon him at Rio
de Janeiro it was soon evident that he had no realization of the
dangers which menaced the independence and integrity of the countries of the New World, and even less understanding of the determination of the majority of the other American republics to do
everything within their power to eliminate these dangers within the
Western Hemisphere. He gave me the strong impression of believing
precisely what he wished to believe and no more.

Assuming that the prestige and influence of his own country
among the other American nations was still what it had been during
those years when the destinies of the Argentine nation were guided
by such towering figures as former Foreign Ministers Estanislaos
Zeballos, José Luis Murature, Ernesto Bosch, Honorio Pueyrredón,
Carlos Saavedra Lamas and Julio Roca, Dr. Ruiz Guiñazú had
arranged, before the conference, to confer in Buenos Aires with the
Foreign Ministers of Bolivia, Paraguay, Uruguay, and Chile. He had
hoped to create a bloc which would unitedly oppose the objectives of
the United States, whose policy had already been made known confidentially, but with complete frankness, to the other governments. In
that expectation, however, he was doomed to disappointment. Dr.
Guani, the Foreign Minister of Uruguay, had refused even to discuss
any variation in the policy already determined upon by his own government, which was to break relations immediately. The Foreign
Ministers of both Paraguay and Bolivia had stoutly refused to make
any commitment. Only in the case of Chile had Dr. Ruiz Guiñazú
found any comfort.

In the many conversations which I held in the first days of the conference with the Brazilian Foreign Minister and with the representatives of the republics which had already either declared war or broken relations, we agreed that, while the practical steps necessary to ensure the safety of the hemisphere must by all means be taken, every effort should likewise be made to prevent any break in the unity of inter-American relations. We were convinced that no greater encouragement could be afforded the Axis governments than for them to learn that united action had proved impossible and that the Americas would be divided against themselves. We furthermore agreed that the main issue of the conference—the breaking of all relations between the Americas and the Axis powers—should be discussed first of all and that all other questions should be regarded as subsidiary.

A resolution that the American republics—because of the act of aggression committed against one of them by Japan and the subsequent declaration of war upon that republic by Germany and Italy—should unanimously sever all relations with the Axis powers, was introduced jointly by the delegates of Colombia, Mexico, and Venezuela. Because they had already, spontaneously, taken the action proposed, they were, of course, the most appropriate governments to introduce such a resolution. In order to obtain unanimous action, the delegates of the governments which had as yet taken no action were at once consulted as to the attitude they would adopt with regard to the proposed resolution.

By this time the Argentine Foreign Minister had had full opportunity to learn the views of his colleagues. As a result of word sent directly by the President of Peru to his brother, the Peruvian Ambassador in Rio de Janeiro, he had learned that the Peruvian government stood firmly for the resolution. He had found out, too, that the government of Ecuador was favorably disposed, although it wanted an agreement providing for a satisfactory settlement of the boundary dispute with Peru before taking any action; that, while the governments of Bolivia and Paraguay had not as yet finally determined upon their policy, sentiment on the part of their delegations was overwhelmingly in sympathy with the objectives sought; and that consequently, since Dr. Guani had already publicly announced that Uruguay was in favor of the resolution, the Chilean government was the only government which might oppose it.

At this juncture the Brazilian Foreign Minister, after repeated conferences with both the Argentine and Chilean Foreign Ministers, informed me that in his opinion both delegations would be disposed to sign the resolution as proposed. Three days after the opening of the conference, at a meeting in the beautiful Itamaraty Palace, attended by all the chiefs of delegations, the Argentine Foreign Minister stated that he would, in the name of his government, approve the resolution in its original form, and the Minister for Foreign Affairs of Chile stated that he would recommend its adoption to his own government. It seemed that evening that the resolution would receive the official approval of the conference on the following day.

On the following morning, however, I was advised that the President of Argentina had sent instructions to Dr. Ruiz Guiñazú disavowing the approval given by his Minister to the resolution on the preceding afternoon.

At an urgent meeting which Dr. Aranha immediately summoned in his office, Dr. Ruiz Guiñazú attempted to persuade the other delegations to agree to a substitute resolution which not only would have wholly circumvented the purposes sought, but which likewise would have stultified the entire proceedings. For hours a number of us worked over an alternative draft which would achieve our purposes and at the same time prevent a breakdown of continental unity which, in the minds of all of us, would have had the gravest consequences. Finally the Argentine and Chilean governments agreed to the new draft.

The compromise draft finally adopted read, in its essential paragraphs:

> The American Republics reaffirm their complete solidarity and their determination to co-operate jointly for their mutual protection until the effects of the present aggression against the continent have disappeared.
> The American Republics, in accordance with the procedures established by their own laws and in conformity with the position and circumstances obtaining in each country in the existing continental

conflict, recommend the breaking of their diplomatic relations with Japan, Germany and Italy, since the first-mentioned state attacked, and the other two declared war on, an American country.

In our judgment, while the wording of the original resolution was preferable because it was more decisive and clear-cut, the purport of the substitute was the same. Any American government subscribing officially to the second draft would not only be recommending the severance of diplomatic relations with the Axis to the other American states but would be officially recommending such action to itself. It seemed to us inconceivable, therefore, that any sovereign American government which officially recommended a step of this grave character could do other than sever all relations with the Axis, as soon as its own constitutional procedure made it possible.

It seemed reasonable to allow the Chilean government, in view of its provisional character, to await the election of the new President and the establishment of a permanent Cabinet before undertaking the decisive step.

Resentment against the attitude adopted by the Argentine government was keen not only in the United States but in many other parts of the Western Hemisphere. There was a strong demand that the nineteen republics disposed to sign the resolution in its original form do so, leaving both Argentina and Chile to pursue a separate course. Some of the delegates of the republics which had already declared war were, momentarily at least, inclined to such action. Yet it has always seemed to me, as it did to my associates who participated in drafting the second resolution, that such a course would be inexpedient from the long-range point of view, and highly unwise from the practical and immediate standpoint.

The future of the inter-American system depends upon unity. If any two republics were to be read out of the American family of nations in a matter of basic policy, their governments would certainly put forth every effort to strengthen their own position. As a result there would be a constant playing for position between one group and the other—a kind of inter-American political jockeying— which would develop to the disadvantage of everybody. No concerted inter-American policy could possibly prosper under such conditions. The strength of the New World will come only from united action. Without it no inter-American system can survive.

Another disquieting possibility, if Argentina had felt that she was being flagrantly ostracized, was that powerful forces in the Argentine Army, incited by Nazi officers of high rank resident in that republic, might deliberately create an acute and ugly situation on the Brazilian and Uruguayan frontiers. It was extremely doubtful whether, under such conditions, the Brazilian government would have felt it possible to break relations with the Axis. It is hardly necessary to add that, had the Brazilian government felt it impossible to take such action, the policies of other republics bordering upon Brazil might have been modified accordingly.

It would be premature for me to write as yet of all the currents and crosscurrents affecting this resolution of the conference. I can merely state that I am today more than ever confident that the action taken was wise in the light of the conditions then existing; that the determined effort to maintain unity among the American nations was necessary not only in order to preserve a true Pan-American front, but also in order to safeguard the security and safety of the Western Hemisphere in its gravest hour.

Notwithstanding the defeatist opinion in certain quarters in Washington that the resolution was so weak that none of the republics that had as yet taken no action in opposition to the Axis powers would carry out its recommendations, the government of Peru announced immediately after the resolution was signed that it had broken relations with the Axis. The government of Uruguay took action almost simultaneously; the government of Bolivia followed suit the next day; the government of Paraguay a day later, and at the exceedingly dramatic session which closed the conference, in one of the most impressive addresses I have ever heard, Dr. Aranha announced to the delegates and to the world at large that Brazil had broken relations with Germany, Italy, and Japan. Like action was taken immediately thereafter by the government of Ecuador.

Today, all the American republics have severed relations with the Axis powers. That would never have occurred if unity had not been preserved at Rio de Janeiro.

Among the other significant decisions reached by the conference

—and there were many—were the resolutions providing for the severance of all commercial and financial relations between the American republics and the Axis nations; the creation of an inter-American committee to remain in session at Montevideo throughout the war in order to recommend joint measures for the control of subversive activities within the New World; a resolution providing for consultation between the American governments concerning postwar problems, and a resolution providing for common adherence to the principles of the Atlantic Charter.

Inter-American conferences prior to the meeting of Rio de Janeiro had all in a certain sense been preparatory. The Consultative Meeting at the Brazilian capital demonstrated in practical form the first fruition of the seeds which had been sown earlier, and encouraged to grow by the principles of the good neighbor policy. The conference at Rio de Janeiro brought to life a real unity between twenty-one sovereign nations confronted by a common danger. It established the effective means by which they could co-operate for their mutual protection in the face of that danger.

In any study of Argentine policy at and since the Rio de Janeiro conference, it is only fair to recollect that fate has not been kind to the Argentine people in these later years. Incapacitating illness, soon to prove fatal, removed Dr. Roberto Ortiz from the Presidency just at the moment when the world crisis arose. His influence, if he had continued as President, would probably have succeeded in aligning the Argentine Republic with the other American nations in open opposition to the forces of aggression in Europe and Asia. Moreover, three of the most powerful leaders of Argentine public opinion, former Presidents Alvear and Justo and former Vice-President Roca, all opposed to Argentine neutrality, died almost at the same time. The censorship imposed over all sources of information by the Castillo government and by the military junta which overthrew the Castillo government in June 1943, headed first by General Ramírez, and later by General Farrell, has deprived Argentine public opinion of accurate knowledge of world affairs. The Argentine people lack particularly accurate knowledge of the reaction of the other American republics to the line of policy which Argentina has recently pursued.

During the past six months relations between Argentina and the United States have deteriorated to such a state of open tension as had not existed for more than a generation. Sadly enough, this development has resulted in a major rupture of inter-American unity at a moment when the need for hemispheric co-operation and comprehension was never more necessary.

The situation is due primarily to the effort of the Department of State to use the act of recognition as a diplomatic weapon, and as a means of exerting pressure in order to shape political developments in Argentina. The policy pursued by the Department of State has been not only unwise and inexpedient. It has been catastrophic in its effect upon Argentine public opinion, and has created in other American republics open sympathy for a reactionary and dictatorial regime which had hitherto been regarded with aversion. It has strengthened the ultranationalist elements throughout the nations in the southern part of the hemisphere.

The Ramírez dictatorship had broken relations with the Axis. It had also, however, connived in the revolution which broke out in Bolivia at the end of 1943. This notorious intervention in the domestic affairs of Bolivia, counter to the treaty obligations of all the American governments, had resulted in the decision of the other American republics to withhold recognition from the new government of Bolivia at least until it had purged itself of this defect in its composition.

The Ramírez government was soon afterwards overthrown by a movement within the Argentine Army, and General Ramírez was replaced as the Chief of State by General Farrell. It was then that the United States government refused to recognize the new Argentine regime. The reasons advanced in Washington for this step were that the Argentine authorities had not yet taken satisfactory measures to check Axis activities. The situation complained of was, of course, due to the defective administration of the preceding Ramírez government, which this government had recognized. It was obvious throughout South America that the decision at Washington was really the result of the State Department's belief that if it withheld recognition, the Farrell regime would be ousted and a more satisfactory government installed in its place. No one with any knowledge of Spanish-American psychology, and particularly of Argentine psychology, could have favored such a course. There can only ensue one of two possible results. Either the Farrell government will be overthrown, in which event even the most democratic elements in Argentina, and those most opposed to that obnoxious dictatorship, will be greatly embittered against the United States for thus flagrantly interfering in their internal affairs; or else the reaction of all elements in Argentina against an attempt at coercion on the part of the United States will be so strong that the Farrell dictatorship will be strengthened. In either event the hostility against this country which our recent policy has created throughout Argentina will persist for years to come.

The Department of State has endeavored to oblige all of the other American governments to follow our lead. The governments of Chile, Paraguay and Bolivia have refused to do so. The governments of Brazil and of Peru, and particularly of Uruguay, have been gravely embarrassed. It is their desire to stand foursquare with the United States, but in this case they have felt not only that our policy was in the highest degree unwise, but also that it took no account of their own political and economic difficulties. How long, for example, could Uruguay be fairly expected to withhold recognition from the Argentine government, when the bulk of her commercial and financial ties are with that neighboring country, and all of her tourist trade comes from Buenos Aires?

The result is, therefore, that by this grave error the Department of State has broken the unity of the hemisphere, maintained against all obstacles for more than ten years. It should be proof that the act of recognition should never again be employed in inter-American relations for political purposes, and never again be exercised as a means of coercion. Had the American governments agreed to adopt the Estrada Doctrine of recognition in their hemispheric relations the present situation could not have developed.

Up to now the influence of the Spanish Falange and the subversive activities indulged in by various agents of the Franco government in Spain have been of no real danger to the Americas. They have only occasionally assumed some significance among the most reactionary political, clerical, and professional elements in a few republics. But if the present rupture of the unity of the Americas continues, if an Argentine dictatorship is stimulated into combating every policy of the United States, and if this country can be truthfully and fairly charged with reverting to the domineering and coercive policies of the old days, the influence of Falangist emissaries and of all other anti-American elements in the New World will be enormously and immediately strengthened.

Of course, no one can ignore the fact that the traditional trend of Argentine foreign policy has always been strongly in favor of close political ties with Great Britain and with other European powers rather than toward any full and genuine participation in a purely inter-American system. This has been partly owing to the valid consideration that, because of United States commercial policy during past generations, Argentina's commercial and financial ties with Great Britain and other European nations have been far more important in her national economy than her ties with the United States.

Much has been written and probably more has been said, both in Argentina and in the United States, about the restrictions imposed by this government upon Argentine meat imports. The policy of the United States in this regard has been by no means as black as it has been painted in Argentina. The truth of the matter is that the hoof-and-mouth disease has for generations been endemic on Argentine cattle ranges. According to the best scientific advice available to our own government, no safe means has yet been found whereby chilled or frozen beef can be imported into the United States without the risk of contagion to our own herds. And in the United States, as in any other uncontaminated regions, the disease that is endemic in Argentina becomes virulently epidemic when it breaks out in the country to which it is brought. Under such conditions the sanitary embargoes imposed until now by the United States government are wholly justified.

On the other hand, it cannot be contended that other restrictive measures imposed by the United States possess equal justification. The hoof-and-mouth disease cannot be introduced through canned beef. Nevertheless, the tariffs now imposed upon canned beef and the quota restrictions limit our imports of this commodity to a very small amount. Other restrictions upon certain other types of Argentine agricultural products, of which we consume more than we produce, lack any equitable economic basis.

The chief difficulty lies, of course, in the fact that the United States and Argentina are both competitors in world markets for agricultural exports and, until that form of normal and healthy triangular trade which existed prior to the first World War is re-established, commercial relations between the Argentine Republic and this country must be given every form of official encouragement possible. The United States would, therefore, be well-advised to remove all remaining restrictions upon imports not obligatory for reasons of quarantine, and the Argentine authorities would be equally well-advised either to encourage the discovery of some safe means by which the danger of contagion can be eliminated from their frozen or chilled beef exports, or to stamp out the hoof-and-mouth disease on their own ranges.

Recent Argentine governments appear not to have realized that there is nothing intrinsically incompatible in the existence of an American nation, such as Argentina, as a world power, and its full and genuine participation in an effective inter-American system. Since the resignation and death of President Ortiz, Argentine policy has become more and more provincial and more and more blindly nationalistic. It is a far cry from the enlightened and far-sighted policies pursued in the proud tradition of Argentina during the earlier decades of the century.

The people in this country who have so vehemently urged this government to adopt a policy of coercion, or at least of retaliation, toward Argentina are advocating a course which will have completely opposite results from those they seek. Not only do the basic principles of existing inter-American agreements and the good neighbor policy itself preclude an attempt on the part of any American nation to dictate the policy of another, but also any such attempt will provoke a reaction upon the part of the Argentine people which may well create a permanent rupture. Such measures could do incalculable damage to the interests of the Western Hemisphere during the uncertain years which lie ahead. If we believe in the efficacy of democratic principles and in the ultimate power of public opinion, then we must permit the Argentine people to determine their own destinies for themselves. I know that the passion for individual freedom on the part of the average Argentine citizen is at least as strong as that of any other American. The present dictatorship which has imposed itself upon the Argentine people is pursuing the fatal fallacy which Mussolini conceived and which the Italian people made their own in the years immediately after the first World War, but experience will soon show that authoritarian regimes of that nature cannot survive in the modern world. They can survive least of all in this New World.

The inter-American system, as it has now developed in the Americas, has its roots in the common recognition of the sovereign equality of all the American states, and in their joint belief that they find individual advantage in co-operation. The good neighbor policy has made it possible for this regional system to be developed. Continued participation by the United States in this system should become the permanent cornerstone of American foreign policy. Hemispheric unity, and the security and welfare of the United States itself depend on it. It should, therefore, be always above the play of internal politics within the United States.

I believe that the regional system of the Americas must be an indispensable part of any international organization which may be established after the war. The ideals of the Western Hemisphere, our liberties, and our democratic institutions can all play a vitally important part in that new World Order. The resources of the Americas are unlimited. They can be developed to the benefit of each nation, with a resulting increase in living standards, if all the Americas share in the enterprise.

To accomplish this, many practices and theories of the past must be thrown aside. United States capital must no longer be invested in other American republics in such a way as to create an empire within another sovereign state. Healthy nationalism would in no event permit such conditions to continue. The only practicable plan is for capital from this country always to be associated with capital obtained in the country where it is invested. That kind of partnership will eliminate the political and economic evils resulting from foreign control of the national resources or public utilities of a country, and will enable the peoples of countries where industries are being developed or natural resources exploited to derive their full and just share of the benefits.

I foresee that, in spite of the problem now presented by the Argentine situation, the peoples of the American nations will draw progressively closer together during the years to come. The expansion of civil aviation, of maritime communication, and the speedy conclusion of the Pan-American Highway not only will bring about a far greater physical familiarity, but will necessarily stimulate a far greater measure of cultural interchange.

If this closer association is to take place without friction and misunderstanding, the new inter-American regional system, both political and economic, must be encouraged to develop upon those foundations of equality, tolerance, and respect laid down during the past ten years.

CHAPTER VI

# The Area of Discord:
## Eastern Europe and the Near East

IN ANY consideration of the problems which are developing in the Near East, in the Eastern Mediterranean, and in Eastern Europe, the future role of the republic of Turkey is a logical starting point.

It is hard to realize that this new dynamic Turkey is the same power which, throughout the past century, was considered a decadent nation and was commonly referred to as the "sick man of Europe." It is equally difficult today to appreciate the profound influence which the question of Turkey has had in shaping the history of Europe during the hundred-year period which terminated in 1914. It was the warp in the fabric of British foreign policy throughout the Victorian era. It provided the dramatic climax to the long career of England's most vivid Prime Minister, Lord Beaconsfield. It was the question of Turkey that, troubling the restless conscience of Mr. Gladstone, brought him forth in his old age from his political retreat to another decade of political leadership. For, as James Bryce has said:

Nothing lay nearer to his heart than the protection of the Christians of the East. His sense of personal duty to them was partly due to the feeling that the Crimean War had prolonged the rule of the Turk and had thus imposed a special responsibility on Britain, and on the members of Lord Aberdeen's Cabinet which drifted into that war.

Nor can the younger generation of today readily conceive of the horror with which Turkey was regarded by a great portion of the civilized world, a horror due in no small part to the anathema hurled against her by the great British Liberal leader. I can well remember as a child looking with trepidation at the flaming cartoons prevalent in the nineties after the Bulgarian and Armenian massacres.

The importance of Turkey in its period of apparent senility lay, of course, in the fact that Russia wanted to control the Dardanelles and thus become a Mediterranean power. The British government consistently and the French government occasionally shaped their policies so as to block any such development. Russian supremacy in the Eastern Mediterranean would have threatened Great Britain's communications with her Eastern possessions as well as her position in Egypt, acquired in the closing decades of the nineteenth century. Russian preponderance in Turkey would have checked the expansion of France's traditional interests in Asia Minor. For these reasons, and because the imperial government of Turkey, in its latter stages, was corrupt and inefficient, she was subjected to increasing pressure by the European nations as they jockeyed for influence. And the overpowering desire of the great powers of Europe to share in the legacies of the supposedly "sick man" would unquestionably have brought about his demise had the would-be heirs been able to agree upon the portion each should inherit.

When William II of Germany came to the throne, he and his successive Chancellors regarded Turkey as the most important link in the chain of Germany's flamboyant "Drang nach Osten" policy. German domination of Turkey was essential if the dream of the Berlin-Baghdad railroad was to be realized and if Germany was ever to expand to the Persian Gulf.

German diplomatic policy in the post-Bismarck period has often —and I think accurately—been termed shortsighted, badly implemented, and consequently ineffective. Yet I think it must be generally admitted that German policy with regard to Turkey during the early years of the twentieth century was singularly successful. Not only were the German Ambassadors to Constantinople usually well-fitted for their complex task, but German political, commercial, and financial dealings with Turkey were most efficiently coordinated. In any event, if the quality of diplomacy can most readily be gauged by the success which it achieves, German policy toward Turkey in the years immediately prior to 1914 was far more successful than that of the other European powers.

From 1841 to 1914 the status of the Dardanelles required that the Turkish government, so long as it remained at peace, prevent the admission of any foreign naval vessels into the Straits. The violation of this status had been largely responsible for the Crimean War, as well as for subsequent serious crises in European power politics.

In the early period of the first World War the French and British governments were confronted with the possible defection of Imperial Russia. In view of the extreme gravity of their own military situation, they were compelled to enter into a secret agreement with her providing that, upon the defeat of Germany and Austria, Russia would be permitted to annex the European coast of the Bosporus, the Straits, and the Turkish capital. With the Russian revolution of 1917, and the pronouncement of the new Soviet slogan of "No annexations and no indemnities," these secret commitments were not only made public but were officially denounced at Moscow.

The effect upon Turkish public opinion was immediate and far-reaching. The Turkish people developed not only a warm sympathy for the new Russian regime, which later crystallized in the Russian-Turkish Alliance of 1921, but also a deep-rooted and—it cannot be denied—well-founded suspicion of the Western European powers. This suspicion persisted for many years after the war. Moscow's publication of the treaty likewise spurred into active life that acute phase of ultranationalism which swept Turkey after 1918.

It should be emphasized that the Turkish revival, brought about in great part by the genius of Kemal Pasha Ataturk, was purely nationalistic and in no sense Pan-Islamic. Its basic result was to divorce the Turkish people from their thousand-year-old traditions of the Mohammedan caliphate and Pan-Islamic doctrines. The rulers of the New Turkey were determined to lead their countrymen along the road from the East to the West. In the details, such as the abolition of the fez and the veil, as well as in the major aspects, such as the creation of at least the form of republican and representative government, Ataturk forced his people to turn their backs upon the East.

No reference to the new Turkey can be made without paying tribute to that strange genius who created it, whose towering figure is already rapidly becoming enveloped in the mists of rumor and folk tradition. An Albanian Turk by birth, educated from early youth under military discipline, persecuted by Abdul-Hamid, Ataturk was closely associated during the first World War with the German General, Liman von Sanders, but became later as prejudiced against Germany as he already was against the British and the French. Most important of all, he knew how to seize the opportunity to strike at the psychological moment for the freedom and integrity of what was left of his country. He struck with entire success at the very moment that the Peace Treaty of Versailles was about to be concluded.

Had he not acted when he did, and had he not dared to confront what would have seemed to any observer the crushing superiority of the victorious Allied powers, Turkey could never have achieved the untrammeled independence which is hers today. For in 1919, with the approval of the British and French governments, Greek forces had already taken possession of Smyrna, while Italy, as an inducement to forego the full control in the Adriatic which had been assured her by the secret treaty of London, had been permitted to occupy Adalia and other parts of western Turkey.

The moves and countermoves of Kemal Pasha against the authority of the League of Nations and of the great powers during the four years that succeeded the signing of the Treaty of Versailles and the Treaty of Sèvres make one of the most enthralling and intricate stories of European power politics in recent times. His task was made easier by the fact that Great Britain and France fell out over their conflicting interests in the Near East. In this crisis, France showed a greater measure of realism than Great Britain. The new Turkish government, greatly strengthened by its alliance with the Soviet Union, had no fear for its eastern frontiers and was able to concentrate its military forces in western Turkey. It had also received considerable quantities of arms and ammunition from its new Russian ally. Most important of all, Turkey was fully aware that Great Britain, forced by domestic pressure to demobilize, was in no position to embark upon any further military involvements. France, left to bear alone the military burden of confronting the German threat, was neither able nor disposed to undertake any new adventures in the Near East.

In fact, the French government went so far in its overtures to Turkey as to conclude a separate treaty with her in the latter part of 1921. The treaty not only violated French pledges to Great Britain, since it provided for a separate rather than a common peace with Turkey, but it likewise violated the Covenant of the League of Nations itself, for France ceded to Turkey a considerable region of Syria, over which France possessed only the rights of a mandatory.

By 1922 the Italians had long since departed bag and baggage from western Turkey. In October of that year the Turkish armies destroyed the last remaining Greek forces in Anatolia. Ataturk had gained a remarkable triumph.

The end of the chapter was written at Lausanne in July of 1923, with the conclusion of a new treaty of peace between the Turkish Republic and the Allied powers, through which Ataturk's Foreign Minister, Ismet Inonu, today President of the Turkish Republic, obtained Allied recognition for the majority of Ataturk's aims. The Treaty of Lausanne re-established Turkey's jurisdiction over Constantinople and the Straits, and laid firm foundations for the future growth of the new republic. It thus was possible for Turkey to emerge as the vital force it has now become in Southeastern Europe and in the Eastern Mediterranean.

The status of the Dardanelles, as then established, permitted the free passage of merchant vessels at all times as well as the free passage of ships of war, provided only that no force larger than that maintained within the Black Sea by Russia or Turkey be sent there from the Mediterranean. In any war in which Turkey remained neutral this restriction would not be applicable to the ships of belligerent nations. Likewise it was determined that the Straits were to be demilitarized, and an International Straits Commission was agreed upon as a general agency of supervision.

Thirteen years later at a Straits Conference held at Montreux, at a moment when the clouds of the second World War were already high on the horizon, Turkey demanded and obtained sole control of the Straits with authority to refortify them. The special interest of the Soviet Union was solved by the common agreement that Russia would henceforth be able without restriction to send warships into the Mediterranean.

The United States has had a greater influence on the rapid modernization of Turkey than is generally realized in this country. For a long time past the activities of American missions have met with singular success, partly because American missionaries were welcomed at a time when Turkish officials were inherently suspicious of the ulterior aims of the nationals of any European power, and partly because the great institutions of learning established in Turkey by American donations have been directed by men of devotion, tact, and high ability. They have been sources of Western liberal culture where many thousands of young Turks now active in public life have found the inspiration they sought. For this reason, and because the United States is the one nation among the great powers of which Turkey has never had any reason to be suspicious, the relations between the two countries have a solid character that should be utilized to common advantage.

The fact assumed greater significance after the outbreak of the war in Europe. By 1940, the Turkish position had become highly insecure. Turkish-Soviet relations had cooled to the point of frigidity during the months prior to the German occupation of Western Europe. The mission of Saracoglu to Moscow for the purpose of clarifying the atmosphere had proved unfruitful. German and British competition, in which the United States later joined the British, for the exclusive right to purchase vitally needed strategic materials, such as chrome, had created an increasingly difficult position for the Turkish government. The tactics of German Ambassador von Papen—tactics which have made him notorious in every part of the world where he has engaged in them—had upon occasion created crises—such as that provoked by the mysterious attempt at his assassination by alleged Communist agents—which had brought Turkey to the point of a rupture with several of the European belligerents.

It is perhaps not surprising that during those days of 1940 to 1942, when the prospects seemed very grim indeed for Turkey, her emissaries in Washington and in other capitals of the United Nations should have indulged, presumably by direction from Ankara, in urgent and almost pathetic enquiries as to whether some basis for a compromise peace was not possible. They insisted that in the view of the Turkish government a stalemate could be the only outcome of the second World War; and that the continuation of the war would plunge the belligerents and the few remaining neutral powers into complete social and economic chaos.

At the outset of the present war Turkey had decided that her security lay in her ability to maintain a neutral position. After protracted negotiations in order to assure herself that, in the event of a German attack, she would have at least some support from the Western powers, she signed a mutual assistance treaty with Great Britain in 1939, and almost simultaneously a nonaggression agreement with the Soviet Union. In 1940, to balance these agreements, at a time when the chances of war appeared definitely to favor the Axis cause, Turkey signed a treaty of friendship with Germany and entered into subsidiary arrangements to exchange strategic materials produced in Turkey for munitions to be provided from the armament factories of German-held territory.

The incentive for this latter agreement was increased by the fact that the British, even after the United States had entered the war and lend-lease material began to be available, were unable to provide the armaments and airplanes which Turkey had expected as a result of her 1939 treaty with Great Britain. There was still another factor in the situation. During that period the United Nations were hard-pressed in the Eastern Mediterranean, and things looked threatening throughout the Near East. From a strategic point of view, the United Nations did not consider it at all desirable that Turkey should enter the war, and thus expose herself to a German march through the regions of western Turkey, a possibility appearing more than likely at the time in view of the inferiority of Turkey's military defenses and the inability of the Allies to afford any material protection. This point of view was officially stated upon several occasions by British spokesmen in Parliament.

The policy of the Soviet Union was far more forthright. The Soviet government, in fact, was anxious for Turkish participation as a means of ensuring a threat to the flank of the German forces engaged on the Black Sea littoral.

The desire of the Turkish government for peace and neutrality, however, proved to be preponderant. After the conference at Tehran in November, 1943, and the subsequent meetings between the President of Turkey and Chiefs of the Western powers, the latter commenced vigorously to urge that Turkey now undertake actively to assist in the campaign against Germany. But Turkey's neutral position has so far been maintained, modified only by her recent decision to ban the export of chrome to the Axis.

Turkey has, however, given definite indications that she intends to have a voice in the postwar adjustment of those issues regarded by her as vital in the future, such as the Bulgar frontiers and the balance of influence in the Balkans. Consequently, since Turkey occupies the dominating position at the eastern head of the Mediterranean and her government represents the will of a virile people, whatever part she may play in shaping the postwar arrangements for the Balkan Peninsula and the Danube Basin will prove of prime importance.

Any study of the forces determining the destinies of the peoples in the blood-drenched lands of Eastern Europe can at best be but superficial in this brief survey. They are so intricate, so inextricably bound up with religious, racial, and economic causes, and with traditional antagonisms that generalizations are liable to be misleading. Yet for well over a century the storms which have swept Europe have usually been signaled by clouds that have first arisen over the peoples of Southeastern Europe.

Even in the most modern times the Balkan nations, and the Succession States which came into being after the first World War, have been made the arena for the so-called power politics of the great powers of Europe. Religious and racial hatreds, grinding poverty, a high percentage of illiteracy, the lack of any prospect of a better future, and, above all else perhaps, the passionate striving for liberty, are all partly responsible for the proverbially chaotic conditions in Eastern European nations. But if there is to be any hope of an ordered and peaceful Europe in the future, some solution of these age-old problems has to be found. Upon that depends not only peace between Western and Eastern Europe, but peace in the Near East as well.

The salient factors in the situation in the Balkans before the outbreak of the second World War may be summarized as follows:

In 1919 Rumania had suddenly become transformed from a small nation of several million people to a country containing almost eighteen million inhabitants. Prior to that time, the Rumanian people had depended very largely upon agriculture for their livelihood. Now, the rapid development of Rumania's Black Sea oil fields provided not only a material addition to Rumanian national income but also stimulated industrial development on a considerable scale. To the original territory of Rumania had been added Transylvania, the Bukowina, the Banat, and Bessarabia. To the problems of racial and religious diversity were added far greater and more serious problems. There was, for instance, the effort to control the unyielding and unassimilable Hungarian population incorporated within the new Rumania, and the religious controversies arising from the consistent attempt of the Orthodox Church and Rumanian officials to whittle away what the new religious minorities considered their inherent right to religious autonomy.

All farsighted Rumanians realized that a day of reckoning inevitably lay ahead. Rumanian governments invariably demonstrated a marked sense of uneasiness about Bessarabia, for example. For generations Bessarabia had been under the sovereignty of Russia, and at the Peace Conference it had been torn from her without the formality of a "by your leave" to the Russian people.

I recall that from the earliest days after 1920 it was almost impossible to talk to any official of the Rumanian government without finding oneself involved in a discussion of what was alleged to be the clear right of Rumania to possess the territories of Bessarabia and the historic justifications for Rumanian sovereignty. The amount of Rumanian governmental funds expended on the publication of books upholding this contention must have been considerable, judging from the liberality of their distribution. Without question the supreme arbiters in Paris in 1919 were convinced that the people of Bessarabia desired to be incorporated into Rumania. But it has seemed for many years very questionable whether the chance they were afforded to make their wishes known was in any sense sufficient to offer any real opportunity for self-determination.

Given these peculiarly intricate and frequently embarrassing problems, only a highly efficient government, controlled by patriots of vision and self-abnegation and imbued with a large stock of common sense, could have brought the new Rumania successfully through the stormy past quarter of a century. But Rumania was notoriously unfortunate in that respect.

Patriots of high caliber have not been wanting. Maniu, the leader of the Peasant party, is a good example. Unhappily, they have rarely been in a position where they could exercise authority. Government has succeeded government. The majority of them have suffered the additional handicap of having been condemned to govern in the lurid light shed by the singular escapades of the members of the royal family. The conditions of the Rumanian people themselves and the stability of their governmental institutions have constantly deteriorated. Corruption in Bucharest has been more apparent than in any other European capital.

Popular government has never in reality existed, and there has been no real foundation for the establishment of popular authority. The government has all been superstructure—and superstructure of the shoddiest variety. That is why, in the late thirties, we saw the final collapse of national authority into such grotesque forms as the Goga and Antonescu governments; such Nazi-inspired aberrations as Codreanu and the Iron Guard; and the hysterical resort, through Hitler's influence, to such hideous atrocities as those committed upon the Jewish people.

As a contrast, the story of Yugoslavia, brought into being by the Treaty of Versailles, has been far more admirable. The internal problems, however, have been even more difficult to solve than those confronting the government of Rumania in 1920. The peoples of Yugoslavia—Serbs, Croats, and Slovenes—have always proved themselves far more passionately devoted to the cause of their individual liberty than the Rumanians. For this very reason, the problems within Yugoslavia have given rise to unusually bitter rivalries and deep-rooted antagonisms. The Serbian people themselves belong for the most part to the Orthodox Church, whereas most of the Croats and Slovenes are members of the Roman Catholic Church. Yugoslavia also has a considerable number of Moslems. Throughout the existence of Yugoslavia as a new state, the Serbs, in the tradition of their proud and extraordinarily valiant history, have sought to secure a dominating position within the kingdom. They have consistently opposed the continued demands of the Croats and the Slovenes for regional autonomy under a nominal federative authority.

But these problems have always taken second place in their attention when foreign danger seemed to threaten: when their lively fears of Hungarian revindication or Austrian preponderance or, in more recent years, of Italian Fascist ambitions appeared to call for renewed vigilance. In fact, the Yugoslav state survived in the face of endless obstacles. The maladjustments resulting from the Treaty of Versailles and from the highhanded incursions of Italy, which brought many bitterly hostile Yugoslav nationals under Italian rule, have created a restlessness along the eastern shores of the Adriatic. They have also done much to promote political and economic insecurity. The adjustments laid down for Trieste, Fiume, and the Istrian Peninsula as a whole settled nothing. They ensured but one thing, and that was the certainty of instability.

The territorial limits laid down for Bulgaria gave rise immediately to a general Bulgarian demand for revindication. As a result, Bulgarian relations with Rumania and Yugoslavia and, in particular, with Greece have been profoundly shaken. By tradition, and by sentiment, Russia has been and is today regarded as the proven friend of the Bulgars. Even the reigning Coburg dynasty and the success of the Axis powers in once more forcing Bulgaria to become a satellite of Germany have not created any fundamental change in the deep-rooted pro-Russian popular sentiment. Throughout the present war official relations between Sofia and Moscow have been maintained. Even the Nazi-dominated Bulgarian government would not have dared to risk the popular uprising which a break would have occasioned.

The Balkan countries have long been a stage for the rivalries between the great powers. Not only have conflicting political influences been constantly at work, but financial and commercial interests have found the Balkan nations a fertile ground for their activities. The investment of foreign capital has made possible rapid development of the oil and mineral resources of both Yugoslavia and Rumania, but it has also encouraged official corruption. These foreign financial interests, operating with unmeasured cynicism, have in no small degree contributed to instability.

In all the Balkan countries the standard of living is pitifully low. Bulgaria is almost entirely an agricultural region. In both Yugoslavia and Rumania, agriculture is the chief livelihood of the masses. It was principally this fact which enabled Germany, during the last three years before the second World War, to obtain so rapidly its predominance in Balkan affairs. By the middle of the 1930's, subsidies, the mechanization of the farms, and the development of mass production methods in many of the food-producing countries in other parts of the world had put an end to the ability of the Balkan farmers to find a world market for their output.

The most acute phase of this crisis coincided with the last stage of Hitler's preparations for the World War. The barter arrangement then proposed by the German government to the Balkan nations, by which the latter would find at least some compensation for their agricultural products, seemed to them the one means of preventing a complete economic and financial collapse. For that reason they accepted the commercial schemes handed to them by Dr. Schacht. Within a very brief period, Germany dominated their markets. From 1936 to 1938, she exported to Yugoslavia and to Rumania more than forty per cent of the total imports of those two countries, as against approximately twenty per cent in the preceding years. With such a degree of economic control, Germany necessarily gained the political control which to her was even more important.

Even had the United States adopted at that time a positive policy designed to check the growth of Nazi domination in Europe, it would have had little to offer to the Balkan governments to offset the economic arrangements proposed by Germany. The trade agreements program—constructive as this was—was of little practical service, for the agricultural products upon which the economy of the Balkan nations depended to so large an extent were not required by American importers. And the British and French governments, having themselves embarked upon a wholly artificial policy of subsidizing an uneconomic production of food supplies within their own territories (necessary as this might be from the standpoint of national defense), were in no position to combat effectively Germany's economic policies.

The poverty of the masses underlies every problem of the Balkan peoples. Only through a higher standard of living can they develop the social foundation upon which to construct stable national governments. It is the only way they can permanently prevent the intrusion of those foreign influences which have kept them economically and politically inferior. The magnificent capacities inherent in all of them can in no other way find scope for independent development.

But so long as the economic barriers, which existed during the period between the two great wars, are maintained, there is not the slightest hope of increasing Balkan living standards. A customs union is only a partial answer to the problem, although it would improve existing conditions. What is even more urgently required in the postwar world is an economic union in which the units of the Soviet Union might in whole or in part participate. Such a union not only would level customs tariffs but would likewise afford an opportunity, through co-operative methods, for intraregional economic development. A regional stabilization of currencies under the supervision of the international organization would provide a tonic stimulus. Joint control of transportation, air, rail and maritime, would still further reduce unnecessary and stifling obstacles to trade, both within the area and with countries outside.

The potentialities inherent in some vast power project which might be established in the Danube Valley are almost unlimited. The electrical power derived from such an installation, cutting across all the national lines of Eastern Europe, could within twenty years create an entirely new industrial civilization in the area. What is perhaps even more important, it would result in a far higher standard of living in every home throughout that part of Europe. There were those who scoffed at the Tennessee Valley Authority when it was first planned. They regarded such men as George Norris and Franklin Roosevelt as impractical visionaries. Today the people of the United States can see for themselves how the lives of hundreds of thousands of American citizens have been benefited by that experiment. Through such co-operative arrangements production could be not only profitably intensified, because of increased regional purchasing power, but profitably diversified. Cheap electrical power readily available under such a scheme would do much to stimulate industrial production and to improve living conditions. But the attainment of all these aims depends primarily upon the reaching of regional agreements for the establishment of freer trade, a freer movement of capital, and an intraregional control of communications and power.

The political and economic difficulties in bringing about a fundamental realignment in Eastern Europe such as I have outlined could scarcely be exaggerated. But is there any other practical means of encouraging the development of stability and at least relative prosperity in the area in the reasonably near future? The obstacles will by no means be found solely within the region. Powerful financial interests in Western Europe will still want to enjoy the profitable opportunities for exploitation presented by a fractionized Eastern Europe. The Soviet Union is apparently reluctant even tacitly to approve any attempts at a federative order among the peoples along its western frontier, unless it is under direct Soviet influence. The obstacles will continue to be insuperable unless the new international organization is directed by statesmen farsighted enough to realize that if the peoples of this region are not helped to obtain a higher living standard these vast areas will continue to be a primary source of danger to the peace and order of the world.

An economic union such as I have described might be composed of one unit, two, or even three. Workable arrangements could be envisaged by which Greece, Albania, Bulgaria, Rumania, and Yugoslavia would form one unit, Poland and Czechoslovakia a second, and Austria and Hungary a third; or with Poland, Czechoslovakia, Hungary, and Austria comprising one unit, and the Balkan nations and Greece a second. A third alternative would be an economic union composed not only of all the nations listed, but one in which Turkey likewise would take part. In all of these possibilities it seems evident that the Soviet Union, in whole or in part, must be included.

It is only realistic to assume that any such arrangement would at first cause the Soviet Union serious misgivings. Conceivably, the major powers of Western Europe also might be alarmed by the political ties which would inevitably be formed.

On the other hand, if as the years pass economic union has the beneficial results envisaged, improved living standards would create an extremely profitable market for a great volume of exports from the Soviet Union and the other exporting nations in Europe.

Given a world organization in which the major powers play their full and corresponding part, the close co-operation of the East European nations could carry no threat to the physical security of Russia or any other country. Under those conditions, economic union could not fail to hold tremendous short-term as well as long-term advantages.

Surely nothing could be more intrinsically detrimental to the future stability of Europe than the creation of a so-called "cordon sanitaire" by the dominant powers of Eastern Europe or by the Western European democracies. But it is equally certain, if a stable order is to be created, that the people of Eastern Europe must be given the opportunity to achieve at least those standards of existence which modern civilization regards as minimum. The experience of the past twenty-five years has shown clearly that that objective cannot be attained so long as the whole economy of the East European nations is fractionized, and so long as the economic policies practiced during the past quarter of a century persist.

In 1919 the Peace Conference of Paris set up the so-called Succession States and then cast them adrift, together with their regional neighbors, to sink or swim. It required no prophet to foresee that under their economic system they could survive only so long as artificial support was given them. This the League, and the great powers, occasionally provided. And when this was no longer possible, the inevitable catastrophe took place. Surely this next time the states of Eastern Europe must be afforded the only sure means by which they can become a self-sustaining and constructive entity in world society.

The drama of the Balkan Peninsula has never been more deeply tragic than during the past five years. The Italian occupation of

Albania on that Good Friday morning of 1939 and the Italian and German attacks upon Greece in the early months of 1941 make a chapter in history which will shame the Italian people for generations to come.

Along the southern shore of the Mediterranean and throughout the Near East, problems very similar to those in the Balkans will confront the world of the future. A survey of these problems, which arise from the complex situation existing in the Arab countries, necessarily involves a review of the decisions reached in connection with the Near East by the victorious Allied powers in 1919, and in the years immediately thereafter.

The disillusionment of the Arab leaders after Versailles and the disillusionment of many brilliant British soldiers who had fought at their side during the first World War, need not now be emphasized. It is sufficient merely to state that the Arab leaders have been persuaded that the British government has not lived up to the commitments it made to them. No small part of the complexities and uncertainties of recent Arab history derives from this fact.

The chief cause of complaint was the failure of Great Britain to carry out the promises which the Arabs alleged were contained in the communications exchanged in 1915 between Sir Henry MacMahon and the Sherif Hussein, father of Prince Feisal, later the first King of Iraq. The so-called MacMahon agreement constituted in part a mutual assistance pact, and likewise stipulated that upon the conclusion of the first World War Great Britain would recognize the Arab caliphate and the independence of all the Arab lands with the exception of Aden. Great Britain, in return, was promised preferential economic relations.

The arrangement was flagrantly contravened in the following year by the secret agreement between Great Britain, France, and Russia. According to this, not only was Russia to be given Constantinople and the Straits but, what was far more important from the point of view of those who planned for Arab independence, France was to obtain as outright colonies Syria and the Lebanon as well as the Mosul oil fields now incorporated within Iraq. In the head-on collisions which took place during the Paris Conference and the three years thereafter between Great Britain and France over their respective interests in the Near East, Arab hopes for an independent Arab federation went by the board. At the San Remo Conference in April, 1920, the Arabian claims were finally disposed of by the decision of the major Allied powers, with the approval of the League of Nations, that France should obtain mandatory powers over Syria and the Lebanon, and that Iraq would be placed under a British mandate. Great Britain likewise was granted a mandate over Palestine.

The history of the Arab states since that time is a story of maladjustment and dissatisfaction. The mandatory powers consistently had recourse to policies of expediency rather than to policies devised to settle basic issues. The vendetta of the French against Feisal and his subsequent selection by the British as the first King of Iraq; the designation through British influence of another son of the Sherif Hussein to control the destinies of Transjordania; and King Ibn Saud's consolidation of his control over Saudi Arabia through sheer force of character are all stories which have many times been told. But none of these developments is necessarily permanent. An independent Arab federation or even a series of independent Arab states does not exist.

There is as yet no system, no order, which grants to all the Arab peoples the chief objectives they seek and for which they have fought. Their demands for the rights and privileges of self-determination are rapidly growing. Unless the victorious powers at the conclusion of the second World War can settle the problems which they left so hopelessly unsettled at the end of the first World War, a focus for grave dangers to world order will exist in the heart of the Near East.

Apart from the very critical problem of Palestine, the question of French influence in Syria and the Lebanon, the future position of Iraq, the future relationship between Syria and the Lebanon, Iraq, Transjordania, and Saudi Arabia, and the relations between these Arab states, including Egypt, and the future state of Palestine will all demand final settlement.

Egypt is in a special category, even though the policy of the Egyptian government in recent years has been stanchly directed toward the creation of a Pan-Arab federation and the inclusion of

Egypt therein. But Egypt in many ways is a law unto herself. While Cairo's pre-eminence in the Islamic world and the religious prestige of the University of El Azhar will unquestionably preserve for Egypt a leading place in any association of the Moslem nations, her ties with the Arab states to her east are in some ways not even so close as those which in the past have linked Morocco with the states surrounding the Holy Places.

After a struggle of many decades and much vacillation on the part of Great Britain, a treaty concluded in 1936 with the British government granted Egypt the greater part of her demands for the full recognition of her sovereignty. Her independence was recognized by the world at large upon her entrance into the League of Nations in 1937. During the present war, Egypt's position has been strengthened rather than weakened, in spite of the difficulties which have inevitably arisen from the presence in Egypt of British troops.

The long and tireless efforts of the Egyptian nationalists, carried on primarily by the Wafd, have at length borne fruit. Egypt's immediate problem at the close of the present war will undoubtedly be the adjustment of her existing treaty arrangements with the British government. Some of the bitter controversies arising from Anglo-Egyptian relationships—and it must be admitted that these have frequently been of a very personal character—have eaten deep into the soul of Egyptian officialdom and, I have no doubt, of British officialdom as well.

But Egypt's basic problems have in great part been met. The grinding poverty of the people and the desperately low standards of education, of sanitation, and of general living conditions were greatly ameliorated during the last decades of British rule. The major improvement that has taken place in the general economy of the country during the past fifteen years promises prosperity for the years to come.

Upon the conclusion of the present war, Egypt will presumably revert to her prewar status in her relationship with Great Britain. Nominally she will enjoy the position of an independent and sovereign nation bound to Great Britain by the terms of a treaty of alliance through which Great Britain is granted the right to take far-reaching measures to protect the Suez Canal and for that purpose to station within certain areas in Egypt such British forces as may be required. Vitally necessary as these treaty arrangements may be for the protection of British interests, the situation in which Egypt finds herself as a result of her alliance is anomalous, as the present war has so frequently shown. These war conditions have undoubtedly stimulated Egyptian nationalism and have made it certain that the Egyptian political parties will demand further modifications of the existing treaty of alliance in the postwar period. The only final and satisfactory solution will lie in the assumption by an international organization of the security rights and privileges which Great Britain has hitherto claimed exclusively for herself.

No account of the French mandate over Syria and the Lebanon can be agreeable reading. The mandatory system as it was conceived at the Paris Conference was one thing. The manner in which it was permitted to operate in the present instance was quite another. The history of French relations with the peoples of Syria and the Lebanon must be read in the light of France's disappointment when it failed to obtain complete sovereignty over those regions and the consequent attempts of successive French governments to interpret their responsibilities as a mandatory power as if these conferred upon France the rights of sovereignty over the peoples involved. I have already referred to the treaty negotiated by M. Franklin Bouillon for the French government with the Turkish government by which an area of Syria was ceded to Turkey. That situation was at least partly corrected by the opposition of Great Britain and the negotiations of 1923 at Lausanne. But in the concluding years of the mandate, the French government, by a later agreement with Turkey, actually ceded to the latter that strip of Syrian territory which included the important region of Alexandretta.

The French mandates in the Near East have been far from satisfactory. Their history is full of regrettable errors of policy and of judgment on the part of French agents. Public opinion in the Near East has not, for example, forgotten that, as a result of the continuing divergence of French and British policies, in 1925 more than ten thousand native Christians were massacred by Jebel Druses and Moslems in the French-mandated territories. Not only was this a shocking commentary upon the manner in which the mandate system was being carried out by the League, but it was likewise a cause for bitter complaint regarding the authority and efficacy of the mandatory power.

In her colonial relations with the native peoples of Central and West Africa and Morocco, France has exercised her authority in the co-operative spirit which the authors of the League had intended should exist between a mandatory power and the peoples under its care. But she has not displayed this spirit in the Near East.

The result has been that the highly civilized, able, and freedom-loving peoples who for the most part make up the population of Syria and the Lebanon have increasingly, and ever more vehemently, demanded their independence. Their appeals have met with response from French statesmen of liberal views and vision. During the first months of Léon Blum's premiership, for example, the French government and representative authorities in Syria and the Lebanon entered into a treaty modeled after the one earlier concluded between Great Britain and Iraq, by which both Syria and the Lebanon were promised their independence in the year 1939.

The outbreak of the European war prevented France from carrying out these treaty obligations. The resentment on the part of the Lebanese and Syrians of their earlier treatment at her hands and their hostility toward Great Britain, undoubtedly fanned by Axis propaganda, were hardly likely to result in their putting any serious obstacles in the way of the Vichy government when, in the spring of 1941, the question arose of granting Germany air bases and other military facilities in Syria. So serious had the danger become that, notwithstanding the major difficulties then confronting the British, their forces together with Free French troops invaded Syria and wrested the control of Syria and the Lebanon from the Vichy government. Simultaneously, both British and Free French authorities guaranteed the postwar independence of the peoples of Syria and the Lebanon, and the government of the United States emphasized in the letters of credence issued to its first diplomatic agent in Syria its official concurrence in these assurances.

It was all the more disheartening, therefore, when in November, 1943, the French Committee of National Liberation at Algiers, under the aegis of General de Gaulle, permitted its High Commissioner in Syria to imprison the newly elected President of Syria and the members of the newly formed Syrian Cabinet. It was one of the most inept and stupid acts recently committed. As a result of stern admonitions from both London and Washington, the action was revoked and the Syrian government was once more permitted to function, but the effect upon Syrian public opinion is not difficult to imagine. Only the certainty that their future independence will be guaranteed by an international organization and that the influence of France will no longer be predominant in their territory can wipe out their long-existing hostility and antagonism to the Western powers.

British policy in Iraq during the past quarter of a century has been far more enlightened. Difficulties and friction have existed, it is true, but in 1930 Great Britain voluntarily arranged to terminate her mandate over Iraq, in return for the assurance that, when she was endangered, she would obtain within the territory of Iraq "all facilities and assistance . . . including the use of railways, rivers, ports, airdromes and means of communication." This is one of the few cases in which the mandatory system, as conceived in the Covenant of the League of Nations, has functioned to the advantage of the people of the mandated territory.

Notwithstanding the wise policy which the British government had followed, Iraqi nationalism steadily increased. When in May, 1941, as the result of German subversive activities, the government of Iraq was overthrown by the pro-German Rashid Ali and British troops were sent in, strictly in accordance with the treaty provisions, to crush the danger which had thus developed, popular hostility made it questionable whether they would succeed. It was only after a month of serious fighting that the usurping government was ejected and that the beleaguered American Legation, within which many of the British officials had taken refuge, could release its inmates.

Moreover, some of the worst phases of Axis doctrine appear recently to have become prevalent in Iraq. The bitter hostility to the Jewish people, repeatedly demonstrated in the past two years by the government of Iraq, has grown so acute that so enlightened and stanch a friend of the United Nations as Nuri Pasha, the Prime Minister, refused a year ago to permit transit to Palestine through Iraq of five hundred Jewish refugee children. These were children who had been enabled to escape to Constantinople from Axis-occupied countries, and whom it was thought unsafe at the time to send to Palestine by sea. In former years there had never been any anti-Semitic feeling in Iraq. The Jews who were resident there were treated without discrimination. No racial problem had created any difficulty. The attitude recently taken by the government, therefore, will provide a new complication in determining the future status of Palestine.

The southern part of Arabia constitutes one of the most extensive states in the Arab world. King Ibn Saud has become a legendary figure within his own lifetime. For the independent kingdom of Saudi Arabia is strictly his own creation. The great number of the children he has raised, the iron discipline with which he has reared them, his towering stature, his avid interest in modern mechanical inventions, and the shrewd ability with which he has now for so many years played off one great power against another have all formed the subjects of innumerable stories written about him in the Western press. Back of all these sensational aspects of an unusually vivid personality, however, are to be found the characteristics of an exceptionally able and devoted ruler of the Arabian people. King Ibn Saud has given his people the strong-handed austere rule to be expected from a man of his vigorous and forceful personality, and from a man who is, furthermore, a devoted adherent of the puritanical Wahhabi sect of the Moslem faith. Throughout the war he has kept his country nominally neutral, although openly favorable to the cause of the United Nations.

The development of Saudi Arabia has been rapid. Revenues from the oil concessions granted to American companies and advances from these companies have done much to counterbalance the loss to the national income occasioned by the wartime lack of pilgrimages to the Holy Places. The desire of the chief authorities for American assistance in carrying out the engineering and construction problems necessary to the continued development of the country's resources has received as large a response from Washington as military exigencies have made possible.

Saudi Arabia is making strong progress and today is potentially the most powerful factor in the Pan-Arab world. The use which can be made of that factor in promoting the stability and development of the Near East will depend upon the nature of the plans drawn up by the United Nations when the war is over.

The surest method through which the Arab states can become constructive members of any new world organization is for the Arab peoples to be given precisely those basic rights and opportunities which they thought they were going to get by the MacMahon agreement of 1915. An Arab federation composed of the independent states of Syria, the Lebanon, Transjordania, Iraq, Saudi Arabia, and the smaller autonomous Arab states, joined by practical political and economic ties, would in all probability become an increasingly prosperous and peaceful part of the world. There is, however, one essential proviso to this prediction: that equitable treatment be accorded by an Arab federation to the Jewish Homeland of Palestine.

The problem of Palestine, and the underlying problem of Zionism itself, has come to the attention of the modern world only since it took shape at the First Zionist Congress, held in Switzerland in 1897 upon the initiative of Theodore Herzl. It came to its first great milestone just twenty years later.

To Dr. Chaim Weizmann more than to any other one man is due the attainment of that objective. It was through the untiring efforts, the extraordinary persistence, and the remarkable ability of this great Russian Jew, who later became a British subject, that outstanding leaders of the British government, notably Lord Balfour, were persuaded of the justice of the Zionist cause. The Balfour Declaration of 1917, an official pronouncement of the British government stated:

His Majesty's Government view with favour the establishment in Palestine of a National Home for the Jewish people, and will use their best endeavours to facilitate the achievement of this object, it being clearly understood that nothing shall be done which may prejudice the civil and religious rights of the existing non-Jewish communities in Palestine or the rights and political status enjoyed by Jews in any other country.

Only Dr. Weizmann himself and the few others who still remain of those who took part in the negotiations could properly relate the long series of events which led up to the Declaration. Originally almost all the members of the British government were opposed to it. Many of the most influential Jews in Great Britain and the United States were violently antagonistic because of their fear that the creation of a Jewish Homeland would result in increasing anti-Semitism, even in those countries where discrimination against Jews had ceased. When Lord Balfour came to the United States on his first official visit in 1917, he held determining conversations with a number of prominent American Jews, chief among them Justice Brandeis; and finally, he succeeded in winning over a majority of the British Cabinet to the proposed Declaration. Subsequently, a wave of enthusiasm swept over the Jewish people in all parts of the world, even those who were passing through the first stages of the Bolshevik revolution in Russia. And only Dr. Weizmann today could give a worthy account of the hopes, discouragements, and burning faith which he and his chief associates have experienced during the twenty-five years that have since elapsed.

History repeats itself in strange and tragic ways. One of the chief reasons why Dr. Weizmann was able to get the attention of the British government in the first World War was that as a scientist of genius he had placed at its disposal his knowledge of and inventions for the manufacture of high explosives. In the second World War, the chief reason why he came to the United States and was enabled to discuss with the highest members of this government his hopes and plans for the future of Palestine was his ability to offer outstanding scientific assistance in the manufacture of synthetic rubber, which in the early days of 1942 was a matter of vital concern in the war effort of the United States.

In such conversations as I myself have had with the world's leading figures I have rarely perceived such qualities of sincerity, real statesmanship, ability, and underlying humanity as I have seen in Dr. Weizmann. If any human being can find a solution for the problems which still beset the final establishment of the National Jewish Homeland, Dr. Weizmann will find it if he is given the chance.

Even the most fervid Zionist can hardly assert that the British mandate in Palestine has been a failure. Foundations at least have been laid. The Jewish people have been given the opportunity to accomplish, even though under the greatest of handicaps, one of the real miracles of modern times. Granting all that the more vehement critics of the Palestine experiment may say, granting that the economy of Palestine during the past twenty years has been largely artificial, granting that no permanent economic solution is yet visible, the amazing achievements of the Jewish people in Palestine are there for all to see. Such evidences of their genius as the great modern city of Tel Aviv, the extraordinary efficiency they have developed in agriculture, and the amazing examples they have set in social and industrial development cannot be overestimated. Had it not been for the British mandate, these achievements could not have been realized.

British authority in Palestine can chiefly be criticized on two counts: first, the small number of truly sympathetic or really qualified men whom British governments have sent as administrators to the mandated area; second, the woeful inability of the British administration in Palestine to cope with the immigration problem in general and with the problem of refugee immigration in particular. I have no doubt that the conflict within the British government itself, as between the Colonial Office and the Foreign Office, and as between military and civil officials, has complicated an already unduly confused situation. But I think it cannot be denied that the White Papers issued by the British government on this matter have been neither constructive nor sufficiently regardful of the misery and distress of a sorely afflicted race.

I cannot see any possibility of a permanent solution through the continuation of a British mandate. The mandate in itself is a temporary arrangement. It is provisional by its very nature. What seems to me essential is an international agreement upon a program that leads step by step to the independent status of Palestine as the National Home of the Jewish people.

Jewish opinion in the United States is widely and bitterly divided over the desirability of an independent Palestine. Many eminent and patriotic citizens of the Jewish faith strongly believe, as did Edwin Montagu when he was a member of the British Cabinet in 1917, that the establishment of an independent Palestine would be highly dangerous to the well-being and security of the Jewish people in all other parts of the world. But it seems to me the time is past when that fear should be allowed to block the attempt to find a permanent solution of this question. For Zionism has become an impelling and overwhelming force. It represents the passionate conviction of many millions of Jews throughout the world and of several millions of American citizens. It has become a spiritual problem which must be solved. If it is not solved, it may well become a disruptive force which would certainly impair the ordered stability of the kind of world we desire to see organized in the years to come.

An infinite number of solutions have been proposed. The extremists who demand the emigration of all Arabs from Palestine and unlimited immigration of Jews into Palestine seem to me to be as unrealistic as the extremists who pessimistically maintain that no Homeland can ever be created because of Arab opposition, and who insist that any additional immigration of Jews into Palestine will create a situation, for an indefinite period, controllable only by armed force.

That a practical solution can be found I am firmly convinced. I am equally persuaded that it will be found along the lines proposed by Dr. Judah Magnes, President of the Hebrew University of Jerusalem. He suggests a union of Jews and Arabs within an autonomous Palestine, and a federative system, political as well as economic, comprising Palestine, Syria, the Lebanon, and Transjordania.

It seems to me that for practical reasons any such federation should be an integral part of any general federative union which may be set up in the Near East. During at least a relatively long experimental period the lesser federation in which it is proposed that Palestine would participate should be placed under the auspices of an international trusteeship, rigidly supervised by the international organization which I hope will be functioning when the second World War is over.

The opportunities for economic development in such a union are manifold. Power and irrigation systems could be developed on a scale not otherwise possible. Furthermore, the artificial character of Palestine's present economy, nourished, as it is, in part by contributions from abroad, would become a thing of the past. Palestine might readily, through such economic arrangements, become self-supporting, and thus offer opportunities for additional hundreds of thousands of the Jewish people to find economic security in the Homeland of their race.

The problem of Palestine necessarily raises the question of the resettlement of many thousands of the Jewish people after the conclusion of the war. Even under the most favorable circumstances it is improbable that Palestine can hope to offer ample opportunities for a new life and an assured economic future to more than a small percentage of the Jewish people who will be destitute or homeless when the victory is won. It is wholly true, as many say, that one of the objectives in the battle being waged by the United Nations is to make it safe and possible for all peoples to return to the land of their origin and there to be treated without discrimination and upon a basis of full equality with their fellow citizens. But to many refugees a return to the surroundings of the past will not be acceptable. In the case of some, the personal tragedies which they have undergone will make them wish to find a new home. In the case of others, their destitution will make them prefer to find in other parts of the world some opportunity for profitable employment.

This great problem of resettlement of all the individuals who fall within these categories is one of the most urgent questions with which the United Nations should deal when the war is done. It is not a question that can appropriately be handled by the United Nations Relief and Rehabilitation Administration. It is the specific problem for which the President called into being in 1938 the Intergovernmental Committee on Refugees. During the early period of the war the Intergovernmental Committee was unable to make more than a modest start in carrying out its responsibilities. Shortage of funds, shortage of shipping facilities and more than all else, the preoccupation of all governments with the conduct of the war rendered it a highly difficult matter for the Intergovernmental Committee to do more than plan for the future. But it is imperative that the committee be continued and that funds be made available to it by all of the governments represented so that it can be prepared to carry out its essential obligations as soon after the war as may be possible. There are vast regions in Africa ideally suited for the resettlement of hundreds of thousands of refugees. These regions possess climates wholly adapted to peoples of European origin. They contain natural resources whose exploitation would grant a profitable livelihood to the new settlers. If the United Nations lend their active support to the Intergovernmental Committee and provide it with the facilities which it requires, its work could greatly simplify the solution of difficult problems which will inevitably confront many nations of Eastern Europe in the postwar period. It would at the same time provide a means of salvation for a very great number of human beings.

Another problem which will affect many parts of the Near East is the development of oil resources. At the present time British capital, operating through the Iranian-Persian Company, has a controlling voice under the Iranian government in the development of the Persian oil fields. By a concession granted originally in 1933 to the Standard Oil Company of California, American interests have a controlling voice in the development of oil resources in Saudi Arabia. In Iraq, the Iraq Petroleum Company, dominated by British interests but representing other nationalities also, determines the output. American oil interests, with British supervision, maintain control in Bahrein, and in Kuwait, at the head of the Persian Gulf, American and British possess joint control, although during the war period all production has ceased.

In the postwar period the production of the Near Eastern oil fields will be a matter of vital concern to the United States and the great powers of Western Europe, because the oil resources of this country are diminishing and it is probable that the remaining oil resources of Central and Northern South America are far smaller than was originally anticipated. The whole question is now under active discussion between the United States and British governments. Necessarily the Soviet Union and the other powers most directly concerned will have soon to share in the determinations of policy now being explored. By reason of the principles for which the United

Nations today are fighting no one nation can maintain its right to any exclusive or monopolistic control over the vast oil resources of the Middle East. The part of wisdom, in so far as this government is concerned, lies in expediting an equitable agreement upon the major issues of policy involved, which will fully protect the legitimate interests of the United States. The longer such a decision is postponed the more dangerous will become the opportunities for postwar discord between the major members of the United Nations.

For some time to come, however, the world's oil production will be greater than is required for immediate needs. It is important, therefore, that some general principles be agreed upon to provide for the proper distribution of oil and to ensure that the peoples of the nations to whom these subsoil resources belong receive their fair share of the profits. Only those who have actually seen what the riches produced by oil can accomplish in the development of a barren land and in raising the standard of living of its people can appreciate how vital it is that this means of ensuring prosperity and orderly development in the regions of the Near East should not be overlooked.

In the extreme southeast of the Near East region, Iran has for more than a century and a half been the scene of an intense rivalry for the expansion of British and Russian influence. The interests of the Persian people have increasingly suffered. Time and again disinterested governments have offered their services to the Persian government in correcting abuses in the internal administration of Persian natural resources, and in establishing sound foundations for the maintenance of law and order, only to be finally snubbed for their pains. American experts, appointed by Iranian governments for the very reason that they had no political advantages to gain, have been hastily shown the door upon the demand of foreign governments which feared the undermining of their own influence.

Through it all, as in Turkey, the altruistic and persistent efforts of American missionaries have gained for this country the trust and regard of the Persian people, a factor of positive value now and in the years to come. It is consequently all the more important and encouraging that at the conference in Tehran held in November, 1943, between the chiefs of government of the Soviet Union, Great

Britain, and the United States, a joint declaration was made with regard to Iran declaring that these governments "count upon the participation of Iran together with the other peace loving nations in the establishment of international peace, security, and prosperity after the war in accordance with the principles of the Atlantic Charter to which all four Governments have continued to subscribe."

And what from the standpoint of Iran was in all probability of almost equal significance, the three governments agreed with the government of Iran that "any economic problem confronting Iran at the close of hostilities should receive full consideration along with those of the other members of the United Nations by conferences of international agencies held or created to deal with international economic matters."

. If this declaration is carried out in practice and is supported by the international organization of the future, Iran will become a stable factor in the Near Eastern picture, instead of being, as she unfortunately has been for many generations, a disintegrating element which afforded periodic inducements for political and economic competition by the great powers of Europe.

# CHAPTER VII

## The Japanese Threat and the Problem of Peace in Asia

ON THAT autumn day in 1915 when I first arrived in Japan, where I was to spend more than two years in the American Embassy in Tokyo, I saw a country in many ways far different from the one which has thrust itself upon the attention of an outraged humanity during the past decade.

The first Japanese with whom I had occasion to talk, during the train ride between Yokohama and Tokyo, was Dr. Takuma Dan, later Baron Dan, for many years the guiding force of Mitsui and Company. He had come to the port to meet our party. He was an outspoken example of that liberal group which believed in constitutional government and in the assimilation of the best that Western civilization had to offer.

During this first talk he spoke with intimate familiarity of political and business conditions in the United States and in Western Europe. He showed particular interest in the political problems which President Wilson was then confronting and, somewhat to my surprise, much enthusiasm for the progressive policies which the President was so vigorously maintaining. While a representative of the largest business interests in Japan, Dr. Dan was at the same time a man who quickly made it plain that, in his point of view, the best interests of the Japanese people would be promoted by a gradual evolution along the lines of liberal self-government. Only a few years ago he was assassinated during a moment of nationalistic mass murder because he was regarded as a powerful leader of those who were opposing the policies of brutal military violence then fast coming to the fore.

In 1915 the control of governmental policy was still largely in the hands of those who had turned Japan to the West. They believed that Japan could best achieve pre-eminence in the Pacific and in the Far East by utilizing the position as a world power which she had achieved by her alliance with Great Britain and by her defeat of the Russian Empire in 1905. They advocated co-operating with the other great powers and working toward their own future greatness by concentrating upon a liberal parliamentary system of government rather than upon domestic policies which were essentially autocratic and reactionary.

In the Japan of 1915, foreign policy was being laid down by men as completely familiar with the ways of the Western world as Count Ishii, who was then the Foreign Minister, and Baron Shidehara, the Vice-Minister for Foreign Affairs. The leaders of thought believed it wise to encourage the incipient trend toward liberalism and constitutional government because they were confident that the rapid industrialization of the country would inevitably act as a counterbalance to the rapacious ambitions of the military classes and to the blind reaction of the ignorant peasant population. The teachings of such outstanding modern thinkers as Dr. Inazo Nitobe and the progressive group with which he was associated still possessed some influence.

Dr. Nitobe had married a Philadelphian lady who was devoting herself, like her husband, to the task of breaking down the barriers of incomprehension between the Eastern and Western worlds. In their charming, half-Japanese, half-European house were to be found the most progressive thinkers from the universities and from among the writers and artists of modern-day Japan. Their home was also a meeting ground for political leaders from the House of Peers as well as from the Lower House in the Diet who wished to know more of Western culture and of Western political thinking. There were many other centers as well where in those days the effort was being made in all sincerity to build the bridge which would create a surer understanding between the people of Japan and the people of the Western nations.

Japan at that time was intensely proud of its recognition as a world power by the United States and the great European nations, and jealously anxious to prevent any word or act by a Japanese official which could be interpreted as indicating that the standards of culture and of civilization in Japan were in any sense inferior to those in other parts of the civilized world. No one could then have foreseen the extent of Japan's degradation today.

In those days the real guiding force in Japanese governmental life was exercised behind the scenes by that unique body known as the Genro, or Elder Statesmen. This self-constituted and self-perpetuating oligarchy had been originally composed of the most trusted advisers of the Emperor Mutsuhito. Together with the Emperor—the one member of the imperial family over a period of many centuries to show any outstanding ability—they had been responsible for the transformation of Japan within the miraculously short space of sixty years from a turbulent Oriental recluse into one of the most powerful forces in the modern world. They had all of them gone as young men to study Western civilization at first hand in the United States or in Europe. They had proved to be apt pupils. Prince Ito, their great leader, had died some years before my arrival in Tokyo. He had demonstrated many of the qualities of first-rank statesmanship, and it was to him primarily that Japan owed her rapid emergence as a great power.

The number of the Genro had by my time dwindled to a handful. The most potent was Prince Yamagata, with Marquis Matsukata and Marshal Oyama as rather silent partners. Prince Saionji, Prince Yamagata's disciple, who led the Japanese delegation at the Peace Conference at Paris in 1919, was not yet recognized as a full-fledged member of the Genro. He achieved that distinction, however, before Prince Yamagata's death and became, in turn, the last surviving member of the body.

In 1915 the influence of the Genro, while necessarily wholly undemocratic, was neither blindly reactionary nor exaggeratedly militaristic. Obviously they sought only the greater power and material glory of Japan. But, for the most part, the members of the Genro had convinced themselves that there were benefits to be derived from Western civilization. Almost without exception, and notably in the case of Prince Saionji himself, they had become imbued with what was an international, rather than a nationalistic, viewpoint.

The policy of the Genro in its broader aspects was guided, I think, by those provisions of the oath which the Emperor Mutsuhito took as Emperor of the new Japan in 1868:

A Deliberative Assembly shall be summoned and all measures shall be decided by public opinion; high and low shall be of one mind in the conduct of the Administration; the vicious and un-civilized customs of antiquity shall be broken through, and the great principles of impartiality and justice . . . shall be the basis for action.

When the Genro disappeared, the Japanese people reverted to the "vicious and uncivilized customs of antiquity." This reversion took place after the years of which I write, for then there was relatively little evidence, even in the interior, of those tendencies which set Japan on the barbaric course she has pursued during the past fifteen years.

In 1915 the American Embassy undertook to represent the German interests in Japan, which it continued to do until the United States severed its relations with Germany in the following year. During that period I was entrusted with the supervision of the German prisoners of war stationed in the many prison camps throughout the Japanese Islands. Consequently, I had the opportunity of seeing for myself not only the decency and consideration with which the Japanese authorities treated the prisoners whom they had captured in the German outposts in China, but likewise the real friendliness which the Japanese people showed a foreigner even in the remote districts. The hatred of foreigners characteristic of the Japanese in the years of their hermitlike seclusion and more recently did not at that period exist. The degenerate barbarity with which present-day military authorities of Japan have treated American, British, and other prisoners of war could not have been conceived of by anyone who, like myself, had visited their prison camps thirty years ago.

Nevertheless, even at that period when the Japanese were apparently making rapid and firm strides toward the assimilation of Western civilization, it would have been a very casual observer indeed who did not realize that behind all the veneer lay a primeval military instinct, and that the basic reality of Japan rested in the war machine which had been created. In every part of Japan the Army or the Navy was the dominating factor in daily life. Obligatory military service, the constant encroachment of the Army and Navy leaders upon civil government, and the glorification in the minds of the youth of purely military exploits were already creating the Frankenstein which would soon cause the ruin of the Japanese people, and would crumble into ashes those more worthy ideals of the generation which first made Japan a modern power.

Because of this fact, I cannot now assert with any assurance that the apparently liberal trend of the years between 1896 and 1926 was rooted in reality. However sincere the liberal leaders of Japan may have been, it is probable that the progress made was merely a façade behind which physical force and military aggrandizement remained the determining factors in the Japanese polity.

Moreover, Western Foreign Offices have known for a long time that as far back as the last decades of the past century several projects, such as the Tanaka Memorial, were drawn up with the approval of the Japanese military and naval general staffs. They set forth the aims which Japan should seek to achieve during succeeding generations as time and circumstances made it possible. These plans vary only slightly from those made known to the world during the past three years as the so-called "New Order in the Far East"—the mistermed "Japanese Co-Prosperity Sphere." The original plans envisaged not only the seizure of Korea and Manchuria, the Islands of the Pacific, including the Philippines and the Netherlands East Indies, but the ejection of all European influence from the Pacific regions, the subjection of China, the elimination of Russia as a Pacific power, and the relegation of the Western Hemisphere to a subordinate position. The Tanaka Memorial may not actually have been the bible for Japanese official policy, but succeeding Japanese governments have unquestionably taken every opportunity offered by the temporary embarrassments of the other great powers to realize, piece by piece, the achievement of this total plan.

Another blot on Japan's record was the presentation at the time of the first World War of the twenty-one demands upon China. This took place in May, 1915, notwithstanding Japan's solemn engagements with the other directly interested powers with regard to the independence and integrity of China, and at a time when her then allies were at the most precarious stage of their common war against the Central powers. Chinese acceptance of these demands was successfully blocked by the pressure exercised by the other Allied governments. This failure brought about the downfall of the Japanese Cabinet, which was headed by that impulsive and erratic but brilliant, old man, Marquis Okuma, relentless in his vitality, notwithstanding the fact that his body was all but shattered by an assassin's bomb. Nevertheless, the Japanese government was permitted to make some progress toward securing the economic stranglehold which it desired ultimately to obtain in China.

The agreement of the Japanese government to enter into the Nine-Power Treaty and the other engagements undertaken at the Washington Conference of 1922, which laid equitable foundations for an adjustment of Pacific problems in a manner which should have been satisfactory to Japan, brought about the first open and violent opposition by the Japanese military and naval leaders to the continued control of policy by civilian Cabinets. From that time on, notwithstanding the granting of full manhood suffrage to the people in 1928, plots to assassinate the more liberal and Western-minded members of Japanese governments rapidly increased. As a result of the agreements reached at the London Naval Conference in 1930, Prime Minister Hamaguchi was assassinated. In fact, the growth in influence and number of the reactionary secret societies, of which the Society of the Black Dragon is a familiar example, made it all but impossible for progressive civilians who still held office in Japanese Cabinets to exercise any real influence on Japanese policy. Assassination became the rule rather than the exception in Japanese public life.

By the autumn of 1931 the purely militaristic elements in Japan had gained control. To make sure that the other great powers would not interfere, the Japanese government once again shrewdly selected for its next move toward Asiatic domination a moment when the nations of Europe were deeply preoccupied with other questions. During the summer of 1931 world-wide economic depression had reached a culminating point, accentuated by the collapse of the Austrian Credit Anstalt. Its repercussions in the financial circles of the European countries had hit the United States hard as well. So serious had the situation become that President Hoover had proposed a one-year moratorium in the payment of all international obligations. It was under such conditions, and with the full realization of the effect of the growth of isolationism in the United States upon American influence in world councils, that Japan launched her long-planned assault upon Manchuria in September, 1931. The city of Mukden and other populated areas in southern Manchuria were occupied.

The timing could not have been better. Not only was the government of the United States fully preoccupied with other problems, like all the major powers, but also neither the Department of State nor American representatives in the Far East had, prior to the invasion, any accurate or realistic conception of Japan's true intentions. Yet all during the summer months Japanese military officials had been blatantly frank about their intentions, and the extent of their military preparations had been by no means concealed. The United States was caught by surprise in spite of these warnings.

China immediately set the machinery of the League of Nations in operation by invoking Article II of the Covenant. For three weary months the optimists still hoped that a miracle would occur: that a League which had no force of its own, whose members—though theoretically obligated to make such force available—were unable or unwilling to take any practical action whatever, would successfully be able to dictate to one of the largest standing armies in the world. These optimists hoped that the League could force an army led by officers already entirely out of the control of the civil government to withdraw from the enterprise of conquest upon which it was fully embarked, and for which it had long been planning!

By January of 1932 Japan had completely succeeded in her aggression upon Manchuria. The Japanese Army and Navy continued their attack upon China through assaults at Shanghai and through the valley of the Yangtze, for the announced purpose of breaking up the economic boycott which the Chinese people were directing against Japan. While these assaults resulted in a stiff defeat for Japan, that defeat halted only temporarily the steady invasion of the vast territory of China which has in one form or another continued to this day.

Secretary of State Stimson was the one figure in the Hoover Cabinet who saw clearly what effect the Japanese invasion would inevitably have upon the peace of the rest of the world. In February, 1932, he urged the British government to join with the United States, in view of the failure of the League to cope with the situa-

tion, in invoking the Nine-Power Treaty of 1922. He felt that concerted pressure upon Japan by all the signatories of that treaty was
the one possible means of achieving any practical results. As is well
known, the British government, through Sir John Simon, then
Secretary of State for Foreign Affairs, tacitly made it clear that it
was not disposed to take the action suggested. The British government permitted it to be understood that, inasmuch as she was a
member of the Council of the League and the League was already
attempting to deal with the situation, she would weaken the effectiveness and the prestige of the League if she were to join with this
government by invoking either the Nine-Power Treaty or the
Kellogg-Briand Pact. This attitude did much to create in this country hostility toward British policy and many otherwise objective
persons placed the blame for the almost unlimited evils arising out
of Japan's successful aggression in Manchuria squarely upon the
doorstep of the British government. It has always seemed to me that
this effort to place the burden of blame exclusively upon the British
government is not only unfair but unrealistic. I have no doubt whatever that powerful City influences in London were bitterly opposed
to any action by their government which could create a breach between
Japan and Great Britain, with a consequent loss of British trade
and hobbling of British influence at a time when freedom of action
was necessary. But, in judging the policy of the British government
on this occasion, it must be remembered that neither the second
article of the Kellogg-Briand Pact nor Article 7 of the Nine-Power
Treaty invoked by the American Secretary of State justified anything more than a consultation between the powers primarily concerned. They did not offer the slightest assurance to the British
government, or to any other government in the League, that the
United States was prepared to take any action of a minatory character which would be of the least effect.

It must also be recalled that the whole course of American policy
from 1920 until 1932 had made it more and more evident that the
American people were determined to evade any responsibility for the
use of force in maintaining peace in the rest of the world. The fact
that the action taken by Secretary Stimson was bitterly criticized
throughout the country and was assailed in many quarters as being

"warmongering" pure and simple is a case in point. The Japanese government itself was fully aware of the position.

The Report of the Members of the Lytton Commission, who were sent by the League of Nations to Manchuria, was the only practical result which the League of Nations achieved. The Lytton Report at least clarified for public opinion throughout the world the actual circumstances of the invasion. In so far as the United States was concerned, the courageous position taken by both President Hoover and Secretary of State Stimson in announcing as official policy that the United States would refuse to recognize the acquisition of territory gained as a result of aggression likewise served some useful purpose at a moment when the standards of world morality had reached a depressingly low point.

Ultimately the whole world saw that Japan had succeeded in the first stages of a war of conquest. It saw the creation by Japan of the puppet state of Manchukuo, dominated completely by the military forces of Japan as a conquered province; it saw the continuous increase in the number of Japanese troops sent to China and in the areas which they occupied. The people of China themselves were soon convinced that the world organization, as it had existed, was impotent to protect them. They were compelled to accept the bitter truth that their traditional friends, at the moment of their greatest danger, limited their action to the enunciation of phrases of eloquent, but highly ineffective, sympathy.

The rape of Manchuria marked the failure of the League of Nations as it was conceived and as it was brought into being in 1919. The unwillingness of the great powers to act and the impunity with which Japan was able to proceed upon her course and withdraw from the League were the direct causes for the decision reached two years later by the Italian government to undertake the conquest of Ethiopia. They also contributed to the decision of Adolf Hitler, when he came to power a year later, to embark upon the creation by force and violence of his "greater Germany."

The blindness and the stupid selfishness of all of us in those years is amazing as we look back. It is not, I think, that we actually believed the Japanese propaganda to the effect that the "Chinese Adventure" was only temporary, and that the liberal and business interests in Japan would sooner or later put the Japanese militarists in their place. It is rather, I fear, that we wanted to believe it. It was so much more comfortable for all of us to make ourselves feel it was true. And in a period of great depression, Japanese trade represented a tangible reality hard to give up. Nor can we overlook the influence of the big business representatives in the Far East, still smarting under the impact of youthful Chinese nationalism, who were shouting to high heaven that Japanese authority in China would teach the Chinese a lesson and greatly assist the course of businessmen in China in the future.

Modern history shows few more wholly admirable passages than the story of the resistance of the Chinese people to the overwhelming armed superiority of Japan during the past twelve years. Forced to realize that no effective assistance could be expected from the League, they had to steel themselves time and again, while fighting for their lives and for their freedom, against the utter disillusion of finding that the great friendly powers either looked the other way or substituted well-meaning but empty words and gestures for effective action.

It is true that the United States, prior to its entrance into the second World War, and subsequently Great Britain, made large loans to the Chinese government. But even the real help which these measures afforded to a government enmeshed in the crushing problems of inflation, and requiring the wherewithal to purchase sorely needed supplies abroad, was outweighed in the opinion of the Chinese people by the continued willingness of our government to permit the export of strategic materials, including oil, to Japan. The Chinese were well-aware of the fact that these exports greatly accelerated the growth and speed of the Japanese war machine and that they were being made at a time when American exports of similar supplies could reach China only in comparative trickles because of Japan's de facto blockade of Chinese coasts.

It is astounding that the Chinese government, though incessantly active in furthering Chinese interests, could nevertheless have displayed throughout this period of dire necessity such great moderation in all its dealings with our government and with the other friendly powers. This attitude demonstrated a measure of self-control almost unique.

The performance of the Chinese is all the more remarkable in view of the fact that until very recent years China was a nation of loosely knit units—of families and villages, of towns and cities, of provinces and localities—rather than a closely knit organism like the vast majority of other powers. The nationalism of modern China is a new phenomenon and has been stimulated by the tragedy which she has undergone during the past quarter of a century, and by her sufferings since the invasion of Manchuria. The violent nationalism flaming now in China has, as is usual in such a situation, passed through a stage of violent xenophobia from which even the United States, the traditional friend of China, has not been exempt. However, it has made the China of today, so far as one can determine from existing signs, far more nearly a nation of a unified people than it ever was before. This unification will enormously assist the leaders of the new China in the task of restoration and rehabilitation which lies before them.

Since we have been fighting at the side of China, we have heard much bitter criticism and complaint that her government today is far from being a real democracy, that it is no more than an oligarchy, and a family oligarchy at that. Actually it cannot be denied that the China of the present, with the great bulk of its industrial and agricultural regions in the hands of Japan, with all of its seaports closed by Japanese force to the outside world, and with the major part of its population in slavery, is not functioning as a constitutional democracy. But what is so often overlooked is the magnitude of the problems which the Kuomintang has had to solve since the downfall of the Manchu Dynasty, and the material success it has achieved. One cannot overestimate the peculiar difficulties which any Chinese government would have had to confront in carrying on the war successfully. The Kuomintang had first to liquidate the final vestiges of the last imperial government, and next to obliterate the iniquitous regimes established by local war lords, many of them purchased body and soul by the Japanese government. It was only after these first steps had been taken that any measures of popular government could be imagined. And the miracle is that it was possible to make some progress in this direction even during the years that the government was apparently faced with inevitable subjection to Japan.

From time to time the government had had trouble with this or the other element in China which was supporting the conduct of the war, notably with the Communist forces. However, it has not permitted these difficulties to check in any way its course toward the supreme objective of withstanding the Japanese onslaught, and of continuing to resist until China's partners among the United Nations are in a position to provide more substantial support.

With the defeat of Japan a period of readjustment in China is inevitable. Internal conflicts which have up to the present been composed will come again to the surface. China may again pass through a chaotic period, as she did in the earlier years of the twentieth century. New men and new political forces will come to the surface. But the groundwork for the future has been effectively laid by Sun Yat-sen and Chiang Kai-shek. Whatever political structure may be erected in China, to these two men must be attributed the undying glory of having made it possible for a unified Chinese nation to exist.

With the exception of the Generalissimo himself, the guiding figures in the present government of China are known to many people in this country. Few individuals have in recent years created so profound an impression upon American public opinion as Madame Chiang Kai-shek. She has an amazing knowledge of the elements which determine public opinion in the United States and a keen appreciation of the very real admiration and friendship which the American people have for the people of China. Her quiet dignity, her beautifully modulated eloquence, and her apparent frailty mask an ardent national fanaticism and an unquenchable faith in the future destinies of her people. But more than that, she is, in the most real sense of the word, a citizen of the Far East as well as a citizen of China. She is no less a citizen of the world itself.

Not many months ago I spent the better part of a morning talking with Madame Chiang Kai-shek, while she was a guest at the White House. Many statesmen of the modern world might well envy her detailed knowledge of international affairs and the clarity of her perception of the underlying trends in modern politics. She knows precisely what kind of Far East of the future will best safeguard the permanent interests of the Chinese people. She sees also, very clearly, I think, the most practical methods by which these objectives can be secured. Chief among them will, in her judgment, be a continuous relationship between China and the United States founded on a community of interests. A Chinese government that represented the views and beliefs which she expressed to me could only be a mighty contributing factor to a stable Far Eastern structure, founded upon practical principles of justice.

In the same way her brother, the present Foreign Minister, Dr. T. V. Soong, is a constructive influence. Brilliant, tough, resilient, he is Chinese to the core, notwithstanding his Harvard education and his wide and detailed knowledge of the world. Dr. Soong, during the years that he has divided his time between Chungking, Washington, and other world capitals, has been tireless in serving the interests of his country. But in serving them he has always seemed to me to be serving as well the interests of a future Pacific region in which all the other powers of the world, particularly the Western and Eastern powers most directly interested, could find full opportunity for co-operation, and for building a new kind of world order which would eliminate the basic causes for ruinous antagonisms between the West and the East.

Other outstanding figures in the long list of distinguished men sent by the present Chinese government to this country are Dr. Sao-ke Alfred Sze, the perennial and extraordinarily able Ambassador of China to many foreign countries, and that admirable philosopher and teacher, Dr. Hu Shih. They have performed outstanding services in bringing home to the whole American people what the resistance of China has meant to this country, not only in the larger sense, but from the very practical standpoint of our own interests.

Policies of nations are determined more often than is generally supposed by the ability of the statesmen of one country to understand the essential problems, needs, and concerns of other countries. President Roosevelt has shown such understanding in this government's relations with China. In spite of the fact that United States policy toward China has been seriously circumscribed at certain times during this Administration by legislative enactments, such as the Neutrality Act, limiting the President's freedom of action, he has, nevertheless, never failed in his sympathetic understanding of Chinese difficulties and of Chinese reactions. In that he has been greatly assisted by the unflagging interest of his own Treasury Department, under the inspiration of Henry Morgenthau, and by the services of such outstanding members of the present Chinese government as those I have mentioned. The maintenance of common understanding has required patience and unswerving sympathy on the part of the President when the Chinese government has made what seemed in Washington unreasonable complaints or inordinate requests. It has required equal moderation and understanding on the part of the Chinese government at times when our government seemed unable or unwilling to take action which would assist it in moments of grave peril. The fact that these difficulties have on both sides been overcome, and that the relations between the two governments are perhaps better today than they have ever previously been, is a tribute to the statesmanship and vision of the men who have been guiding the destinies of the two countries during these more than usually difficult years.

What has, of course, made the situation especially difficult has been the barbaric nature of Japanese aggression and of Japanese occupation in China. Compared with the publicity given the brutal atrocities committed upon Americans by the Japanese forces, relatively little has been made known to our public about the nature and extent of Japanese atrocities in China. Occasionally, as in the earlier days of the attacks upon Shanghai or the subsequent occupation and looting of Nanking, eyewitness accounts of Japanese barbarism have been published in the American press. However, these represent but an infinitesimal percentage of the total of similar atrocities which the Japanese occupying forces have been inflicting in China day in and day out for more than a decade.

Rape, looting, destruction, torture, and murder of civilian populations, total disregard for those elementary principles of modern warfare to which Japan had pledged herself in innumerable international agreements: the records of hostilities in modern times have no equal.

Another element in the Japanese occupation has not been sufficiently emphasized in current accounts. That is the all-pervading corruption of the officers and noncommissioned officers composing the forces of occupation. It is notorious that every military unit in the Japanese invasion armies, as soon as it becomes established in any given locality, devotes its attention primarily to the organization of graft. The incomes which all those in authority thus obtain are many hundreds of times greater than the stipends they draw from their own government. This situation had become so firmly rooted by 1938 that it was a matter for well-founded conjecture whether, even in the event that any negotiations between Japan and the Western powers for the evacuation of China were to prove successful, the Japanese forces would be willing to obey the orders issued from headquarters. As a result of this widespread corruption, not only has occupied China been devastated to an even greater degree than would otherwise have been the case, but the entire military structure of Japan has been so honeycombed with corruption as to make any effective discipline a thing of the past.

This country, like most of the Western powers, has had many good reasons to suspect Japan's ultimate designs ever since the influence of the last liberal elements in Japanese government was liquidated. For some years Japan was given the benefit of the doubt as to the nature of her activities in the Japanese Mandated Islands, notwithstanding her consistent refusal to permit officials of the League of Nations or officials of other powers to visit those territories. But in more recent years it became a matter of actual knowledge to the United States that Japan, in flagrant violation of her treaty obligations and of her obligations as a member of the League, had undertaken on a vast scale the fortification of the most strategic islands in the mandated areas. Several factors made it extremely difficult for the executive branch of the government at Washington to take any course which would have given Japan pause. One was the reluctance of Congress to approve naval appropriations for the fortification of our own Pacific outposts, even after the agreements entered into in Washington in 1922 had become obsolete. Another was the overwhelming reluctance of the American public to be persuaded that for the sake of their own security any policy other than one of isolation was necessary. In this critical situation Japan's intelligence services in this country have proved as effective as their diplomacy in other parts of the world has proved faulty. She was thus fully cognizant of our military and naval situation in the Pacific region, and just as fully aware of the significance to be attached to the public's widespread disapproval of the President's "quarantine" speech in Chicago in October, 1937.

For American diplomacy or foreign policy to have been effective during the five years preceding Pearl Harbor, American public opinion would have had to express its readiness to support positive acts on the part of the government. It would have had to make clear its willingness to defend its legitimate rights throughout the Pacific, and to prevent Japan, by force if necessary, from obtaining a strategic position from which she could suddenly strike. But no such popular support for a positive policy existed. The American people were repeatedly told by self-appointed spokesmen and by certain sections of the press in all parts of the country that what went on in China was none of their business, that Japan's aims, clear as they might be and regrettable as they might be, were no direct threat to the interests of this country. Moreover, Washington's ability to maneuver was almost ended by legislative enactment, and the conduct of foreign affairs practically ceases without such latitude. Nevertheless, the President did what he could, hampered as he was by the provisions of the Neutrality Act which provided that when war broke out between two foreign countries he should proclaim the existence of such a war, in order that the embargoes stipulated by the Act should become effective. The President assumed the responsibility of not making any such declaration in the case of China and Japan in 1937 because that would have prevented sadly needed exports of munitions from going to China. This course of action was technically possible only because the Chinese government refrained from declaring war upon Japan for fear of the invocation of these embargoes, and because Japan refrained from declaring war upon China because of the similar fear that the supplies of war materials which she was obtaining from the United States would automatically be cut off.

It has lately been said that this government should have shown greater vigor when the Japanese sank the United States river gunboat *Panay* on the Yangtze River in December, 1937. I have always felt that the President, who handled the entire incident personally, could, under the conditions which then existed, have shown neither greater wisdom nor greater determination. His message, sent directly to the Japanese Emperor, was admirably couched. The Japanese disavowal and offer to pay full indemnity was complete and immediate. The prestige and dignity of this country were fully upheld. Short of bellicose action, for which this government was not prepared and to which the American people would not have been receptive, the President could have taken no more positive step.

In the last months prior to Pearl Harbor, when Congress had finally removed many of the obstacles to executive action, the adoption of a more positive policy was made extremely difficult by the increasing probability that the policies of the European Axis would eventually force this country into war. The insistent demands of our highest military and naval authorities that diplomacy prevent any hostilities with Japan until the last possible moment, in order that the United States might not find herself confronted with a war in both oceans, were regarded—and I think rightly—as the paramount consideration. That was the compelling reason why the Administration continued to permit until only three months prior to Pearl Harbor the exportation of certain grades of oil and scrap iron to Japan. That is the explanation for the President's subsequent use of the much criticized expression "babying along" in connection with our policy toward Japan in that period.

The wisdom of any foreign policy can generally be determined only by its results. Any impartial estimate of our policy during those crucial years from 1936 to 1941 must, therefore, be appraised in that light. Our objectives essentially were those laid down for the government by its chief military and naval advisers, and in my own judgment our policy did delay the Japanese attack for at least a brief period.

The entrance of Japan into French Indo-China as a result of pressure brought by Germany upon the Vichy government in July of 1941 was the last overt danger signal. Obviously, the occupation of Indo-China was not really, as the Japanese claimed, for strategic operations against China. It could only be regarded as an immediate threat to the British position in Burma and Malaya, and as a thrust at the highly vulnerable position of the United States in the Philippines. The time which passed between that move and the actual outbreak of war between Japan and the United States was so much time saved for military preparations by this country.

The last stages of the history of the relations between Japan and the United States prior to Pearl Harbor are of fascinating interest. The appointment in January, 1941, of Admiral Nomura as Ambassador to Washington was the first step in this episode. Admiral Nomura had previously served as Japanese naval attaché many years before in Washington and for a brief period had likewise been Foreign Minister. He had generally been regarded both in this country and in Japan as well-disposed to the United States and as the proponent of a policy of conciliation. In my first conversations with the Ambassador after his arrival in Washington, I obtained the definite impression that he, at least as an individual, was sincerely seeking an adjustment of what he recognized as the most acute crisis that had ever arisen in Japanese-American relations. I also thought he was far from optimistic that the path to any such adjustment could be found. A man in his late sixties and singularly tall for a Japanese, with a missing eye lost in a bomb explosion in Shanghai in 1932, moderate and conciliatory in his manner of speech, Admiral Nomura consistently appeared to seek during the first six months of his mission the way around rather than the path into the obstacles.

I have always had reason to believe, and I have not changed my opinion, that the selection of Admiral Nomura as Ambassador to this country was a blind. The blind was made more effective by the fact that for some time Admiral Nomura himself was not aware that he was being used for that purpose. But it is unquestionable that he must have known the true situation in the final days of his mission, whether he was so informed or not by that ill-famed emissary, Mr. Kurusu. Long before the end of the protracted series of conferences which he held during the greater part of the spring and summer months of 1941 with the Secretary of State, Admiral Nomura, being by no means an unintelligent man, must have drawn his own conclusions that an attack by his country upon the United States was inevitable. Granting that the Ambassador tried to be as entirely sincere as the Secretary of State, it must have been obvious that the points of views of the two governments were clearly irreconcilable. If the United States abandoned the basic principles which it had maintained, it would not only betray China but likewise its own highest national interests. Consequently, since this government would not agree to depart from these principles, either the Japanese military dictatorship would have to recede from its position and withdraw from China and Indo-China, which was all but unthinkable, or war between the two countries—bearing in mind the agreements entered into between Japan and the European Axis powers—would be unavoidable.

My own views at that juncture—for I took no part whatever in the conversations between the Secretary of State and Ambassador Nomura—can most clearly be illustrated in these excerpts from a conversation which I had on August 4, 1941, with Mr. Wakasugi, the Minister Counselor of the Japanese Embassy, who has recently died:

I said that the policies of my Government had been made clear time and again in our interchanges with and in our communications to the Government of Japan since the spring of 1933. I referred to letters exchanged between the Secretary of State and the Prime Minister, to public statements made by the Secretary of State and by the President and other officials, and by innumerable other clear-cut and detailed analyses of our position with regard to the Pacific and more specifically, vis-à-vis Japan. I said that in addition to all of this, the policy of this Government had been made completely clear in the most painstaking way by the Secretary of State himself in the conversations which he had held during the past five months with the Japanese Ambassador. Finally, I said, the policy of this Government was clarified and summarized to the fullest extent possible by the proposal which the President himself had made to the Japanese Ambassador on July 24 and to which this Government had not as yet received any reply.

I said that I doubted whether in the history of the past 50 years any great power in its dealings with another great power had consistently shown such utter and complete patience as had the Government of the United States in its dealings with Japan.

At this point Mr. Wakasugi nodded his head.

I said that if Mr. Wakasugi nevertheless desired me once more to summarize the policy of this Government, I should define it succinctly as a policy which contained, as its fundamental premise, the maintenance of peace in the Pacific; the renunciation by all of the powers interested in the Pacific of force and of conquest as their national policy; the recognition of the rights of independent and autonomous peoples of the Pacific to independence and integrity; and equal opportunity and fair treatment for all, and exclusive preference or privilege for none. I added that it seemed to me that the policy of the United States made it fully clear to the Government of Japan that the American Government and people desired in no way to impede or to limit the equal rights of the Japanese people to economic and commercial opportunity, either in the Pacific or, for that matter, throughout the world, or the enjoyment of equal opportunity in obtaining free access to raw materials and food supplies required in the national economy of Japan; and afforded Japan complete assurance that so long as Japan adopted similar policies the United States could never remotely be regarded as endangering by military or naval force the national security of the Japanese Empire.

I said that I wished to emphasize by repeating the fact that American policy, if Japan followed an identical course, afforded Japan the fullest measure of security both physical and material. However, I said, at the same time that this policy had been enunciated over and over again to Japan, Japan had been following more and more openly a completely diametrical tendency.

The result was that during these recent years our national policies, instead of converging, had been moving steadily apart and the result was that today this Government was forced to the conclusion that the policy finally and definitely adopted by Japan was a policy of expansion through the use of force and by conquest. I said that I wished, therefore, to make it very clear to Mr. Wakasugi that in my considered judgment, if Japan continued on an aggressive policy of force and undertook moves of expansion which would result in acts of aggression upon additional peoples in the Far East, in the south or in other regions of the Pacific, the aim of Japan could only be regarded by the United States as the creation of a military overlordship of the Japanese Empire imposed over all of the peoples of the Far East, the Southern Pacific, and perhaps over other areas as well. If this were in reality the objective of the Japanese Government, I thought it necessary at this stage to say that in my judgment such a situation as that would inevitably be regarded as intolerable by the

United States and by other peace-minded nations having direct interests in the Pacific, and that, consequently, whether it came tomorrow, or next month, or next year, or even later, the pursuit of such an objective by Japan would inevitably result in armed hostilities in the Pacific.

At this point Mr. Wakasugi interjected to say that what I had stated confirmed his own fears that the situation would now reach an exceedingly critical stage. He said that there were certain underlying factors which the Japanese people could never explain to themselves. He said that when Japan first awoke in the middle of the last century from her long sleep of isolation, she found herself completely surrounded by the imperialistic encroachments which occidental nations had made, not only in China, but in all the Pacific region as well. He said that the United States had been a rapidly expanding and growing country but that Japan was likewise a rapidly expanding country, obviously not on the same scale as the United States, but nevertheless on the same general trend. He said that the Japanese people could not indefinitely be confined to their own poor land and that they had to find, in view of their ever increasing birth rate and their rapidly rising power as a great nation in the world, some means of expanding outside of their own territories. At the very moment that the Japanese people were beginning to realize their situation along these lines, he said, the other great powers of the world had been undertaking exactly the same kind of action, by acquiring colonies and dominating other less advanced peoples, which we, the United States, were now reproaching the Japanese people for undertaking.

I said it would be ludicrous for me to attempt to argue with regard to the policies and measures undertaken by the great powers of the world in the last century but that I was certain that in the years when I had first known Japan, Japan and the United States both agreed that a new and better era in the world was possible and that while, unfortunately enough, a better era had not been realized, I saw no reason for a retrogression in international policy which Mr. Wakasugi seemed to be recommending as a justification for the policy of conquest upon which his country now seemed to be embarked. I said that if it came to a question of expansion, I could quite understand the need for an energetic, able, and rapidly growing race like the Japanese to undertake in their own national interest certain forms of expansion outside of their own national boundaries, but I said that in the considered judgment of this Government the people of Japan would be infinitely more benefited and rendered infinitely more secure by the kind of expansion for which this Government stood than by the policy of expansion for which the present Government of Japan stood. I said that the kind of expansion which I had in mind was the kind of peaceful and productive expansion which resulted in the expansion of Japanese commercial activities in other countries along the lines of equality and non-discrimination which had been for so many years now upheld by the United States. I said I could conceive of no way in which greater prosperity, and contentment and security could come to the Japanese people than by utilizing their great gifts for commercial enterprise and thereby enjoy the great markets which China and other nations of the Far East as well as other nations in other sections of the world offered for peaceful commercial enterprise of this character. I asked him to compare the situation of Japan today, bled as she had been by the militaristic efforts she had been making in one form or another since 1931, with the position which Japan would occupy today if she had embarked upon the other course which I had indicated. I said surely there was great accuracy in what the Japanese Ambassador himself had stated a few days ago when he said that by the occupation of China, Japan had been putting everything into China and getting nothing out. I said that almost inevitably that was the sole result which Japan could gain from her present militaristic course and that the eventual outcome would be, I felt, economic prostration, and possibly social and financial collapse.

I also made very clear my own belief that the United States was confronted by a situation of the utmost gravity in a speech which I delivered on Armistice Day at the tomb of Woodrow Wilson. I reiterated that belief in an off-the-record speech which I made that same month as the guest of the Overseas Press Club in Washington. The forces which were gathering both in Europe and in the Far East had clearly reached the point where they could not much longer be controlled. It seemed to me that any official who possessed any position of responsibility in connection with the conduct of foreign relations had an obligation to make his beliefs known, not in an alarmist spirit but so that the people of the United States would realize beyond any shadow of a doubt how dark the international skies had become.

In Tokyo, Ambassador Grew had done his utmost, in conditions of extreme delicacy—and, at times, of appalling difficulty—to make clear to the Japanese government and people how grave the situation was becoming. There is no foreign post where it is more difficult for an American Ambassador to learn the truth than Tokyo. The reports of Ambassador Grew from the outset of his mission to the last days— seen in the light of the present—reflected with amazing accuracy the true trend of events.

In the United States, the executive branch of the government, besides being obligated to take such measures to prepare for war as are permitted by the co-ordinate branches of the government, is equally obligated to fight for peace until the last moment. I think it can with all certainty be said that the United States government in this instance did just that. It is easier today, of course, than at that time to determine how much of Japanese policy from January to December of 1941 was a "blind" and how much was sincere. Then at least, in order to fight for peace, it was necessary, in addition to seeking pacific solutions, to obtain every shred of intelligence by which the sincerity of the Japanese protestations could be appraised.

Upon two occasions during those final months the President received urgent, detailed requests from Prince Konoye, then still Prime Minister, to meet with him at some point in the Pacific in order to try to solve through personal conferences a situation becoming more and more insoluble as the weeks passed. Prince Konoye was a highly civilized Japanese statesman, weak and vacillating in character but imbued with at least some of the moderate tendencies of his great mentor, Prince Saionji, and he must have appreciated far more accurately than any of his colleagues the tremendous odds Japan would face if she gambled on war with the United States. I myself am not certain to this day of the purpose behind those requests: whether he hoped to utilize the solemn significance which would attach to any official agreement into which he entered with the President of the United States as a means of overriding his fanatical military and naval war lords; or whether this again was a deliberate ruse upon the part of the Japanese government to secure for itself a better striking position. It must also be admitted that it is conceivable, in view of the treacherous nature of the attack upon Pearl Harbor, that the Japanese

may have had some even more sinister purpose in seeking this conference with the President. The plan for a meeting between Roosevelt
and Konoye is at least a tantalizing subject for speculation, particularly if one bears in mind the President's extraordinary ability to
achieve practical results by personal conference with the heads of
foreign governments. In any event, he determined not to venture
upon what seemed a forlorn hope.

With the removal of Prince Konoye as Prime Minister in October,
1941, and the appointment of General Tojo as his successor, any possibility of such negotiations vanished. From that time on the die had
been cast.

For that reason the notorious Kurusu mission becomes even more
fantastic in retrospect. Mr. Kurusu came to Washington in the role
of the goat tethered as bait for the tiger. He was undoubtedly selected
for that purpose because of the mistaken belief of the Tojo Cabinet
that his familiarity and personal ties with the United States, the
acquaintances he possessed in official circles in the American capital,
and the capacity he had demonstrated at other times in dealing with
Western governments would facilitate his mission of deceit. As a
matter of fact, no responsible official in the Administration was ingenuous enough to believe for an instant that any practical benefit
could be gained from Mr. Kurusu's mission. Nor did his oily manner,
his inability to present any convincing reasons for his sudden mission,
the more than naïve protestations of sincerity and of good will which
he so frequently made to members of the Diplomatic Corps in Washington for the obvious purpose of having them repeated to high
authorities in our government, add any conviction to the official conversations in which he attempted to engage. His last call at the Department of State, at the very moment that word was received of the
attack on Pearl Harbor, was thoroughly in keeping with the despica-
ble nature of the job he had been sent to perform.

I imagine that every detail is burned into the memory of anyone
who had any participation in the events of that Sunday of December 7, 1941.

I had many occasions to see the President during the hours between the time the announcement of the attack upon Pearl Harbor
was made and the early hours of the following morning. Sitting

calmly at his desk in the study of the White House, receiving constantly the reports of what was one of the blackest and most tragic episodes in all of American history, he demonstrated that ultimate capacity to dominate and to control a supreme emergency which is perhaps the rarest and most valuable characteristic of any statesman. With complete grasp of every development, with full composure at the receipt of early, and fortunately, unfounded reports that Japanese landing operations in Hawaii were under way, with full realization of all that Pearl Harbor implied and all that it might still further imply to the future of the American people, the President never for one split second ceased to be master of the fate of his country. In all of the many times that I have seen the President I have never had so much reason to admire him. Before the evening of Sunday had passed the President had personally handled every detail of the situation which his military and naval advisers laid before him. He had also approved the nature and text of the declaration of war to be submitted to the Congress of the United States.

At that moment this country entered a new, and what will perhaps be appraised as the most difficult, epoch in its national existence.

Throughout the year 1942 the situation in the Pacific continued to grow worse. The onward rush of the Japanese military and naval forces was unchecked. The people of the United States and the Filipino patriots passed through those grim days which ended in the tragedies of Bataan and Corregidor and in the complete domination of the Philippine Islands by the Japanese troops. The infiltration of Japan into Thailand, accomplished by treachery and by corruption, later terminated in British disaster, the capture of Burma and Malaya and Singapore. Notwithstanding the stout resistance of the Dutch forces in the Netherlands East Indies, these were likewise soon added to Japan's spoils. Finally, her occupation of the strategic islands in the Southwestern Pacific brought her within easy striking distance of Australia and New Zealand. Before 1942 was ended it seemed quite possible that Japan was both able and prepared to invade not only Australia but India as well.

It was only by one of the most admirable feats in the military record of the United States that the Australian, American, and Allied forces obtained in record time and over vast distances the quantity

and quality of arms and ammunition required in order to cease re-
treating and undertake a counteroffensive. They were able finally not
only to prevent the Japanese invasion of the Dominions of the South
Pacific, but likewise to forestall the grave danger of Japanese expansion through and beyond the Indian Ocean. For the danger that the
German and Japanese forces might effect a juncture seemed very
imminent indeed during a great part of that black year.

However completely the physical results of the Japanese attempt to
dominate the Pacific and Asia may be obliterated, it must frankly be
recognized that one psychological development—the growth of nationalism among the peoples of the Far East—has been greatly
accelerated by their triumphs of 1942. It was not only the quick collapse of British resistance in Burma that struck Eastern observers in
that year, but also the apparently incredible rapidity of the surrender
of the great British naval base at Singapore, and the general elimination of all Western resistance to Japan. This nationalistic development is due in part to healthy and spontaneous growth, as represented
by the birth of a greatly unified China and by the demands of the people of India during the past quarter of a century for the right of self-
government. But it has likewise been stimulated by Japanese propaganda during the past five years or more, in all of which much
emphasis has been laid upon the issue of "Asia for the Asiatics."

The inherent justice of that thesis, if divorced from the fact that
it has been put forward to serve their own ends by a people who
have shown the most cynical disregard for the rights of others, has
necessarily made an appeal to all the peoples of the Far East. For
that matter, it has appealed to many peoples in other parts of the
world as well.

Moreover, during the years between 1920 and 1940 a period in
the history of the Asiatic and Pacific peoples was in any event drawing to its close. The startling development of Japan as a world power,
and the slower but nevertheless steady emergence of China as a full
member of the family of nations, together with the growth of popular
institutions among many other peoples of Asia, notably India, all
combined to erase very swiftly indeed the fetish of white supremacy
cultivated by the big colonial powers during the nineteenth century.
The thesis of white supremacy could only exist so long as the white

race actually proved to be supreme. The nature of the defeats suffered by the Western nations in 1942 dealt the final blow to any concept of white superiority which still remained.

Another factor in the Asiatic situation, which we of the West must constantly bear in mind, is that, quite apart from the fact that we cannot logically expect any people to derive satisfaction from their domination by an alien power, the colonizing powers of Europe have only in a few instances used their authority with any regard for the rights or interests of the people over whom they have ruled. Resentments, as a result, are deeply rooted. They have their roots not only in the memory of early brutalities and shocking injustices, but also in such recent horrors as the massacre at Amritsar. They find their origin likewise in the very natural human reaction to the contemptuous treatment usually accorded a subject people by its overlords.

The British government, like the government of the Netherlands, has undoubtedly demonstrated a desire to deal justly with the people within the British Empire, and the spirit of devotion, of decency, and of self-abnegation shown by many thousands of British colonial administrators can only be admired. Yet only too many British representatives in the Far East have demonstrated that type of thinking which is so well exemplified in the words of a high British official in India at the outset of the present century when he expressed a conviction which he asserted "was shared by every Englishman in India, from the highest to the lowest . . . the conviction in every man that he belongs to a race whom God has destined to govern and subdue."

These words might well have been spoken in this present year of grace to the German people by Hitler, or by one of his Nazi associates. They assert the existence of a master race, and the right of that master race to "govern and subdue." We ourselves, the British people, and all free peoples are at the present moment fighting and dying in order to show the intrinsic falsity of any such philosophies as these.

It is hardly surprising, therefore, that as the peoples of Asia have become increasingly conscious of their own individual virtues, of their own national strength, and of their own national resources, any such doctrine as that should become more and more intolerable. If the assertion of these alleged rights has already proved to be so completely unbearable to peoples ruled by the most humane and the least tyrannical of the colonial powers, how far more unbearable it must have proved to peoples dominated by colonial nations mainly bent upon the exploitation of the subject populations.

Some nations, like China, have in the past been only partially subject to foreign domination; others, like the Philippines, have been voluntarily granted their freedom and independence. To the present-day enlightened leaders of such nations, the continued exercise of colonial jurisdiction over the peoples of Asia by European powers has become morally repellent. Also, they necessarily regard it as a source of future peril to the steady development of their free institutions and as a continuing danger to the peace and stability of Asia.

Upon the conclusion of the present war a radical readjustment of international relationships throughout Asia and the regions of the Pacific is indispensable if there is to be any hope at all of political stability, economic security, and peaceful progress. The situation is replete with highly explosive factors. The dynamics of the situation can be regulated, provided the major European and Western powers make the radical readjustments which are necessary. If they do not, it is difficult to foresee any other prospect in the Far East than a century of chaos and general anarchy.

I believe that these new forces of nationalism can successfully be canalized into peaceful and constructive channels only if the powers of the world, in a future international organization, are willing to adopt the basic principle that no nation possesses the inherent and unlimited right to dominate alien peoples. They must recognize that the so-called colonial powers are obligated to prove to world public opinion, as represented by an international organization, that their administration over alien peoples is to the interest of the governed, and has for its chief objective the assumption of self-government by these peoples. Once that great principle is established, it will still be necessary to construct machinery capable of carrying it out.

An international trusteeship of the kind suggested must be first of all responsible to the political executive body established by the world organization. For reasons of efficient administration, under the over-all authority of this supreme executive agency, regional authorities should be set up with jurisdiction over certain stated areas of the world within which local administration of subject peoples is exercised by a colonial power. Finally, representatives of the regional authority should reside within each colonial area in order that the authority may have, in addition to such reports and information as the administering power may be required to present to it periodically, the impartial and objective reports of individuals responsible solely to the international trusteeship.

I will have occasion in a later chapter to deal more specifically with this general problem of an international trusteeship, as a substitute for the discredited and unworkable mandate system provided for by the League of Nations. The trusteeship principle, it seems to me, must be resorted to in any plan looking to future stability in the Far East.

The problems with which any organization such as I have outlined would immediately be faced in the Far East fall into four main categories.

First, the problem presented by the people of Korea. In the Declaration issued at Cairo by Roosevelt, Churchill, and Chiang Kai-shek, with which the Soviet Union must clearly have been in accord, it was stated that the powers concerned would see to it that, upon the defeat of Japan, Korea would regain its independence "in due course." These words "in due course" have created much disquiet among certain Korean patriots. It must be clear, however, that, after a ruthless domination and exploitation such as the Korean people have suffered at the hands of Japan during the past thirty-seven years, a certain period of time must necessarily elapse before the last vestiges of Japanese rule can be wiped out and the independent economy of the country can once more be set up. The Korean people will need sufficient time to strengthen the atrophied muscles of self-government. It is equally clear that some friendly hands must be available to render the assistance required until all of the mechanics of self-government can be supplied by the Korean people themselves.

Such assistance must be given, under the ultimate jurisdiction of the world organization, by powers directly concerned in the welfare of the independent Korea and in the successful stabilization of the Far Eastern situation. In this case it would appear logical that the governments called upon to participate should be China, the Soviet Union, and the United States.

The trusteeship would last until the Korean people demonstrated their ability to walk alone. Until such time the trustee countries, through local administrators who might well be nationals of other countries, would undertake the task of expediting the return of the Korean people to the responsibilities of self-government.

The second category would comprise those peoples of the Far East now under the control of a colonial power, but believed to be capable of enjoying autonomy in the immediate future. Within this category would come India.

There is no useful purpose to be served by debating whether or not the people of India are capable of self-government, since upon several occasions since the conclusion of the first World War, notably two years ago during the special mission to India by Sir Stafford Cripps, the British government has officially announced its intention of granting self-government to India. As recently as January 28, 1944, that most enlightened and liberal-minded of Indian Viceroys, Lord Halifax, publicly stated in the name of the British government:

> We hope that India, in what we believe to be her own highest interests, will wish to remain within the British Commonwealth. But if, after the war, her people can establish an agreed constitution and then desire to sever their partnership with us, we have undertaken not to overrule such decision. . . . If India cannot yet agree to move forward as a single whole, we are prepared to see her large component elements move forward separately. We recognize all the objections to a rupture of Indian unity, but we also believe that stability cannot be found through compulsion of the great minorities. . . . This attitude is in complete conformity with the principle of the Atlantic Charter.

Thus it is clear that, provided the people of India and the British government can reach an agreement as to the basis upon which an independent government of India can be established, a solution for this ever-increasingly intricate and dangerous problem can be found. Such a solution will not be made easier by intemperate outpourings from Downing Street, nor by equally intemperate insistence by pundits in the United States that the way to solve the problem is for British authority to remove itself bag and baggage from India between dawn and night. Obviously the ideal method of solution is through direct negotiation between the British government and the representative leaders of India. It is a method which has already frequently been adopted. However, should these efforts continue to fail, the executive council of the international organization, through its agencies, should stand ready to assist in composing the difficulties which might still exist.

Neither die-hardism in England nor ultraliberalism in other countries, such as the United States, can change one salient fact, and that is that the people of India are determined to obtain self-government. A continuation of the present impasse after the war will seriously endanger the peace and stability of all of the Far East. The independent peoples of the Far East today, let alone those still under alien rule, not only view the aspirations of the Indian leaders with the utmost sympathy, but regard the disposition to be made of India after the war as the acid test of the intentions of the Western powers as set forth in the Atlantic Charter.

Equally clearly within this category fall the Netherlands East Indies. But I am inclined to believe that this problem has probably been solved already. In 1942 the Netherlands government-in-exile announced its decision that upon the liberation of Holland a new federal constitution would be promulgated under which the peoples of the Netherlands East Indies would be guaranteed precisely the same constitutional rights of self-government and individual liberty as the people of the Netherlands themselves. If this pledge can be carried out, the peoples of the Netherlands East Indies will have ample means of determining their own destiny, and any question of international trusteeship in their case should not arise.

The third category would include the problems of Burma, Malaya, and French Indo-China. The peoples of these countries have all passed the first milestone along the road toward self-government; but they have not as yet reached a stage of development where they can successfully undertake the exercise of those rights. In such cases the world organization, operating through the supreme agency of the international trusteeship and the regional authorities to be created, must assert its right to hold the present administering powers responsible for the nature of their administration. This will ensure that every practical step is taken to accelerate the course of these countries toward independence. I would further propose that the regional authority in this instance be entrusted to the present colonial powers, namely, Great Britain and France, and that China, Australia, New Zealand, and the future republic of the Philippines likewise participate in such regional authority. It seems to me logical, and from many standpoints highly desirable, that the seat of the executive agency of the regional authority should be at Manila.

The fourth category would comprise those colonial peoples of the Southwestern Pacific who are still uncivilized and as yet clearly incapable of governing themselves. The aborigines of the islands of the South Pacific, such as the peoples of New Guinea, would be an example. As in the case of the peoples comprised within the third category, the supreme agency of the international trusteeship, through a regional authority, should exercise ultimate control over the local government of the administering power. This will ensure that the peoples governed are treated with humanity and justice, that their natural resources will be exploited primarily for their benefit rather than for the benefit of the administering power. It will also make certain that all possible steps will be taken for their physical and moral improvement and for their education, until such time as their descendants may demonstrate their ability to exercise autonomy.

In this brief survey of possible future dispositions in the Pacific, it is of course assumed that the promises made in the Declaration of Cairo will be carried out. There it was announced that the territory seized from China during past generations by Japan would be restored to the sovereign jurisdiction of the republic of China, and that the Pacific islands over which Japan obtained jurisdiction as a mandatory upon the conclusion of the first World War would be utilized by the international organization primarily for purposes of international security.

Apart, therefore, from normal and continuing participation in Pacific affairs by the nations of North and South America and by the Soviet Union, the New Order in the Far East, far different from that envisaged by Japan, will comprise the republic of China, restored to the control of the territories of which it has been robbed; the Dominions of Australia and New Zealand; the independent states of the Philippine Republic and Korea; India, as a self-governing Dominion or as an independent nation; the Netherlands East Indies, as an autonomous and integral part of the kingdom of the Netherlands; and a diminished Japan, to be placed, for at least a period of years, under some form of rigid international control exercised through the world organization.

The statesmanship of the United States government and the essential wisdom of the American people in the field of foreign affairs will be tested as they have never been before when the time comes to decide on the policy to be followed in regard to a defeated Japan. The future of the American people will in great part depend upon the nature of these decisions. Of one thing they can be everlastingly sure: that upon the United States will be concentrated the lasting resentment of the Japanese people for their defeat.

In Hallett Abend's admirable book *My Life in China*, the author quotes the Japanese Consul General at Hong Kong, Okasaki, as having said in the spring of 1941:

> One of our formally adopted policies now is to "get even" . . . Our whole literate population feels this way—a slumbering, smoldering hatred because America is blocking our moves in East Asia. And as a people, we do not forget.

How much more bitter that hatred and that resentment will be upon the conclusion of the present war we can readily conceive.

There can be no question but that Japan must be deprived of her stolen territories. The Japanese criminals, high or low, who have been guilty of the hideous atrocities perpetrated upon our own nationals and upon those of other countries during these war years must be relentlessly punished. Japan must be disarmed, and prevented from rearming, under a continuing form of international control. But, as Ambassador Grew has wisely said with regard to this very problem, if steam is confined in a vessel from which there is no outlet, there will be an inevitable explosion. Neither sentimentality nor softness, therefore, inspires my considered conviction that one of the factors determining whether the United States will in the future be secure, and whether a lasting world organization can be created, will be the manner in which the Japanese people are handled.

The people of Japan have demonstrated their power and their ability, however evil the purpose to which these may have been applied. They have shown their willingness to subordinate themselves as human beings to what they conceive to be their national interest. They can exist and prosper at an incredibly low standard of living. They breed fast. They are governed more directly as a national unit by blind hate and by the spirit of revenge than any other major people of the earth. Those are facts which cannot be brushed aside.

There is not the shadow of a doubt that the Japanese military and naval high commands, submerged though they will be after Japan's defeat, will keep alive their organization, precisely as the German General Staff will endeavor to keep alive its organization, and plan for the eventual day of revenge. In making our peace decisions, as in shaping our long-range policy, these facts should be kept uppermost in mind.

In my opinion there is but one constructive approach to the problem. This involves three major objectives which should be pursued consistently, whether or not the majority of Americans are once more lulled into a false feeling of security. First, an unswerving determination to make every necessary contribution toward the existence of an effective world organization. Second, the continued disarmament of Japan. Third, the establishment by international agreement of liberal economic policies which will afford the Japanese people an outlet for their abilities and for their enterprise. That is the only course by which they can gradually improve their standard of living, without at the same time endangering the peace of the rest of the world.

# CHAPTER VIII

# The Constructive Power of the U.S.S.R.

IN THE first postwar years the two greatest powers, both from a material as well as from a military standpoint, will be the United States and the Union of Soviet Socialist Republics. Frank recognition of this fact must underlie any consideration of the policy which this government should pursue toward the Soviet Union.

The maintenance of world peace and the progress of humanity is going to depend upon the desire and the capacity of the peoples of the two countries to work together. It will depend upon their ability to replace their relationship of the past quarter of a century, which has not only been negative but marked by fanatical suspicion and deep-rooted hostility on both sides, with one that is positive and constructive.

During the period between the two wars the people of the United States lacked even the desire for a common understanding with the Russian people. Popular opinion in this country was molded by an almost unanimous detestation for Communism in all its aspects —particularly for its doctrine of world revolution—and by the violent and justifiable revulsion against the bloody excesses of the Soviet government, especially during the first years after the Bolshevik revolution of 1917. Furthermore, the people of the United States were profoundly repelled by the steps taken by the Soviet government in its vain attempt first to deny and then to destroy religion.

For their part, the Soviet leaders and the Russian people as a whole have seen the United States and the other so-called capitalist countries erect against them a wall of political antagonism. Quite naturally, they have been prone to interpret this in the light of the open efforts of the Allied governments, upon the conclusion of the first World War, to assist reactionary elements within Russia to overthrow the revolutionary government and to substitute for it a conservative regime subservient to the desires of the Western world. They have also seen the Western powers agree to the transfer to other peoples of territory which had for many years formed an integral part of greater Russia. They had some reason to believe not long ago that the Western nations, in the hope of keeping the robber powers out of their own preserves, were ready and willing to sanction the notorious plan of the German General Staff to divide additional spoils torn from Russia between Germany and Japan. And at one time they were led to the conclusion that the policy of this country was dominated by those financial interests which demanded the full payment with compound interest of the debts incurred by the imperial governments of Russia, and that, until this condition was met, the people of the United States would continue to look with jaundiced eyes upon their efforts at regeneration. In the years when Hitler was poising himself for his final thrust against the rest of civilized mankind, statesmen as well as important newspapers in all the Western countries loudly proclaimed that were Hitler to overwhelm Communist Russia the rest of the world would be the gainer thereby.

In brief, the record is far from one-sided. Recent events, political trends, the very conditions in which the world has lived during this past generation have all tended to create in each country a mass of deep-rooted resentments and prejudices which only statesmanship of the highest order and joint determination can hope to eradicate.

Far too many influential figures in this country have been glibly announcing that the fact that our two nations are joined today in the war against Hitlerism is sufficient to ensure complete understanding and enduring friendship in the years to come. No talk could be more intrinsically harmful. Such assertions tend to blind public opinion to the thorny truth that there is as yet no common understanding; that there are major problems to be solved before any such understanding can be achieved; and that our foreign policy today has no more difficult task before it. Unless both governments and both peoples make a sincere and determined attempt to find a new foundation for the relationship between the two nations, the

very cornerstone of any future international organization will be
lacking.

Such an effort on our part will be made much easier if we keep
in mind certain salient factors in the history of the Russian people,
as well as the policies of their governments both before and after
the revolution of 1917. For one thing must be remembered, however much it may be denied by a few apologists for Soviet policy, and
that is that, during the last fifteen years of the Soviet regime, the
policy of Russia toward the other nations of Europe and the world
objectives sought by her strikingly parallel the policies followed and
the objectives sought by Russian governments during the preceding
two centuries. The basic truth of this assertion is not changed by
the fact that the Soviet government, primarily as a weapon for
defense, has sought at times to utilize the Communist International
to further a world revolution. That hope, incidentally, was obviously
becoming more and more a fantastic and forlorn delusion in the
years prior to this war.

Too many of us are apt to forget that, until the year 1861, the
overwhelming majority of the Russian people were serfs. Until
that time Russia was a vast sprawling territory, only brought into
actual contact with the Western world by Peter the Great at the
close of the seventeenth century, and ruled by the most autocratic
governments which modern history has known. The masses of the
Russian population were no more than the chattels of a small oligarchy of nobles and members of the gentry.

The tidal waves which recurrently swept Europe as a result of
the French Revolution in 1789 and which culminated in the revolutionary year of 1848 were barely felt within Imperial Russia. The
servitude of the masses and their total illiteracy made it possible for
successive Czars to close Russia's doors hermetically to any foreign
revolutionary doctrines. Even the earlier liberal tendencies of Alexander I were transformed before his death into policies as autocratic, reactionary, and devastating as those followed by his grand-
mother, Catherine the Great, or by his brother and successor
Nicholas I.

It was only after Alexander II emancipated the serfs in 1861
that a tremendous social force began to ferment in Russia. From

time to time appearing upon the surface during the closing years of the nineteenth century, it had its being largely underground. It culminated finally in the Bolshevik Revolution of 1917. It is true that during the first half of the nineteenth century a few within university circles were influenced by contemporary Western thought, and that in Michael Bakunin there is found the originator of the later school of Russian anarchism, but only with the generation which came to maturity after the year of emancipation did there develop the school of Russian intelligentsia that paved the way for the people's revolution of today.

Each attempt during the nineteenth century to accomplish a gradual transformation from absolutism to constitutional monarchy was subsequently reversed by ukase. Even the halfhearted effort in the reign of the last Czar, Nicholas II, to lay rudimentary foundations for constitutional government by the creation of the Russian Duma was frustrated by the elements of black reaction surrounding that weak and unhappy monarch.

What must not be forgotten, therefore, is that before 1917 the Russian people as a whole never had the slightest voice in the policy of their government. Only in the past twenty-five years has the determining force within Russia come from the masses as well as from an autocratic few at the top. It is easy to assert that the Russian, as an individual, is still merely a cog in the wheel turned by a highly centralized dictatorship. From the standpoint of our Western tradition, that is superficially true. From the standpoint of the Russian people, it is a hopelessly inadequate appraisal. The Russian people today are satisfied that their government is devoted to the popular interest. While the methods by which popular reactions are made apparent within the Soviet Union are totally different from those within the Western democracies, and particularly within the United States, the Soviet government today is guided by the popular will, and ultimately depends upon that will for its existence. Certainly in the immediate future the foreign policy of the Soviet government will continue to represent what the people want. Therein lies its claim for recognition by the people of this country as representing a real and permanent force.

Various aspects of Russian foreign policy during the past two and a half centuries are strangely significant in the light of the present. It was Peter the Great who wrought the first great change in Russian history. By wresting the Baltic Provinces from Sweden, he obtained for Russia the "windows to the West"—the vital outlet to the Baltic Sea without which she could scarcely have become a European power. Catherine the Great and Potemkin gained from Turkey mastery of the Black Sea, and by doing so began that long duel with Great Britain for control of the Dardanelles which in Russian hands would have made Russia a Mediterranean power. It was Catherine who was primarily responsible for one of the greatest international crimes of history, by conniving with, and even inducing, Prussia and Austria to participate in three successive encroachments upon the territory of Poland. Finally, through the third partition in 1795, Poland ceased to exist; all of her people had been divided between the three predatory powers. Paul I, in conjunction with Napoleon, planned for the overland invasion of India, and thus engendered that continuing series of nightmares which disturbed the sleep of all British Prime Ministers and Viceroys of India throughout the nineteenth century.

Every successive Czar during two centuries, from 1689 to 1869, fostered the gradual, steady expansion of the Russian people through the Siberian wastes to the Pacific Ocean. This finally resulted in the firm establishment of Russia as a Pacific power with full domination as far south as the banks of the Amur River.

While successive imperial governments, during the earlier part of the nineteenth century, had intervened repeatedly on behalf of the Slavonic Christians, who were still suffering under Turkish rule over the Balkan Provinces, it was under Alexander II and Alexander III that Russia's Pan-Slavic doctrines were first proclaimed as cardinal principles of Russian foreign policy.

The significance of these aspects of Russia's traditional foreign policy and of their hold upon the imagination of the Russian people themselves should not be minimized, for much of European history has turned upon these policies of the past. In my opinion such policies will soon again play an important part.

By the time the Russian people finally rose to overthrow the hopelessly incompetent government of the last Czar in 1917, Russia had not only assimilated her territorial acquisitions, but she had even been assured by the Allied governments that at the close of the war she would at last be given control over the Dardanelles.

After the Bolshevik government had been forced to conclude the Treaty of Brest-Litovsk with an apparently victorious Germany in March, 1918, she was stripped of all the territories in Central and Eastern Europe which she had obtained since the time of Peter the Great. Immediately thereafter Finland, by force of arms, won its independence of Russian control, an independence sanctioned by the Soviet government itself. The Baltic provinces of Latvia and Estonia likewise achieved their freedom. The remaining province of Lithuania was granted its independence by the Treaty of Versailles. So Russia's entrance to the Baltic, obtained for her by Peter the Great, was closed.

By the Treaty of Riga, which the Soviet government was forced to conclude with the reconstituted Poland in 1921 after the Polish armies, assisted by the French, had defeated the Russian troops at the gates of Warsaw, she was deprived of vast additional territories. They had at one time been under Polish sovereignty, it is true, but in a great portion of them the Polish population did not exceed ten per cent of the total. Much of the Ukraine was thereby wrested from her. By the Treaty of Versailles the province of Bessarabia had already been incorporated within the new Rumania.

Russia thus entered the postwar period, under her new revolutionary government, stripped of far-reaching territories in Eastern Europe. She regarded these not only as vital to her security but as indispensable to her position as a European power. At the same time her Siberian provinces were being invaded by Japan and other Allied powers bent upon fostering that counterrevolution which it was thought might result in the establishment of a more responsive and amenable government in Moscow.

Granted the history of the Russian people, and the fact that the masses themselves now believed that they were at last on the path to the enjoyment of popular rights, it is hardly surprising that they should have been fertile ground for propaganda against the "predatory capitalist nations" of the West.

There was, of course, one way in which the breach between the

Soviet Union and the Western powers might have been avoided. It was the way Woodrow Wilson advocated. But it called for sufficient vision and constructive statesmanship on the part of the powers represented in the Council of the League of Nations to realize that a League without the Soviet Union could not long function successfully in Europe.

Postwar Europe was a desperately shaken community. That same strange contagion of panic which swept Europe at the close of the eighteenth century again gripped the continent in the early twenties of this century. Governments and the wealthier classes saw the specter of Bolshevism in every sign of unrest, political or social. Not only the British and French governments, but this government as well, were firm in the illusion that through a rigidly enforced quarantine the miasma emanating from Moscow could be prevented from spreading its ills abroad. Both the British and French governments, therefore, steadfastly refused to consider the possibility that the League of Nations should be called upon to deal with the Soviet government except at very long range indeed. It must be admitted, however, that Lenin's anathema of the League as a tool of the capitalistic powers was not conducive to a change of sentiment on the part of the Council of the League.

When Soviet delegates were permitted to come to Rapallo in 1922 they were isolated as if they were lepers. Their conclusion there with Germany of the Treaty of Rapallo made it evident to some of the more clearsighted leaders in the Western powers that the German General Staff was far from moribund, and that Germany had been enabled to gain a great advantage, tragically and shortsightedly rejected by Great Britain and by France. German foreign policy throughout the Stresemann period used this understanding with Russia as its chief card in all dealings with the Western European powers. Russian policy was thereby turned back from the democratic West, and encouraged to brood for more than a decade upon the destructive dogmas of world revolution rather than upon the constructive possibilities of world co-operation inherent in the League.

But in any event Russia was at that time principally concerned with her internal problems. Bolshevism had been founded upon the doctrines of Karl Marx, which were first made known in Russia in

1872, and which were applicable, in the concept of their author, to economies that were primarily industrial. The new government had to adjust the Marxist theories to a national economy where the industrial population was only an infinitesimal percentage of the agricultural population. The impossibility of applying the pure Marxist philosophy, under such conditions, and the violent rivalries, both individual and doctrinary, which were constantly coming to the fore, demanded the first attention of the revolutionary leaders. As the one practical solution of these initial problems, Lenin assumed dictatorial authority in 1921. Upon his death in 1924, the supreme control passed into the hands of Stalin, Kamenev, and Zinoviev.

Any hopes that Lenin or the more doctrinaire of his associates may have had that Communism in its revolutionary aspect would spread throughout the world were shown to be illusory. In none of the Western powers of Europe, much less in the United States, did the doctrines of world Communism meet with any popular support. Even among the sorely beset and suffering peoples of Central and Southeastern Europe the flare-up of Communism lasted but a brief moment.

Russia itself gradually swung back from the early and fantastic extremes of the Trotskyist school of violence. The execution of the leaders of the Roman Catholic Church, and the deposition of the famous patriarch of the Orthodox Church, Tikhon, resulted, by the admission of the Soviet leaders themselves, in their realization that religion could not be stamped out of the Russian heart.

In the realm of economics, the stubborn refusal of the Russian peasant to produce more than he required for his own consumption unless he were permitted some reasonable profit, after a series of famines and highly disruptive disorders, forced a return to a more rational basis for collective farming.

The 1920's were necessarily dedicated to the readjustment made necessary by the growing breach between the Soviet leaders, such as Zinoviev, who were determined to concentrate upon the plans for world revolution, formulated by the Comintern, and the leaders who followed Stalin in desiring to set the course back toward the establishment of a workable form of state socialism. The long-protracted and bitter controversy ended only in 1928 with the final victory of Stalin, and the expulsion of Trotsky from Russian soil.

The year 1929 marked the turning point in modern Russian history. In that year the Five-Year Plan was announced to the Russian people. It had as its chief objective a self-sufficient Russia— self-sufficient not only in an industrial sense, but likewise in a military sense. For Stalin already saw clearly that unless the Russian people themselves could rapidly produce the necessary means of self-defense, through their internal economy as well as through their armies, the country would be unable to survive the dangers ahead.

Under the conditions which then existed, the rapid industrialization of Russia could be achieved only by means of foreign credits. In view of the Soviet government's repudiation of the national debts incurred by preceding governments, and in view of the suspicion with which the West still regarded any contact with Russia, credits, except on the shortest terms and at an inordinate rate of interest, were almost unprocurable. The situation, however, had to be met, and it was met in large part by the exportation of raw materials, desperately needed at home, in payment for what was required from abroad.

To satisfy the more extreme of the doctrinaires, further efforts were made, even during this critical period, to put an end to religious education as well as instruction in independent schools which refused to make Communism the basis for their teaching. But, as in the earlier years of the revolutionary period, both efforts proved futile and were slowly abandoned.

The success of the Five-Year Plan, however, exceeded all expectations and was viewed with incredulous amazement in other parts of the world. Industries increased each year at a fantastic rate. Whole new towns sprang into being in every part of the Soviet Union. The Five-Year Plan became, in fact, the subject of almost idolatrous devotion on the part of Russian youth. It was for them the first concrete evidence that the people's revolution was bringing results, not only for the people's benefit but also for the greater glory of Russia. The Five-Year Plan alone made it possible for Russia twelve years later to resist the German onslaught successfully. Stalin's ability to increase his control over the Soviet regime and to triumph

over those earlier revolutionary leaders who sought to question his
policies was also due largely to the success of this experiment.

Each year that passed marked an advance from the earlier stages
of impractical and unproductive Communism toward state socialism. By 1935 the basis for a practical, rather than an ideological,
state education had been re-established; the staggering percentage
of national illiteracy was being sharply reduced; family ties were
once more respected; and various categories of personal property
were sanctioned. By 1936 a new constitution had been proclaimed
and approved. This established the right to hold property (exceedingly limited in practice, as to both quantities and categories) and,
nominally at least, the rights of universal and equal suffrage, freedom of worship, freedom of the press, and freedom of speech and
assembly. While it is true that the exercise of these rights was ini-
tially greatly restricted, it is noteworthy that their enjoyment has
expanded each year since the Constitution was proclaimed. The
right of religious worship is today far more nearly actual than theoretical.

During the decade 1930-1940, the leaders of the Soviet government were compelled by circumstances to devote more and more of
their attention to the course of events in Europe and the rest of
the world.

The election of President Roosevelt in 1932 brought with it the
end of a sterile chapter in American foreign policy. The refusal
of this government during the preceding twelve years to maintain
any official relations with the government of Russia raised some
grave questions as to the realism of the policies of the American
statesmen who had been shaping the foreign policy of this nation.

In the early days of the Republic the United States accorded recognition to a foreign government as soon as that government seemed
to have established itself in power, to possess evidence of popular
support, and gave assurance that it was prepared to abide by its
international commitments. The refusal of the United States to
recognize the revolutionary government of Russia was based primarily upon the unwillingness of the Soviet government to recognize
the validity of debts incurred by preceding Russian governments,

and upon the proclamation by the state-fostered Communist International of world revolution as its objective.

The refusal of the United States to enter into official relations with the Soviet government did nothing to cause it to reconsider its position on these two points. In contrast to our policy, both the British and French governments, with a very practical desire to obtain commercial advantages, had resumed diplomatic relations as soon after the war as they had overcome their fears of the efficacy of Russian revolutionary propaganda. It is true that after Zinoviev was charged with the authorship of a letter inciting Communist revolution in England, a letter which had become a prime weapon of political attack against the British Labor government, relations remained broken between the United Kingdom and the Soviet Union from 1927 to the autumn of 1929, and were only resumed when the British Labor party again came to power. It is likewise true that the French government at the same time dismissed the Soviet Ambassador in Paris on the charge that he was responsible for revolutionary propaganda in the French Army. But both the British and French governments, far more affected than our own by the question of revolutionary propaganda and the problem of Russian debts, had taken what seems a more objective attitude in so far as recognition is concerned: that in questions affecting Russia's relations with other nations, a solution is far more readily available through direct contacts than if no contacts at all exist.

The policy followed by the United States is now shown by experience to have been of no practical value whatever. The Soviet government showed not the slightest intention of reconsidering its position on the subject of the debt payments and such activities as were being carried on by the Communist International were not arrested because of our official attitude.

In fact, our policy became more and more emotional rather than objective. Many of us still remember the hysteria with which Secretary of State Kellogg was wont to react to any mention of the Soviet Union. Both he and President Coolidge were so swayed by their detestation of Communism that all the other issues involved went by the board.

Our policy was tantamount to an assertion that the United States regarded as nonexistent the government of a nation of one hundred seventy million people, occupying the greatest single area in the world, a nation of the utmost potential importance to the people of this country from the standpoint of our legitimate interests in both Asia and Europe.

Our people overlooked the fact that with no major power have our interests in the past collided less frequently, and that at various critical moments in our own national history the policies pursued by Russian governments have been of the highest value to us.

For example, the Russian government adamantly refused to favor or participate in the plans to propose a European mediation in the American Civil War, then under discussion between the British government and the government of Napoleon III. Neither the government of Lord Palmerston nor that of Napoleon III would have been at all averse to seeing a division of the American Federal Union, for that would have diminished for all time the potential power of the United States. If Russia had not withheld her approval, the mediation would have taken place with incalculable consequences to the future of our people. This attitude was obviously in no sense due to any love for the United States or its institutions on the part of Alexander II or his advisers. It was of advantage to Russia that a powerful United States should continue to exist in the world as an offset to Great Britain. For similar reasons, Russian policy has frequently paralleled that of this country.

Few people today recall that in 1780, at a most critical moment in our War of Independence, the Russian government, together with Portugal, Austria, and the two Scandinavian nations, Denmark and Sweden, formed a bloc of armed neutrals which refused to accept the supremacy of British sea power. This bloc, under Russian inspiration, insisted that neutral ships should be permitted normal communications with belligerents unless blockades were instituted, and that such blockades need not be recognized unless they were effective; that only arms and ammunition should be considered contraband; and that a neutral flag should cover belligerent goods except for contraband. The determination of the armed neutrality bloc that these rules should be established was of vital assistance to the struggling American colonies.

From a practical as well as from a historical standpoint there was every reason in 1933 to seek an end to the deadlock between the two countries. President Roosevelt, prior to his inauguration, had determined, as a basic part of his foreign policy, to rectify this condition. It was, of course, necessary for him to be guided during the negotiations by the clear requirements of legitimate United States interests. But he had also to take into consideration the almost insuperable wall of public prejudice which had been built up against everything relating to Soviet activities. The moment the possibility of establishing any relationship with the Soviet Union was even mentioned, a loud clamor arose. It was claimed that such a course would open the door to a flood of Communist agents.

Tentative soundings taken during the summer of 1933 gave assurance that a reasonable foundation existed for the resumption of official relations between the two countries, and in the late autumn of that year the Soviet Foreign Commissar, Maxim Litvinov, came to the United States. In the ensuing conversations, the President and the Foreign Commissar reached satisfactory agreements on the question with which popular opinion was then chiefly concerned: the guarantee that subversive activities within this country would not be undertaken by agents, indirect or direct, of the Soviet government. However, they came to no satisfactory understanding on the question of the debts incurred either by the Imperial Russian governments or by the short-lived Kerensky government. This matter was consequently postponed for settlement at a future time.

Official relations were immediately established by the reciprocal appointment of Ambassadors. If the two governments had shown more concern in following up this beginning, they might well have reached a satisfactory working understanding far more speedily than they did. Unfortunately, the supervision of Soviet-American relations in both Washington and Moscow was largely entrusted by this government to men who proved incapable and unsympathetic to the task of bettering the ties between the two countries. Nor, it must be frankly stated, were more friendly relations encouraged by the continued subversive activities of Communist International agents in other parts of the Western Hemisphere, notably in Mexico, Uruguay, and Brazil.

The fact is that official relations between the two countries were purely nominal and almost entirely static until Joseph E. Davies was sent as Ambassador to Moscow by President Roosevelt in the first days of 1937. I doubt whether people in this country as yet realize sufficiently the concrete value of the work accomplished by Ambassador Davies during his relatively brief mission to the Soviet Union. Entirely devoid of any ideological sympathy for Communism, and by no means captivated by certain policies of the Soviet government, Ambassador Davies brought to his task an open mind, a completely objective point of view, and a wealth of political and practical experience. Above all else, he was governed by a deep-seated conviction that, in view of the increasingly dark international horizon, a way must be found to remove every unnecessary obstacle to the establishment of a closer understanding between the two peoples. He has himself written about his mission. But his achievements can properly be evaluated today only in the light of the war years. Had the foundations not been laid, the efforts of both governments to find a common meeting ground in 1941 would have been far more difficult.

It was during the years before Munich that Maxim Litvinov at last had an opportunity to demonstrate the quality of his outstanding talents. For it was then, with her internal conditions well in hand, that Russia at last sought to play a more co-operative part in European affairs. And Great Britain and France now finally, although hesitatingly, accepted her co-operation. In 1934 she became a member of the League of Nations and immediately, through the energy and inspiration of Litvinov himself, became a prime factor in League affairs.

These were years of constantly mounting difficulties for the Soviet Union. The dangers in the world situation were always obvious to the realistic vision of Stalin and Litvinov. In the Far East, Japan, by her invasion of Manchuria, threatened the vital interests of Russia in her Siberian reaches. With the consolidation of Japanese control in North China and in Inner Mongolia, the Soviet government was forced to relinquish its interest in the Chinese Eastern Railway. Although Russia assumed protection of Outer Mongolia and Chinese Turkestan, she was pushed back by Japanese encroachments to the line of the Amur River. Even this tactical withdrawal did not prevent constant border clashes with the Japanese militarists, any one of which might unexpectedly have proved the forerunner of a major conflagration.

In Europe, first the growth of Fascism in Italy and then the far graver peril of Hitlerism in Germany only too obviously threatened the existence of the Soviet state. It did not need the conclusion of the Anti-Comintern Pact between Germany and Japan to tell the Soviet leaders that the German General Staff was planning the dismemberment of Russia through simultaneous attacks by Germany on one side and by Japan on the other. The German Army's perpetual ambition to rob Russia of the Ukraine, even though a part of Ukraine territory had now become a portion of the new Poland, was once more uppermost.

To guard against these dangers, the Soviet government attempted both to reinforce the power of the League of Nations and to achieve a measure of security through the negotiation of special agreements with France and other powers directly allied to France. The Protocol of Mutual Assistance, signed by France and Russia in 1934, was supplemented by a further pact in May, 1935, together with a Soviet-Czechoslovak Pact of Mutual Assistance signed on May 16 of the same year.

The ability of the Soviet government to complete its task of internal reconstruction, in order to be ready to defend Russia against what seemed an inevitable war in the East as well as in the West, depended upon its ability to gain time and to make the Western democracies realize that they themselves were endangered.

Litvinov became the foremost prophet of the basic principles underlying the Covenant of the League of Nations. No responsible European statesman in the decade of the thirties saw more clearly or spoke more truly. Unfortunately, he proved to be a prophet crying in the wilderness. His insistence that peace is indivisible fell on deaf ears. His demand that the Western powers join with the Soviet Union in recognizing the dangers inherent in the rearmament of Germany was disregarded. In the light of present events, no statesman of those years, with the exception of Winston Churchill, has been proved more consistently right.

The difficulty, of course, was that in Great Britain Mr. Baldwin was still maintaining that there was no danger of a new German aggression and that only rearmament by his country could create such a danger. And in France, the days of degeneration were already approaching their climactic tragedy. The work of the agents of the German General Staff was bearing fruit. In so far as the United States was concerned, the doctrines of isolation were paramount; the very idea that the ground swell already resulting from Hitler's early moves to create the greater Germany could ever break upon the shores of the United States was regarded in many quarters as sheer nonsense.

In those prewar years, great financial and commercial interests of the Western democracies, including many in the United States, were firm in the belief that war between the Soviet Union and Hitlerite Germany could only be favorable to their own interests. They maintained that Russia would necessarily be defeated, and with this defeat Communism would be destroyed; also that Germany would be so weakened as a result of the conflict that for many years thereafter she would be incapable of any real threat to the rest of the world.

This stupendous lack of realism on the part of the so-called realists did incalculable damage in its effect upon the sentiments of the Russian people and the policies of the Soviet government. By the end of 1938 the Soviet government had reached the conclusion that it could not expect any sincere assistance from the Western powers, and that such armed assistance as they could give, even were it definitely forthcoming, could be of only minor avail.

Internally, Stalin had already cleaned house. The notorious and much-dramatized purges had eliminated from positions of authority within the Soviet Union, and particularly within the Soviet Army, those individuals who had been suborned by the German General Staff.

From the standpoint of foreign policy, a radical readjustment was determined upon. The views of the Soviet government in 1938 are concisely set forth in a report sent to Washington by Ambassador Davies at that time.

Litvinov's position and the attitude of this country definitely is that a Fascist peace is being imposed on Europe; that ultimately Europe will be completely Fascist with the exception of England and the Soviet Union; and that finally Italy will desert Germany as she did during the great war; that Soviet Russia must count on no outside aid and in fact must be and is completely self-contained and independent; that France cannot be depended upon; that there is no hope for the maintenance of law and order based on public morality between nations until the reactionary elements in England in power are overthrown; that they see no immediate prospect of this.

The agreements of Munich confirmed the conviction of the Soviet government that the Western powers strove to keep Germany from the west only by turning her to the east.

Through an official pronouncement of the Communist party, the Soviet government declared in the spring of 1939: "Relying solely on its own strength it will be able to withstand the attack of any coalition, and to destroy the enemy on his own territory."

In March of 1939, in an address delivered to the Party Congress of the Soviet Union, Stalin seized the opportunity to warn the Western powers finally that continued appeasement of Hitler and of the Fascist government of Italy would end in ruin. He added a characteristic blunt declaration that Russia would under no conditions pull the chestnuts out of the fire for the Western powers. That was the last warning given. Early in May, Molotov replaced Litvinov as Foreign Commissar and the first steps were taken toward finding the basis for an uneasy truce between Hitlerism and the Soviet Union.

The replacement of Maxim Litvinov under these conditions had been inevitable. In the councils of Europe, Litvinov had gained an outstanding position. He had won for himself recognition of his real, if frequently brutal, sincerity. He had seen clearly and he had spoken the truth. But the policy for which he stood was the policy that "peace is indivisible"—which he had in his hoarse and guttural voice preached so often to deaf ears at Geneva. He was identified, consequently, with a policy of international co-operation for which the League of Nations stood, but which, through no fault of his, it had failed to carry out.

It is interesting to recall a similar maneuver in Russian foreign policy that took place some one hundred thirty-two years previously. During the early years of the Napoleonic Wars, Russia had been steadfastly aligned with England and her allies in withstanding Napoleon's attempt to dominate Europe. On land the chief burden of the contest fell primarily upon the Russian armies. Disheartened by the weakness and double-dealing of a majority of his allies, Alexander I saw that Russia could not long continue the hopelessly unequal struggle. After he had signed with Napoleon the Treaty of Tilsit in 1807, as a result of which Russia deserted England, Prussia, and Sweden, the Emperor Alexander said to a friend: "At least I will gain time." For five years thereafter the Russian government held aloof. When it re-entered the struggle against Napoleon in 1812 its participation was decisive.

In the summer of 1939, the Soviet government not only believed her potential allies to be weak and ineffective, but also feared that, should war break out, they would seek to throw the major burden upon the Russian people.

The history of the negotiations undertaken in the early spring of 1939 between the British and French governments and the Soviet Union for the purpose of agreeing upon joint action in the event of German aggression anywhere in Europe makes painful reading. The negotiations lasted four months. Ostensibly they collapsed because the Western democracies were unwilling to let Russia impair the integrity of the smaller countries of Eastern Europe. Actually they broke down because the Soviet government had already determined that two could play at the same game. It suspected that the Western powers were doing everything they could to turn Hitler to the east and therefore decided to checkmate them by turning him to the west. The protracted ostracism of Russia, her abstention from the League until five short years before, the hostility with which the Soviet government had long been treated in the West, had all combined to create so much suspicion and distrust on both sides that any real agreement was impossible. No greater error in policy was ever committed either by the Soviet Union or by the Western democracies.

Throughout the discussions with the British and French representatives the Soviet government was secretly bargaining with Germany. The end came while the representatives of Great Britain and of France were still in Moscow. On August 23 agreement between Germany and the Soviet Union was proclaimed to the world. Nine days later Hitler launched his attack on Poland.

This agreement was profoundly alarming to everyone in this country who believed that it might well result in the defeat of Great Britain and France. But from a practical standpoint it is important to observe how it enabled the Soviet government to achieve advantages which proved to be of inestimable value to her two years later when the anticipated German aggression finally took place, and to note how Soviet diplomacy consistently hoodwinked Hitler and his egregious Foreign Minister von Ribbentrop. The secret agreements concluded with Germany in August and during the second visit of Ribbentrop to Moscow in September, while giving Hitler temporary security on his eastern frontier, gave Russia some vital advantages. She occupied the Baltic States. She occupied Eastern Poland. She occupied Bessarabia. And with the reluctant acquiescence of Germany, Soviet troops on November 30 invaded Finland. Through the terms of the Armistice concluded with that republic in March, 1940, the Soviet government obtained military control of strategic territory which later enabled it to prevent Germany from occupying Leningrad.

Employing precisely the same methods, Stalin in April, 1941, further checkmated Germany by concluding a Neutrality Pact with Japan's Foreign Minister Matsuoka. This immediately blasted the hopes of the German General Staff for an attack by Japan upon the Soviet Union when Hitler should determine that the time for it had come.

I have never been surprised, in view of this extraordinary demonstration of the ineptitude of Japanese policy, that Stalin speeded the departure of his Japanese official guest by appearing personally at the railway station in Moscow and exhibiting far more exuberance on that occasion than he is generally credited with showing. Soviet diplomacy had triumphed completely over both the chief partners in the Anti-Comintern Pact. While the Japanese signature to the Neutrality Pact was obviously not worth the paper it was written on, it was evidence that Japan was not prepared to follow her German partner blindly.

What made the conclusion of this Neutrality Pact at that time seem to me all the more amazing was the fact that the plans of the German General Staff definitely called for a German attack upon Russia the following summer, as the Department of State was already well aware, and as I had advised the Soviet Ambassador in Washington in January of that year.

History will demonstrate, I believe, that Hitler's fatal errors were his failure to invade England after the collapse of France in June of 1940, his failure to achieve any satisfactory working agreement with Japan, and his determination, even without Japanese support, to attack Russia on June 22 of the following year. Supposedly, the strategy of the invasion of Russia was due to the same erroneous estimate of Soviet power that existed both in Washington and in London at that time. The underestimate of Russia's military effectiveness, of her fighting morale, and above all else, of her amazing ability to remove her industrial machinery from exposed cities to points well behind the Russian lines, and thus not only continue but constantly expand military production, was due to the precautions previously taken by the Soviet government to prevent the German intelligence services from obtaining accurate knowledge of the state of her military preparedness.

It is no longer a secret that even the highest military authorities in this country and in Britain did not believe in the summer of 1941 that Russia could possibly resist the German onslaught for any appreciable length of time. They had been persuaded that alleged inferiority in Russian military equipment and what they believed was a lack of effective discipline within the Russian Army would necessarily bring about, sooner rather than later, an inevitable Russian collapse. They had refused to listen to the repeated reports on the strength of Soviet morale and on the might of Soviet mechanized equipment and aviation sent to them by General Philip Faymonville, long stationed as a military attaché in Moscow. Of all our observers at that time, General Faymonville was by far the best qualified to speak, for he possessed a sympathetic understanding of the Russian people which did not distinguish many of his colleagues, who were hypnotized by a belief in Nazi invincibility. Fortunately, General Faymonville's predictions, and not those of the majority of the high military authorities of the Western powers, were justified, as Hitler has now found to his cost.

The achievements represented by the victorious struggle of the Soviet Union during the past two years have never been excelled by any other nation. They would not have been possible save through the efforts of a united and selflessly patriotic people. Maurice Paléologue, French Ambassador to Russia during the first World War, said very truly of the Russian: "He is capable of the most splendid impulses and the most heroic sacrifices. And his whole history proves that he is always true to himself when he feels himself really called on." That has never been demonstrated more conclusively than during the present war. For in this war, more than at any other time in Russian history, it is the Russian people themselves who have been called on.

When the United States was brought into the war six months after the attack by Germany upon the Soviet Union, this government immediately made every effort to establish closer relationships between Moscow and Washington in the political, as well as in the military, sphere.

After an initial delay, due largely to Russia's unfamiliarity with the operating methods of the American government, an increasingly workable arrangement was found to supply the equipment and raw materials so urgently needed by the Soviet authorities. It was long, however, before anything approaching satisfactory arrangements for the interchange of military information took place. In the political field, not until very recently—in fact, not until the conferences at Moscow and Tehran in October and November, 1943—has there been any satisfactory opportunity for a joint clarification of the war aims and peace aims of our two countries.

At the moment when I write these lines, there have suddenly developed glaring evidences of a tragic lack of accord between the Soviet Union and the British Empire and the United States concerning the solution of various fundamental political problems—fundamental in that they directly affect not only Russia's vital interests, but likewise the ability of the United Nations to construct a durable and workable international organization when the war is won.

As I have emphasized before, there are no traditional or material grounds for antagonism between the Russian people and the people of the United States. And, although only a tentative beginning has been made, the United States is the one major power, from Russia's point of view, with whom an enduring friendship should be most easily possible. As yet, however, little real progress has been made in this direction. The time for it, of course, was while our partnership in the war was young, and before any of the major powers had assumed open and intransigent positions on important political questions. Recollections of Western policy during the past twenty years and the necessary but ingrained caution of the Soviet civil and military authorities about permitting alien governments to obtain accurate or detailed information on Russia's internal and military affairs have created among the Russian people a deep suspicion of all Western powers, including the United States.

This prejudicial state of affairs has been overcome partly by the highly important military assistance given the Soviet government by the United States, and partly by President Roosevelt's never faltering insistence that in the interest of both countries and of the world at large a personal relationship be instituted between Marshal Stalin and himself.

His insistence was rewarded at the Moscow Conference, and at the conference a month later at Tehran, when the President and Marshal Stalin finally met face to face. The Four-Power Declaration was the first marker on the road toward the establishment of a workable international organization in the postwar period, for it pledged the four major powers to continued co-operation not only until the war was won but afterward. The announcements made as a result of the Cairo Conference, which obviously could not have been released without the prior agreement of the Soviet government, proclaimed the postwar objectives of the United Nations in the Far East. The Declarations of Tehran gave a heartening indication that the Soviet government intends to fortify the independence of Iran in the years to come and is apparently wholehearted in its desire to collaborate with the two major Western powers in postwar reconstruction. Unfortunately, these Declarations were followed a few weeks later by danger signals indicating that the Soviet government was bitterly opposed to any intervention by the Western powers in Russia's relationships with the nations of Eastern Europe.

Had the government of the United States determined in the early days of 1943 that time would not permit any delay in establishing, at least in rudimentary form, an executive council of the United Nations, in all probability most of the problems which now loom so large could have been avoided. An executive council composed of representatives of the four major powers and representatives of the smaller powers could have paved the way for a more comprehensive organization in the future and in the meantime could have threshed out and settled political questions as they arose, at least in principle. It was hardly wise to postpone the effort to solve so extremely delicate a question as the Polish frontiers, for example, until the armies of triumphant Russia had actually occupied the territories involved or to put off creating an international agency, which would have simplified the solution of such questions, until the various governments concerned had taken stands that made any joint solution highly doubtful.

In recent years the Soviet government has discarded many of the more radical forms of political organization which time and experience have proved to be inefficient. This has been particularly noticeable in the Army, which has recently adopted the methods of organization and discipline that centuries of experience have shown to be conducive to efficient military procedure. Even the traditional titles have been resumed. With the successful progress of the Soviet campaign against Germany, the Russian Army has assumed an increasingly important place in the Russian state. Stalin's assumption of the title of Marshal a few months ago has made this clear, if any confirmation were required. Consequently, any conjecture as to the future international policies of the Soviet Union must take into account the opinions and ambitions of Russia's military leaders.

What does Russia want? On the answer to that question depends the ability of the United Nations to set up an international organization that will be able to keep peace in the world and successfully undertake the task of reconstruction. And in the success or failure of that adventure will be found the answer to the question which underlies all others: Is a third World War ahead of us?

I do not wish to overstress the parallel between Russian policy during the past one hundred fifty years and the policy which the Soviet government may follow in the years to come. Nevertheless, I believe it would be singularly unrealistic to assume that because the Soviet government in 1918 and 1919 decried indemnities and annexations, it would today be guided in any literal sense by those pronouncements. So far as one can judge, the Soviet government is reverting to the concept of Russia's world interests that was held by her governments prior to 1918 and 1919. In exploring the future it is well to keep in mind the historical Russian objectives.

It seems to me that in the Pacific the Soviet government, at the conclusion of the war, will seek first, either by actually joining in the war against Japan or by facilitating her defeat by the other three major powers, to reduce her to a position where she can no longer threaten Russian supremacy. The United States, Great Britain, and China have declared that Japan is to be forced lock, stock, and barrel out of the Asiatic mainland. In such event, it would be logical for the Soviet Union to demand that Russia be restored to the position she occupied in Northeastern Asia prior to 1906, which included sovereignty over the whole of Sakhalin, that her present position in Sinkiang and Outer Mongolia be confirmed, and that her financial and commercial interests in Inner Mongolia be fully protected. It also seems not only logical but eminently desirable that the Soviet government be assured of her rightful place in any international trusteeship which may be established on behalf of the Korean people. Finally, Russia's legitimate interests in the fisheries of the Northwestern Pacific must be fully protected.

I also hope that under a future world organization the Soviet Union will be willing to share with the United States, the Dominion of Canada, and China the responsibility for safeguarding peace in the regions of the Northern Pacific.

In the Near East, the Declaration of Tehran concerning Iran seems convincing proof that the Soviet Union desires only equal protection with other powers of her legitimate trade in the regions north of the Persian Gulf. It is more difficult to forecast Russian policy in Eastern Europe and the Balkans. At the end of 1916 both the British and French governments officially informed the Imperial Russian government that the question of the Straits and of Constantinople would be settled in the manner Russia had so long desired. That assurance was given because of the participation of Turkey in the first World War against the Allied powers, and was later nullified as a result of the Russian Revolution of 1917. At the same time the Imperial Russian government demanded a part of East Prussia and a western frontier on the Carpathians, which would have brought Galicia and a large part of the Bukowina under Russian sovereignty. The changes which she then apparently desired in the Balkans would have assured her of a political "sphere of influence" without, however, any direct acquisition of territory within that area.

From present indications, the ambitions of the Soviet government today are by no means dissimilar. It refuses to discuss the matter of the incorporation within the Soviet Union of the three Baltic republics, which had been an integral part of Russian territory until the termination of the first World War. In so far as Poland is concerned, the Soviet government has made it clear both publicly and privately that, while it desires to see Poland reconstituted as a strong, independent state, it will insist that the Polish eastern frontier run more or less along the lines set down by the so-called Curzon Line of 1919.

In this the Soviet government is adopting an attitude similar to that assumed by the short-lived Kerensky government of 1917, which likewise proclaimed the independence of Poland and announced that "the creation of an independent Polish state, comprising all lands inhabited by a majority of Poles, [was] a reliable guarantee of peace in a future renovated Europe." The Curzon Line, drawn at the Versailles Peace Conference, was from the outset protested by the new Polish state on the ground that the frontiers of Poland as they existed prior to the first partition of Poland in 1772 should be re-established. When the Allied governments in 1920 refused to alter their decision that the new republic of Poland should incorporate only territories which were indisputably Polish in their population, Marshal Pilsudski attempted to satisfy Polish aspirations by armed force. After initial successes and, subsequently, more serious reverses, the Polish armies with French assistance finally forced Russian capitulation in the autumn of 1920, and in March of 1921 the Peace of Riga was concluded between the Polish and Soviet governments. As a result of that treaty, the Polish frontiers were so drawn as to incorporate Russian, White Russian, and Ukrainian populations amounting to many times the strictly Polish population of those areas.

There is nothing sacrosanct about the Polish eastern frontier as established by the Peace of Riga. The Curzon Line would establish a boundary far more in accordance with the principle of self-determination, and consequently far more likely to assure stability in that grievously afflicted portion of Eastern Europe.

Every impartial observer must have great admiration for the magnificent faith and patriotism of the Polish people. These qualities have survived a century of national extinction and all the efforts of the most brutal and reactionary forces of Europe to suffocate them. But the Polish people can hardly maintain that the nations of the world must today consider as sacred the Polish frontiers of 1772, which had themselves been established by shifting tides of conquest. Even in the modified form laid down by the Treaty of Riga, supposing it were conceivable that the Soviet government would agree, these frontiers would today bring under Polish sovereignty peoples violently hostile to such an arrangement.

The maintenance of Poland's western frontiers, as they existed in 1939, would offer even less assurance to the peace of Europe. The arrangement which gave Poland her only access to the sea through a Corridor separating one portion of Germany from the rest, promised trouble from the moment it was made.

A surgical operation will be required to lay down frontiers that will ensure the existence in the future of that "strong" Poland which both the Soviet government and this government desire to see. That operation will involve the elimination of the Polish Corridor, the humane and orderly transfer, under international regulation, of German populations from East Prussia and their replacement with Polish nationals, and an adjustment of Poland's eastern frontier with Russia in such manner as to incorporate within Eastern Poland

only areas in which Polish majorities predominate. The true friends
of Poland can only favor a solution which by fixing permanent
frontiers will at last give a homogeneous Polish people the opportunity to turn their thoughts to the peaceful development of their
resources.

The Soviet government has made repeated announcements, recently confirmed by President Beneš of Czechoslovakia, that Russia
desires the independence of Finland, Austria, Hungary, Rumania,
and the remaining Balkan States. In so far as her frontiers with
Finland are involved, Russia will undoubtedly demand as a minimum a confirmation of the frontiers established by the Armistice
of 1940 as a measure of security upon which she must insist. The
lamentable unwillingness of the Finnish government to make peace
with the Soviet government when it could in April, 1944, may result
in far more onerous terms later on. In the south the Soviet government will recover, and should recover, the province of Bessarabia
wrested from her in 1919.

The Slavophile policies pursued by the imperial governments of
Russia in the first decade of the twentieth century have by no means
been abandoned. At the end of the present war Russia will undoubtedly seek to have the Balkan States set up governments whose policies are in harmony with hers.

As for the Dardanelles, for so many generations a dominating
factor in Russian foreign policy, the development of aviation has
considerably reduced their strategic significance from the point of
view of Russian security. I can see no reason why a continuation of
the Montreux Agreement, which governed the status of the Straits
prior to 1939, should not prove satisfactory. Only if there is no
world organization in which the Soviet Union takes part, and
Turkish policy appears to menace Russia's vital interests, need the
historic question of the Straits once more provoke trouble.

The Soviet government is as legitimately entitled to promote a
regional system of Eastern Europe, composed of co-operative and
well-disposed independent governments among the countries adjacent to Russia, as the United States has been justified in promoting
an inter-American system of the twenty-one sovereign American
republics of the Western Hemisphere. I can only assume, until evi-

dence to the contrary is presented, that the recent constitutional modification of the Soviet Union, as a result of which a federal system of sixteen nominally autonomous Soviet republics has been established, is the first step in this direction, motivated by the Soviet government's belief that regional arrangements can thus more readily be perfected.

If the Soviet Union attempts to use such a regional system for the purpose of imposing a series of protectorates, as a preliminary to their subsequent incorporation within the Soviet Union itself, the other nations of the world can only regard it as an unmistakable sign that Russia is embarking upon a policy of expansion, whether by military force or by the domination of the internal affairs of independent states. If, on the other hand, such a system is based upon the same general foundations as the inter-American system, in which the sovereign independence of each state is assured, it should readily become one of the cornerstones of a stable world organization.

The foreign policy of this government should support these principles: The Soviet government is entitled to determine its frontiers with a view to its essential security and with regard for the right of self-determination on the part of the peoples inhabiting the regions concerned. It may be that the peoples of the Baltic States desire to form an integral part of the Union of Soviet Socialist Republics. It must be admitted, however, that the manner in which the plebiscites of 1939 were conducted by the Soviet Union gave but little assurance, even to those animated by a friendly spirit toward the Russian people, that they did anything more than mask a military occupation. To remove all grounds for justifiable criticism and to make doubly sure that the frontiers of the future Russia will incorporate willing, rather than unwilling, Soviet citizens, the Soviet government would be well-advised to permit open plebiscites to be taken in every instance where there is a dispute as to the will of the majority, and to permit all individuals who do not wish to become Soviet citizens to depart freely with their possessions, and with due compensation for the real property they are obliged to abandon.

Our second principle should be that the Soviet government is entitled to take such steps as it may judge best to create a regional system of Eastern Europe or, should a regional system be set up for the whole of Europe, to enter into pacts similar to that recently concluded with Czechoslovakia, providing for close co-operative relationships between the Soviet government and the governments of the nations in its vicinity. Only if the Soviet government were to intervene directly in the internal affairs of those nations would the United States, in my judgment, be entitled to object. For in that case the very basis for any healthy international organization would be destroyed, and the other nations would be compelled to take steps to safeguard their own security.

If, however, as I believe will be the case, Russia acts on the theory that her prosperity and security can be assured only through an international organization capable of maintaining world peace, there are innumerable ways in which the United States can help the Russian people in their task of reconstruction and industrialization. The needs of Russia in the immediate postwar period for credits, for expert services, and for machinery and equipment of many kinds will be great. At the same time, the commercial opportunities which such a situation will offer to American enterprise and to American export trade are almost unlimited. In a two-way trade lies an effective means of assuring a strong and healthy relationship between the two countries, and one that will immeasurably enhance the political and material well-being of both.

Maurice Paléologue wrote, while he was still French Ambassador in Russia: "The Russian nation is so heterogeneous in its ethnic and moral composition, it is formed of elements so incongruous and anachronistic, it has always developed in such defiance of logic, through such a maze of clashes, shocks and inconsistencies, that its historic evolution utterly defies prophecy."

Those words were written when the Russian people had no control over their own destinies. They have now secured this control. Many examples of Russian policy which seem to us inexplicable, often illogical, and occasionally even brutal are, however, due to the factors set forth in Paléologue's appraisal. For the Russian people are still in the process of transition.

Russia can become the greatest menace that the world has yet seen. It is potentially the greatest power of the world. It can equally well become the greatest force for peace and for orderly development in the world. It is, I think, no exaggeration to say that Russia's future course depends very largely on whether the United States can persuade the Russian people and their government that their permanent and truest interest lies in co-operating with us in the creation and maintenance of a democratic and effective world organization.

CHAPTER IX

## The German Menace Can Be Ended

A BASIC decision affecting the stability of the postwar world
and the problem of maintaining peace is the part which the
German people are to be permitted to play in the world of the future.
Much will depend upon the practical wisdom displayed by the United
Nations in dealing with this question.

One conclusion is inescapable. During a period of some two hundred years, the Germanic peoples, and specifically the Prussian people,
have been a destructive force in the family of nations. Throughout
that time they have never made any constructive contribution to
regional or world peace.

But it is a singular fact that no people contributed more to the
philosophic, scientific, literary, and musical heritage of modern
civilization. The "Elysian fields of Weimar" are peopled with those
whose genius brought about the culmination of the Romantic movement. The German universities, still vibrant with the vital forces
which originated in the liberal movements of the early nineteenth
century, seemed to hold the promise of becoming the source of inspiration for a new intellectual Renaissance. And in the field of
municipal government, the Germans set a high standard of efficiency
and of civic responsibility which, as an example, proved of material
benefit to many other countries.

For these reasons, and because of the admirable virtues of many
individual Germans, the world has been prone to extenuate the
measure of the havoc which the German nation has wrought.

So long as Prussia was no more than one member of the German
Federation, and so long as the German people were not a homogeneous mass, capable by their dynamic vigor and sheer weight of
numbers of disrupting the equilibrium of European stability, the
danger, while it existed, was not necessarily fatal. But when Germany

became unified the destructive nature of German tendencies and German policies soon made itself felt.

The first opportunity for Prussia to exercise hegemony in the German Federation occurred in 1848. Strangely enough, it was a German Parliament elected by universal suffrage that offered the imperial crown to Frederick William IV of Prussia. But it was not at all surprising that the refusal of the King to accept the crown was due to the Parliamentary source of the offer. The dictatorial control which Prussia already desired to exercise would have been gravely weakened had the King of Prussia accepted an imperial prerogative coming to him from what his advisers termed "revolutionary sources."

In the political field, Bismarck is the one outstanding genius the German people have produced since the time of Frederick the Great. For that reason, Bismarck's analysis of the course of Prussian policy has peculiar significance. In his judgment the first indications of a "national German tendency" came to life with the outbreak of the French Revolution. But the first steps toward achieving a unified Germany were taken not by Germans, but by those who claimed to be Prussian particularists. Again to quote Bismarck, it was only when Prussia had attained a position where it could itself become Germany, rather than Prussia, and when it had "a fully equipped force behind it," that the driving urge toward domination and expansion finally swept all before it.

For what became the motivating force of Prussian ambitions, operating through the brilliant but brutal genius of Bismarck, what actually made possible the creation of the Greater German Second Reich of 1914, was the germ brought to life by a handful of Prussian military scientists, thinking and writing in the dawn of the nineteenth century, of whom Clausewitz is the archetype. It is their teaching and their concept which made Germany during the past one hundred years the bane of Europe, and today the curse of the entire civilized world. It is their unholy inspiration that brought into being the German General Staff. And that instrument is responsible for the havoc which Germany has been able to wreak upon mankind during the present century.

What is the record of the German people since Bismarck first undertook to carry out the policies of Prussian militarism?

The war of aggression against Denmark in 1864.

The war of aggression against Austria in 1866.

The war of aggression, based on falsehood and misrepresentation, against France in 1870.

The attempt to wage a further war against a too rapidly recuperating France in 1875, averted only through joint British and Russian pressure.

The continuous effort between that date and 1906 to weaken France by insidious interference in her internal affairs, such as at the time of the Dreyfus case, and finally the ultimatum checkmated only by the Conference of Algeciras.

The Agadir incident of 1911, which for long months had Europe trembling on the brink of a general war.

The policies of political and military aggrandizement having as their inevitable consequence the outbreak of the first World War in 1914.

Finally—with the German General Staff using Hitlerism as its tool—the policies and acts which have plunged the peoples of the earth into the second World War.

Throughout this long chapter Germany has to offer in extenuation not one act on her part resulting in a contribution to world peace or to international stability and progress.

In 1899, as well as in 1907, at The Hague, when for the first time the international conscience sought through co-operation to curb the forces threatening the civilized world, Germany was the power which prevented any constructive achievement.

Throughout this period the German people have invariably shown themselves willing, in the words of Bismarck, "to fight, like their forefathers, before they knew what was to be fought for." While Bismarck declared that it was the German Emperor for whom they fought, we now know, as he knew then, that the authority to which the German people have so often and so disastrously responded was not in reality the German Emperor of yesterday, or the Hitler of today, but the German General Staff.

It will be said that this insistence that the German General Staff has been the driving force in German policy is a dangerous oversimplification. I am not disposed to minimize the importance of other factors in German history. They all have their place. But I am convinced that each of them has played its part only in so far as it was permitted to do so by the real master of the German race, namely, German militarism, personified in, and channeled through, the German General Staff.

To the average American the German General Staff has been nothing more than a board of army generals appointed to determine military strategy, similar in nature to the French, British, or American General Staff. It is there that the basic error has existed. All German foreign policy during the past seventy-five years, and to a considerable extent German internal policy as well, has either been initiated by, or has required the approval of, the German General Staff. This body has not been an agency of secondary importance in times of peace, as in the case of democratic states. Nor did it evaporate, as so many of us were led to believe, in the years after Germany's surrender in 1918. Though it went undercover, the organization remained quite as intact and cohesive as during the years prior to Germany's defeat.

Whether their ostensible ruler is the Kaiser, or Hindenburg, or Adolf Hitler, the continuing loyalty of the bulk of the population is given to that military force controlled and guided by the German General Staff. To the German people, the Army today, as in the past, is the instrument by which German domination will be brought about. Generations of Germans may pass. The nation may undergo defeat after defeat. But if the rest of the world permits it, the German General Staff will continue making its plans for the future. The country as a whole at this very moment has confidence that eventually, whatever may be the outcome of the present war, its Army will survive to become the agency through which the master race will ultimately triumph.

It must be admitted that almost every act of the Allied nations, subsequent to 1918, strengthened this determination on the part of the German people. The policies of the Western nations played right into the hands of the German military authorities.

The United States held back from all participation in world affairs.

Great Britain and France differed continuously over carrying out the provisions of the Versailles Treaty. The measures for the control of German disarmament laid down by the treaty were never effectively applied, and the course pursued as to reparations was muddled, contradictory, and wholly unrealistic. The Allied governments, whether individually or through the League of Nations, were unable or unwilling to adopt a policy designed to strengthen the hands of the few liberal leaders in Germany. During the early years after Versailles these German Democrats and Socialists saw better than anyone else what the continued predominance of the German General Staff meant. They were struggling feebly to persuade the people to follow the road to constitutional government and partnership in a cooperative Europe. But Allied support was given time and again to the old-line military organizations because it was thought that these alone could prevent Germany from going Communist!

Inflation was permitted to destroy many of the soundest classes of German society. Every German placed the blame squarely upon the Allied effort to collect unpayable reparations.

It was because of these facts that the only policy which before long had any appeal for the average German was one of aggressive nationalism. If the Allied governments in the year 1919 had frankly gone into partnership with the German General Staff in order to help it carry out its designs, they could not have succeeded better.

As the years passed, German rearmament became flagrant. British public opinion, like the public opinion in our own country, preferred resolutely to close its eyes and to refuse to admit the existence of what it did not wish to see. No more typical instance of that could be found than when Stanley Baldwin, as Prime Minister, forced at last to take cognizance of the jeremiads delivered in the House of Commons and in the press by Winston Churchill, flatly denied that Germany was arming.

In France, also, war weariness, abetted by the astonishing effectiveness of German propaganda, persuaded the people to look the other way until after Hitler had come into power and the German General Staff had again succeeded in making Germany the strongest military power on the European continent. Only a handful of French

Parliamentarians and a group of French Army leaders saw what was happening.

In this country we showed ourselves singularly susceptible to German propaganda. German propagandists hammered home the theme that all that the German people wanted was to be treated on a basis of strict equality with other peoples, and that if the discriminations against them contained in the Treaty of Versailles were only removed, they would automatically become decent members of international society.

At the same time financial and commercial interests in the United States poured into Germany hundreds of millions of dollars in the shape of loans. The greater part of the money was spent on public works and municipal buildings. It came as a godsend to the German General Staff, since it gave employment to hundreds of thousands of workers until the time was ripe for them to be used in munitions factories.

Nor was it a very practical contribution when, in 1937, this government, through its Secretary of State, requested Hitler to subscribe to a series of pious principles as a basis for international relationships. This action was taken at a time when the aggressive forces in Germany were about to break out openly.

Neither as a government nor as a people can we claim to have taken an effective part in preventing the rise of the new German threat to world peace.

In retrospect we can see more clearly that it was futile for the Western democracies to have tried to repress by mere words an irresistible and dynamic force, to keep within bounds by gestures or with the broken weapon of the League a virile, warlike people bent upon revenge and upon military dominion. Only an international organization, with armed force at its disposal, and the willingness to use it, could have successfully controlled the rising danger.

Hitlerism is the most shameful manifestation that has taken shape in any civilized country in modern times. In type, in antecedents, and in their common ends there is no difference between Hitler's agents on the gauleiter level and the craftiest, most brutish racketeers to be found in the United States. With but a few exceptions, the men who have surrounded Hitler and who have carried out his orders have come from the dregs of humanity, have utilized their positions primarily to enrich themselves, and have resorted to the lowest gangster methods.

The handful of those who have directed Nazi destinies are without exception of the criminal type. Some of them, like Hess, Himmler, and Hitler himself for that matter, are criminal paranoiacs. Others, like Goering, while they have sought profit at every turn, are even more avid for power. Still others, like Ribbentrop and Goebbels, are motivated by malignant inferiority complexes. But all of them embody within themselves unadulterated evil.

This handful of men, as well as those individuals of the older and more respectable regime of Imperial Germany—men of the type of von Neurath, Schacht, Meissner—who have prostituted their talents to serve Hitler, have furnished but a veneer for the monster racket. It is this criminal machine, directed by a demagogue who came to the surface of Germany's caldron at an opportune moment, that the German General Staff has utilized for its own purposes. It is to this vicious enterprise that the patriotism of the German race has responded.

Throughout the past one hundred years, whether the rallying point for German patriotism was the venerable figure of William I, Bismarck, the superficial and spectacular William II, the Marshal President Hindenburg, or, in most recent times, Hitler himself, public opinion in this country has always been prone to take the figurehead as the reality. It has overlooked the fact that German policy during the past eighty years has been inspired and directed, not by the Chief of State, but by the German General Staff. It is this living, continuing, destructive force that must be extirpated if the German people are ever to make a constructive contribution to the stability of Europe, and if any organized international society is to be able to safeguard the security of free peoples in the years to come.

The German General Staff is already well-aware of Germany's inevitable defeat. It is playing for time in the hope that the present war, if sufficiently protracted, will stimulate differences between the United Nations in such a way as to benefit Germany and make a compromise peace more likely. It has, however, made detailed plans for a later renewal of its attempt to dominate the world. Measures have already been taken throughout the globe to facilitate the execution of these plans when the favorable moment arrives, whether that moment be ten years or two generations from now.

The General Staff itself is only one-half visible. Half the mechanism is secret and will so remain. The General Staff considers the Anglo-Saxon powers the only antagonists that will be permanently and inevitably opposed to it. It bases all its preparations upon the cynical assumption that the policies of the Anglo-Saxon nations will not long remain consistent. And, lastly, it is confident that the reasoning of Anglo-Saxon peoples is solely a posteriori, whereas it conceives of its own reasoning as being invariably a priori.

With this in mind, the German officers who are to prepare the way for the next war will be guided by the following assumptions. They have been told that the war which Germany forced upon the world in 1939 will be lost solely because the material resources of the German Armies were insufficient; that although the German Armies greatly excelled their adversaries in strategy, in tactics, and in audacity, their superior intelligence and bravery was finally outweighed by the superior industrial production of the United States, which her geographical isolation made possible. Therefore, in order to overcome this purely material handicap, the German General Staff must prepare for the new war by taking as its basis of operations the whole of Europe rather than Germany itself. All the industrial and scientific contacts and knowledge made available in the countries of Europe which Germany has occupied during the past four years must be turned to advantage.

To do this, the economic and political sections of the German General Staff have perfected the theory of "indirect complicity." By putting this theory into practice, primarily in the countries of Europe but throughout the rest of the world as well, and by no means least in the Western Hemisphere, the German General Staff plans to complete its domination of the world.

The theory of "indirect complicity" is simple in conception but extremely complicated in detail. According to the bland assertions of German officers captured in the present war, it will prove so incomprehensible to the Anglo-Saxon mind in its entirety that the idea will not be fully grasped.

The German reasoning is as follows: Experience has shown that a purely military occupation by no means results in the complete political and economic domination of a conquered country. Only through actual possession of the key industries and through direct accomplices in the political life of the occupied country can satisfactory control be exercised. If such foreign intervention becomes known to the public, it is bound to provoke a patriotic reaction difficult to overcome. If, however, it is undertaken secretly by indirect accomplices, preferably nationals of the country over whom a sure measure of control can be exercised, there can be constructed without any unfavorable public reaction a system which slowly, little by little, can impose itself upon the life of the entire country.

When, as in the case of occupied France, Germany is able by imperceptible degrees to reach a point where there remains little practical difference between secret domination and open and avowed domination, she can pass from one system to the other without danger of an open revolt.

In any modern war, the German military authorities maintain, a victory is possible only after indirect complicities have been created. But, they say, this arm devised by the German military brain can be successfully wielded in the economic and political fields only under military control, since only under military authority can it maneuver with the required rapidity.

Finally, according to the German belief, the employment of this weapon against the Anglo-Saxon powers will be made much easier by reason of the fact that Anglo-Saxons react primarily to accomplished facts and only rarely to abstract theories. Neither the British nor ourselves are regarded as capable of understanding "indirect complicity."

The agents of the German General Staff will believe fanatically that theirs is a "life mission," for the accomplishment of which they are responsible to no one save to their superior officers. They will endeavor to carry out this mission so long as there is breath in their bodies, no matter what upheavals or political changes may take place within Germany herself.

At first glance the theory of "indirect complicity" seems very simple and easy to deal with. It obviously implies the use by a foreign power for its own ends of the nationals of another power without their conscious knowledge. But it would be disastrous to dismiss the danger lightly because of a belief that we can readily construct the necessary legal safeguards, or that we can meet it solely by expanding our existing intelligence agencies.

The principal danger is that after the present war the people of the democracies, and particularly of the United States, will wish once more, as in 1920, to plunge themselves into the oblivion of "normalcy." We will be inclined to believe that because the war has ended with our victory there need be no continuing process to maintain the safety won at so huge a cost. We will be inclined to accept at its face value the propaganda which will once more emanate from German sources and, unfortunately, from many wholly sincere and patriotic American sources susceptible to the influence of German propaganda. The very nature of the German plan will, in peacetimes, seem fantastic.

The German General Staff will seek to put its theory into practice in three principal ways: (a) It will try to create doubts among the people of each country as to the ability, integrity, wisdom, or loyalty of their leading statesmen; (b) in critical moments it will attempt to paralyze or to diminish the capacity for cool thinking by the people as a whole; and (c) it will search in each country for men who, through ambition, vanity, or personal interest, will be disposed to serve the causes which the German General Staff desires at that particular moment to further.

In order that these plans may be carried out without interruption and with complete efficiency, agents of the German General Staff have already been naturalized, usually in two successive countries, so that their future activities will be less suspect. The majority of them are being trained to appear as men of large commercial or financial interests, who will be able to dispose of considerable amounts of capital derived from the reserves which the German General Staff has already, during the past years, deposited under one guise or another in neutral countries. These agents will be fully trained to follow at least two entirely distinct pursuits. They will have a direct and active part in large-scale industrial or commercial enterprises.

In this way, each agent will be able to cultivate a circle of indirect and unknowing accomplices, nationals of the country where he is stationed, who can determine opinion, control industrial production, and even influence the results of elections.

The German General Staff is convinced that over a period of years it can gain a controlling influence in labor unions, in the banking world, in Chambers of Commerce, and, through these channels, an indirect influence in the press. It believes that it can thus discourage the growth of industrial systems disadvantageous to Germany when Germany strikes again, and, when the right time comes, stimulate internal dissension sufficiently to destroy the morale of the people in those countries marked as victims.

The technique that the German General Staff has used in the occupied countries differs only in that it is simpler. Its inner workings are now becoming known. We are ready to recognize that "fifth column" activities contributed greatly to the speed of German military victories in 1940. We are too ready, however, to think of those activities as being carried on only by the Quislings and other direct accomplices. We are consequently too inclined to believe that that "can never happen here," because the American citizen, with rare exceptions, is not apt knowingly to become a traitor. The danger lies in our failure to recognize that the German General Staff looks for the weakest spot in the political structure of each country, and that in the Anglo-Saxon democracies the weakest point is not the direct accomplice, but the indirect accomplice.

The German high command had many indirect accomplices in the United States prior to Pearl Harbor. Some of them were American-born citizens who had gained high distinction in this country. For the most part they were wholly sincere; entirely patriotic according to their own lights. To this day the majority of them do not realize how they were being used, and what harm they did to our national interest.

In thinking about how to deal with the German menace in the future, it is necessary to take as a starting point the assumption that a practical world organization will be established at the close of the present war, and that it will have the power to enforce decisions believed by us to be expedient and wise.

Germany became a menace to the rest of the civilized world only after two major developments in her history. The first of these was that the German people came to believe in German militarism as the supreme glory of the race, a concept implanted and fostered by Clausewitz and his school, and in Pan-Germanism as an ideal which German militarism alone could achieve. The German General Staff became the agency for bringing about these objectives.

The second development was the centralization of authority over all the widely divergent peoples of the German race. The unification of the German peoples, first envisaged in 1848, actually begun in 1866, consistently furthered during the four decades of the Second Reich, and forced to its final completion by Hitler himself, has coincided with the rise of Germany as a threat to the rest of the world.

Neither development, however, could have proved a major danger without the other. With each successive stage in the centralization of authority, the power of the German General Staff was correspondingly increased. Without such centralization it could not have attained its position of supremacy in 1914. If Hitler had not abolished all the remaining barriers between the former German states, German militarism could never have carried out its policies so successfully in the years between 1933 and 1939, nor could it have obtained the complete control which it had acquired when the war finally began.

The unification of Germany, with the centralization of all power in Berlin, has made possible the building up of Germany's destructive power.

It has enabled a central government to stereotype the education of all German youth in order that it might voluntarily become the tool of Pan-Germanism.

It has destroyed the opportunity, and even the capacity, for individual thinking in German universities and schools, which might to some extent have operated as a counterweight to purely military influence.

It weakened the ability of Germans as individual citizens to think for themselves, and made possible that persistent official encroachment upon the liberty of the press and all other means of popular information which had its climax in the total control over all sources of information by the Nazis.

Finally, it has eliminated all the earlier countervailing balances to stark Pan-Germanism.

The power of religion, whether Catholic or Protestant, to influence the German people against Hitlerism was gravely weakened as soon as a centralized government was able to stamp out religious freedom. That a Bavarian government, for example, could never have accomplished in Bavaria. The different peoples within Germany had the chance to resist being dragged into military adventures and to withstand the contagion of mass hysteria only so long as they retained their autonomy, and remained primarily Bavarian, Saxon, or Hessian. Once these age-old safeguards had been broken down, the German peoples as a whole became a malleable instrument for the use of their overlords.

The abolition of local government, with the substitution of authoritarian rule from Berlin, destroyed the last vestiges of regional autonomy which had remained from the days of the Empire and of the Republic, and completed the obliteration of German individual liberty.

Centralization also stimulated the unhealthy growth of those vast financial, commercial, insurance, and shipping combines which have spread their tentacles throughout the world during the past two generations. They have proved one of the most effective agencies for the schemes of the military high command.

No world organization, however effective, will be able to combat the danger which will exist if after the war a centralized Germany continues to be subject to German militarism. The purely military controls imposed by the world organization will inevitably become weakened as time passes, as the ravages of the present war are partially effaced, and as the instinctive human desire to forget becomes intensified. When that day comes a centralized Germany will start another war of revenge, waged this time in the light of the experience gained by the German military commanders in the present war.

Many people will agree that German militarism must be crushed and are satisfied that the major military powers should take care of this as soon as Germany is occupied. They say, however, that there is no similar justification for destroying her present unification. Many responsible Americans are already maintaining that any partition of the German peoples is inherently unjust and will prove unworkable. They insist that the major powers will be unwilling to enforce the partition at the time when the German people clamor to be reunited. And they are confident that enforcement will require a continuing military force of occupation which none of the major powers will be disposed to furnish. These are the main arguments against a partition of Germany:

First, the centripetal urge among the German people is so great and so persistent that any attempt on the part of a world organization to prevent German unity would soon result in a new form of eruption.

Second, partition would develop an inferiority complex similar to that which it is claimed the German people contracted as a result of the war guilt clause in the Versailles Treaty. Any such sense of inferiority, it is said, will prevent their ever becoming co-operative citizens in a new Europe.

Third, partition of Germany would mean the economic ruin of the people, with such unemployment and distress as to give rise to some dangerous form of Communism.

Fourth, any partition of Germany into separate units would be answered by concerted efforts at evasion, and, owing to their great organizing ability, the Germans would soon find satisfactory means to get around it and prepare for a new attempt at unification whenever the moment seems propitious.

I would be the last to underestimate the force of these arguments. My whole individual predisposition is in favor of the unity of the German people. It is only because of my conviction that German unity means a continuing threat to the peace of the entire world that I have reached the conclusion that partition is the only way of offsetting the German menace in the future.

The so-called centripetal urge on the part of the German people is far from being the powerful force that so many have claimed during the past twenty years. The vociferous demand for the reconstitution of the German Reich and the unification of all the German peoples has been largely stimulated by the German General Staff. It has provided Hitler with some of his most effective propaganda in consolidating his own regime. Certainly the unification of the German peoples is by no means a prerequisite for the happiness and prosperity of individual Germans. The several German nations were both happy and prosperous during the nineteenth century. Even under changed economic conditions this situation can be brought about in our time.

Those who favor the continued unification of Germany are inclined to overlook for how brief a period the German states have been governed by a central authority, and how bitterly many of the German peoples struggled against unification.

Doebert, the modern German historian, in his book on the unification of Germany, *Bayern und die Bismarckische Reichsgründung*, refers to Bavaria, for example, as "one of the oldest European States . . . which, in the opinion not only of Bavarian statesmen but of Bismarck himself, possessed in the highest degree everything that entitled it to an independent existence—an immensely ancient political tradition, a fourteen-centuries-old political unity, a dynasty that had been part and parcel of the land and the people for a thousand years, a population with an intense political self-consciousness, an indigenous, firmly rooted, vigorous people with an ancient culture of its own, with its own markedly individual characteristics of social and of business life."

Bavaria came under Prussian control seventy years ago, and has been a part of the present form of German state for barely a decade. As against this short span, the Bavarian people for over a thousand years had maintained their independent national existence. Is it conceivable that those deep roots established during a millennium of independence and autonomy have been destroyed in less than three-quarters of a century? Is it possible that the Bavarian people have so soon forgotten their struggle against Prussian domination, and their hatred of Prussia, even though they have fought with her in several wars?

It is equally unbelievable that many of the older generations in the former German states do not also still prefer their former autonomy.

The point made with regard to the creation of a national inferiority complex within Germany, if partition is undertaken, is undoubtedly true. But that complex, with all its unfortunate psychological effects, will exist in any event as a result of German defeat, whether Germany remains a centralized unit or is separated into several entities.

If the economic prospects of the German people were to be irreparably damaged by partition, the objections raised on this score would be conclusive. But there is no valid reason why they should be. In my opinion no greater safeguard can be devised against future German military aggression than measures that will afford every German equality of economic opportunity with the citizens of other European countries. He should be assured that he need not look ahead to the same dark and uncertain future that he faced in 1919. Such economic security can be obtained only if basic economic arrangements which ensure the eventual prosperity of the German people are taken into full account in any division of the present German Reich. Next to the military considerations, these appear to me to be the determining factors.

As for the final objection, there is of course not the slightest doubt that many Germans for one or two generations to come will make every effort to evade the results of partition and to pave the way for a renewed unity. The precise manner in which to deal with these attempts may only be determined in the light of future conditions. For some years they will have to be forcefully repressed by the future world organization. But the surest guarantee of permanence will lie in the kind of partition undertaken. It will be effective only if it proves practicable from the economic and political standpoints, and is based upon economic, political, and cultural considerations.

The possibility of a partition of Germany has undoubtedly received close study from many of the governments of the United Nations. A number of plans have been devised, varying from the reconstitution of the old German Federation, as it existed prior to 1848, to the inclusion within a federation of Western Europe, as an autonomous state, of the industrial regions west of the Rhine, leaving the remainder of Germany, except for slight frontier rectifications, much as it was prior to 1936.

Arguments can be advanced in favor of many such schemes. If

one proceeds, however, upon the theory that Germany is to be divided solely to prevent her from again becoming a military menace, and that at the same time individual Germans must be given every opportunity to achieve economic security and ultimately to comprehend, and to enjoy, popular government, the following basis for partition is probably the one best calculated to procure these results.

Exclusive of East Prussia, Germany should be divided at the time of the armistice into the following three separate states, the boundaries being determined primarily by cultural, historic, and economic factors:

A new state of Southern Germany, comprising the former sovereign nations of Bavaria, Wuerttemberg, Baden, and Hesse-Darmstadt, together with those regions which may roughly be defined as the Rhineland and the Saar. It will be noted that the populations which would be comprised within this division are predominantly Catholic.

A state consisting of the following old German subdivisions, together with the smaller subdivisions contiguous to them: Upper Hesse, Thuringia, Westphalia, Hanover, Oldenburg, and Hamburg.

A state, omitting the enumeration of small contiguous political subdivisions, composed of Prussia (exclusive of East Prussia), Mecklenburg, and Saxony. It will be noted again that in the second and third states the populations are predominantly Protestant. In each one of these three new states the historical, as well as the religious and cultural, divisions which existed during the centuries prior to the creation of the Third Reich have been maintained.

In that connection it is desirable that certain fundamental characteristics of the German people be borne in mind. These words of Bismarck are apt:

> In order that German patriotism should be active and effective, it needs as a rule to hang on the peg of dependence upon a dynasty; independent of dynasty it rarely comes to the rising point, although in theory it daily does so in Parliament, in the press, in public meeting; in practice the German needs either attachment to a dynasty or the goad of anger hurrying him into action; the latter phenomenon, however, by its own nature is not permanent. It is as a Prussian, Hanoverian, Wurtemberger, a Bavarian, or a Hessian, rather than as a German, that he is disposed to give unequivocal proof of patriotism;

and in the lower orders in the Parliamentary groups it will be long before it is otherwise.

(Bismarck, *Reflections and Reminiscences,* Vol. 1, page 320)

These words, written in his final years by Germany's only great modern statesman, demonstrate, I think conclusively, that the centrifugal urge within Germany has only recently been overlaid by the propaganda for centralized unity.

Furthermore, by this suggested division a complete economic balance, both agricultural and industrial, would be established within each of the three states, and the proportionate relationship within each state of the prime economic factors, such as agricultural and industrial production, and mineral resources, would be roughly equivalent to that in each of the two others. If, as I hope may prove to be the case, the end of the war sees the lowering of customs barriers within Europe, and the creation of customs unions, the new German states should be afforded free opportunity to take part in such customs unions.

The capacity for economic development in each one of the proposed states is almost unlimited. What would vanish would be the giant combines which could be used again as a means of military penetration in other countries. It cannot be claimed that the existence of these huge cartels were in any sense necessary to a healthy German national economy.

The problem of the disposition of East Prussia affects world security not only with regard to Germany, but with regard to Eastern Europe as well. There are four main points to consider:

First, it is now generally recognized that the Polish Corridor, far from providing a permanent solution of Poland's need for an outlet to the sea, was, on the contrary, a major source of danger to her. The Corridor was an alien sovereignty separating one portion of Germany from the other. While one can appreciate the difficulties which confronted the treatymakers of 1919, one must equally recognize that no statesman familiar with European history and politics could even then have regarded the Corridor as anything but a makeshift. The solution was repugnant to the Polish as well as to German nationalistic forces. It left Poland at the mercy of Germany whenever

Germany felt strong enough to close the gap which the Corridor created.

Second, the legitimate requirements of the future Polish state include unimpeded access to the sea, without the complications resulting from such artificial arrangements as those involved in the international control of Danzig, and from the juxtaposition of Danzig and Gdynia.

Third, we must take into account the insistence of the Soviet Union that the eastern frontier of Poland, as it existed in 1939, be rectified to include within Russian territory the regions inhabited by non-Polish populations living to the east of the Curzon Line.

Fourth, inasmuch as these boundary changes would deprive Poland of a considerable portion of her eastern territories, some equivalent restoration must be made if she is to become that "strong and independent Poland" which not only the United States and Great Britain are pledged to see reconstituted, but which likewise has been proclaimed officially by the Soviet government as an objective of its own policy.

The only solution of these four questions is to give Poland the province of East Prussia, at the same time readjusting the frontier between Western Prussia and the old Polish Corridor so as to give the new German state, of which Western Prussia will form a part, an area of the old Corridor. This will leave the seaports of Danzig and Gdynia in Polish hands. The exact frontier between the new state of Eastern Germany and the western flank of Poland can be determined only after an actual survey in which the question of populations and availability of land for agricultural purposes should be deciding factors.

In any readjustment of so radical a character, the resultant transfers of population must take place over a reasonable period of time under the direct supervision of the international organization. Any individual who desires to remove from one sovereignty to another must be afforded free opportunity to do so, with a guarantee of full and equitable compensation for such property as he is unable to remove, or of which he may be deprived.

It is roughly estimated that one-third of the population of East Prussia consists of individuals who are either Polish nationals or of

Polish descent. The human problem involved in a transfer of populations on so vast a scale is very great. However, in the only instance in recent times—the exchange of populations between Turkey and Greece, after the first World War—the transfer was not only humanely and successfully carried out, but is today recognized by both Greece and Turkey as having been beneficial to both.

What is proposed in this readjustment of German and Polish frontiers is in the nature of a surgical operation. But that is the only remedy which gives any promise of permanence. Certainly the adjustments made in 1919 were productive of only harm. At the conclusion of the present World War, the Soviet Union, as well as Germany and Poland, will be concerned in the final settlement. If the situation is not wisely resolved, it will grow once more into a festering sore bound in the years to come to create renewed dangers.

It will of course immediately be alleged that any such adjustment as that proposed would constitute a flagrant violation of the assurance contained within the Atlantic Charter relative to the right of self-determination of all peoples. As I interpret that assurance it would prevent the transfer of peoples against their will from the jurisdiction of one sovereign government to that of another. It should make it impossible for Germans to be forced to become Polish nationals counter to their own free decision. It should prevent Poles from being compelled to live under Russian sovereignty, or vice versa. That, it seems to me, is the essential freedom implicit in the promise held out in the Atlantic Charter. If the assurance of the Atlantic Charter were to be so construed as to make impossible any orderly transfer of territories in any part of the world, there could be undertaken at the close of the war no remedial measures to provide for the solution of problems which have afflicted Central and Eastern Europe for many centuries, and the continuation of which in the postwar years would make impossible the creation of a stable and peaceful Europe.

In the adjustment proposed with regard to East Prussia there is no suggestion that peoples be transferred, like cattle, from one sovereignty to another. On the contrary, it is specifically recommended that every individual who desires to retain his former nationality be given full right to do so, and that any individual who, for that reason, is obliged to migrate be compensated in full for the losses he may incur by such removal.

Any transfer of populations results in hardships, and in human suffering. But in such a case as that under consideration the eventual benefits to the peace and stability of the whole of Europe would outweigh many thousands of times the temporary distress which might be created.

Partition will do more than anything else to break the hold which German militarism has on the German people. But it is also certain that the plans of the militarists have taken this possibility fully into account, and that the General Staff, as such, will continue its activities for many years to come.

There is only one sure way by which this danger can be blotted out of existence. A wholly new spirit must be brought to life within the German people, and a totally new concept of what is worth living and striving for. But I fear it would be as softheaded as it would be softhearted for the United Nations to assume that such a change can be brought about during the lifetime of the present generation. For that reason all preventive measures which the victorious powers take to guard against German military activities in peacetime must be persistently enforced for many years.

The effective use by the German General Staff of indirect accomplices demands that the precise nature of their operations be kept secret. The best counteractive measure will be full ventilation through the press and radio of the United Nations of every detail of such activities as they are brought to light.

In order that such facts can be made known, their existence must be ascertained and verified. This requires efficient intelligence services. The precise nature of such services is a matter which can be determined only by each government. However, it can readily be seen that all governments must have far more definite knowledge than in the past of the origin of capital investments made from abroad, as well as of the individuals of foreign origin taking part in the industrial and financial life of the nation.

To many of us, when peace is restored, these precautions will seem fantastic and altogether unnecessary. But it would be foolhardy to forget what the past has so clearly proved. The only proof that such precautions are no longer necessary will lie in the ability of the Germans to convince the other peoples of the world that they have permanently discarded the gods they have been taught to serve by their own war lords.

After the first World War, when the Allied Nations were told that, with the establishment of the Weimar Republic, the freely expressed voice of the German people would now be heard, they tacitly accepted the truth of these assertions. I should be the first to deny that Fritz Ebert and his immediate associates were either insincere or undemocratic in their beliefs. But the events of the past twenty-five years have shown conclusively not only that the German people were not responsive to democracy, but also that the Allied governments did nothing to stimulate the growth of democracy within Germany.

We already hear many Germans, refugees in the United States, insisting that the way to assure Germany's good behavior in the future is to give the German people another opportunity to establish a true democracy within a unified Germany. More and more citizens of the Western democracies, many of them advanced liberals, are publicly professing the same conviction.

One of the chief reasons why it is difficult for some close observers of recent German history to accept this view is the fact that when Germany is defeated this time conditions will be far less propitious for the creation of a real democracy than they were at the end of the first World War. Since Hitler gained control of the German Reich, the youth of Germany has been hopelessly corrupted. It would be an optimist indeed, no matter how deep his sympathy for the German people, who would have any hope that the younger generation will ever be able even to understand what democracy is. During their formative years the younger Germans have had no education other than that given them by the Nazi machine. They have been taught to believe in no ideals other than that of the master race and the inherent right of the Germanic peoples to dominate the world. They have watched with enthusiasm the consistent and effective efforts of their leaders to reduce the population and the future population of the peoples of the occupied countries. They have had inbred in them a total contempt for religion, and a brutal hatred for other races.

These millions of Germans will be at the prime of life during the next two decades. They will be a controlling force within Germany. Theirs will be a force of fanaticism and of revenge.

The brutalities of Hitlerism have become a daily commonplace to all generations of present-day Germans. They have necessarily produced a coarsening of the national psychology which cannot be modified overnight solely by such a change in governmental structure as took place in 1919.

By the time the war is over, the Nazi regime will have succeeded not only in destroying the value of the savings and property of all classes in the occupied countries, but, through its domestic policies and the war requisitions, in obliterating all but real property within Germany itself. Everyone save the higher authorities in the Nazi machine will be destitute. The misery and starvation will be far greater than it was in 1918.

In all probability, the first stratagem of the German military command will be to stimulate throughout Germany the growth of Communism in its world-revolutionary form. Conditions will favor it. The establishment of Communistic governments of such a type is a foregone conclusion, provided the United Nations forces of occupation make no objection. Many well-intentioned liberal elements within the United Nations will hold that the creation of such governments is proof positive that the German people have seen the light and have at last set foot upon the road leading to popular self-government.

This would by no means necessarily be the case. The establishment within Germany of Communism of the Trotskyist, or world-revolutionary, type would give the German General Staff precisely the advantages it will seek. For, after the war is over, all the occupied countries of Europe and many countries in other parts of the world will be seething with social unrest as a result of economic prostration. A new German Communism, furthering the doctrines of world revolution and directed by the cold and ruthless brains of the German General Staff, would find in many parts of the world a situation made to order for the purpose of Pan-Germanism. The kind of governments, therefore, that the German people are to be permitted to install must be decided by common agreement between the United

Nations with full regard for the dangers which may arise from any hidden military schemes of the General Staff.

The United Nations must continue to occupy various regions of Germany for a considerable period after the war, under the supreme authority of the future world organization. The war criminals must first of all be tried and sentenced. The return to self-government must be gradual, commencing with the establishment of municipal administrations, after all Nazi officeholders have been eliminated. Furthermore, until the immediate distress of the postwar period within Germany has been relieved, and until the German people can once more put their industry and agriculture on something approaching a peacetime basis, it would be extremely inadvisable, as well as against their best interests, to hasten their resumption of self-government. Certainly Germany must be both socially and economically stable, even under an alien occupation, before the United Nations can safely permit other than local governments to be established.

Even then, certain safety measures will have to be enforced. There must be a system of controls, organized and carried out by the world organization, to make sure that German rearmament is impossible and that every store of arms and munitions remaining at the time of the armistice is delivered into the hands of the United Nations. There must this time be no such fatal inefficiency in this matter as existed in 1920. In the same manner and for the same purpose, controls must be imposed over German mining and heavy goods industries. The controls must likewise be exercised over German imports. Finally, if all Central European communications and sources of power development, including railroads, coastal and fluvial shipping, radio and telegraph, and electric power facilities, were to be internationalized, no development could prove of more practical value from a purely economic standpoint, as well as in preventing the German people from using these instruments for military purposes.

All the safeguards that have so far been considered are in a sense negative. They are preventive measures. What will in the last analysis be far more important are the constructive measures which may be taken to encourage the German people to become of their own initiative co-operative members of human society.

For as I see it, if the treatment accorded to the German people is to result in the strengthening of the foundations of world peace, such treatment must not be punitive. It should be the result of the adoption of a policy by the world organization which is remedial as well as precautionary. It should prepare the German people for true popular self-government when they have actually learned to value such a form of government as the one best calculated to assure their welfare.

The policy to be followed should be designed not to destroy Germany, but to construct out of Germany a safe and co-operative member of world society.

The start in this direction must be made from the first moment after Germany's defeat, even though it may be a long period before the German people can again be safely permitted to walk alone. But first it is essential to canvass the salutary forces within Germany which, if encouraged and strengthened, may provide the means of her salvation.

As I see them, there are, first of all, the forces which will spring from a renewal of religious freedom. Among the few admirable figures who have appeared upon the German scene during the years of Hitlerism are those who have dared to speak in the name of the churches. The spiritual reformation which can result from freedom of religion in Germany may be very great.

Freedom of information, which is indispensable, also can become one of the great constructive forces in the creation of a new German national conscience. To a people deprived of the means of access to the truth during the past ten years, full freedom to learn the truth will come at first as a bitter shock. It may well become eventually a means of national regeneration.

The freedom from fear which will come through the establishment of an effective world organization and the freedom from want which will be assured by the establishment of a sane economic policy with regard to the German people will have their stabilizing effect upon the German mind.

Many German nationals now in exile because of their hatred of Nazism are disposed to work for the ultimate salvation of their people. The United Nations should give them every encouragement, as soon as the time is ripe, in order that their voices may be heard by their fellow countrymen.

Already the organization of "Free Germans" and the groups of well-intentioned, liberal-minded citizens of the United States who support the efforts of these organizations are moving rapidly to create a state of mind on the part of public opinion within this country which will hold that the fourth German Reich can be trusted, provided German "democrats" are aided in seizing and holding the reins of government. I would count myself a member of this body of opinion if I could believe that democracy could really determine the destinies of the German people within a foreseeable future. The basic point to remember is that democracy cannot be imposed upon any people. It can only exist in reality when it springs from the consciousness, and from the will, of a people. There is no proof which can be offered, worthy of credence, that the history of the German people during the past twenty-five years holds even a spark of promise that democracy would become a true, or a predominant, force within Germany so long as the tragically poisoned German youth of the Hitler years remain a majority of the German people.

If, after the years of trial have passed, and a new generation of Germans comes of age under conditions which make the new Germans conscious of what the word "liberty" really means, we may all hope democracy—true and not artificial—will prevail in every region of Germany. When such a time comes the German people should once more be afforded by the international organization as full an opportunity to determine freely their political destinies as any other people of the earth. But until that moment comes, even the most idealistic of the liberal groups within the United Nations should pause to remember the bloody pages of the history of the past decade.

The treatment accorded Germany by the United Nations when their victory is won should be neither Draconian nor vengeful. It should be formulated, however, in the light of the stark reality that Germany has twice within a quarter of a century brought war and devastation to mankind. The peoples of the world are obligated, to ensure their own survival and the survival of all those things which they hold most dear, to see to it that the German race cannot again so afflict humanity.

# THE TIME FOR DECISION

## PART THREE

# CHAPTER X

# World Organization

FOR centuries past civilized man has been groping for some means of preventing war. Time and again during the past four hundred years there has been held up as the ultimate ideal the conception of an association of nations co-operating for their common good and bound together for the fundamental purpose of making war impossible.

Many of the plans which have been drawn up for this purpose have, even today, more than merely academic or historical interest. The searchers of today may find much of inspiration and, for that matter, much of practical value in such conceptions as those embodied in William Penn's plan for a federal union of Europe, made known in 1693, or in the singularly modern scheme for a federation of free and democratic peoples published in 1795 by the author of the *Critique of Pure Reason*, the philosopher Immanuel Kant.

The bloody and chaotic period inaugurated with the French Revolution and ending twenty-five years later with Waterloo gave an added impetus to the quest. But the only solution forthcoming was that proffered by the Congress of Vienna in the form of the Holy Alliance. This effort to maintain lasting peace through a military alliance for the repression of human freedom, and for the perpetuation of a wholly reactionary status quo, was necessarily foredoomed to failure. In the popular revolution which flamed over Europe in the 1840's the last vestiges of the Holy Alliance vanished. During the latter half of the nineteenth century the peoples of Europe were spared any general war as a result of the armed truce brought about by the British-sponsored and British-maintained balance of power system.

Some progress at least was made toward international co-operation as a result of the suffering caused by the Crimean War. International agreements for the adoption of more humanitarian standards in the conduct of war were concluded at the Conference of Paris of 1856.

The first major accomplishment in the field of international cooperation for the elimination of the causes for war came, however, through The Hague Conferences of 1899 and 1907, held upon the initiative of the Russian government. The agreements reached in these two conferences provided machinery for the pacific adjustment of international controversies through the arbitral tribunals established at The Hague. Progress would also have been made in the field of international disarmament if, as I have pointed out earlier, it had not been for the unyielding opposition of the German government.

During the years between 1900 and the outbreak of the first World War in 1914, public opinion in Europe and in the Americas was rapidly gathering momentum. There began to grow up a widespread demand for the creation of effective methods of preventing war or for limiting its repercussions. It is noteworthy that one of the most advanced proposals was made at the second Hague Conference by the government of Uruguay, then as always in the vanguard of progressive and liberal governments.

In our own country, the trend had become rapid. The movement was wholly nonpolitical in character, supported by leaders in both parties as well as by outstanding figures in the churches, the universities, and the professions. This swift tide of opinion, developing into a general popular demand that the influence and the prestige of the United States be exerted to realize this high aim, reached its full climax immediately after the outbreak of the first World War.

As far back as 1910 Theodore Roosevelt, when he addressed the Nobel Prize Committee in Norway, declared:

It would be a master stroke if those great powers honestly bent on peace would form a league of peace, not only to keep the peace among themselves, but to prevent, by force if necessary, its being broken by others. The supreme difficulty in connection with the developing of the peace work of The Hague arises from the lack of any executive power, of any police power to enforce the decrees of the court.

And in 1915 Theodore Roosevelt again reiterated the thesis, quite as applicable today as it was thirty years ago:

The one permanent move for obtaining peace which has yet been suggested with any reasonable chance of attaining its object is by an agreement among the great powers, in which each should pledge itself, not only to abide by the decisions of a common tribunal but to back with force the decision of that common tribunal. The great civilized nations of the world which do possess force, actual or immediately potential, should combine by solemn agreement in a great world league for the peace of righteousness.

It was worthy of note that Senator Henry Cabot Lodge, with precision and clarity, expressed the same conviction in the Chancellor's Address at Union College which he delivered that year.

Nineteen hundred fifteen also saw the creation in Philadelphia of the League to Enforce Peace, composed originally of a thousand leading Americans, among whom ex-President Taft was a guiding spirit. It supported the same ideals as those announced by Theodore Roosevelt and Henry Cabot Lodge.

It was also in 1915 that President Wilson, through the agency of Colonel House, undertook to bring into being an inter-American league of nations, to be founded upon the first provision of the Monroe Doctrine. While this effort proved abortive, and for that matter was never even pressed beyond a nebulous preliminary stage, it served the purpose of crystallizing in Woodrow Wilson's own mind the principles which later were set forth in the Covenant of the League of Nations.

Like all products of the human intellect, the Covenant of the League of Nations is imperfect. Its imperfections have been plainly seen during the years which have elapsed since it was adopted in Paris in the winter of 1919. Many of those imperfections can be fairly attributed to the compromises which President Wilson was forced to accept because of demands arising out of our own internal political conditions. Among these, of course, was the reservation covering the Monroe Doctrine, in which reference was made to the latter as a "regional agreement," which, of course, at that time it was not. Moreover, the increasing reluctance manifested by leaders of both parties in the United States Senate to support even a limited and circumscribed employment of force by the United States resulted in a material watering down of the Articles in the Covenant that had to do with the imposition of sanctions and the contingent employment of force to check aggression. Had President Wilson been able to agree during the early stages of the debate in the Senate to the so-called "mild reservations," this country would have entered the League. In all probability, adjustments could then have been made over the course of the years which would have solved any real difficulties created by these reservations.

One would have to be blind indeed to fail to realize that the hope of an overwhelming majority of the American people—and of great numbers of the men who risked their lives for this country—that this nation would assume its full share of responsibility for preventing future wars was betrayed as a result of the national elections of 1920.

At the cost of infinitely greater sacrifices, this country has now, twenty-five years later, a new chance to see to it that the tragedy shall not reoccur. By a strange coincidence, this great issue must again be determined in the turmoil of a Presidential election. It would be too much to assume that human nature has so changed that some political leaders may not again attempt to make political capital out of the situation, notwithstanding the fact that the way in which this issue is decided may well be a matter of life and death to the United States. I believe, however, that the men in our armed services and their families, the workers and the taxpayers of the country, will have learned from our experience since the last war that the issue transcends all party politics. I am confident that they will demand that this supreme question be determined solely upon the basis of how we can most surely prevent the present tragedies and losses from "happening again."

What steps are necessary if this government is to make sure that in the years to come the United States will be able to live freely and to prosper in an orderly and peaceful world?

Many people have recently advocated a world order built upon the same foundations as the existing inter-American system. I am the first to maintain, as I have so often publicly stated, that the present agreements between the twenty-one American republics have resulted in the most advanced regional system ever to have been evolved. The system can worthily serve as a successful example of what free peoples can achieve. I am hopeful not only that the present inter-

American system will continue in the years to come but, even more,
that it may become better integrated and more fully effective. But
it cannot be taken as an exact model for an effective international
organization, since the inter-American agreements now in effect
include no provision for the use of force to prevent or to check war.

The whole inter-American structure rests upon four basic principles: the recognition by each American republic of the sovereign
equality of all the twenty-one republics; nonintervention on the part
of any American republic in the internal or foreign affairs of any
other American republic; the commitment on the part of all the
republics that they will resort solely to pacific methods for the solution of controversies which may arise between them; and, finally,
the agreement of all that any danger or threat of danger originating
outside the hemisphere and menacing the peace of an American
nation will be regarded as an equal danger to all American countries,
requiring such joint action as may be determined through consultation.

The inter-American system provides the machinery for the conciliation, mediation, or arbitration of all controversies which may
develop between members of the American family of nations. It is
conceivable, although by no means certain, that the present consultative procedure might result in an agreement to use force should
one of the American republics endanger the peace of the hemisphere.
Up to the present time, however, there is no provision as to when, or
how, or if, force is to be used to repel either an extracontinental
aggression or an aggression arising within the hemisphere itself.

Danger of attack from abroad has for more than a century been
covered by the provisions of the Monroe Doctrine. Any threat by a
non-American power to the integrity or independence of any American nation has been regarded as an immediate menace to the vital
interests of the United States, calling for the use of the full measure
of its resources. Furthermore, the only world power, besides the
United States, in a dominating position in the Atlantic has been
Great Britain, and for many generations she has been regarded by
the United States as well as by the other American republics as a
friendly power from whose naval might no danger need be expected.

Those, therefore, who have suggested that the inter-American

system could be taken as an exact model for an international organization have, as I said before, overlooked the fundamental fact that
it does not make specific provision for the use of force in preserving
peace, or else they have assumed, what to me cannot be assumed,
that an international organization can maintain peace without having
at its disposal such armed force as may be required to prevent the
outbreak of war or to take punitive action against a lawbreaker.

Other people are urging that the League of Nations, properly
modified, be brought into service again. Among them are several
outstanding statesmen of the United States. It would obviously be
the height of folly for the United Nations to fail to salvage whatever
they can from the League of Nations or to refrain from profiting
by the lessons gained through the operation of the Covenant. There
is every practical reason to regard the Covenant of the League as
a standard by which the efficacy of a new world organization may
be determined. But it seems to me that it would be disastrous, in the
light of the experience of the past twenty-five years, to attempt to
build up anew on precisely the same foundations.

I have long felt that a major reason for the failure of the League
was the fact that the Covenant came suddenly into being as a completed and detailed international charter. It was not a carrying-over
into the time of peace of the alliance which had been created during
the war. It did not grow gradually as a result of actual experience.
Furthermore, because the Covenant came full-grown into being,
peoples everywhere were apt to persuade themselves that a final and
real peace already existed. It was impossible for their governments
to arouse them to the truth that the Covenant was but paper, and
would remain so unless each of the major powers was willing to use,
if necessary, sufficient armed strength to carry out the provisions
both of the Covenant and of the peace treaty itself, especially during
the first turbulent postwar years.

After this war a wholly different approach seems indispensable.
It is essential that, before the war ends, the United Nations agree
to a transition period to follow the surrender of their enemies. Its
length would be fixed later by common agreement and would depend
on their progress in laying the foundations for a world of peace.
During this transition period the United Nations would have a

chance to complete the first and most urgent military steps required; to correct the cardinal territorial errors of the past; to carry out such transfers of populations as may be necessary; to conclude the more immediate programs for rehabilitation and reconstruction; and to pave the way for their ultimate assumption of international trustee-ship over such dependent peoples as are not yet ready to enjoy the rights of self-government. During this period, as the hatreds and bitternesses engendered by the war years gradually burn themselves out, the United Nations can, little by little, determine the specific machinery needed for a permanent and effective international organ-ization.

But, long before the conclusion of the war, the United Nations must agree upon a provisional organization to knit them firmly together, and to become the embryo of the perfected organization of the future. First of all, before and during the transition period, there must be effectively functioning some executive agency of the United Nations able to make political and military decisions for all of them. At the present moment no such executive agency exists. In the Moscow Agreements the four major powers among the United Nations took the first essential step, through an agreement to co-operate after the victory as well as throughout the war. They expressed their common determination to create a permanent inter-national organization.

They also set up a Mediterranean Commission composed of repre-sentatives of the British, Soviet, and United States governments and, contingently, of certain other members of the United Nations specially interested in the Mediterranean region). And they estab-lished in London a European Advisory Commission composed only of subordinate British, Soviet, and United States officials, which is supposed to decide political questions that may arise in Europe. These two commissions are in no sense representative of the United Nations as a whole. The only completely representative agencies so far set up are the International Relief and Rehabilitation Admin-istration, created to provide relief for the populations of the countries ravaged by the war, the Food and Agriculture Committee, and the group of experts which has been formulating plans for the solution of the great problem of postwar finance.

There could be no more fatal error than for the United Nations to enter the transition period without having previously established some executive agency to represent all of them and to act in their names in the determination of the problems which not only will arise immediately after the cessation of hostilities, but which actually have already arisen. It is lamentable that this executive agency should not have been set up for some time in order that it might carry over from the war into the post-armistice period. It would have gained invaluable experience and have had time to shake down into a working organization before being confronted with the violent stresses which will characterize the critical period immediately after the war.

Of the United Nations, the four major powers primarily responsible for winning the war and for preventing renewed outbreaks after the armistice must necessarily assume the basic responsibility for making and carrying out all military decisions. At the present time, all agreements of this sort are reached by the Combined Chiefs of Staff or through the commissions set up by the General Staffs of the major powers. During the transition period, some more permanent mechanism evolving out of the existing organization of the Combined Chiefs of Staff should be functioning effectively so that necessary steps can be taken without delay, and without the danger of friction or misunderstanding. In order that the military authorities of the major powers may neither take nor prejudice the taking of purely political decisions, which should be made by all the United Nations, some means must be found of co-ordinating political and military agencies.

As soon as the transition period commences, the United Nations will have to occupy the Axis countries for an indefinite period and even before that time, they will be obliged temporarily to occupy the countries seized by the Axis until their legitimate governments can resume control of the local administration or until the people can freely elect the governments of their choice. Also all the United Nations will have to decide upon the nature and the duties of the armed force that they will make available to enforce peace until such time as that obligation devolves upon a permanent international organization.

In the purely political field, every variety of problem, within the defeated Axis countries as well as within many of the occupied countries, will call for immediate action. Likewise, decisions relative to boundaries and the movements of populations will have to be made within the briefest time possible.

The executive council of the United Nations must also create the new agencies, or continue the already existing agencies, necessary to lay the foundations for economic and financial reconstruction.

I have mentioned only a few of the outstanding problems confronting the United Nations. Were there in existence today an executive council representing all those nations, one could view with a greater measure of equanimity the prospect for their effective and wise solution. And it is inconceivable that the United Nations as a whole will acquiesce willingly in having decisions outside of the purely military sphere made solely by the four major powers.

There is a considerable body of opinion in this country, and a few of our ablest authorities on foreign affairs are included in it, which maintains that all that is really required in the way of international organization after the war is a continuing military alliance between the Soviet Union, the British Commonwealth of Nations, and the United States, together with China when Asiatic questions are involved.

It seems to me that the proponents of this theory overlook two indisputable facts. The first of these is that in all human history no military alliances have lasted for more than a few short years. National policies and ambitions change, individual leaders are replaced, and rivalries or antagonisms develop between the very partners in the alliance. The second fact is that the other members of the United Nations, let alone the few remaining neutral states, will never reconcile themselves to being dominated for an indefinite period by a dictatorship composed of the four great powers. They are not fighting a war to liberate themselves from the domination of Hitlerism solely to replace the Axis tyranny with a new form of world dictatorship.

This same school of thought insists that the pledge on the part of the major powers to co-operate in using force to keep the peace after the war should be strictly limited to the enforcement of the peace treaties to be imposed upon Germany and Japan, and that the charter of any future world organization should contain no pledge on the part of any power to use force to prevent war. It likewise holds that all that the world organization should amount to should be an agreement on the part of the nations composing such an organization to consult together. No principles of conduct—no stipulations as to the nature of their obligations—should be agreed to when the organization is created.

If any such form of international organization as this is all that is constructed by the United Nations as the outcome of the second World War, the people of the United States would have little ground to anticipate the maintenance of world peace for more than a few uneasy years.

No international organization can conceivably survive unless it is supported by the opinion of free men and women throughout the world. That support will not be forthcoming unless the new international organization assures them all of national independence and liberty—not an overlordship; unless it is based upon those principles of international conduct which mankind has learned can alone establish a decent world; and unless it is so constituted as to offer the promise that peace will no longer be merely the subject of consultation, but that it will actually be enforced as the foremost obligation of all nations.

If there is any hope of a permanent international organization in the future, the path leading toward it must be prepared now. For that reason, while, as I have said, any provisional executive council of the United Nations must enable the major military powers to discharge effectively their responsibilities of a purely military character, it must at the same time afford the other members of the United Nations full right to share in all other decisions.

The most effective means of reconciling these two indispensable requirements may be found in establishing the executive council of the United Nations in the following manner:

A. The Provisional United Nations Executive Council must be created by agreement among all the United Nations upon the firm pledge that a permanent international organization shall be established for the maintenance of peace and for the promotion of human welfare as soon as they agree upon a practicable time when such a step could be taken. Until that time the Provisional United Nations Executive Council should function in the name of all the United Nations as the supreme authority which is representative of them all.

B. This Provisional Council should be composed of eleven members, including a member designated by each of the four major Allied powers, namely, the United Kingdom, the Soviet Union, China, and the United States; two additional members chosen by the group of European states; two additional members chosen by the group of American states; one by the group of Far Eastern states; one by the group of states of the Near and Middle East and of Africa; and one by the British Dominions.

C. The members of the Executive Council representing the regional groups of states would be elected for a term of one year by all the states comprised within that region, from a panel consisting of two nominees designated by each state within the regional group, such nominees being chosen from among the nationals of any of the states within that region. Members of the Executive Council elected regionally should represent the interests of the region as a whole rather than the specific interests of the state of which they may be a national.

D. The Executive Council should be charged with the following major duties:

1. The determination of the procedure to be adopted for the pacific settlement of any dispute which may arise subsequent to the armistice and which threatens the peace.

2. Should pacific methods of settlement prove ineffective, reference of the dispute, actual or threatened, to the police agencies functioning under the authority of the Executive Council.

3. The assumption of responsibility for determining the form of the administration of any Axis territory from the date upon which the military authorities of the major powers which have occupied that region agree that the purely military objectives in that region have been attained.

4. The formulation and recommendation to all the United Nations of the completed plan for a permanent international organization, and of any preliminary steps desirable in expediting its creation.

E. The Executive Council should immediately establish a Security and Armaments Commission as well as an Armaments Inspection Commission to which should be entrusted the following responsibilities:

1. The Security and Armaments Commission should be composed primarily of military, naval, and aviation representatives of the states and regional groups of states represented on the Executive Council.

2. It should advise the Council in any emergency as to the steps which should be taken in order to maintain international peace and security and it should act as the agent of the Council in the taking of such measures as may be required for that purpose.

3. It should supervise the execution of all armaments stipulations, including control over the manufacture of and trade in arms, which may be required of the defeated states by the terms of surrender, or which may subsequently be adopted by the members of the United Nations themselves or the states later associated with them in preparing for the permanent world organization.

4. It should recommend to the Executive Council the plans necessary for a general limitation of armaments.

5. It should likewise recommend to the Council any modifications considered desirable from time to time in such armaments limitation agreements as may be decided upon.

6. It should control and supervise the work of the Armaments Inspection Commission to be appointed by the Executive Council.

F. The Armaments Inspection Commission should likewise be composed primarily of technical military, naval, and aviation experts who should be designated preferably from among the nationals of states other than those of the major powers which will be individually represented on the Executive Council. It should regularly report to the Security and Armaments Commission on the armaments and armaments potential of all states, and should be charged with the responsibility of maintaining a continuous inspection of the armaments and of the armaments potential of the defeated Axis nations, and of the states represented in the Executive Council in accordance with any agreements which may be entered into between them providing for the limitation of armaments.

G. The Executive Council should give preferential consideration to an early agreement among all the member states for a general limitation of armaments in order that there may be established through such agreements a maximum and minimum level of armaments to be maintained by all states for the preservation of internal order and for the discharge of such obligations as they may incur for the maintenance of regional or general security.

H. The Executive Council should establish such technical agencies or other committees as may be required, and should appoint as its chairman, or "moderator," an individual of outstanding international experience and authority who would likewise serve as the Executive Director of all the administrative agencies and commissions which the Council may establish. He should, however, have no vote within the Council.

The Executive Council should remain in permanent session, but might sit at such places as it may consider most expedient. It should establish its own rules of procedure. But it should not be empowered to take any action save by at least a two-thirds vote of its voting members, which determining vote should include all the members designated by the four major powers.

I. The Provisional United Nations Executive Council should come into being as soon as the protocol providing for its creation has been ratified by at least twenty states, members of the United Nations, including the United Kingdom, the Soviet Union, China, and the United States. Provision should be made within the protocol for the adherence of other sovereign states, not originally members of the United Nations, subsequent to the termination of the present war.

It should be emphasized again that this plan is intended to reconcile the two basic problems which proved difficult of reconciliation in the Covenant of the League of Nations and which are today perhaps even more difficult to reconcile.

It is to meet the first of these problems—the need to give the four major powers scope for military action—that I have proposed to give them direct representation in the Provisional Executive Council and further to make it necessary that their votes be cast affirmatively before any action is taken by the Executive Council.

The second problem—to give full representation and protection to the interests of the smaller nations—will, I believe, be met by building the world organization upon a foundation of regional systems. This plan may also help to solve many other difficulties which in varying degree were partially responsible for the breakdown of the League of Nations.

It will be maintained, I have no doubt, that the foundation of any permanent world order upon regional systems runs counter to the third of Woodrow Wilson's five points, namely: "No alliance within any League of Nations" and to the warning contained in his oft-quoted words: "There must be, not a balance of power, but a community of power; not organized rivalries, but an organized common peace; all nations henceforth (must) avoid entangling alliances which would draw them into competitions of power."

The dangers envisaged by President Wilson in these warnings cannot be overemphasized. However, they will exist only if the nations of the world seek to employ regional systems as offensive or defensive alliances, or as political or economic "spheres of influence" to be exploited for the individual ends of the great powers dominant in each region.

The surest way to prevent this is to make the Provisional United Nations Executive Council an agency capable of exercising a continuing control so that it can check instantly any development of the regional system which might threaten to engender regional rivalry. By giving each region full representation in the Executive Council, and by guaranteeing to the Council supreme authority, any trend toward regional antagonism, and any tendency to use the regional systems for the aggrandizement of an individual power should be successfully combated. The greater the participation of the smaller states in the Executive Council the more remote will become the dangers which Wilson foresaw. Moreover, from the standpoint of preserving world peace and expediting world order and stability, regional systems have great practical advantages.

It is obvious that the states composing each region are far more familiar with their local problems than states geographically distant from them. They are more competent to work out constructive solutions and to take the initial steps necessary to prevent the growth of controversies. The history of the League of Nations has demonstrated this fact innumerable times. Nationals of distant countries who dealt with crises in Central Europe, notwithstanding their high motives, proved as unsuccessful as the European nationals who dealt with the peculiarly regional problems of the Chaco controversy between Bolivia and Paraguay. If at any time, because of local antagonisms, the states of a given area are unable to find satisfactory solutions for controversies within their region, the Provisional United Nations Executive Council will be available to take whatever measures may be required to keep the peace.

The nations of the Western Hemisphere would not willingly abandon the inter-American system—which has functioned effectively and will, if permitted to do so, grow stronger as the years pass —as a prerequisite to their participation in a world organization. If it continues to exist, the machinery which has already been created will render unlikely the rise of controversies within the Americas that would result in war. However, should war break out between two American republics and should the present pacific methods for the solution of such controversies fail to prove effective, none of the American republics, it must be frankly stated, would willingly see British or Soviet or Chinese troops or airplanes sent to the Western Hemisphere to quell the outbreak. They would unquestionably prefer to try to settle the conflict within their region through the use of a strictly inter-American force, one designated for such a purpose by agreement between the American republics and yet operating in accordance with the provisions of an over-all plan laid down by the supreme international organization.

For very much the same reason, the European nations would not care to have United States troops and airplanes used to check hostilities within Europe. It must be also admitted that the people of the United States would not be willing to have American soldiers or airplanes utilized whenever a Balkan controversy flared up or whenever minor disputes outside the world areas in which the United States is directly concerned required police action.

By the establishment of regional systems whose members would be charged with the initial responsibility of keeping the peace among themselves, this country would be directly committed to use its armed forces only in co-operation with other American countries to prevent the outbreak of war in this hemisphere. Outside of the

New World, it would take concerted action with the other major powers only when regional machinery to enforce peace broke down, or when such action by this government was necessary to prevent the outbreak of major wars which threatened the maintenance of world peace and consequently the security of this country. The issue of the Monroe Doctrine would not then be raised, as it was in 1919, nor would the United States be required to send its troops to the four quarters of the globe whenever minor trouble arose.

Founding the world organization upon regional systems would also remove a deep-rooted objection which existed in the minds of many Americans when the Covenant of the League of Nations was presented to them for their approval. They insisted that in the Assembly or Council of the League the United States should at no time have less voting strength than any other power. The question arose from the fact that, because of the representation given to the self-governing Dominions, the British Empire could have been assumed to possess in the Assembly of the League a voting strength of six as against one vote for the United States.

By using the regional system of representation the United States, under the plan proposed, would be given one vote in the Provisional United Nations Executive Council through its individual representative, and the United Kingdom would also be given one individual vote. In addition, the United States would have the right, as one of the sovereign republics of the Western Hemisphere, to participate in the election of the two representatives from this hemisphere, who would sit on the Executive Council together with the individual representative of the United States. In the same manner the United Kingdom, in addition to its individual representative, would have the right to vote for the two regional representatives from Europe. It would also have the right to participate in the selection of a representative of the British Dominions.

Complaint will be made that the United States would have a voice in only three votes on the Executive Council, while the British government would have a voice in four. This complaint would, in my judgment, be based upon a failure to appraise conditions realistically. In the first place, it should be borne in mind that the Soviet Union as a member of the regional system of Europe would also be entitled to vote for the two European representatives on the Council. It is inconceivable that the United Kingdom could so influence the selection of the representatives from Europe that these votes would be cast solely to the selfish advantage of Great Britain. Nor does it seem probable, granted the highly developed nationalism of the self-governing Dominions of the British Commonwealth of Nations, that the British government would ever be able to use the representative of the Dominions as the individual agent of Downing Street in the determination of crucial questions.

Finally, and most important of all, it must be remembered that under the proposed terms, which make any action by the Executive Council impossible unless it is voted for by all of the four major powers, the United States retains a veto right.

Regional systems, moreover, would greatly encourage the development of constructive economic and financial policies in each area. In Eastern Europe, in many parts of the Americas as well as in Africa, Asia, and the more highly developed area of Western Europe, there is almost unlimited opportunity for co-operative measures to remove artificial and prejudicial trade barriers, to unify currencies, to distribute electric power—all essential steps in promoting a rise in living standards. Over a period of years, regional systems would inevitably do away with the more restrictive forms of ultranationalism in the economic and financial field. In short, they are a device that in innumerable ways would make it far easier to maintain peace— which is, after all, the most important function of the Executive Council.

It is proposed that the Security and Armaments Commission to be designated by the Executive Council, and to function under its control, act as the agent of the Council whenever armed force is necessary to keep the peace or to enforce the Council's decisions.

There are two ways in which these responsibilities can be carried out. The first is through the creation of an international police force under the control of the Executive Council and its agencies. The second is through the agreement of the major powers that each will contribute its military, naval, or air strength whenever that becomes necessary to check or prevent hostilities, which they have assumed the obligation to repress. I do not believe that the first of these alternatives—the creation of an international police force—is either feasible or desirable. It is not feasible because, I believe, no one of the great powers will be willing for many years to come to reduce its own armed strength to a level lower than that of an international police force over which it does not possess full control. And unless an international police force is superior in strength to the military, naval, or air power of any nation, and even to the combined power of several nations, it will serve no practical purpose.

The second alternative seems to me the only practical solution. It would be both expedient and wise, therefore, for the nations within each region to agree upon the manner in which they will make force available, should it be required to prevent the outbreak of war within that area. The plans must, of course, be subject to the approval of the Executive Council and its Security and Armaments Commission, which will co-ordinate them with whatever over-all agreement for world security it may have devised. Take as a concrete example the Western Hemisphere. The twenty-one American republics would appoint by common agreement the nations of the New World which were to make force available, and the precise obligations of each in such an event. They would designate air or naval bases within the Americas which would be available to them. If, notwithstanding the use of such regional force, a local war should threaten to endanger the peace of the rest of the world, the Executive Council of the International Organization and its agencies would employ such additional force as might be required to stamp out the flames.

The major powers, through the Executive Council, would thus be called upon to contribute their armed force only after the regional system has failed to put an end to regional controversies. For this purpose, there would have to be set aside, in addition to regional bases, air and naval bases throughout the world to be used whenever world security is threatened.

As I have already publicly said, I believe that two great moral principles must from the very outset be an integral part of the constitution of even a provisional international organization. The first is the recognition by all nations of the inalienable right of every people on earth to enjoy freedom of religion, of information, and of speech. There can be no peaceful or free world of the future unless every nation recognizes these freedoms as human rights. Every government, before it joins the world organization, should be obligated to demonstrate that its citizens are enabled to enjoy these rights through effective guarantees contained in their national constitution.

The second principle is equal in importance. Hundreds of millions of people at the outset of the present war were under alien sovereignty as colonial subjects of the imperial powers. Can we conceivably envision a peaceful or a stable world if it is to continue, when the war is won, half slave and half free?

The peoples of Asia, of the Near East, and of Africa are waiting to see what the victory of the United Nations is going to mean to them. They will regard the decisions taken by us as an acid test. Unless the forces of nationalism, which are fast growing more and more powerful in all these vast areas of the earth, are canalized into constructive channels, a devastating state of chaos will ensue. The determination of some of these peoples to secure their freedom cannot longer be thwarted.

The international organization must consecrate in a practical form the basic principle that no nation has an inherent or unlimited right to govern subject peoples. The colonial powers must recognize that their control is to be exercised first of all to prepare these peoples for self-government as soon as they are capable of exercising this right; and that until they are fitted for autonomy the colonial power will be regarded by the international organization solely as an administering power—as a trustee—and as such must be responsible to world public opinion through the international organization itself. Peoples capable of self-government must be given this right by the international organization whatever their race or color, or whatever the vested interests of any present colonial power may be.

The United Nations must not evade this problem as the Allied powers evaded it in 1919 by creating on paper a mandate system, and then washing their hands of all further responsibility. No power on earth should again be permitted to ignore the obligation to demonstrate that its control of subject peoples is being exercised to expedite their fitness for autonomy, and that, until such time, its administration of their affairs is primarily in their interest.

The Provisional Executive Council of the International Organization must obtain agreement upon these principles. What is more, it must at once create the machinery necessary to put these principles into practice.

Directly under the Executive Council, and responsible to it, must come the Superior Agency of an International Trusteeship, the members of which would be appointed by the Executive Council. Under the authority of the Superior Agency, there should be created in every region where there are dependent peoples a Regional Council of the International Trusteeship, composed of representatives of all powers of the region. It would be responsible for keeping in continuous touch with all developments affecting the dependent peoples within its territory, and would have whatever authority it required to carry out the decisions of the Superior Agency. The Regional Council should sit permanently in some central place in the region where it possesses jurisdiction.

Finally, the Regional Council should have as many agents as it may need, who would remain permanently in each territory as observers and as advisers to the local authorities. Where present colonial powers remain as administering powers in a colony, their administrative staff should continue to act as the local administrators, but with the obligation to facilitate the duties of the representatives of the Regional Council.

The administrative expenses in each region would be the first charge upon the revenues of that territory.

In cases where dependent peoples at the close of the war will no longer be under the control of an administering power, as in the case of Korea, or where the present colonial power has proved unworthy or incompetent, the International Trusteeship, through its regional councils, should undertake the administration of their affairs.

The International Organization, upon the advice of the International Trusteeship, would determine broad policies for the welfare of dependent peoples, and would decide when they are fitted to exercise partial, or complete, autonomy.

During the transition period the United Nations, through the Provisional Executive Council, should likewise at the earliest moment install a World Court to which justiciable matters could be referred.

The Court established by the League of Nations might well be retained, with such amendments to its existing faculties and duties as circumstances may require. To the Court would be brought international controversies or problems whose solution it would be unnecessary to refer to a political body such as the Executive Council itself.

The Executive Council should also prepare the way for the creation of a World Congress in which every sovereign state may be individually represented, and in which even the defeated Axis states may have representation as soon as their period of trial has ended and they have had the opportunity to select popular governments.

The specific powers of such a World Congress should be determined by the Executive Council only after most of the world is once more at peace. First must come radical political and territorial readjustments, which only the Executive Council and its Security and Armaments Commission can effectively make, and an advanced degree of economic rehabilitation. But when that time is at hand, an international forum (whatever its powers) in which every nation can be heard will provide a safety valve for world public opinion, the practical value of which should not be underestimated.

With the creation of these agencies, the Provisional United Nations Executive Council, the Security and Armaments Commission, the World Court, and the World Congress, the four bodies indispensable to any permanent world organization will have been established. It would be unwise to attempt at this stage to define more precisely the final details of their correlation and of the manner in which they would fit into the permanent world organization itself. Those are questions that can best be settled in the light of the experience which will be gained during the first postwar years.

Measures of relief and of rehabilitation for the peoples of occupied Europe and of occupied Asia will be of prime urgency as soon as the war ends. The United Nations Relief and Rehabilitation Administration will be prepared to move as soon as military conditions make it possible.

The United Nations must also determine upon co-operative economic and financial measures which will enable the nations of the world as rapidly as possible once more to take up a normal international life.

The first great problem confronting the proposed provisional organization is the stabilization of currencies, for until this is done international trade cannot be successfully carried on. Except in a limited sense and for a limited time, a resort to barter will be no solution. Until normal healthy international trade is resumed, the industrial lives of those nations which have depended primarily upon their export trade to maintain their national economies cannot be resumed. Much less can any nation hope to return to real prosperity. The agreement of the experts of the thirty-four United Nations in April, 1944, upon the principles through the employment of which world currency stabilization can be secured is a great step forward. It may be hoped that the governments themselves will soon ratify the plan proposed.

The solutions of this problem cannot be improvised. And they will not be found in projects cleverly devised to further the selfish interests of one nation, or of one group of nations. The United Nations will find themselves in a desperate predicament unless such projects as this are agreed upon prior to the conclusion of the armistice and unless they are both workable and soundly conceived.

The economic and financial agreements reached must take into account the—I hope, temporary—practices of certain governments, such as the Soviet Union, by which the state itself wholly controls export and import trade. Furthermore, they must prevent the resumption of that destructive authoritarian practice in international trade which utilizes the financial and economic policies of the government for political purposes.

As soon as possible, the Provisional Executive Council must stimulate the creation of international agencies to recommend to all governments co-operative measures in the realms of agriculture, finance, communications, aviation, shipping, and electric power development. It should immediately provide for the continuation, if possible on an even more extensive basis, of the International Labor Office. And it should prepare for the establishment of agencies to encourage international cultural activities.

There are many others, but these, in my judgment, are the most

important and most necessary steps to be taken by the United
Nations prior to the winning of the victory and during the years
subsequent thereto. Only after a period of years, during which peace
must be maintained; only after a Provisional United Nations Executive Council and its Security and Armaments Commission have
carried out their preliminary tasks; only after a World Court and a
World Congress are functioning; and only after the defeated Axis
powers are under control and definitely on the path to regeneration
can, in my judgment, the final steps safely be taken to complete that
permanent world organization which the peoples of the world are
seeking.

Time is passing swiftly. The longer the United Nations fail to
agree upon the measures they will jointly take in order to achieve the
objectives set forth, the less likely it will be that the tragic sacrifice
of life and treasure which this war has imposed upon the free
peoples of the earth will ever be compensated for by a sure promise
of security and peace—the only kind of compensation which we of
today can offer the generations of tomorrow.

CHAPTER XI

# The Part We Must Play

IN ANY attempt to project the future foreign policy of the United States, it is profitable to recall the broad lines of our foreign policy in the years of our youthful independence. By doing this we avail ourselves of an invaluable touchstone. For our policy in those early years was fashioned by the ablest Americans who have ever assumed that responsibility, and it has proved its worth beyond any latter-day dispute.

The genius shown by the two great Virginians, Thomas Jefferson and James Madison, and the great New Englander, John Quincy Adams, who so largely determined our foreign policy during the forty years between 1789 and 1829—when the world was suffering from convulsions strangely similar to those of the present day—was not equaled even by the great figures who guided the destinies of Europe at that time. And those were the decades when the younger Pitt, Castlereagh, and Canning were at the helm of British foreign policy; when Talleyrand was weaving the devious mesh of French diplomacy, under the Consulate, under the Empire, and under Louis XVIII; when Metternich was in the midst of his protracted attempt to hold back the tides of democracy, and when Alexander I was pursuing the paradoxical policy that marked the course of Russia during the first quarter of the nineteenth century.

Today we too rarely attempt to appraise justly the immense dangers and difficulties with which this country was beset after the years of its birth. The slightest misstep at that time would inevitably have involved the United States in European Wars. But when we do undertake such an appraisal we are forced to render tribute to the amazing skill with which those three great Americans succeeded in achieving the basic objectives upon which the safety and future welfare of this country depended. In its formative years our nation could not afford to become involved in international controversies.

It needed time in which to weld together the diverse elements comprised in the original colonies, and in which safely to gain the additional territory needed for expansion and security. As a sovereign nation, the United States had also to preserve intact its rights upon the high seas so that American trade and industry might prosper. None of these prerequisites to future power could have been secured had this country permitted itself to be drawn into the European wars, particularly when it had already been shown that the European allies of one day were more than likely to become the European antagonists of the next. "Entangling alliances," under such conditions as these, were no temptation to the farseeing.

In the history of the diplomacy of the United States, there are no two accomplishments which had a greater long-term effect upon the growth of the American nation than Jefferson's acquisition of the territory comprised within the Louisiana Purchase, and the extraordinary feat of John Quincy Adams in securing the Florida Territory from Spain through negotiations into which he entered with hardly a card in his hand.

Certainly mistakes were committed during those years. It was good fortune rather than foresight that prevented the War of 1812 from bringing in its train disastrous consequences for the people of the United States. Nor were the embargo measures for which Jefferson and Madison were responsible any more sagacious in their conception than the embargo measures imposed by this government in very recent years.

But throughout those four decades the foreign policy of the United States was consistent, unflagging in its initiative, and farsighted. It magnificently accomplished the ends sought. It made it possible for the thirteen colonies to become one united nation and to gain the additional territory needed to transform the small and struggling Republic into one of the great powers of the earth. It concerned itself solely with the interests of the American people. It abjured the temptation of adventures in which only a powerful country could afford to engage.

In our democracy a few individuals generally shape foreign policy. Domestic policies are far more often determined by public opinion operating through the legislative branch of the government. It is only occasionally that one sees the sharp imprint of the individual leader upon them. In the field of foreign policy, on the other hand, while from time to time popular opinion forces the government into a course of action, as in our war with Spain, it is usually the President and his Secretary of State who initiate and mold the course of the government. Except in a moment of crisis, most of the people are prone to leave the determination of their foreign policy to their executive authorities.

During the past century it has become almost second nature to many United States citizens to believe that one of the most useful attributes that can be possessed by those whom they select to guide foreign relations is a lack of any personal acquaintance with peoples in other countries. I suppose that this conviction arises in part from that inferiority complex which was so plainly shown by the thunderous applause which always greeted the gibe of the elder Will Rogers when he used to say that the United States never lost in a war and never won in a conference. It is due to the fear that the average American is no match in diplomacy for the wily foreigner. It also springs, perhaps, from the long-standing feeling that the best way to be truly American is to avoid any contact with foreigners. I remember very well how Senator Borah, who was certainly one of the most popular figures of his generation in the United States Senate, used to take especial pride, while he was Chairman of the Foreign Relations Committee, in the fact that he had never left the shores of the United States. He was convinced that for that reason his thinking had not been affected by the insidious propaganda of foreigners. He felt that he was thus far better fitted to determine the true needs of his own country.

In the light of this feeling, it is worth recalling the special training of the fathers of this country who so brilliantly shaped and conducted the foreign policy of the United States in its infant years. Benjamin Franklin was not only as much at home in London and Paris as he was in his native Philadelphia, but he was appreciated even more highly in Paris than he was at home. The veneration with which he was regarded in France was equaled in the more liberal circles of England. Both Jefferson and Monroe had served the United States for long years in diplomatic missions in Europe. So had

Henry Clay and many other leading Senators and members of the House of Representatives. No man in the history of the United States has been a more able, a more successful, and a more patriotic Secretary of State than John Quincy Adams. He proved himself, in fact, more than the equal of the European statesmen with whom he was successively forced to come to grips. No man in our history has possessed a more specialized training for the office which he later occupied. He had served as secretary to his father, John Adams, during the latter's European mission; he was then appointed Minister to the Netherlands, and subsequently to Russia; he was Commissioner in the negotiations which resulted in the Treaty of Ghent, and ultimately Minister to London before becoming Secretary of State. The men who successfully shaped the history of the United States during its first four decades, and who by their own initiative laid down the course it followed in its relations with other countries, were men intimately familiar with European affairs, personally acquainted with most of the statesmen of Europe. They possessed a knowledge of the languages and customs of other countries. Thus time and again they knew what kind of reaction to expect under given circumstances.

Our earlier statesmen not only understood the trends and cross-currents of world politics, but also, as one can see from their diaries and correspondence, considered such knowledge to be essential in determining the course the United States should pursue.

After the Jackson Administration, a majority of the people, as well as their chosen leaders, gradually came to regard Europe as of remote interest and concern. The growing strength of this country made the threat of danger from abroad less probable. It encouraged the belief that our security was enhanced by a mental insulation from affairs in Europe as much as by physical remoteness. After the days when Henry Clay kindled a brief but very real sympathy for the struggling nations of the other Americas, the rest of the Western Hemisphere became of even less interest to the average citizen of this country. And it was only at the turn of the present century that the nations of the Far East became anything more than a name to most Americans.

Everything tended to foster the spirit of isolation which became ingrained in the American way of thinking. Prior to the outbreak of the War between the States, the attention of the American people was riveted solely upon two all-absorbing problems—the question of slavery and the question of industrial and physical expansion.

During the years of our Civil War even the flagrant violation of the Monroe Doctrine, when Spain occupied the Dominican Republic and Napoleon III intervened in Mexico, was all but ignored. Between that time and the war with Spain in 1898, except for the vision and initiative of Secretary of State Blaine when he urged the need for establishing an economic Pan-Americanism, the people of the United States lived in an isolated world of their own. The physical power which this country already possessed, and the fact that the greatest maritime power in the world, Great Britain, held no ambitions which ran counter to our own security, together with the safety which we then still derived from our transoceanic position, all combined to instill the unshakable conviction that we were secure no matter what happened in the rest of the world.

During the fifty years between the Van Buren Administration and the Administration of President McKinley, our foreign policy was almost consistently negative. It was static. It is at least a coincidence that the Secretaries of State throughout that period, let alone the Presidents, were with but the rarest exceptions such as Daniel Webster and James Buchanan, wholly devoid of any personal knowledge or experience of the rest of the world.

When this government during that period ventured into the field of positive diplomacy it threatened disaster. William H. Seward was an able man, but no Secretary of State with even the slightest knowledge of European affairs would have submitted his notorious memorandum, in which he urged President Lincoln, on the very eve of our Civil War, deliberately to provoke a war with the great powers of Europe. Fortunately President Lincoln, who possessed the sure grasp which only genius provides, ignored it. Cleveland's last Secretary of State, Richard Olney, was correct in his vigorous assertion of the Monroe Doctrine in our dispute with Lord Salisbury's government over Venezuela's boundaries. But a Secretary of State with more accurate understanding of what was then going on behind the European scene could very readily have

secured the full recognition of the American demands without risk-
ing an open clash with a power that was already thwarting German
ambitions for expansion in the Western Hemisphere.

With the conclusion of the Spanish War, a brief wave of imperialism hit the United States, and hit it hard. For a transitory moment
the people of this country and their government were afflicted with
the contagion of the "white man's burden" virus. The corollary to
the Monroe Doctrine announced by Theodore Roosevelt, which
created such havoc in inter-American relations, was concrete evidence of the reforming spirit with which a portion of American
public opinion suddenly became imbued.

While the majority of the people of this country were stimulated
by their experience in imperialism, as represented by their acquisition of the Philippine Islands and of Puerto Rico, and by the basic
change wrought in their status through the acquisition of Hawaii and
the later construction of the Panama Canal, they were slow to grasp
the full implications of their position as a world power. Yet two
successive Presidents did all that they could to hasten public realization of this reality. Both President Theodore Roosevelt and President Taft repeatedly urged that the prestige and influence of the
United States should be used to help maintain world peace. They
early saw that a major war in Europe would inevitably affect the interests of this country and of the entire Western Hemisphere. President Theodore Roosevelt's part in bringing about the Conference
of Algeciras was striking proof of his realistic vision. And he
rendered the service at a time when such constructive participation
in European affairs was regarded by the bulk of his fellow citizens as
extremely dangerous.

The failure of the American people to understand the force which
the United States had come to represent in the modern world was
fully demonstrated with the outbreak of the first World War. The
months between 1914 and 1917 were months of travail for the
American spirit. It was through the enlightenment and the inspiration which the American people received from leaders in both political parties that they were at last prepared to heed the inspired
phrases of Woodrow Wilson when in 1917 he summoned them to
assume their obligations as citizens of the world, and to recognize

their own responsibility for preserving the free institutions which had made this country great.

The people of the United States responded magnificently. Never since the days of the Civil War had their moral conviction been stronger. They also seemed to see clearly that the triumph of the policies Wilson urged on them was indispensable if they were to safeguard their own future welfare. Yet within the two years between April, 1917, and the midsummer of 1919 their fervor vanished. The moral issue had been obliterated. Their just estimate of where their own individual interests lay had become obscured.

In the history of our foreign policy this is probably the most ominous chapter. It requires a somewhat more extended consideration than that which has been already given it in this book. Errors in political appreciation on the part of the President, the maneuverings of his opponents, the weaknesses of human nature, all contributed to the result. And all these factors are peculiarly worthy of our study in the crisis with which this nation is faced today.

It was a mistake for President Wilson personally to attend the Peace Conference at Paris. His influence both abroad and at home would have been far greater had he remained in Washington. It was unfortunate that he refused to appoint to the Peace Delegation men who were capable of following an independent line of thought. For with the exception of Colonel House, Wilson rarely obtained the advice of any save "yes men." It was unfortunate that the President stubbornly refused to appoint to the Peace Commission outstanding representatives of the Republican party, able because of either their position or their personal influence to speak with authority for the opposition party. It was even more unfortunate that he had not previously consulted with leaders of both parties in the United States Senate, and in the House of Representatives as well, so as to obtain their co-operation, if possible, in bringing about the participation of the United States in the League of Nations. The consent of the Senate to the treaty in which the Covenant of the League was to be inserted was indispensable. The assistance which the Senate leaders might have given rendered an effort to secure their support advisable from every standpoint. For membership in the League of Nations implied that under certain contingencies the

United States would have to join in the use of force to prevent war outside of the Western Hemisphere. Clearly, for this country to embark upon a policy totally distinct from that which it had followed prior to the year 1917 was not a question of party politics. It was patently a question that rose above all party considerations. It is, of course, true that President Wilson had already commenced his bitter personal feud with Senator Lodge, who, as a result of the elections of 1918, had become Chairman of the Senate Foreign Relations Committee. But President Wilson had available to him the services of such other outstanding Republicans as former President Taft or former Secretary of State Root, both of whom still possessed great influence in the councils of their party, and both of whom fully supported Wilson's foreign policy. The President's decision disposed the rank and file of the American people to regard the League of Nations issue as political. After the Treaty of Versailles was signed, this belief was sedulously encouraged by political leaders on both sides.

The point of view that a great number of the men in the armed services adopted upon their return home swelled the changing current of popular sentiment. The government had done little, if anything, during the war months to keep the men in the Army or Navy informed of the great issues involved in the League Covenant and Peace Treaty, and of the reasons for their government's policy. Although our men by the hundreds of thousands had gone to the war on fire with enthusiasm for the ideals which Woodrow Wilson had held up before their eyes, they returned home in a far different frame of mind. The idea that their sacrifices were only half paid for by their victory had never been hammered home to them. They had not been given the chance to realize that the contributions in blood and treasure made toward winning the war could only be fully justified if the people of the United States insisted that their government adopt a policy designed to prevent these sacrifices from being again demanded of themselves or of their sons. Nor must it be overlooked that the occasional friction arising between our armed forces and the peoples of the Allied powers prejudiced many of our men against everything "foreign."

However, even as late as the Presidential campaign of June, 1920, public opinion had by no means receded to such an extent that the leaders of the Republican party thought it expedient to make a clear-cut issue of participation in the League as against straight-out isolationism. Any member of the Republican party who went to the polls the following November was fully entitled to believe that, while the Republican party was opposing both the Treaty of Versailles and the Covenant of the League of Nations in their existing form, the Republican party, as well as the Democratic party, was committed by its platform to the principle of effective, practical co-operation on the part of the United States with the other great powers of the world to prevent future wars. Notwithstanding the propaganda against the League of Nations as such, and the opposition which centered on the terms of Article X of the Covenant, any citizen was further justified in believing that existing objections to the original form of the Covenant would be removed by means of amendments or reservations, and the United States would then take its full part in the League as well as in the tribunals and agencies to be established by it.

What happened, of course, was that a group of leaders of the Republican party, composing an alliance between the sincere out-and-out isolationists of the Borah and Hiram Johnson school and the old bosses of the Republican machine led by Senator Boies Penrose of Pennsylvania, saw to it that the pledges contained in the Republican party platform remained pledges and nothing more. During the time between the elections of 1920 and the inauguration of the Harding Administration in March, 1921, this group, ably abetted by all the extreme anti-British elements in the country, conducted an exceedingly effective campaign against the dangers alleged to be inherent in the Covenant of the League. Before long millions of Americans believed that the elections of 1920 had been in fact a solemn referendum between a policy of international co-operation and a policy of complete isolation. To many of the more unthinking, the League of Nations had become a symbol of the Devil incarnate.

Within this brief period, therefore, popular support for the foreign policy of Theodore Roosevelt, Taft, and Wilson vanished. The policy of international co-operation, evolving rapidly during the war years and culminating with the signing of the Treaty of Versailles, had now suddenly been replaced with a foreign policy which called for no co-operation of any character with other nations. And there can be no question that by 1921 public opinion in this country strongly supported that change.

In view of this total reversal it is not difficult to understand why the other powers of the world were in the following years so reluctant to place any faith in the permanence of our international commitments. Fully familiar as they were with our constitutional system, it was not surprising that they had grave doubts as to where the United States, in any given contingency, might actually be found.

One of the great questions which we as a people must answer before we can decide upon our postwar role is whether a different United States foreign policy during the years between the wars could have prevented the catastrophe of 1939. I am one of those who believe that the present World War would not have cursed mankind had the United States followed a different course during the past quarter of a century.

Our cardinal error was our refusal to take any part in the League of Nations. No one can deny that, even with the exclusion of the United States from the League of Nations, the League should have accomplished far more than it did. Had the major powers been willing to forge a common policy to guide the functioning of the League, had they refrained from playing power politics, had they been willing to place their common welfare above their individual selfish ambitions, and had the statesmen of the world who were directing the Council of the League been possessed either of greater vision or of higher intelligence, many of the calamities of the past two decades might have been avoided.

But if this country had been willing from the outset to take part in the League, many of these very causes for disaster would surely have been eliminated. The eventual failure of the League was a foregone conclusion unless the United States and the Soviet Union, or at least one of them, participated in its activities during its formative years.

But, granting that the basic error in our foreign policy was made by 1921, there were other times during the past twenty-five years when this government might at least have helped to avert, or lessen, the final catastrophe.

If the Weimar Republic was to have had any chance of success, German reparations should have been based upon a just appraisal of what the German people could pay and still maintain a standard of living and a level of employment that would prevent a breakdown in the social and economic life of the country. No Republican regime, attempting to govern a people unaccustomed to and uninclined toward democratic institutions, could carry on successfully in the face of the insuperable obstacle which the Allied handling of the reparations question represented.

The internal political problems which confronted the European governments when they tried to agree upon a realistic plan, taking into account these German complexities, made it impossible to bring about any constructive solution of the reparations problem. And yet the future stability of Europe in part depended upon finding a satisfactory answer. The men who were directing the policies of the United States were fully aware of this fact. They also knew that, unless the government itself took an active part in these decisions, no politically expedient result would be achieved. However, the popular fear of becoming involved in the "disputes of Europe," added to the belief that official participation by this country would also result in the refusal of the European debtor nations to repay their war debts, created an issue of such magnitude that the Harding Administration limited itself to announcing that, while United States citizens might take part as individual experts in reparations discussions, the government itself would hold aloof. It was not difficult to forecast the outcome. Not only did the treatment of Germany in the matter of reparations make it far easier for German militarism to consolidate its grip upon the German people, but it was also one of the reasons why the war debts owing to the United States by the Allies later fell into default. If in 1921 the United States government had been willing to take an official part in deciding the reparations question, particularly since we had renounced all reparations for ourselves, the course of events in Europe would have been greatly modified.

At the end of September, 1930, when coming events in Europe were already so clearly foreshadowed, Eugene Meyer, then Chairman of the Federal Reserve Board, urged President Hoover to

propose to all the governments concerned a cut of fifty per cent in the
reparations payments then being made by Germany. At that time
Germany had already been exceedingly hard hit by the first waves
of the world-wide economic depression, and insistence that she continue to pay at the scale then fixed meant either unilateral repudiation, with the consequences which that implied, or social upheaval.
Nevertheless, President Hoover refused to consider Meyer's suggestion. He feared the political repercussions in this country as a result
of a corresponding cut in the Allied war debt payments to us. In
January, 1931, that stormy petrel of German finance, Dr. Hjalmar
Schacht, then in Washington, officially assured this government that,
even at that late date, the step proposed would make it possible for
the German government to prevent a social and economic collapse.
Nothing, however, was done. In June, 1931, President Hoover finally
suggested the one-year moratorium, which obviously implied abandonment of all reparations payments and of all war debt payments.
It was then too late. Had the halfway measure proposed been taken
the preceding September, it is well within the bounds of possibility
that the tides which commenced to run so rapidly in Germany during
the ensuing months, and which swept Hitlerism into power, might
have been diverted.

I am not so confident as some who insist that the policy pursued by
the United States at the London Economic Conference of 1933,
which is alleged to have been responsible for the breakdown of the
conference, had a conclusive effect in determining the conditions
which led up to the second World War. Hitlerism had by then been
entrenched in Germany for five months. Control by the Nazi party
and by the German General Staff had already reached such a point
that any change in German policy was by no means certain, even if
the Economic Conference had been successful. However, those nations not already bent upon autarchy might have been persuaded to
join in alleviating the deplorable stalemate of world commerce. But
it must be confessed that the inability of the world's greatest power
to join in presenting any practicable proposals for international
economic and financial co-operation does not make a page in their
country's record in which the American people can take much pride.

I have already expressed my belief that the position adopted by this government with regard to the Civil War in Spain, during the years between 1935 and 1938, constitutes the greatest error in the foreign policy of this country during the past twelve years. Had the United States then adhered to its traditional policy and permitted the legal government of Spain, which we officially recognized as such, to acquire from us the arms and munitions which it so desperately needed in its own defense, the Soviet government would undoubtedly have made even greater efforts than it did to render similar assistance. Presumably the British and French governments would have reconsidered their policy of so-called "non-intervention." Granted such assistance, it is improbable that the German and Italian governments would have been in any position to defy the sentiment of so large a part of the rest of the world and to intervene in the Spanish struggle on any such scale as they actually undertook. Had the Republican government survived, Italy would have been less likely to have entered the war against France and the military course of the war in Western Europe might consequently have proved quite different.

This summary survey of some of the chief errors in the conduct of our foreign relations in the years between the wars emphasizes the justice of the criticism which has been so often directed by other nations against our foreign policy. As they say, it has been neither logical nor consistent. Consistency is a prime requisite in any country's foreign policy. It is as indispensable in ordering the dealings between nations as is credit in commercial and financial enterprise. Until we have a consistent foreign policy, all other nations must necessarily discount the commitments into which we may enter, or the assurances we may give. British foreign policy is open to many strictures. It has, however, for a century and a half been premised upon certain well-recognized and thoroughly established principles, and the consistency of British policy, whether Cabinets in London have been Conservative or Liberal, or Labor or Coalition, has not faltered. British policy has varied in the handling of specific questions. It has never changed with regard to essentials. It has always possessed as its fundamental objectives the maintenance of a European balance of power, British control of the high seas (modified in latter years by a recognition of the friendly association of the

United States Navy), and the prevention of any danger to the freedom of British access to the British Dominions and Colonies.

If we wish to recapture for our foreign policy that logical consistency which it had in the first decades of our independent life, the people of the United States must determine now what it is that they seek in their relations with other peoples, and must see to it that their elected representatives pursue those basic objectives, no matter to which political party they may belong. Given the constitutional system of the United States, these decisions must transcend all party lines. They should be accepted by both our traditional political parties as the foundations for the policies they will pursue when they are entrusted with power by the people. For they involve the supreme interest of the nation and are circumscribed by no partisan considerations. In the entire history of the United States since 1823 there has been but one basis of our foreign policy which has been supported by all the people of this country and to which all political parties have consistently adhered, and that is the Monroe Doctrine. The time has come when, for the sake of the safety of this nation, the broad foundations of all aspects of our foreign policy should be laid down in the same way, and in similar fashion be fixed by popular decision so that no party disputes within a foreseeable future may hamper its fulfillment. At no time within the past quarter of a century has the moment been more favorable for such a determination. Both major parties are clearly dominated by a similar conception of what the main objectives of our foreign policy should be.

It is axiomatic that the foreign policy of the United States, like that of any other nation, should be based upon enlightened selfishness. It should be determined from the standpoint of what is of most advantage to the long-range interest of its people. It should be shaped so as to save the lives of our sons. It should be molded so as to relieve the burdens of the taxpayers.

There would today be little dispute, I believe, that the people of this country wish their government's foreign policy to procure for them the following assurances:

The maintenance of the peace of the nation; the preservation of the independence and integrity of the United States; the certainty that our democratic institutions will not be jeopardized; full oppor-

tunity for the United States to make its power and influence felt
in shaping the future course of world events; untrammeled encouragement for the American people to advance their standard of
living and to progress in social development; and the assurance that
they may trade, and utilize the air and the high seas on a basis of
complete equality with the peoples of other nations.

It must by now have become plain to all of us that not one of these
objectives can be surely achieved unless the world is free from
the dangers which have twice within a short quarter of a century
threatened to overwhelm us. It must be a world in which the political, social, and economic forces that have their origin in other
countries are canalized into channels that will permit us to attain
our own objectives.

For a period after the conclusion of the present war, and this
period may be long or short, disordered world conditions will make
it imperative for us to keep within our own grasp the military, naval,
and air power necessary for our self-defense. This is an elementary
precaution for which no foreign policy, however wise, can find any
substitute during such a transition period.

Our foreign policy should therefore be designed to meet two requirements. The first requirement, in the transition period, is to
hasten as quickly as possible the establishment of a world order that
would give the United States security. The second requirement, to be
met after an international organization has been created and the
immediate postwar adjustments have been made, is to further the
achievement of the long-range objectives of our foreign policy outlined above.

The only way in which this government can fill the first requirement is by unswerving concentration, by unremitting initiative,
and by the blunt admission that far too much time has already been
wasted. It will never be done by limiting ourselves to saying publicly
and officially that an international organization to keep the peace
is desirable and that we want it. It will never be done by official repetition of windy and platitudinous generalities. This government has
the power necessary to accomplish this purpose if it wishes to accomplish it. But it will do so only by unflinching effort, and through
acts rather than through words.

Every month that has passed since we entered the war has made it more difficult to set up the foundations for a future international organization. The understanding between the governments of the Soviet Union, Great Britain, China, and the United States necessary to create a United Nations Executive Council, in which all the United Nations would be represented, could readily have been reached early in 1942. It has grown progressively more difficult as the military aspects of the war changed, and as the major powers publicly took definite stands concerning political and territorial questions. But the necessary agreement can still be reached if the United States wants it to be reached.

These lines by an Englishman are as applicable today as they were when they were written twenty-five years ago:

> All conquerors in a great war show the more despicable side of human nature. Those who have been sworn allies in the face of a common foe invariably have disagreements, more or less deep, when the work of the soldiers is finished and the politicians begin to apportion the spoil.

Unless the United States succeeds in the immediate future in establishing the basis for an international organization, such as that outlined in the preceding chapter, we will drift into the armistice period to find ourselves once more in the position that President Wilson occupied in Paris in January, 1919. But this time our government will possess neither the prestige nor the influence which Wilson then held.

The second requirement—that involving the long-range objectives of the people of the United States—must of course be carried out by policies supplementary to our basic one of active participation in an international organization. It is the supplementary policies, founded always upon a consistent American course of international co-operation, that in their total constitute the completed structure of American foreign policy.

First in the list of these parts of the whole must always come the maintenance of the independence and integrity of the nations of the Western Hemisphere, and the continuous perfection of the existing inter-American system. These are the aims of the Monroe Doctrine. But this country has now wisely realized that they can be more readily secured through the multilateral approach provided for in present inter-American agreements (by which all the American republics are full partners in a joint enterprise) than through the unilateral approach maintained by the government of the United States for over a century. Our earlier insistence that we alone would interpret the Monroe Doctrine not only prevented the growth of any real inter-American community of interest, but aroused wholly legitimate suspicions and antagonisms among our American neighbors which greatly weakened our capacity to preserve the safety of the hemisphere.

The growth of the present inter-American system was continuous from the autumn of 1933 until the autumn of 1943. At this moment it has been arrested—only temporarily, I hope—by the shortsighted attempt of the Department of State to utilize inter-American machinery for the purpose of coercing the Argentine Republic. There is no room for the coercion on any American state by another in the present system of inter-American understanding. If this course is persisted in it will inevitably destroy all that has been accomplished during the preceding ten years. Further, the United States must continue wholeheartedly its present policy of economic co-operation with its American neighbors. Such bread cast upon the waters will come back to the citizens of this country a hundredfold. One of the most profitable opportunities for American investment and for American trade lies within the neighboring republics of this hemisphere.

As a part of its responsibility as a member of both the inter-American system and the World Organization, the United States must retain sole authority to maintain and defend the Panama Canal. That authority must be limited only by the provisions of its treaty with Panama of 1936, which gave the people of Panama both the right and the obligation to co-operate with the people of the United States in that enterprise.

If outlying islands of the Western Hemisphere, now under the exclusive sovereignty of one of the American nations, are required for world or regional security, they should be placed, by agreement with the nation possessing sovereignty over them, under such inter-American security control as the American republics may determine.

This government should exercise its rights in the naval and air bases leased to it in British territories in the Atlantic and in the Caribbean in such a way as to make sure that the eastern coast of the United States and the eastern approaches to the Panama Canal will be safe against an attack for many generations to come. The United States should obtain such additional air and naval bases in the Pacific Ocean as may be required to assure the safety of its outlying Pacific possessions, of the west coast of the continental United States, and of the western approaches to the Panama Canal. Such steps should be co-ordinated with whatever agreements the United States may make with the other American Republics for the maintenance of regional peace, and with the major world powers entrusted by the International Organization with the preservation of world peace. These agreements, of course, must envisage the joint inter-American use of regional bases, and joint use by the United States with the other major policing powers of strategic bases located in the Atlantic and in the Pacific areas.

The continued existence of the British Commonwealth of Nations (as distinct from the British Empire) should be one of the objectives of United States policy. So long as naval power continues to be a factor of major importance, the existence of the United Kingdom, as one of the greatest maritime powers of the world, ensures that we will share the control of the Atlantic with a friendly navy. However, what will be even more important to this nation as the years go by is that the association of the self-governing Dominions of the British Commonwealth will assure us of the existence in every part of the globe of friendly democracies with which we will never have any insuperable difficulty in reaching an understanding. Their economic prosperity is a bulwark to our prosperity. It is therefore highly desirable that this government and the governments of the British Commonwealth of Nations reach an early understanding which will remove deep-rooted causes for antagonism in their respective commercial policies.

The United States must play its full part in coming to a close understanding with the Soviet Union. As rapidly as possible, it must try to expand its volume of trade and other economic relations with Russia. From the standpoint of size, the Russia of the future will become the greatest of the world powers, greatest because of its vast and rapidly increasing population, greatest because of its territorial extent, and greatest because of its as yet largely undeveloped material resources. It will derive additional power from the dynamic energy of its component peoples. The present Soviet government has made it clear that world revolution, as a means of establishing the supremacy of Communism, has at least temporarily been abandoned as part of its national policy. Upon the conclusion of the present war, the Soviet government undoubtedly will have to dedicate its chief energies for a term of years to the rehabilitation and reconstruction of its devastated cities and territories, to the problem of industrialization, and to the achievement of a rise in the popular standard of living. That period will determine whether the Russian people, contrary to their history since the time of Peter the Great, will become, as they readily can, the greatest destructive force in the world of the future, or whether they will become one of the most powerful constructive forces. It is of first importance to a stable world order that the Russian people co-operate with the people of the United States in the supreme task of helping to make a safe and peaceful world, as they are today co-operating in the war against Germany. The closer the ties between them during the transition period the more constructive a factor will Russia become in building up the world of tomorrow.

The policy of the United States toward China should be similar. The Chinese have an immense population, extraordinary fortitude, and an ability to live on an infinitesimal fraction of what is needed by other peoples. They can become a disruptive force of incalculable danger in the future world unless their almost unlimited potential power is directed toward building a new and peaceful Asia, a task for which they are supremely qualified. For generations, and in particular during these war years, the only power of the world upon which China has been able fully to depend for friendly and equitable co-operation is the United States. There are innumerable ways in which we can help the Chinese people in the years to come to develop their resources to our mutual advantage, but primarily in order to raise standards of living in China; to stabilize and perfect through their own efforts the forms of government best suited to Chinese needs; and to come successfully through the period of readjustment which they inevitably must confront in the first postwar years. The future stability of Asia and our own security as a Pacific power will depend largely on the wisdom of our policy toward China in those years.

The policy of this government should be directed toward helping the French people resume as rapidly as possible the position which for centuries they have occupied as one of the great powers of the world. We may as well candidly admit that for various reasons our policy toward France since June, 1940, has not been a happy one in retaining the confidence and co-operation of the sorely shaken French people. During the nineteenth century, and until the outbreak of the second World War, there was no power of Europe with which we had closer ties. With no great European power had we had less cause for antagonism, and less misunderstanding. At the present moment the temper of the French people toward this country, both within and without France, tends to be resentful and suspicious. It is entirely proper to admit that these conditions are partly due to the attitude assumed by Frenchmen who now hold positions of transitory authority, and to propaganda emanating from other than French or American sources. However, should these conditions not be rectified, Franco-American understanding, which would be to both peoples of positive value during the postwar years, as well as during the foreseeable future, will be nonexistent. We should, therefore, make it doubly clear today that our influence will be exerted to furnish them with a free opportunity to determine their own constitutional form of government and to select the Frenchmen by whom they desire to be governed. We should make it unmistakably plain that in our own interest we want to see France become again the great constructive force in the world that she was prior to her defeat of 1940; and that no aspect of American policy will cause the French people to be deprived of one iota of what is rightly theirs.

The treatment to be accorded the people of Germany and of Japan has already been dealt with at some length. The detailed character of that treatment is not a matter which the United States can determine by herself. It will be decided by the common agreement of the powers by whom the Axis nations are defeated. The peaceful nations of the world are confronted in this case with the need to control what are two of the most dynamic races of the present day. It is easy enough in the terms of the approaching treaty, or in the announced war aims of the United Nations, to stipulate that the Japanese people shall in the future be confined within their own islands and that the Germanic peoples shall be enclosed within the limits of a reduced or a partitioned Germany. Realism demands full understanding of the fact that any effort to enclose the Japanese or German people means, unless some outlet is afforded, an inevitable explosion later on. The United States and the other members of the United Nations cannot permit these explosive forces to find their outlet through military expansion, or through any other kind of physical domination. Statesmanship requires that some constructive outlet be found so that these forces are put to a desirable use, and do not again plunge the world into chaos. The peoples of the earth have long since discovered that the constant pleas of both the Japanese and the German people that they require additional territories to which to send the surplus of their rapidly expanding populations were insincere and fallacious propaganda. Neither Japan nor Germany, while it possessed them, has ever really utilized the territories acquired by conquest for emigration. The practical safety valve for these forces will be found in the realm of economics. Both Japan and Germany have already proved that they can prosper and steadily progress in their internal development by making use of the legitimate advantages which they possess in their national genius for certain forms of industrial production and in international trade. What is required—and imperatively required—is an agreement by the other nations upon an enlightened approach toward the establishment of a basis for international trade, of such character as to afford a fair and safe outlet to the peoples of the defeated Axis. If this basis is not found, no kind of control, short of the continuous and unlimited exercise of force, can prevent the recurrence of the disaster of 1939.

United States policy in the economic field cannot be defined except in very general terms. It should be sufficiently elastic to be adaptable to precise conditions which cannot now be foreseen. However, there are certain observations to be made. If, at the conclusion of the second World War, we again raise our tariffs as we did in the 1920's and refuse to admit that our prosperity depends upon that of the rest of the world, if we decline to buy as well as to sell, none of the basic objectives of our foreign policy can be achieved.

The people of this country must remember that in the postwar years not only will by far the greatest portion of the civilized earth be devastated and economically prostrate, but in many countries of the Western Hemisphere, as well as in many countries of Europe, such as the Soviet Union, industrialization will proceed at an exceedingly rapid pace. If the United States adheres to the policy it has so often pursued, of attempting to shut its doors to foreign imports, it will once more contribute toward a world depression of a staggering size.

It has become a fetish in the United States on the part of many groups that the industrialization of other countries automatically cuts off export trade from the United States and that this tendency should be blocked at all hazards. The truth is, of course, that industrialization automatically raises the standard of living and that this country is always benefited by an increase in the living standards of other peoples. For the higher their living standards the greater is their demand for those products of our own factories and farms which we here are able to produce more efficiently and in better quality than anyone else. It is absurd for some of us to think that great, developing countries such as Brazil and the Soviet Union can be persuaded or compelled to continue to buy steel rails or lard from us when they are able to produce such products themselves more cheaply and quite as efficiently. The realistic policy which we should adopt is gradually to concentrate upon the manufacture for export of such articles, and there are many of them, which we can make better than any other country in the world. We have never yet attempted to make the most of our continuing capacity to invent and perfect products which, in fair competition, can always command the world market. The essential thing is for us to make sure that fair competition in the world market will be possible. Readjustments in our domestic economy and in our industrial and agricultural production will be required, not only for our own well-being but also in order that other nations can follow truly liberal trade policies. Only if we are willing to see that such readjustments are necessary will we be able to prevent the recurrence of disastrous economic depressions. For they have often had their origin in our own insistence, and in the insistence of other nations, upon raising every form of financial and commercial barrier to the free movement of goods between countries.

The Ottawa Agreements, providing for a system of imperial preferences between the members of the British Commonwealth of Nations, constitute an obstacle to any healthy flow of trade between the nations of the world. But we would have no leverage to press for the abrogation of these policies should we ourselves revert to the economic isolationism which we pursued during the twelve years after the first World War.

There has already been much discussion in this country as to the policies which the government of the United States should pursue in the field of civil aviation. The term "freedom of the air" has had many interpretations. Many American citizens who have been discussing this problem seem to think that the term "freedom of the air" should mean freedom of the air in all parts of the world for the United States, but no freedom of the air for anyone else. There is, of course, nothing more necessary than that civil aviation, in which we have persistently shown such marked ability and which we so largely originated, should afford unlimited opportunities for the expansion of American passenger and commercial air-borne traffic in the postwar years.

Like any other sovereign great power, we must preserve free from foreign entry by air such regions under our own flag as we may consider necessary to our military, air, or naval defense. Apart from this, we must be prepared to grant to other powers possessing civilian aviation interests, on a basis of reciprocity, the same rights for their commercial aviation as we desire to obtain in their territory, or in the regions where they may today possess exclusive air rights.

There undoubtedly must be established, under the general supervision of the International Organization, some international air transport authority. Its powers should be limited to securing common requirements for safety and quarantine regulations, weather reporting, and radio communications. It should not be given the authority to fix rates or to parcel out air traffic. If this were to be undertaken, all incentive to excel in competition, for which American aviation interests are superbly qualified, would be removed.

The chief difficulty at this time in solving the international aspects of the problem lies in the fact that our own government has so far reached no decision as to its domestic policy covering American aviation interests engaged in international traffic. Is there to be unlimited competition between such American interests? Can the government provide them with sufficient support if, as purely private corporations, they are obliged to compete abroad with foreign aviation interests which are government-owned and government-operated? Can American companies survive foreign competition if they are not subsidized to the extent to which foreign air transport lines are subsidized? These are only a few of the questions that surround consideration of the whole problem. Until government policy settles these present uncertainties, it is evident that we are grossly handicapped in negotiating any international agreement through which vital American interests would be adequately safeguarded.

United States policy must likewise make sure that in the future the strategic raw materials not produced within our own borders will be always available to us. This country should never again be confronted with a situation similar to that which existed in 1939 and 1940, when it was largely cut off from its normal sources of supply of such materials as rubber and tin. Synthetic rubber will probably play an increasing part in our national economy. However, it cannot be used as a substitute for natural rubber for all purposes. Therefore, the policy of the United States government and the policy of American private industry must be directed toward securing a reasonable volume of natural rubber from certain other American republics. The knowledge that they will have an assured market in this country for natural rubber will greatly assist these republics in improving their national economies. It will provide them with a source for dollar exchange that would otherwise be lacking, and will increase their purchasing power for American goods. The wise policy on our part would be to prohibit tariff rates upon natural rubber which would unduly expand the production of synthetic rubber, and to negotiate some international accord, similar to the international sugar agreement, through which the American rubber-producing countries will be guaranteed, by a quota system, an assured percentage of the American market for rubber. In this way their production of raw rubber would be encouraged and the American consumer would be protected against monopolies. Our policy should aim to prevent, by means of international agreements, the recurrence of the monopolistic practices which existed in the period between the wars. Cartels in the hands of a few individuals controlled the total production of essential commodities and were able to force up the price of rubber and tin and quinine to such artificial levels as to decrease materially the ability of consumers everywhere to benefit from their use.

The government of the United States should participate in the proposed International Bank of Stabilization so that international currencies can be kept steady. Without it, international trade in the postwar years cannot be revived.

The United States must also use its influence to secure the adoption by other governments of trade and financial policies founded upon the principle of nondiscrimination and of equal treatment under equal conditions. It is in that direction that the best interest of this country lies. It is in that way that the peoples of the world can derive full benefit from their own economic capacity and from the capacity of their neighbors.

These are the chief objectives upon which we should fix as the foundation of a permanent foreign policy. The method by which they can best be achieved is the vital question now before the people of this country. I believe that the overwhelming majority of the American people today see clearly that the only way to make sure that these aims are attained is by the creation of an international organization through which the peoples of the earth can co-operate for their security and prosperity, and to which the United States should pledge its wholehearted collaboration.

This, if we have learned anything at all from the past, should become the future cornerstone of American foreign policy. And it must be a continuous and consistent policy.

The United States has a part to play which is both regional and universal. It should be prepared to assume its responsibilities by sharing in regional agreements, both political and military, which will maintain the peace and security of the Western Hemisphere, and of the Atlantic and Pacific oceans. Under an international organization, it must stand ready to employ its naval and air forces, in common with the other police powers, whenever the peace of the entire world is jeopardized.

During the transition period it must make every effort to help restore a sound basis for world stability and to hasten the construction of a permanent world organization in which all peace-loving and law-abiding peoples should participate from the outset. If the regional systems are perfected, and if the United States is able to maintain a close, understanding, and co-operative relationship with the other major powers of the world during the transition period, new major wars will be prevented. The people of the United States will not again be called upon to make the sacrifices they have been compelled to offer twice in the lifetime of my own generation.

Finally the United States must dedicate itself to the task of creating such world conditions as will foster the growth of democratic government throughout the earth. For the progressive growth of democracy in other parts of the world means increasing safety for the United States. The ability of peoples to obtain freedom from fear and freedom from want is contingent upon their ability to want it enough.

The forces of reaction are again stirring. The people of this country should learn that the world revolution is not something they need dread, but rather something that can be made to redound to their own benefit. The world revolution is already here. For that reason it is desperately necessary that the policy of this country should not be directed toward the vain and fatal effort to put back the pieces as best we can, but rather toward seeing that our safety requires that something new can and must be built. More than at any other time in the past hundred years of our history, the American people need to have sufficient imagination and initiative to avail themselves of the opportunity that has been granted them. If they do, they can shape the kind of world in which they are to live in the future. For they have the power and the influence necessary, if they will but use them.

The United States is the most powerful nation on the globe. Its people cannot afford to await, as a few within this country are urging, the decisions of other peoples before they chart their own course. It is for them to assert their full right to seize the initiative. Prudence and caution are admirable characteristics of any foreign policy. But they are deadly when they prove to be only synonyms for indecision and timidity.

The people of the United States are once more afforded the chance to offer their co-operation and their leadership to other nations. They are granted another opportunity to help to make a world in which they, and all peoples, can safely live. The decision they now make will determine their destiny.

# Appendix

*UNFORTUNATELY, space precludes more than this brief mention of the men who contributed so greatly to the success of the Third Consultative Meeting of the American Foreign Ministers at Rio de Janeiro in January, 1942. From the following list of delegates Dr. Enrique Ruiz Guiñazú of Argentina is omitted since, owing to the critical state of United States–Argentine relations, I have dealt with him at some length in Chapter V.*

Dr. Aranha, Brazilian Foreign Minister and Chairman of the conference, is one of the most brilliant statesmen the New World has produced. Even in that long line of exceptionally qualified Foreign Ministers who have so greatly contributed toward making Brazil the world power that she is today, he is outstanding. An orator of rare eloquence and extraordinary intuition, whose mind works with unexcelled rapidity, he holds an unswerving conviction that Brazilian-American amity is a necessary keystone of practical Pan-Americanism. More than by all else, he is impelled by his confident belief in the assured destiny of his own people.

From Uruguay came its then Foreign Minister and present Vice-President, Dr. Alberto Guani, a profound student of international affairs, deeply imbued with a knowledge of the fateful events in Europe of the preceding twenty years, which, as his government's representative, he had watched at so many meetings of the League of Nations. He was a stanch supporter of the cause of Pan-Americanism, and an optimistic realist in all that involved the future of the New World.

Panama sent its young and dynamic Foreign Minister, Dr. Octavio Fábrega, who, as a result of his many years in the United States, speaks English with perfection. From the Central American republics came the able jurists and diplomats who have so frequently contributed force and capacity and enthusiasm to the task of perfecting the inter-American system. Haiti and the Dominican Republic delegated their two Ministers of Foreign Affairs, both highly qualified to interpret the spirit of co-operation and determination with which their two governments were inspired.

The governments of Ecuador and Peru sent, in addition to their two Foreign Ministers, large missions of advisers and of technical experts, because they realized that the other American nations would make every possible friendly effort to obtain a final solution of their boundary dispute before the termination of the conference.*

I have seldom had the privilege of meeting a statesman of greater intellectual integrity than Dr. Tobar Donoso, who was then Ecuador's Minister for Foreign Affairs. A devout Catholic, he impressed me deeply throughout the conference by the sincerity of his devotion to the interests of his own country as he saw them. Never swayed by considerations of his personal popularity at home, he did all that he could to bring about the final solution of the boundary dispute. The solution he sought might not bring with it all that the most clamorous of his fellow countrymen demanded, but it would be inherently equitable and, by bringing peace and stability to the two neighboring countries, would permit his own people to devote themselves to the development of their great national resources and to the tranquil evolution of their political life.

His colleague from Peru, Dr. Solf y Muro, had been throughout his life an intimate friend of the family of President Prado. A distinguished lawyer of ability and pertinacity, he showed the same spirit as his associate from Ecuador in his desire to put an end to the controversy between the two adjoining nations. For more than a century, the boundary dispute had done untold damage to the highest interests of the two peoples, and had only recently flamed out again in open conflict.

The government of Paraguay was represented by its Foreign Minister, Dr. Luis Argaña, who, throughout the conference, distinguished himself by the great clarity with which he envisioned the world situation and by the courage with which he insisted that the best interests of his own nation were inextricably linked to the destinies of the Western Hemisphere.

The Minister for Foreign Affairs of Bolivia, Dr. Anze Matienzo, a young and able statesman who had passed many years of his life in active diplomacy, never faltered in his conviction that the security of his own country could not be divorced from the security of the other American republics. He contributed greatly to the work of the conference.

For special reasons, however, the representatives of four republics of the north occupied a peculiar place in the conference. Cuba was represented by its Ambassador in Washington, Dr. Aurelio Concheso. Cuba had, of course, already declared war upon the Axis, and the Cuban delegate played the exceptional part that has come to be expected of her representatives at inter-American gatherings.

Closely associated with him at all times were the Minister for Foreign Affairs of Mexico, Dr. Ezequiel Padilla, the Minister for Foreign Affairs of Venezuela, Dr. Caracciolo Parra Pérez, and the delegate of Colombia, Dr.

* Outside the actual scope of the conference itself, the boundary dispute was finally settled through the efforts of the representatives of Argentina, Brazil, Chile and the United States; and the protocol containing the solution was then signed in the Itamaraty Palace.

Gabriel Turbay, then Ambassador in Washington and later Minister for Foreign Affairs of his country.

The three republics, Mexico, Venezuela, and Colombia, had already broken relations with the Axis powers. They believed firmly that their own security, as well as the security of the entire New World, could be effectively safeguarded only if similar action were taken by the other American republics. The brilliantly persuasive efforts of these three delegates contributed decisively to the final results of the conference. Dr. Parra Pérez of Venezuela is one of the keenest statesmen of the Americas today. With long experience in Europe, he has nevertheless always been an ardent supporter of Pan-Americanism, and his untiring efforts to bring about a united front in Rio de Janeiro will always be gratefully remembered by his associates there. Dr. Gabriel Turbay, because of the years of his service in Washington, has innumerable friends in the United States, as well as in all other parts of the Western Hemisphere. Like most Colombians, he is an orator of the first order, and the architectural structure and the logic of his speeches are profoundly impressive in their effect. He again, passionately convinced of the need for the realization of the Pan-American ideal, made a major contribution in the work of the conference.

There was, however, little oratory at the meeting at Rio de Janeiro. But those who were there will always remember the speeches made by Dr. Ezequiel Padilla in the name of Mexico at the opening and closing sessions in Tiradentes Palace. It was not only his extraordinary eloquence, the beauty of his voice and of his delivery, nor the remarkable literary quality of the phrases he used which made his name a household word in every American country at the close of the conference. It was even more the power of his conviction, the burning sincerity of his plea for inter-American unity, and his tribute to those citizens of the Americas who had already given up their lives at Pearl Harbor that brought forth so deep and so lasting a response. No man in recent years has done more to draw the Americas together.

From the start of the sessions at Rio de Janeiro, I had realized the difficulties* under which the Chilean representative, the then Minister for Foreign Affairs, Dr. Juan Bautista Rossetti, was forced to labor. I have always believed that Dr. Rossetti himself ardently desired the unity of the American nations, and that, democrat that he is by training, by politics, and by conviction, he wanted his own country to take its stand openly against the Nazi and Fascist dictatorships.

He had had long experience in the political world of Chile, and was also, as he still is, the publisher of a newspaper in the Chilean capital. The existence of a provisional government in Chile and the reluctance of his colleagues in the Cabinet to agree upon any positive course of policy made his position extremely difficult throughout the conference.

*This subject is discussed in Chapter V.

# Index

Abdul-Hamid, 245
Abend, Hallett, 304
Aberdeen, Lord, 242
Act of Havana Concerning the Provisional Administration of European Colonies and Possessions in the Americas, 215-216
Adams, John Quincy, 50, 388, 389, 391
Admiralty, 133
Africa, 155
Africa Corps, Rommel's, 167, 168
Agadir incident, 338
Albania, 257
Alexander I, 308, 323, 388
Alexander II, 308, 310, 317
Alexander III, 310
Algeciras, Conference of, 338, 393
Algeria, 153
Alsace-Lorraine, 114, 123
Alvear, President, 235
American Federal Union, 317
American General Staff, 164
American-German relations, 91, 96, 108
American republics, 78, 205, 207, 219, 226, 227, 229, 230, 231, 232, 233, 236, 240, 379, 405
  Axis propaganda, 209-210, 221
  conference, 225, 231-232, 234
  economic difficulties, 218-219
  effect of German invasion of Netherlands and France, 215
  severed relations with Axis, 234
American Treaty of Guaranty, 11
Amritsar, massacre, 298
Anderson, Sir John, 132
Anti-Comintern Pact, 33, 320, 324
Anti-Semitism, 130, 265
Antonescu, 251
Aranha, Dr. Oswaldo, 208, 227, 232, 415
Argaña, Dr. Luis, 416
Argentina, 205, 206, 214, 218, 220, 225, 229, 230, 233, 234, 236, 237, 240
  relations with U.S., 220, 225, 228, 235-236, 238-239
Arias, Dr. Harmodio, 202
Armaments conference, 54

Armaments Inspection Committee, 376
Armaments limitation agreements, 376
Arnold, General, 174
Atlantic Charter, 176, 178, 235, 301, 302, 355
Atlantic Charter, Proclamation of, 172
Attlee, Major Clement, 133
*Augusta*, U.S.S., 174, 175
Australia, 303, 304
Austria, 81-82, 86, 114, 317, 332
  incorporation into German Reich, 22-23
  invasion of, 36
  Ribbentrop's statement on consolidation, 92
Austrian Credit Anstalt, 277
Axis propaganda in American republics, 209-210, 221
Azores, 180

Bakunin, Michael, 309
Balbo, 146
Baldwin government, 31
Baldwin, Stanley, 131, 321, 340
Balfour Declaration, 264
Balfour, Lord, 5, 43, 264, 265
Balkan Peninsula, 249, 253, 256, 332
Baltic States, 310, 311, 324, 330, 333
Bataan, 296
Batista, Fulgencio, 197, 199
*Bayern und die Bismarckische Reichsgründung*, 350
Beaconsfield, Lord, 242
Beaverbrook, Lord, 172, 176
Beck, Colonel, 38, 93, 94
Beneš, President, 21, 38, 69, 70, 332
Berlin-Rome Axis, 33, 66
Bernstorffs, 99
Bessarabia, 250, 311, 324
Biddle, Anthony, 155
Big Four, 13, 14, 15
Bismarck, 90, 99, 102, 243, 337, 338, 342, 350, 352, 353
Blaine, 185, 392
Blum, Léon, 129, 261

Board of Economic Welfare, 217
Bodenschatz, General, 144
Bohemia-Moravia, 82, 87, 114, 123
Bolívar, Simón, 185
Bolivia, 225, 237, 379
   revolution, 236
Bolshevik Revolution of 1917, 306, 309
Bolshevism, 312
Bonnet, Georges, 80, 113, 114, 125, 127
Borah, Senator, 46, 47, 75, 390, 396
Bosch, Ernesto, 230
Bouillon, M. Franklin, 260
Bourgeois, Léon, 8
Brandegee, Frank, 43
Brandeis, Justice, 265
Brazil, 207, 218, 221, 222, 234, 237, 318, 400
Brenner Pass, meeting at, 139, 142, 143, 144
Brest-Litovsk, Treaty of, 11, 311
Briand, 23, 26, 43, 47
   plan for a European union, 47
British Alliance, 151
British Commonwealth of Nations, 76, 176, 373, 405, 410
British Dominions, 401
British Empire, 104, 134, 298, 326, 380
   Germany's objectives concerning, 93, 114, 134
   relations with Soviet Union, 316
British Labor party, 316
British Parliament, 92
British War Cabinet, 167
Bryan, William Jennings, 43
Bryce, James, 242
Buchanan, James, 392
Bulgaria, 252, 253
Bülows, 99
Burma, 296, 302

Cadogan, Sir Alexander, 132, 174, 175
Cairo Conference, 327
Cairo, Declaration of, 303
Camacho, General Avila, 203, 204
Canning, 388
Cantilo, Dr. José Maria, 208
Capus, Alfred, 4
Cardenas, General, 203
Castillo, Dr. Ramón, 225, 235
Castlereagh, 388
Catherine the Great, 308, 310
Cerda, President Aguirre, 224
Cespedes, Dr. Carlos Manuel de, 196, 197

Chaco, war of the, 225, 379
Chamber of Deputies, 85, 151, 154
Chamberlain, Austen, 26
Chamberlain, Neville, 36, 37, 38, 66, 67, 68, 76, 92, 131, 132, 148
Chautemps, Camille, 125, 127
Chiang Kai-shek, 283
Chiang Kai-shek, Madame, 283
Chicherin, 30
Chile, 188, 218, 220, 224, 233, 237
China, 45, 280, 299, 303, 304
   Communism, 283
   emergence as world power, 297
   financial assistance from U.S. and Great Britain, 281
   Japanese aggression, 31, 49, 277-280, 285, 319
   nationalism, 281
   relations with United States, 281, 284
Chinese Eastern Railway, 319
Churchill, Prime Minister Winston, 66, 92, 133, 135, 151, 155, 163, 171, 172, 173, 174, 175, 176, 177, 178, 320, 340
Cianfarra, Camille, 83
Ciano, Count, 78, 79, 80, 81, 82, 83, 84, 85, 86, 87, 135, 136, 137, 138, 139, 141, 142, 143, 144, 145, 146, 148
   efforts to maintain peace, 143
Civil War, American, 59, 317, 392, 394
Clausewitz, von, 337, 347
Clay, Henry, 185, 391
Clemenceau, 9, 13, 125, 154
   receded from demands on Germany, 11
Coalition party, 400
Coburg dynasty, 252
Codreanu, 251
Colombia, 218, 220, 225
   controversy with Peru, 191
Columbus, 106
Comintern, 313
Communism, 27, 28, 29, 306, 313, 314, 315, 316, 319, 321, 340, 349, 358
Communist International, 308, 316, 318
Communist party, 169, 322
Concheso, Dr. Aurelio, 416
Congress, 43, 46, 54, 55, 56, 60, 61, 63, 72, 77, 148, 286, 288, 296
Congress of Vienna, 365
Conservative party, 400
Consultative Meeting of the American Foreign Ministers, 206, 210, 213, 215, 220, 223, 235

Convention for the Maintenance, Preservation and Re-establishment of Peace, 208
Coolidge Administration, 46, 201
Coolidge, President Calvin, 46, 48, 187, 188, 189, 190, 316
Corregidor, 296
Costa Rica, 219, 225
Coulondre, 125
Covenant. See League of Nations
Cox, Governor, 41, 54
Crewe, Marquess of, 132
Crimean War, 242, 365
Cripps, Sir Stafford, 301
Croats, freed from Austrian domination, 19-20
    unstable adjustment in Yugoslavia, 22, 251
Croce, Benedetto, 28
Cuba, 193, 200, 225
    original treaty with U.S., 194
    Treaty of 1901 with U.S., 198
Cuna, Herr, 25
Curzon Line of 1919, 330, 331, 354
Curzon, Lord, 3
Czechoslovakia, 36-39, 107, 114, 115, 123, 128, 140, 332, 334
    atrocities alleged by Germany, 92
    excuse of Ribbentrop for Hitler's violation of obligations, 93, 95
    internal difficulties, 21, 36
    invasion of, 36-37, 71
    Mussolini's views, 140
    President Beneš, resignation of, 38
    rapid progress after autonomy, 21
Czechs, 114, 123
    freed from Austrian domination, 19

Dakar, 157
Daladier Cabinet, substitution for, 150
Daladier, Prime Minister, 122, 123, 124, 125, 127, 134
Dan, Dr. Takuma, 272
Daniels, Josephus, 189
Danube Basin, 249
Danzig, 82, 87, 93, 114, 115, 354
Dardanelles, 243, 310, 332
Darlan, Admiral, 150, 153, 155, 165, 166
Darmstadt, French occupation of, 18
Davies, Ambassador Joseph E., 319, 321
Democratic party, 42, 54, 396
Denmark, 148, 317
    occupation of, 148
Department of Commerce, 52

Department of State, 52, 60, 61, 72, 149, 162, 170, 171, 188, 217, 236, 237, 278, 325, 404
Destroyers-Bases Agreement, 172, 178
Disarmament, 43, 44, 45, 48, 49, 54, 65, 85-87, 98, 103, 117-118, 124, 128, 137, 140, 145, 305, 366, 382
    armament limitations agreement, postwar, 376
    Hitler's views on, 68, 104, 105
    treaty provisions for German, 16-17, 340
Doebert, 350
Doernberg, Herr von, 91, 101
Dollfuss, 81
Dominican Republic, 186, 392
Donoso, Dr. Tobar, 416
Dreyfus case, 130, 338
Duff-Coopers, 92
Duma, Russian, 309
Dunkirk, evacuation from, 149

East Prussia, 93, 114, 352, 354
Ebert, 101
Economic and financial measures, postwar, 385-386
Ecuador, 218
Eden, Anthony, 59, 68, 92, 96, 132, 168
Egypt, 155, 258, 259, 260
    Anglo-Egyptian relations, 259
Einwohnerwehr, 17
Eisenhower, General, 166
Elizabeth, Queen, of England, 130
El Salvador, 225
Estonia, 311
Estrada Doctrine, 199, 237
Ethiopia, 33, 57, 67, 68, 280
    attack by Italy, 32, 35
    attitude of Great Britain toward Italian conquest, 57
European Advisory Commission, 371
Executive Council of the International Organization, 382

Fabrega, Dr. Octavio, 415
Falange party, 179
Falange, Spanish, 237
Far East, 283, 301, 303, 319
    growth of nationalism, 297
    postwar objectives of United Nations, 327
Farrell, General, 235, 236, 237

Fascism, 27, 28, 58, 59, 78, 83, 179, 214, 221, 322
  effect on Italian people, 88
  emergence of, 27
  triumph in Spain, 32
Fascist policy in Spain, 59
Faymonville, General Philip, 325, 326
Federal Reserve Board, 399
Federation, Danubian, 20, 23
  German, 336, 337, 351, 352
  of major powers, 140, 255
  Pan-Arab, 264
Feisal, Prince, 257, 258
"Fifth column" activities, 346
Finland, Soviet war on, 169, 324, 332
  won independence, 311
First Zionist Congress, 264
Five-Year Plan, Russian, 314
Florida Territory, 389
Foch, Marshal, 9, 14, 17, 24, 152
Food and Agriculture Committee, 371
Foreign Relations Committee, 390, 395
Four-Power Declaration, 327
Fourteen Points, 4, 5, 14, 15
Four-year plan, German, 33
France, ceded region of Syria to Turkey, 246, 260
  collapse of, 149, 155
  controversy with Great Britain over Near East, 245, 260
  entrance of Japan into French Indo-China, 288
  Franco-German relations, 128
  German occupation of Paris, 150
  in postwar world, 303
  negotiations with Soviet Union, 80
  nonaggression pact with Germany, 113, 127
  occupation of Frankfurt and Darmstadt, 18
  relations with Great Britain, 156, 157
  secret alliance with Germany proposed by Stresemann, 127
  special agreements with Soviet Union, 320
  treaties with Syria and Lebanon, 261
  under totalitarian rule, 158
  undermining by German propaganda, 76, 129-130, 157
Franco, 57, 58, 59, 179, 180, 181, 224, 229, 230, 237
Franco-German relations, 128
François-Poncet, M., 83
Frankfurt, French occupation of, 18

Franklin, Benjamin, 390
Frederick the Great, 337
Frederick William IV, 337
Free French, 156, 162, 261
Free French Committee, 159, 160
Free French movement, 163
"Free Germans," 361
French Africa, 167
French Committee of National Liberation, 162, 167, 261
French Committee of Resistance, 158
French Consultative Assembly, 167
French fleet, 150, 153, 155, 159
French Guiana, 157
French Indo-China, 288, 302
French National Assemblies, 154
French Republic, 153
French Revolution, 308, 337, 365
French Senate, 125, 126, 154
French West Indies, 157

Gamelin, General, 125, 151
Gaulle, General Charles de, 151, 156, 159, 164, 165, 167, 262
Gdynia, 354
Geneva Conferences, 45
Genro, or Elder Statesmen, Japanese, 274, 275
George, King, of England, 130
German-American relations, 91, 96, 108
German General Staff, 10, 16, 17, 32, 47, 69, 144, 148, 170, 305, 307, 312, 320, 321, 324, 325, 337, 338, 340, 341, 342, 343, 344, 345, 346, 347, 349, 356, 358, 359, 399
  driving force in German policy, 339, 342
German High Command, 155, 163, 171
German-Italian Pact, 141
German-Italian relations, 80
German Popular party, 24
German Republic, obliteration of, 29
German Socialist parties, 10
Germany, agreement with Italy, 81
  Soviet Union, 71-73, 137, 323-324
  American-German relations, 91, 96, 108
  attack on Poland, 324
  Soviet Union, 171
  basis for confidence, 75
  collapse of, in first World War, 6
  colonial adjustments, demand for, 34-35, 68, 82, 87, 95, 107, 114
  Communism, 358

Germany—*Continued*
declared war on U.S., 224, 231
"Drang nach Osten" policy, 243
economic control of conquered countries, 253
evasion of treaty terms, 340
excuse of Ribbentrop for Hitler's violation of obligations toward Czechoslovakia, 93, 95
"fifth column" activities, 346
foreign policy in Stresemann period, 312
four-year plan, 33
Franco-German relations, 128
"Free Germans," 361
German-Italian Pact, 141
Goering's statement of objectives, 114, 116
inflation in, 340
invasion of Czechoslovakia, 36-39
liberalism, disappearance of, in, 10, 336
Naval Agreement of 1935 with Great Britain, 34, 93, 104
negotiations with France, 127
nonaggression pact with France, 113, 127
  Poland, 32, 93, 127
objectives, 133, 135, 139
  outlined by Hitler, 106-107
policy directed by German General Staff, 339, 342
position in postwar world, 336, 358-361
postwar partition, 349, 351, 352
propaganda of, after defeat, 18
prosperity in, 1925-1929, 29
rearmament, 30, 49, 56, 124, 320, 340
relations with Great Britain, 34, 92, 104, 114, 133
  United States, 96, 108
repudiation of treaty stipulations, 17
secret alliance with France proposed by Stresemann, 127
stipulation before entering League of Nations, 30
subversive activities in American republics, 209-210, 221
ten-year pact with Poland, 39
trade relations, international, 105-108
treatment accorded, by Treaty of Versailles, 8
Treaty of Rapallo, with Russia, 312
unification, 347, 348, 349, 350

Germany—*Continued*
withdrawal from League of Nations, 30
Ghent, Treaty of, 391
Gibraltar, 157
Giraud, General, 164, 165, 166
Gladstone, 242
Goebbels, 34, 109, 342
Goering, Field Marshal, 112, 113, 114, 115, 116, 117, 118, 119, 136, 148, 342
Goga, 251
Good neighbor policy, 50, 55, 190, 192, 200, 207, 209, 235, 240
Gordon, George, 148
Grandi, 146
Great Britain, Anglo-Egyptian relationships, 259
assistance to Greece, 167-168
attitude toward Italian conquest of Ethiopia, 57
controversy with France over Near East, 245, 260
entered commercial relations with Soviet Union, 12
in postwar world, 303
loans to China, 281
Naval Agreement with Germany, 34, 93, 104
negotiations with Soviet Union, 80
Ottawa policy, 85
rearmament, 92
relations with France, 156, 157
  Germany, 34, 92, 93, 104, 114, 133
  Italy, 145
secret treaty of London, with Italy, 245
warning to Germany, 39
Greater German Second Reich, 337
Greater Germany, 93, 123, 280
  Hitler's first move toward creation of, 32
Greece, 167, 168, 257, 355
Greenwood, Arthur, 133
Grew, Ambassador, 293, 304
Guani, Dr., 230, 231, 415
Guaranty, Treaties of, 14
Guatemala, 207
Guiñazú, Dr. Enrique Ruiz, 220, 228, 229, 230, 232

Hacha, Dr., 38, 39
Hague Conference, 366
Haiti, 186, 191

Halifax, Lord, 35, 80, 114, 130, 131, 132, 301
Hamaguchi, Prime Minister, 277
Hapsburg Empire, 20
Harding Administration, 46, 187, 396, 398
Harding, President Warren, 42
Harriman, Averell, 174
Harvey, George, 42, 44
Hawaii, United States acquisition of, 393
Henderson, Nevile, 110
Henlein, 123
Herriot, Edouard, 24, 25, 26, 126-127, 129, 154
Herzl, Theodore, 264
Hess, Rudolf, 110, 111, 342
Himmler, 342
Hindenburg, 101, 339, 342
Hitler, Adolf, 29, 30, 32, 33, 34, 35, 36, 37, 38, 39, 51, 55, 58, 60, 68, 69, 70, 71, 73, 74, 75, 76, 77, 78, 80, 81, 82, 87, 89, 90, 91, 92, 93, 94, 100, 101, 102, 103, 104, 105, 106, 108, 109, 110, 113, 114, 119, 123, 124, 131, 134, 136, 138, 139, 142, 143, 144, 146, 148, 152, 159, 168, 170, 180, 214, 230, 250, 280, 298, 307, 321, 322, 323, 324, 326, 338, 339, 340, 341, 342, 347, 350, 357
explanation of negotiations with Poland, 104-105
fatal errors, 325
first move toward creation of Greater Germany, 32
Naval Agreement with England, 1935, 34, 93, 104
outline of German objectives, 106-107
ten-year pact with Poland, 39
Hitlerism, 28, 30, 61, 71, 76, 96, 119, 131, 169, 179, 214, 215, 307, 320, 338, 341, 348, 358, 360, 373, 399
effect on German life, 89-90, 110
Hoare-Laval deal, 57
Holland, invasion of, 148
Holy Alliance, 365
Hoover Administration, 46, 49, 51, 190, 191, 194
Hoover, President Herbert, 48, 189, 190, 191, 277, 280, 398, 399
Hopkins, Harry, 172, 175
House, Colonel, 14, 367, 394
House of Commons, 17, 340
House of Lords, British, 3, 132

House of Representatives, 178, 391, 394
Hughes, Charles Evans, 43, 44, 116, 187, 188, 189
Hull, Cordell, 55
Hungary, 140, 332
Huntzinger, General, 162
Huntzinger, Madame, 151
Hu Shih, Dr., 284

Ibn Saud, King, 258, 263
India, 297, 301, 302, 304
Inonu, Ismet, 246
Inter-American Conference for the Maintenance of Peace, 61, 208
Inter-American Financial and Economic Advisory Committee, 212, 215
Inter-American Juridical Committee, 213
Inter-American Neutrality Committee, 213
Inter-American relations, 186, 188, 189, 190, 191, 192, 193, 197, 200, 204, 209, 211, 212, 214, 219, 231, 237
Intergovernmental Committee on Refugees, 268
International Bank of Stabilization, 412
International Economic Conference, 51
International Organization, 384, 405, 410
International Relief and Rehabilitation Administration, 371
International Straits Commission, 246
International Trusteeship. See Postwar plan for international trusteeship
Iran, 270, 327, 329
Iranian-Persian Company, 269
Iraq, 168, 257, 262, 263
Iraq Petroleum Company, 269
Iron Guard, 251
Ishii, Count, 273
Ismet Inonu, 246
Isolationism, 42, 43, 48, 57, 61, 63, 71, 75, 277, 286, 321, 391, 396, 410
Italian fleet, entrance into service of Axis, 157
Italian General Staff, 146
Italy, antagonized by Wilson's refusal of demands, 14
   Balkan policy, 136, 144
   declaration of war against U.S., 231
   deterioration of economic situation, 146
   German-Italian Pact, 141
   internal difficulties, 27

Italy—*Continued*
last to embark on autocratic system, 85
out of the war, 180
people opposed to war, 125, 143, 146
policy of non-belligerency, 136
relations with Great Britain, 145
secret treaty of London, 245
stand in regard to Poland, 81
Ito, Prince, 274

Japan, 272, 273, 274
American policy toward, 279, 288
attack on Pearl Harbor, 219, 226, 231, 294
control in North China and Inner Mongolia, 319
corruption in military structure, 286
declared war on U.S., 224
development as world power, 275-276, 297
entrance into French Indo-China, 288
German islands acquired by Versailles Treaty, 45
in postwar world, 304, 329
invasion of Siberian provinces, 311
militaristic elements, rise of, in, 277
policy of aggrandizement, 8, 276, 280, 292
propaganda activities in American republics, 209-210, 221
rape of Manchuria, 31, 49, 277-280, 285, 319
relations with the United States, 289, 291
twenty-one demands on China (1915), 276
withdrawal from Shantung Peninsula, 45
Japanese Empire, 291
Japanese Mandated Islands, 286
Jeanneney, Jules, 125, 154
Jefferson, Thomas, 388, 389, 390
Jewish Homeland, National, 266
Jews, achievements in Palestine, 266
persecution of, 30, 71, 76, 97, 117, 158, 251, 262, 263
Johnson, Hiram, 396
Joint Declaration of Continental Solidarity, 211
Justo, President, 235

Kamenev, 313
Kant, Immanuel, 365

Kellogg-Briand Pact, 26, 46, 47, 48, 279
Kellogg, Secretary, 47, 187, 188, 319
Kemal Ataturk, Pasha, 244, 245
Kennedy, Joseph P., 130, 131
Kerensky, government, 318, 330
King, Admiral, 175
Kirk, Alexander, 90, 100, 112
Knox, Philander, 43
Konoye, Prince, 294, 295
Korea, 304
Krassin, 31
Kun, Béla, 22
Kuomintang, 282
Kurusu, Mr., 289, 295
Kurusu mission, 295

Labor party, 132, 133, 400
Lamas, Dr. Carlos Saavedra, 206, 207, 209, 230
*La Prensa*, 4
Latvia, 311
Lausanne, Treaty of, 246, 260
Laval, Pierre, 153, 158
League of Nations, 4, 8, 11, 13, 18, 19, 22, 24, 25, 26, 28, 30, 31, 33, 41, 43, 44, 45, 47, 48, 49, 56, 67, 70, 140, 186, 245, 259, 260, 280, 281, 286, 319, 320, 340, 370, 378, 385, 394, 395, 396, 397
Assembly, 26, 380
Council, 20, 23, 312, 380
Covenant, 5, 8, 13, 26, 31, 186, 246, 262, 278, 320, 367, 370, 377, 378, 380, 395, 396
League to Enforce Peace, 367
Leahy, Admiral William D., 158, 159, 160
Lebanon, 257, 261
Lebrun, President Albert, 121-122, 125, 154, 155
Léger, Alexis, 125, 151
Lend-Lease Act, 172, 173, 228
Lend-Lease Administration, 170
Lenin, 312, 313
Leticia, controversy between Colombia and Peru, 191
Levinson, Samuel P., 47
Liberal party, 132-133, 400
Liebknechts, Karl, 16
Lima, Declaration of, 209
Lincoln, President, 392
Lithuania, 311
Little Entente, 19, 23
Litvinov, Maxim, 31, 318, 319, 320, 322

Lloyd George, David, 6, 11, 12, 13, 14, 17, 18, 133
Locarno, Treaty of, 26
Lodge, Senator Henry Cabot, 367, 395
London Economic Conference, 53, 54, 399
London Naval Conferences, 45, 56
Lorraine, Sir Percy, 83
Louis XVIII, 388
Louisiana Purchase, 389
Low Countries, 75
  attack on, 148
Loyalists, Spanish, 58
Lytton Commission, Report of the Members, 280

MacDonald, Ramsay, 126
Machado, General, 193, 194, 195, 196, 197
MacMahon, Sir Henry, 257
MacMahon agreement, 257, 264
Madison, James, 388, 389
Maginot Line, 75, 76
Maglione, Cardinal, 142
Magnes, Judah, 267
Malaya, 296, 302
Manchukuo, 280
Manchuria, 31, 49, 277-280, 319
Mandate system, 8
Mandel, Georges, 135, 151, 154
Maniu, 251
Marshall, General, 174
Marx, Karl, 126, 312
Masaryk, Dr., 21
Matienzo, Dr. Anze, 416
Matsukata, Marquis, 274
Matsuoka, 324
Matteotti, 28
Matthews, Herbert L., 83
McKinley, President, 392
Mediterranean Commission, 371
Mein Kampf, 34
Meissner, 101, 342
Melo, Dr. Leopoldo, 214
Mendieta, Colonel Carlos, 199
Mers-el-Kébir, incident of, 155, 156, 157
Messersmith, George, 189
Metternich, 388
Mexican-American relations, 203-204
Mexico, 186, 203, 219, 220, 318, 392
  attitude of U.S. toward, 189
  Chamizal dispute, 203
Meyer, Eugene, 398, 399
Ministry of National Defense, 122

Minorities, 20, 97, 301, 354, 355
  arrangement for treatment of, in Versailles Treaty, 7
  German, 82, 94, 115
  Greek, 20
  Hungarian, 20, 22, 140
  Mussolini's views on, 87
  Rumanian, 20
  Turkish, 20
  Yugoslavic, 251
Molotov, 322
Mongolia, 329
Monroe, 390
Monroe Doctrine, 95, 97, 98, 367, 369, 380, 392, 393, 401, 403, 404
Montagu, Edwin, 267
Montreux Agreement, 332
Moreau, General, 109
Morgenthau, Henry, 285
Morrow, Ambassador Dwight, 189
Moscow Agreement, 371
Moscow Conference, 327
Munich Agreements, 92, 113, 127, 141, 322
Munich, meeting of, 38
Murature, José Luis, 230
Muro, Dr. Solf y, 416
Murphy, Robert, 161, 163
Muselier, Admiral, 162
Mussolini, Benito, 27, 28, 30, 32, 33, 55, 57, 58, 59, 60, 70, 77, 78, 79, 80, 81, 83, 84, 85, 86, 88, 100, 101, 103, 119, 125, 135, 136, 137, 138, 139, 140, 141, 142, 143, 144, 145, 146, 147, 167, 221, 230
  advocated federation of major powers, 140
  statement on rights of Poland, 87
Mutsuhito, Emperor, 274
My Life in China, 304

Napoleon, 16, 109, 310, 323
Napoleon III, 128, 317, 392
Napoleonic Wars, 323
National Socialism, 29, 108, 118, 134
Nationalism, rise of, after Versailles Treaty, 19
Naval Agreement with England, concluded by Hitler, 1935, 34, 93, 104
Nazi party, 29, 36, 110, 111, 112, 399
Nazi policy, 101, 130
  in Spain, 59
Near East, 123, 246, 261

Near East—*Continued*
  controversy between Great Britain and France, 245, 260
  French mandates, 260
Netherlands East Indies, 296, 302, 304
Neurath, von, 342
Neutrality Act, 284, 287
"Neutrality" legislation, 55-56, 60, 77, 122
Neutrality Pact, 324, 325
New Zealand, 303, 304
Nicholas I, 308
Nicholas II, 309
Nicolson, Harold, 3
Nine-Power Conference, 65
Nine-Power Treaty, 66, 277, 279
Nitobe, Dr. Inazo, 273
Nollet, General, 124
Nomura, Admiral, 289, 290
Nonintervention Committee, 58
Norris, George, 254
North Africa, Allies firmly established in, 180
  invasion of, 161, 163
Norway, invasion of, 148
Nuri Pasha, 263

Okuma, Marquis, 277
Olney, Richard, 392
Orlando, Signor, 14
Ortiz, Dr. Roberto, 225, 235, 239
Ottawa Agreements, 85, 176, 410
Ottawa policy, 85
Oumansky, Ambassador Constantin, 170, 171
Oyama, Marshal, 274

Packards, the, 83
Padilla, Dr. Ezequiel, 416
Paléologue, Maurice, 326, 334
Palestine, achievements of Jews in, 266
  problem of, 264-268
Palmerston, Lord, 317
Panama, 201, 202, 210, 211, 220
  Declaration of, 211, 212
  U.S. treaty with, 201, 202, 404
Panama Canal, 157, 202, 393, 404, 405
Panama Conference, 214
Panamanian National Assembly, 201
Pan-American Conference, 187, 199-200
Pan-American Congress, 185
Pan-Americanism, 206, 227, 392
Pan-American Union, 209
Pan-Germanism, 9, 11, 28, 347, 348, 358

Pan-Slavic doctrines, Russia's, 310, 332
Papen, von, 247
Paraguay, 225, 237, 379
Paris Conference, 6, 8, 10, 22, 257, 260
Party Congress of the Soviet Union, 322
Paul I, 310
Peace Conference, 8, 9, 13, 14, 187, 256, 274, 330, 394
Pearl Harbor, 219, 224, 226, 288, 294, 296
Peasant party, 251
Peña, Roque Saenz, 207
Penn, William, 365
Penrose, Boies, 43, 396
Pérez, Dr. Caraccio Parra, 416
Peru, 188, 218, 237
  controversy with Colombia, 191
Pétain, Marshal, 153, 155, 156, 158, 159, 161, 163, 165, 215
Peter the Great, 308, 310, 311, 406
Philippines, 296, 299, 303, 304, 393
Phillips, William, 78, 83, 84, 138
Pilsudski, Marshal, 32, 330
Pitt, 388
Pius XII, Pope, 135, 142
"Platt Amendment," 199
Poincaré, 9, 11, 122
Poland, 20, 22, 39, 75, 76, 94, 114, 115, 127, 320
  aggression by Prussia and Austria, 310
  agreement between Germany and Italy, 81
  attack by Germany, 324
  Goering's explanation of war against, 113-114
  Hitler's explanation of negotiations, 104-105
  legitimate requirements of future state, 354
  minority problem, 22
  Mussolini's views, 86-87, 139
  nonaggression pact with Germany, 32, 94, 127
  plans for reconstitution of, 12, 82
  reconstitution after first World War, 20
  relations with Italy, 81
  stand of Soviet Union, 330-332
  ten-year pact with Germany, 39
  Treaty of Riga, with Russia, 311
Police force, international, 382
Polish Corridor, 22, 32, 38, 82, 87, 94, 114, 115, 331, 353, 354

Polish war, 99, 142
Portes, Madame de, 151
Portugal, 317
  revalidated ancient alliance with United Kingdom, 180
Posen, 87
Postwar plan for international trusteeship, 300-305, 328, 329, 365-387
Potemkin, 310
Pound, Sir Dudley, 132
Prinkipo meeting, 12
Propaganda, German, after defeat in 1918, 18
Protocol for the Pacific Solution of International Differences, 25
Prado, President, 416
*Prince of Wales*, 175
Protocol of Mutual Assistance, 320
Provisional Executive Council of the International Organization, 383-384, 403
Provisional United Nations Executive Council, 374-387
Prussia, 336, 350
Prussian Imperial House, 10
Puerto Rico, 393
Pueyrredón, Honorio, 230

Ramírez, General, 235, 236
Rapallo, Treaty of, 312
Rashid Ali, 262
Rathenau, Walter, 30
Rearmament, British, beginning of, 92
  German, 30, 49, 56, 124, 320, 340
  Italian, 56
  Japanese, 56
  United States, 56
*Reflections and Reminiscences*, 353
Regional Council of the International Trusteeship, 384
Rehabilitation, 385
Reich, 23, 25, 36, 87, 92, 95, 114, 140, 349, 361
  Second, 337, 347
  Third, 120, 211, 352
Reichstag, 36
Reichstreuhandgesellschaft, 17
Reichswehr, 17
Renaissance, 336
Reparations, 10, 14, 16-17, 46, 340, 398, 399
  differences between France and Great Britain concerning, 24

Republican party, 41, 42, 43, 394, 396
Reynaud, Paul, 128, 134, 135, 150, 151, 152, 153, 154, 155, 156
Rhineland, 352
  reoccupation of, 32, 92
Ribbentrop, 80, 82, 90, 91, 92, 93, 94, 95, 96, 97, 98, 99, 100, 102, 104, 108, 111, 113, 114, 119, 127, 128, 135, 136, 137, 138, 139, 142, 143, 144, 324, 342
Ribes, Champetier de, 125
Riga, Treaty of, 311, 331
Rivera, Primo de, 28
Robert, Admiral, 162
Roca, Julio, 230
Rogers, Will, 390
Romantic movement, 336
Roosevelt Administration, 55, 85, 153, 190, 200
Roosevelt, President Franklin Delano, 49, 50, 52, 54, 55, 56, 60, 61, 63, 65, 66, 67, 68, 69, 70, 72, 73, 74, 76, 77-78, 79, 85, 86, 88, 98, 102, 103, 104, 122, 124, 126, 129, 131, 132, 135, 143, 144, 145, 150, 155, 158, 162, 163, 164, 165, 169, 170, 171, 172, 173, 174, 175, 176, 177, 178, 191, 192, 194, 196, 197, 201, 202, 204, 205, 211, 254, 268, 284, 287, 294, 295, 315, 318, 319, 327
Roosevelt, Theodore, 366, 367, 393, 396
Root, Elihu, 43, 48, 185, 395
Rosas, 230
Rossetti, Dr. Juan Bautista, 417
Ruhr, evacuation of, 24, 25
Rumania, 250, 253, 311, 361
Runciman, Lord, 36
Russia, agreement with France and England in first World War, 244
  assumed protection of Outer Mongolia and Chinese Turkestan, 319
  attitude of Allies toward, 11, 307
  Communist, effect of doctrine emanating from, 12
  entered into commercial relations with Great Britain, 12
  invasion of Siberian provinces by Japan, 311
  new constitution, 315
  Pan-Slavic doctrines, 310, 332
  rapid industrialization of, 314
  territories disposed of, 12, 307, 311
  Treaty of Riga, with Poland, 311
Russian Revolution, 244, 330

Russian-Turkish Alliance, 244, 245
Ruthenians, freed from Austrian domination, 19-20

Saar, plebiscite in, 32, 352
St. Pierre-Miquelon incident, 163
Saionji, Prince, 274, 294
Sakhalin, 329
Salazar, Dr. Carlos, 207
Salisbury, Lord, 392
Sanctions, 19, 33, 145, 368
Sanders, Liman von, 245
San Martín, Dr. Ramón Grau, 198, 199, 200
San Remo Conference, 258
Sao-Ke Alfred Sze, Dr., 284
Saracoglu, mission of, 247
Saudi Arabia, 263, 264, 269
Schacht, Dr. Hjalmar, 33, 253, 342, 399
Scharnhorst, military system of, 16
Schmidt, Herr, 90, 102, 110, 112, 113, 114
Schuschnigg, 81
Security and Armaments Commission, 376, 381, 382, 385, 387
Senate Committee on Foreign Relations, 60
Serbs, unstable adjustment in Yugoslavia, 22, 251
Sèvres, Treaty of, 245
Seward, William H., 392
Sforza, Carlo, 28
Shantung Peninsula, withdrawal of Japan, 45
Sherif Hussein, 257, 258
Shidehara, Baron, 273
Siegfried Line, 76
Simon, Sir John, 108, 279
Sims, William Philip, 83
Sinclair, Sir Archibald, 133
Singapore, 296
Sinkiang, 329
Slavophile policies, 310, 332
Slovakia, 82, 87
Slovaks, 114
    freed from Austrian domination, 19-20
Slovenes, freed from Austrian domination, 19-20
    unstable adjustment in Yugoslavia, 22, 251
Smoot-Hawley Tariff Act, 49, 191, 193
Smuts, General, 14
Snell, Lord, 132

Soares, Dr. José Carlos de Macedo, 208
Socialist party, 22
Society of the Black Dragon, 277
Somaliland, British, 146
Soong, Dr. T. V., 284
Soviet-Czechoslovak Pact of Mutual Assistance, 320
Soviet-German Agreement, 71
Soviet Union, 22, 30, 38, 39, 44, 58, 65, 66, 68, 80, 137, 247, 255, 303, 319, 321, 322, 323, 324, 330, 397
    achievements, 326
    agreement with Germany, 71-73, 137, 168, 323-324
    alliance with Turkey, 244, 245
    attitude toward League of Nations, 31
    desertion by great powers, 31
    entered League of Nations, 319
    Five-Year Plan, 314
    future foreign policy, 309, 328-335
    German assault upon, 171
    position in postwar world, 329-335
    recognition by Great Britain and France, 316
    relations with United States, 50, 168-172, 306, 307, 312, 315, 318, 326, 405
    Russian-Turkish Alliance, 244, 245
    special agreements with France, 320
    stand on Poland, 330-332, 354
    Turkish-Soviet relations, 247
    views on Turkey's entering war, 248
    war on Finland, 169
    war materials supplied by United States, 172
    warned by United States of impending German attack, 170-171
Spain, 57, 58, 59, 178, 179, 237, 389
    Axis policy in, 59
    occupied Dominican Republic, 392
    treatment of Catholic Church, 60
    United States war with, 390, 392, 393
Spanish-American republics, 206, 207, 222, 224
Spanish civil war, 57, 59, 61, 400
Stalin, 137, 313, 314, 319, 321, 322, 324, 327, 328
Stanley, Oliver, 132
Stark, Admiral, 175
State socialism, 313, 315
Stimson, Henry L., 48, 49, 191, 278, 279, 280
Straits Conference, 246

Stresemann, Gustave, 24, 25, 26, 126-127
Strikes, general, in Italy, 27
Struwe, Herr von, 89
Succession States, 20, 21, 24, 249, 256
Sudeten Germans, 21, 36, 92
Sudetenland, 37, 38, 68, 114, 123
Suez Canal, 155, 157, 259
Suñer, Serrano, 179, 180
Sun Yat-Sen, 283
Superior Agency of an International Trusteeship, 384
Sweden, 310, 317
Syria, 168, 257, 260, 261, 262

Tacna-Arica dispute, 188
Taft, President, 367, 393, 395, 396
Talleyrand, 388
Tanaka Memorial, 276
Tariff Act of 1930, 209
Tariff rates, high, 46, 85
Tassigny, General de Lattre de, 165
Tehran, Declaration of, 327, 329
Tennessee Valley Authority, 254
Thailand, 296
Tikhon, 313
Tilsit, Treaty of, 323
Times, New York, 83
Tiso, Father, 38
Tojo, General, 295
Tories, 30
Trade Agreements Act, 55
Trade agreements program, 209, 253
Trade relations, international, 98, 103, 106-107, 114, 117, 169-170, 305, 386, 405, 408-414
  Hitler's statement on, 105
Treasury Department, 52
Treaty of 1901 with Cuba, 198
Trotsky, 313, 314, 358
Tunisia, 35
Turbay, Gabriel, 417
Turkey, 168, 242, 243, 244, 246, 247, 248, 330, 332, 355
  alliance with Soviet Union, 244-245
  desire for peace and neutrality, 249
  lost mastery of Black Sea, 310
  region of Syria ceded by France, 246, 260
  Turkish-Soviet relations, 247
  relations with United States, 247

Ukraine, 311, 320
Union, Briand's plan for European, 47
  economic, need for, 254, 255, 256

Union of Soviet Socialist Republics, 306, 333
United Nations Declaration, 178
United Nations Relief and Rehabilitation Administration, 268, 385
United States, acquisition of Hawaii, 393
  American-German relations, 76, 96, 108
  arranged to supply war materials to France, 153
  assistance to Soviet Union, 172
  attitude toward Mexico, 189
    Spanish civil war, 400
  conference of American republics, 225, 231-232, 234
  declaration of war, 296
  early foreign policy, 389, 392
  foreign policy between two world wars, 396-397, 400
  future foreign policy, 388, 401-408
  imperialism, 393
  influence on modernization of Turkey, 247
  in postwar world, 306
  inter-American relations, 186, 188, 189, 192, 200, 204, 211, 214, 219, 237
  loans to China, 281
  original treaty with Cuba, 198
  Panama treaty, 201, 202, 404
  policy in North Africa, 165
    toward Japan, 279, 288
      Manchurian incident, 49
    Vichy government, 156, 157, 158, 160, 163, 178
  promised Germany full co-operation in a just peace, 103
  relations with Argentina, 220, 225, 228, 235-236, 238-239
    Canada, 50
    China, 281, 284
    Germany, 96, 108
    Japan, 289, 291
    Mexico, 203-204
    Soviet Union, 50, 168-172, 306, 307, 312, 315, 318, 326, 405
    Spain, 178, 179
    Turkey, 247
  rights on the high seas, 389
  security endangered by Germany, 133, 149
    endangered in the Pacific, 157

# INDEX

United States—*Continued*
  trade relations in postwar world, 408-414
  vulnerable position in Philippines, 289
  war with Spain, 390, 392, 393
United States "inquiry," 7
United States Senate, 13, 41, 47, 55, 367, 390
Uruguay, 237, 318

Van Buren Administration, 392
Vargas, Getulio, 222, 223
Vasquez, General Horacio, 187-188
Vatican, 27, 142
Venezuela, 218, 220, 392
Venizelos, M., 14
Versailles, Treaty of, 6, 14, 15, 16, 17, 18, 21, 23, 27, 29, 32, 33, 70, 93, 107, 245, 257, 311, 340, 341, 349, 395, 396
  errors of omission and commission, 7
  three major issues, 8
Vichy, 151, 156, 157, 158, 159, 161, 163, 166, 215, 261, 288

Wafd, 259
Wakasugi, Mo., 290, 291, 292
War of 1812, 389

War of Independence, 317
Washington Conference, 44, 45, 277
Washington, Treaties of, 44
Webster, Daniel, 392
Weimar Republic, 16, 126, 357, 398
Weizmann, Dr. Chaim, 264, 265, 266
Weizsaecker, von, 99, 100
Weygand, General, 151, 152, 153, 161, 165, 166
Whitaker, John T., 83
White Books, German, 92
White Papers, British, 266
William I, 342
William II, 243, 342
Wilson, Woodrow, 3, 4, 5, 8, 11, 12, 13, 14, 15, 42, 49, 116, 186, 272, 312, 367, 368, 378, 393, 394, 395, 396, 403
World Congress, 385, 387
World Court, 384, 385, 387
World Organization, 404

Yamagata, Prince, 274
Yellow Book, French, 128
Yugoslavia, 144, 253

Zeballos, Estanislaos, 230
Zinoviev, 313, 316
Zionism, 264, 266

*Set in Linotype Old Style No. 1*
*Format by A. W. Rushmore*
*Manufactured by H. Wolff*
*Published by* HARPER & BROTHERS
*New York and London*